Did Something Begin in the Year 2012 that will Reach Its Apex in 2016?

ZENITH 2016

(The Revised & Expanded Edition of *Apollyon Rising 2012*)

THOMAS HORN

DEFENDER

CRANE, MISSOURI

Zenith 2016: Did Something Begin in the Year 2012 that will Reach its Zenith in 2016?
The Revised & Expanded Edition of Apollyon Rising 2012
Defender
Crane, Missouri 65633
Copyright 2013 Thomas Horn

Printed in the United States of America

ISBN 10: 0984825657
ISBN 13: 9780984825653
A CIP catalog record of this book is available from the Library of Congress.
Cover illustration and design by Daniel Wright.
All Scripture quotations from the King James Version.

When our founders declared a new order of the ages...they were acting on an ancient hope that is meant to be fulfilled.
—US President George W. Bush,
January 20, 2005, second inaugural address

CONTENTS

ACKNOWLEDGMENTS

I wish to acknowledge the following people without whose friendship, inspiration, assistance, and research, this book would have been difficult to finish on time: my lovely wife Nita Horn, Carl and Althia Anderson, David Flynn, Sharon Gilbert, Sue Bradley, J. R. Church, Gary Stearman, Stephen Quayle, documentary filmmaker Christian Pinto, and Dr. Stanley Monteith.

FOREWORD

by Dr. Stanley Monteith

Host, *Radio Liberty* radio program
and best-selling author of *Brotherhood of Darkness*

Why is the world changing? Will things ever return to "normal"? What is the significance of the occult emblems on the back of the dollar bill you use every day? Why did President Bush mention "the angel that rides in the whirlwind" in his first inaugural address (2001) and "the new order of the ages" in his second inaugural address? Who was Apollyon, and why is his story important today? Why do powerful men want to establish a world government? Who directs the course of world events?

This book contains a great deal of new and important information about the occult architecture of our nation's Capitol, the strange ritual performed every year at the Bohemian Grove, the fact that the attack on the Twin Towers of the World Trade Center in New York took place eleven years to the day after President George H. W. Bush gave a speech that promoted a "New World Order," and a great deal of other shocking information.

Tom Horn recounts the story of the mythological god, Apollyon (Apollo), and cites the biblical reference to him. His book notes several references to the fact that there may be a major catastrophic event following the year 2012. Will the spirit of Apollyon be involved in that event? I don't know the answer to those questions, but I am certain we are living in prophetic times, and some of the people who read this book may very well witness the advent of the "man of sin... the son of perdition" (2 Thessalonians 2:3).

You will learn a great deal by reading this book and, hopefully, you will be encouraged to delve deeper into the background of the forces that are shaping modern-day civilization.

Stanley Monteith, M.D.

PREFACE

By Christian J. Pinto

Award-winning filmmaker of the documentary series,
Secret Mysteries of America's Beginnings

M any Christians are repeatedly told by their pastors, teachers, and church leaders that America was founded as a Christian nation. This assertion would not be so bad if it were confined to the arrival of the Puritans at Plymouth and the early development of the new world. If that were the case, it would be an accurate statement, in this writer's opinion.

The problem arises when one marks the foundation of our country at the American Revolution and the establishment of the United States. It is at this point where all Bible-believing Christians should be very wary, since the working of occult societies during this era was at an unprecedented height. Some historians even argue that you simply cannot understand the history of the world for the past few hundred years if you do not take these societies into account. Their members have been the planners, leaders, and engineers of a global agenda, one that they do not readily share with the rest of the world. More importantly, they often use "religion" as an instrument to manipulate the masses, their belief being that the end justifies the means.

Thomas Paine

While often overlooked or marginalized by modern historians, the American Revolution, in many ways, begins with Thomas Paine. The Marquis de Lafayette said, "A free America without her Thomas Paine is unthinkable."[1] Paine wrote the famous pamphlet, *Common Sense*, which is called "by far the most influential tract of the American Revolution" by not a few historians, who also maintain that it influenced Jefferson's writing of the Declaration of Independence.[2] Paine also published *The Crisis* pamphlet series, some of which were read aloud by George Washington to his troops during the Revolution. John Adams is known for saying, "Without the pen of Paine, the sword of Washington would have been wielded in vain." These words (sometimes attributed to Joel Barlow) are engraved on the very tombstone of the revolutionary author, whose words are said to have "stirred the American colonies to independence." Another quote appears on his tombstone, saying: "History is to ascribe the American Revolution to Thomas Paine." With these things in mind, consider that Paine wrote:

> When I see throughout the greater part of this book [the Bible] scarcely anything but a history of the grossest vices and a collection of the most paltry and contemptible tales, I cannot dishonor my Creator by calling it by His name.[3]
>
> What is it the Bible teaches us?—rapine, cruelty, and

murder. What is it the Testament teaches us?—to believe that the Almighty committed debauchery with a woman engaged to be married, and the belief of this debauchery is called faith.[4]

It is the fable of Jesus Christ, as told in the New Testament, and the wild and visionary doctrine raised thereon, against which I contend. The story, taking it as it is told, is blasphemously obscene.[5]

Thomas Jefferson

If there ever were a man utterly ruined and spoiled by vain philosophy, it was surely Thomas Jefferson. Along with Thomas Paine, he was America's greatest deceiver and antichrist—*if you judge him according to the Scriptures.* Jefferson, perhaps more than any other, typifies the last-days "scoffers, walking after their own lusts" warned about in the Bible (2 Peter 3:3, KJV). Jefferson said this about the book of Revelation in a letter to General Alexander Smyth dated January 17, 1825:

> It is between fifty and sixty years since I read it and I then considered it as merely the ravings of a maniac, no more worthy nor capable of explanation than the incoherences of our own nightly dreams.[6]

Through the rest of his letter, Jefferson made it clear to the general that he had not repented of his formerly held view. Some have tried to whitewash Jefferson because he thought Jesus was a fine teacher of morality, but here is what he said in a letter to William Short dated October 31, 1819:

The greatest of all the Reformers of the depraved religion of his own country, was Jesus of Nazareth. Abstracting what is really His from the rubbish in which it is buried, easily distinguished by its luster from the dross of his biographers, and as separable from that as the diamond from the dunghill.[7]

The above passage describes the approach Jefferson took in writing his so-called *Jefferson Bible* (properly titled *The Life and Morals of Jesus of Nazareth*). What he claimed he was attempting to do (and wrote about extensively) was to separate the "true" sayings of Jesus from the things he believed had been added to the Gospel accounts. But he did not really believe in the authority of the Bible, Old Testament or New. In a letter to John Adams dated January 24, 1814, he wrote:

Where did we get the Ten Commandments? The book indeed gives them to us verbatim, but where did it get them? For itself tells us they were written by the finger of God on tables of stone, which were destroyed by Moses.... But the whole history of these books is so defective and doubtful, that it seems vain to attempt minute inquiry into it.... We have a right to entertain much doubt what parts of them are genuine.[8]

As seen earlier, Jefferson's view of the New Testament was no better. In the same letter to John Adams, he wrote:

In the New Testament there is internal evidence that parts of it have proceeded from an extraordinary man; and that other parts are of the fabric of very inferior minds. It is as easy to separate those parts, as to pick out diamonds from dunghills.[9]

When one reads *The Jefferson Bible*, it becomes clear what Jefferson was referring to when he mentioned "dunghills." He specifically removed the virgin birth, the miracles of Christ, the Lord's resurrection, and His ascension into heaven. Needless to say, the entire book of Revelation was omitted. These were among the things Jefferson believed came from "inferior minds." Concerning the Lord Jesus, Jefferson wrote in another letter to Short on April 13, 1920:Among the sayings and discourses imputed to Him by His biographers, I find many passages of fine imagination, correct morality, and of the most lovely benevolence; and others, again, of so much ignorance, so much absurdity, so much untruth, charlatanism and imposture.... I separate, therefore, the gold from the dross...and leave the latter to the stupidity of some, and roguery of others of His disciples. Of this band of dupes and impostors, Paul was the...first corruptor of the doctrines of Jesus.[10]

Benjamin Franklin

One of the most influential founding fathers, and the only one of them to have signed all of the original founding documents (the Declaration of Independence, the Treaty of Paris, and the US Constitution) was Benjamin Franklin. Franklin was responsible for three important phases of America's development: 1) Unifying the colonists in their rebellion against England; 2) Philosophy concerning the rights of mankind; and 3) Facilitating the American Revolution by publishing the writings of Thomas Paine. To Sir Walter Isaacson, Benjamin Franklin was "the most accomplished American of his age and the most influential in inventing the type of society America would become."[11] Ben Franklin was, without question, deeply involved in Freemasonry and in other secret societies. He belonged to secret groups in the three countries involved in the War of Independence: America, France, and England. He was master of the Masonic Lodge of Philadelphia; while over in France, he was master of the Nine Sisters Lodge, from which sprang the French Revolution. In England, he joined a rakish political group founded by Sir Francis Dashwood (member of Parliament, advisor to King George III) called the "Monks of Medmenham Abbey," otherwise known as the "Hellfire Club." This eighteenth-century group is described as follows: The Hellfire Club was an exclusive, English club that met sporadically during the mid-eighteenth century. Its purpose, at best, was to mock traditional religion and conduct orgies. At worst, it involved the indulgence of satanic rites and sacrifices. The club to which Franklin belonged was established by Francis Dashwood, a member of Parliament and friend of Franklin. The club, which consisted of "The Superior Order" of twelve members, allegedly took part in basic forms of satanic worship. In addition to taking part in the occult, orgies and parties with prostitutes were also said to be the norm.[12]

Dead Bodies in London

On February 11, 1998, the *Sunday Times* reported that ten bodies were dug up from beneath Benjamin Franklin's home at 36 Craven Street in London. The bodies were of four adults and six children. They were discovered during a costly renovation of Franklin's former home. *The Times* reported: "Initial estimates are that the bones are about two hundred years old and were buried at the time Franklin was living in the house, which was his home from 1757 to 1762 and from 1764 to 1775. Most of the bones show signs of having been dissected, sawn or cut. One skull has been drilled with several holes."[13]

The article goes on to suggest that the bodies may have been the result of the experiments of Dr. William Hewson, who worked alongside the founders of British surgery and who was a friend of Benjamin Franklin. Hewson apparently ran his medical school from Franklin's home from 1772 to 1774. The suggestion put forth is that the bodies were probably "anatomical specimens that Dr. Hewson disposed of," but investigators admitted they were still "uncertain." For the record, the Benjamin Franklin House currently presents the bones as "the remains of William Hewson's anatomy school," and even has them on display for the public.

The original *Times* article reported that the bones were "deeply buried, probably to hide them because grave robbing was illegal." They said, "There could be more buried, and there probably are." But the story doesn't end there.

Science and Satan: Together Again?

Later reports from the Benjamin Franklin House reveal that not only were human remains found, but *animal* remains were discovered as well. This is where things get very interesting. From the published photographs, some of the bones appear to be blackened or charred, as if by fire. Needless to say, a number of researchers are doubtful about the "medical" explanation and have suggested that Franklin's involvement with the Hellfire Club may be the real answer. It is well documented that Satanists perform ritual killings of both humans and animals alike. Could Franklin and his Hellfire friends have been working with Hewson to provide the doctor with fresh bodies?

The uncomfortable questions are these: If the humans were medical cadavers, why were they disposed of like so much trash beneath the house? Why not give them some kind of proper burial? If grave robbers could sneak into a graveyard to steal a body, they could also sneak in to put one back. Furthermore, why were the human remains mingled with those of animals? It is worth noting that Dr. Hewitt developed an infection from working on one of his cadavers and died from it.

Franklin and the Gospel

What was Franklin's view of Christianity and of the Lord Jesus Christ? He answered that question directly shortly before he died. He wrote the following to Ezra Stiles, who was then president of Yale University. Stiles had inquired about Franklin's views on religion and of the Lord Jesus Christ:

> As to Jesus of Nazareth, my Opinion of whom you particularly desire, I think the System of Morals and his Religion, as he left them to us, the best the world ever saw or is likely to see; but I apprehend it has received various corrupt changes, and I have, with most of the present Dissenters in England, some Doubts as to his divinity.[14]

From the first part of his response, Franklin's views about Jesus seem very similar to those of Paine and Jefferson, making reference to "corrupt changes" in the Gospel record. Like many others, he compliments the "morality" of Christ while rejecting His authority. This was typical of the founding fathers.

John Adams

John Adams was America's third president and a close friend of Thomas Jefferson. Adams, Jefferson, and Franklin worked together on the first committee to design the Great Seal for the United States. While it does not appear that Adams was a member of any secret group, he was a Unitarian and shared views of Christianity not unlike those of Paine, Jefferson, and Franklin. He wrote the following to Thomas Jefferson in a letter dated September 3, 1816:

> I almost shudder at the thought of alluding to the most fatal example of the abuses of grief which the history of mankind has preserved—the Cross. Consider what calamities that engine of grief has produced![15]

George Washington

Undoubtedly, the most famous man to have survived the American Revolution is the veritable "father of our country," George Washington; but was he a Christian? Many die-hard Christian patriots have insisted that he was, but history reveals that questions about his faith did not begin in the modern era. Even during his lifetime, there were many who sought out a clear answer as to what George Washington believed about God and the Lord Jesus Christ specifically. After more than twenty years of being a pastor to George Washington himself, Bishop James White was only able to give a vague testimony of Washington's faith. For obvious reasons, many people sought this man, hoping he could give a clear description of Washington's Christian beliefs. His reply on one occasion was:

I do not believe that any degree of recollection will bring to my mind any fact which would prove General Washington to have been a believer in the Christian revelation further than as may be hoped from his constant attendance upon Christian worship, in connection with the general reserve of his character.[16]

In other words, beyond his generally moral character and the fact that he went to church regularly, there is no other proof that he was a believer.

The assistant to Rev. White was Rev. James Abercrombie, who also ministered to Washington for years. Years later, when questioned by Dr. Bird Wilson, Rev. Abercrombie arrived at the following conclusion:

Long after Washington's death, in reply to Dr. Wilson, who had interrogated him as to his illustrious auditor's religious views, Dr. Abercrombie's brief but emphatic answer was: "Sir, Washington was a Deist."[17]

In Philadelphia, certain Christian clergymen had even tried to obtain a confession of faith, or a clear denial, from Washington during his farewell address as president. Thomas Jefferson commented on this in his journal, saying:

Feb. 1.—Dr. Rush tells me that he had it from Asa Green that when the clergy addressed General Washington on his departure from the Government, it was observed in their consultation that he had never on any occasion said a word to the public which showed a belief in the Christian religion and they thought they should so pen their address as to force him at length to declare publicly whether he was a Christian or not. They did so. However, he observed, the old fox was too cunning for them. He answered every article in their address particularly except that, which he passed over without notice.... "I know that Gouverneur Morris, who pretended to be in his secrets and believed himself to be so, has often told me that General Washington believed no more in the system [Christianity] than he did."[18]

The "Asa Green" mentioned by Jefferson was Dr. Ashbel Green, who was the chaplain to the Congress during Washington's presidency. Dr. Green "dined with the President on special invitation nearly every week."[19] One of his relatives, A. B. Bradford (who was later appointed a consul to China by President Lincoln), gave the following testimony about the event Jefferson had described. Bradford related that what follows was "frequently" told to him by Dr. Green:

> He explained more at length the plan laid by the clergy of Philadelphia at the close of Washington's administration as president to get his views of religion for the sake of the good influence they supposed they would have in counteracting the Infidelity of Paine and the rest of the Revolutionary patriots, military and civil. But I well remember the smile on his face and the twinkle of his black eye when he said: "The old fox was too cunning for Us."[20]

Notice the reference to "Us," as Dr. Green counted himself among the Christian clergymen who were trying to obtain a clear confession from President Washington. The quote continues, as Bradford says of Dr. Green:

> He affirmed, in concluding his narrative, that from his long and intimate acquaintance with Washington he knew it to be the case that while he respectfully conformed to the religious customs of society by generally going to church on Sundays, he had no belief at all in the divine origin of the Bible, or the Jewish-Christian religion.[21]

Sacred Fire?

In recent years, an attempt was made by authors Jerry A. Lillback and Jerry Newcombe, in their book, *George Washington's Sacred Fire*, to prove that Washington was a Christian. They penned a thousand pages of seemingly endless speculation and suggestive possibilities, but the only confession they could produce was a single quote from Washington on "the Religion of Jesus Christ." Moreover, the authors of *Sacred Fire* destroyed their entire hypothesis by revealing the following ecumenical quote from Washington to his fellow Freemason, the Marquis de Lafayette:

> Being no bigot myself to any mode of worship, I am disposed to indulge the professors of Christianity in the church, that road to Heaven, which to them shall seem the most direct, plainest, easiest, and least liable to exception.[22]

Notice how Washington referred to Christianity as "that road to Heaven," as if it were one of many. Washington's words are entirely Masonic, and the quote appears as if he were letting his hair down to a fellow Mason. Furthermore, the quote clearly shows that Washington viewed himself as an *outsider* to biblical Christianity, and suggests that he merely "indulged" the Christians by going to church, etc.

All who knew him would agree that in terms of moral conduct and his code of honor, the world viewed him (and he probably saw himself) as *a man of Christian character*. This did not, however, require that he believe that Jesus is the Christ, the Son of God, or that He died for our sins, and that by faith in Him alone we have eternal life.

Freemasonry and the Founders

In his book, *The Question of Freemasonry and the Founding Fathers*, author David Barton takes up the argument about whether or not the United States was founded by Masons. Despite the overwhelming evidence against him, he diminishes the role of Masonry, saying, "It is historically and irrefutably demonstrable that Freemasonry was *not* a significant influence in the formation of the United States" (emphasis in original).[23]

Nevertheless, in January of 2007, the first session of the 110th Congress (when Nancy Pelosi became Speaker of the House) passed House Resolution 33, which recognized "the thousands of Freemasons in every State in the Nation." The resolution goes on to say specifically:

> Whereas the Founding Fathers of this great Nation and signers of the Constitution, **most of whom were Freemasons**, provided a well-rounded basis for developing themselves and others into valuable citizens of the United States [emphasis added].[24]

Christian Masonry?

Furthermore, Barton makes the assertion that Freemasonry was a "Christian" organization during the time of the founding fathers, but was then later corrupted by men like Albert Mackey and Albert Pike. As shown in the documentary, *Secret Mysteries of America's Beginnings*,[25] American Masonry can be traced to England during the time of Sir Francis Bacon (1561–1626), who is considered the first grand master of modern masonry. Even at this time, the inner doctrine of embracing all the world religions alongside Christianity existed, but they did not publish such things in formal declarations, for fear of persecution. The outer and inner doctrine of secret societies is something overlooked by many researchers who attempt to marginalize the influence of Freemasonry. These same men would also know little of Rosicrucianism, which was the forerunner of Masonry.

Satanic Roots of Masonry

Sir Francis Bacon's close associate during this time was Dr. John Dee, who was the court astrologer for Queen Elizabeth I. It is well known that Dee was a sorcerer who summoned demonic spirits to obtain secret knowledge; a practice used by Rosicrucians (of whom Dee was the chief in England) for centuries. The root word for "demon" means "a knowing one."[26] The Rosicrucians desired to know secrets of science (i.e., knowledge) and consulted demons to get information. Bacon also made contact with demonic spirits, including the goddess Pallas Athena, whom he claimed was his muse or inspiration. In time, Dee handed off the leadership of the Rosicrucian Society to Bacon, who would enfold the secrets of Rosicrucianism into the system of Freemasonry.

Little wonder that Sir Francis Bacon would become the father of the modern scientific method, and that men like Benjamin Franklin and Thomas Jefferson would follow his example in their scientific endeavors. Franklin and Jefferson are both claimed by modern Rosicrucians as being of their order.

Like the Gnostics, the Rosicrucians craved knowledge; it was this desire that led them to worship Lucifer. The secret orders regard Lucifer as the "angel of light" who, in the form of a serpent, bid mankind to partake of the "Tree of Knowledge of Good and Evil" so that their eyes would be open and they could become as gods. This is the inner doctrine of Rosicrucianism, Freemasonry, and all the secret orders—and always has been. In the nineteenth century, when Masons like Pike and Mackey (along with leading occultists such as Eliphas Levi and Madame H. P. Blavatsky) described this doctrine in their writings, they were only admitting in print what had been secretly known for centuries. The difference was that with the revolutionary movements, freedom of religion allowed them to publish such things without fear of persecution.

Secrets in Stone

Centuries before all this, in 1492, Rosslyn Chapel was built by Scottish Freemasons. To this day, the chapel is considered a puzzle because it is filled with carvings and icons of Christian and Pagan religions. Why? The reason is because Freemasons have always had the inner doctrine of amalgamating religious beliefs. Much of this can be traced back to the Knights Templar, who are said to have fled to Scotland when they were persecuted in Europe (circa 1307). In fact, the red cross of the Templars is said to be a point of origin for the rose cross of Rosicrucianism. Furthermore, in the wake of the Scottish Jacobite rebellions of the early 1700s, many Scottish Masons and Rosicrucians fled to America, bringing their occult doctrines with them. One of their power centers was the Fredericksburg Lodge No. 4, whose members included George Washington, James Monroe, and eight of the Revolutionary War generals.

The practice of carving their doctrines in stone continued in the new world with the building of Washington, DC. This is why one will find in our nation's Capitol countless images of gods and goddesses, along with zodiacs, the Washington Monument Obelisk, reflecting pools, and a whole cacophony of pagan imagery. There are no monuments to Jesus Christ, the apostles, or anything having to do with the Christian faith.

The Reason for Masonic Deception

Manly P. Hall has been called "Masonry's greatest philosopher" in America's leading Masonic publication.[27] In his book, *The Secret Destiny of America*, Hall says that in the past, secret orders intentionally made a pretense of Christian faith in order to avoid persecution. He writes:

> The rise of the Christian Church broke up the intellectual pattern of the classical pagan world. By persecution…
> it drove the secret societies into greater secrecy; the pagan intellectuals then reclothed their original ideas in a garment of Christian phraseology, but bestowed the keys of the symbolism only upon those duly initiated and bound to secrecy by their vows.[28]

The "initiated" who were "bound to secrecy" is an obvious reference to those in secret societies. Hall argued that these groups have been operating in America for centuries, and that they were the authors of the American Revolution. Before dismissing his assertion as a conspiracy theory, ask yourself a question: Did *Christians* erect a bunch of pagan monuments to various gods in Washington, DC, and while doing it, just happen to omit Jesus Christ? Or was it done by men who outwardly *pretended* to be Christians, but who inwardly had a hidden agenda, just as their "greatest philosopher" tells us?

Classicism: The Veil of Lucifer

In his book on the founders and Masonry, David Barton defends the use of pagan symbolism with the following argument:

> Americans in recent generations have not been trained in classical literature—a training that was routine in the Founding Era. Therefore, present-day Americans are not inclined to consider structures from the ancient empires (such as the pyramids), or to be familiar with their heroes (such as Cato, Cicero, and Aeneus), or even with their writers (such as Homer, Virgil, Herodotus, and especially Plutarch).[29]

If you take the time to look up the works of Homer, Virgil, etc., you will find that these ancient writer/philosophers were writing about the gods and goddesses of the ancient world. All of these gods are called *devils* in the Bible (1 Corinthians 10:20). The same deception is used to describe the Statue of Liberty, where reference is made to "Liberty's classical origins." The placard on Liberty Island goes on to say that the statue was based on the Roman goddess Libertas. Were the statue judged from a biblical viewpoint, it would tell of Liberty's *demonic origins*. The clever use of the word "classic" is simply more evidence of satanic duplicity. David Barton's incredible delusion seems to be that if Satan and his demons are put in a book designated as "classical literature," then they are somehow sanitized and no longer offensive to God. But in the Bible, God says, "Thus shall ye say unto them, The gods that have not made the heavens and the earth, even they shall perish from the earth, and from under these heavens" (Jeremiah 10:11).

Why would any Bible-believing Christian want to build statues and monuments to exalt spiritual powers that God has condemned to destruction? Clearly, the modern references to "classical literature" by which demons become acceptable learning tools are a clever veil of deception. This danger was defined two centuries earlier by the sixteenth-century scholar Erasmus concerning "classical" studies. He said that, "under the cloak of reviving ancient literature, paganism tries to rear its head, as there are those among Christians who acknowledge Christ only in name but inwardly breathe heathenism."[30]

GAOTU and George Washington

To enable their members to embrace any god they wish, Masonry developed vague terminology when referring to deity. Their favorite title is "Great Architect of the Universe" (GAOTU). David Barton, in his attempts to call early Masonry a "Christian" organization, suggests that this idea developed *after* the founding era. He creates this argument in an attempt to justify the involvement of men like George Washington and others in early American Masonry.

In his book, Barton rightly states that in Christianity, "Only one God is worshipped—and that God is *not* the universalist deistic god that Masonry denotes as the 'Great Architect of the Universe' (GAOTU)."[31] While saying this, he fails to tell his readers that George Washington (whom he insists was a Christian) referred to this same Masonic god when writing to the Massachusetts Grand Lodge on December 27, 1792, when he said, "I sincerely pray that the Great Architect of the Universe may bless you and receive you hereafter into his immortal Temple."[32]

Notice that the idea of GAOTU was not invented by Albert Pike or others who came later. It was well known among early American Masons. Could such a quote be the reason George Washington, in his thousands of pages of written correspondence, never made a clear confession of Jesus Christ? Or could it be that the only quote anyone can find from him makes mention of "the religion of Jesus Christ," but not of faith in the Son of God according to the Scriptures? Could this be why Washington's own pastor called him a *Deist?*

Pythagorean Masonry

While some patriot Christians will scoff at the idea that the Illuminati could have had anything to do with the design of Washington, DC, they are simply unfamiliar with Illuminati symbolism. The Illuminists (an inner circle of Freemasons) were high-minded intellectuals who exalted the teachings of the Greek and Roman philosophers of the ancient world (i.e., the so-called *classical* authors Barton defends). Pythagorean philosophy was chiefly embraced by the revolutionaries of the founding era. The Pythagorean theorem is based on the right triangle of Pythagoras, and (according to Masonic author David Ovason) is the reason Federal Triangle in Washington, DC was designed the way it was.

Dr. James H. Billington, in his book, *Fire in the Minds of Men,* writes about the revolutionary faith that was inspired by the Bavarian

Illuminati. Bear in mind that Billington is not a "conspiracy writer," but the thirteenth Librarian of Congress and a friend of the Bush family. He is as official a historian as you can find. President George W. Bush quoted Billington's book in his 2005 inaugural address after he was elected for his second term. In his exhaustive work, Dr. Billington presents a whole section titled "The Pythagorean Passion," in which he says: "A vast array of labels and images was taken from classical antiquity to legitimize the new revolutionary faith."[33]

Notice his reference to "classical" antiquity (i.e., pagan symbolism). He goes on to say that "Pythagoras, the semi-legendary Greek philosopher, provided a model for the intellectual-turned-revolutionary. He became a kind of patron saint for romantic revolutionaries."[34] Adam Weishaupt, the founder of the Bavarian Illuminati, even named his "final blueprint for politicized Illuminism...*Pythagoras*."[35]

Billington says that the "revolutionaries...repeatedly attached importance to the central prime numbers of Pythagorean mysticism: one, three, seven, and above all five." The number five is significant because there are five points to a pentagram. Pythagoras called the pentagram the *pentalpha,* which is why there are so many Pentalpha lodges in modern Freemasonry. This is also why there is a pentagram in the street layout of Washington, DC, as we detail in our documentary, *Riddles in Stone.*[36]

The Washington, DC Pentagram

All serious researchers contend that the controversy over the pentagram is not about whether or not it is truly there. Aerial photos clearly reveal it. Even the Masons, who deny that they are responsible for it, acknowledge its presence, but argue that Rhode Island Avenue does not extend all the way to complete the figure. As such, the debate is twofold: 1) Was the pentagram intentional, or simply the coincidence of geometric lines? 2) Why is the pentagram incomplete? The answer to the second part seems to reveal the first. As explained in *Riddles in Stone*, the unfinished pentagram is a well-known symbol in Freemasonry. As Manly P. Hall records in his writings:

> The pentagram is used extensively in black magic, but when so used its form always differs in one of three ways: The star may be broken at one point by not permitting the converging lines to touch.... When used in black magic, the pentagram is called the "sign of the cloven hoof" or the "footprint of the devil."[37]

Of course, Hall was writing in the twentieth century, but was this symbolism known by Masons during the founding era? The answer is yes. One of the most famous Master Masons of all time was Johann Wolfgang von Goethe, who made use of such a pentagram in the play, *Faust,* in which the character of Faust summons Mephistophiles (the Devil) to make a pact with him. As the Devil tries to leave, he is hindered. As a result, he and Faust have the following exchange:

Mephistophiles
Let me go up! I cannot go away;
a little hindrance bids me stay.
The Witch's foot upon your sill I see.

Faust
The pentagram? That's in your way?
You son of Hell, explain to me,
If that stays you, how came you in today?
And how was such a spirit so betrayed?

Mephistophiles
Observe it closely! It is not well made;
One angle, on the outer side of it,
Is just a little open, as you see.[38]

The "open" or "broken" pentagram was used by Faust to summon the Devil in a black magic ceremony. The famous author of the play, Goethe, was not only a Mason, but also a well-known member of the Bavarian Illuminati. To this day, Freemasons proudly acknowledge that his writings are filled with Masonic symbolism, while books have been written about his Illuminist involvement.

Goethe published his first edition of *Faust* in 1790 (called *Faust: ein Fragment*), and it was in the next two years that Pierre L'Enfant (with the possible help of Thomas Jefferson) came up with the street design for Washington, DC (1791–1792). It is therefore provable that members of these secret orders were familiar with the idea of an unfinished pentagram *before* the street layout was complete. Admittedly, this does not, of itself, prove that the pentagram was intentional. Yet it is interesting that Goethe's play and the DC design were done during the same period. Because of the close interaction between the Freemasonry of America and that of Europe, it is entirely possible (and likely) that L'Enfant and Jefferson were familiar with the symbol and placed it intentionally.

Were They Masons?

Both Pierre L'Enfant and Thomas Jefferson are thought to have been Masons. The reason for doubting it is because modern American Masonry cannot find the initiation records of these two men. Some believe they were initiated in France and their records were destroyed through the chaos of the French Revolution. Before believing those who deny their membership, bear in mind that Jefferson is listed among the Masonic presidents in the Harry S. Truman Presidential Library. Furthermore, the well-known European publication *Freemasonry Today* maintains unequivocally that Pierre L'Enfant was a Mason: "Washington, DC can fairly be described as the world's foremost 'Masonic City.' Its centre was laid out according to a plan drawn up by the French Freemason Pierre L'Enfant."[39]

Many other Masonic writers similarly state that Jefferson and L'Enfant were Masons, while some Masonic apologists debate the issue. When critics like David Barton or the History Channel *insist* that these men and others of the founding era were not Masons, and then blame the "conspiracy theorists" for passing on misinformation, they are either ignorant or deliberately withholding information.

America: The New Atlantis

In our documentary series, *Secret Mysteries of America's Beginnings*, we show how Freemasonry and Rosicrucianism existed in England during the Elizabethan era, and were directly involved in the colonization scheme. Yes, there were most certainly Christians who came to this country through the Puritan/Pilgrim movement, but they were not alone. With them came the secret societies that saw America as "the New Atlantis" envisioned by Sir Francis Bacon. There is even a 1910 Newfoundland six-cent stamp (with three sixes on it, no less) with the image of Bacon that reads: "Lord Bacon, the Guiding Spirit in Colonization Scheme."

Clearly, there were those who understood that the development of the new world was inspired by Bacon and his occult philosophies.

It was Bacon who said, "Knowledge is power," and the pursuit of knowledge through scientific discovery has guided the success of America. If one reads *The New Atlantis*, where Bacon describes a society with tall buildings, flying machines, weapons of mass destruction, health spas, the magnification of sound, and experiments with poisons on animals for the purpose of curing human beings, it becomes readily discernible that our country has followed his blueprint from the start. Once you understand that Rosicrucianism (the inner doctrine of Masonry) is the mingling of Christianity with paganism, many of the founding fathers make more sense. A Rosicrucian can readily quote the Bible and make references to Christ, Jesus, the Savior, and so forth, but he will also exalt the teachings of Plato and the philosophers of old, and will look upon the gods of the ancient world as examples of virtue and justice.

Bacon's *New Atlantis* has also been called *The Land of the Rosicrucians* (see *A New Light on Bacon's New Atlantis* by Mather Walker), and that is exactly what America has become, thanks to the secret societies. The rise of paganism in our country is no accident; it was planned from the beginning. What author Tom Horn demonstrates in *Apollyon Rising 2012* is that America's great struggle—which is indeed the wound of the whole world—is not against terrorists, communists, or liberals, but is the spiritual war against the one true God, waged in the manifestation of this ancient pagan dream.

Christian J. Pinto

INTRODUCTION

I t was two a.m. when suddenly I sat straight up in bed. A moment earlier, during REM (rapid eye movement) sleep, when most dreams or "night visions" occur, a last piece of an important puzzle had fallen into place, shaking me from slumber.

I had been wrestling with certain images and enigmatic information for years, trying to make sense of what I had found. But not until recently had something deeper troubled me. It was as if an ominous voice somewhere was ready to show me what I was finally able to receive.

Of course, I was very familiar with transcendent subject matter. I had been involved with religious institutions for more than thirty years in official capacities, including as an executive in the largest evangelical organization in the world. During that same time, I had appeared on international television and radio programs with the opportunity to expand my presence to a regular audience, if desired.

Yet it was not until a brief stint working with exorcisms that I had come face to face with authentic supernaturalism, and had finally begun questioning the differences between indoctrination and revelation, knowledge and wisdom, religion and relationship, or good and evil. It was here at last that my arrogant disposition, which had served my significant ego like a triumphant battlehorse for decades, fell weak. The sword of a superb memory that had allowed me to chop down others with proof texts and so-called writs of fact had at once become as empty as the tomb of Jesus Christ.

I wouldn't know until later how necessary that rebirth and change of heart and mind had been. Some of the very people I had mocked as conspiratorial had turned out to be closer to understanding these enigmatic truths than I had ever been. Naiveté and blind acceptance—especially of specific, controlled versions of American history—had kept me in the dark, blinded from the actual course that a frightening network of hidden powers had set our nation upon years before.

Then came "the angel in the whirlwind," and pieces of the puzzle began rapidly falling into place. Things were making sense now—world affairs, changes to US domestic and foreign policies, and a renewed focus on the Middle East, Israel, Iran, Iraq, and Babylon—and I found it astonishing. The words, deeds, gestures, and coded language of the world's most powerful men clearly pointed to an ancient, prophetic, cryptic, and even terrifying reality.

As outlined in this book, the startling truths behind the clandestine society that helped frame the United States and placed within the Great Seal a prophetic secret doctrine can finally be understood. What even the best researchers of the Illuminati and veiled fraternities such as the Freemasons were never able to fully decipher is spelled out herein for the first time. The power at work behind global affairs and why current planetary powers are hurriedly aligning for a "new order from chaos" is exposed. Perhaps most incredibly, readers will learn how ancient prophets actually foresaw and forewarned of this time.

One caution: If you are a person who is happy living in a "matrix," cradled in the warm embrace of illusions, I recommend that you set this book aside and enjoy your remaining days uninformed.

But if, like the millions of others around the world, you have recently awakened with a sense that something foreboding is unfolding on earth, then this book is for you. If you believe that a global event, which, so far, nobody has been able to clearly explain, is on the horizon, this book is for you. If you feel whatever is happening is both physical and spiritual, yet you cannot solve the conundrum of what is stirring beneath the surface, this book is for you. If you hunger to discern the meaning behind the raging turmoil recently enveloping nature, societies, and global politics, this book is for you.

But prepare yourself for the unexpected, including truly startling and often discomfiting information that you have not heard or read anywhere before.

What has been hidden in plain sight for more than two hundred years is preparing to reveal itself to humanity.

The clock is ticking and the hand is closer to midnight than most can comprehend.

Something wicked this way comes.

The occult desire of the ages is here.

And once you understand the secret, you will know what you have to do to survive.

Chapter 1

SUMMONING THE ANGEL FROM THE WHIRLWIND

Some of the biggest men in the United States, in the field of commerce and manufacture, are afraid of something. They know that there is a power somewhere so organized, so subtle, so watchful, so interlocked, so complete, so pervasive, that they had better not speak above their breath when they speak in condemnation of it. —Woodrow Wilson

The real rulers in Washington are invisible and exercise power from behind the scenes. —US Supreme Court Justice Felix Frankfurter

On January 20, 2001, President George W. Bush, during his first inaugural address, faced the Obelisk known as the Washington Monument and twice referred to an angel that "rides in the whirlwind and directs this storm." His reference was credited to Virginia statesman John Page, who wrote to Thomas Jefferson after the Declaration of Independence was signed, "We know the race is not to the swift nor the battle to the strong. Do you not think an angel rides in the whirlwind and directs this storm?"

Five weeks after the inaugural, on Wednesday, February 28, 2001, Congressman Major R. Owens of New York stood before the House of Representatives and prayed to the "angel in the whirlwind." He asked the spiritual force to guide the *future* and *fate* of the United States.[40] Twenty-eight weeks later (for a total of thirty-three weeks from the day of the inaugural—a number invaluable to mysticism and occult fraternities), nineteen Islamic terrorists attacked the United States (according to the official story), hijacking four commercial airliners and crashing two of them into the Twin Towers of the World Trade Center in New York City. They slammed a third into the Pentagon, and a fourth, which had been directed toward Washington, DC, crashed near Shanksville, Pennsylvania. What happened that day resulted in nearly three thousand immediate deaths, at least two dozen missing persons, and the stage being set for changes to the existing world order.

When Bush was giving his second inaugural speech four years later, he again offered cryptic commentary, saying, "For a half century, America defended our own freedom by standing watch on distant borders. After the shipwreck of communism came years of relative quiet, years of repose, years of sabbatical—and then there came a day of fire." A few paragraphs following, Bush added, "By our efforts, we have lit a fire as well—*a fire in the minds of men*. It warms those who feel its power, it burns those who fight its progress, and one day this untamed fire of freedom will reach the darkest corners of our world" (emphasis added).

The phrase, "a fire in the minds of men," is from Fyodor Dostoyevsky's nineteenth-century book, *The Possessed* ("The Devils"), a novel set in pre-revolutionary Russia, where civil resistance is seen championed by nihilist Sergei Nechaev, who tries to ignite a revolution of such destructive power that society will be completely destroyed. The fact that a United States president would quote this phrase in an official speech of record was astonishing to many analysts, given that *The Possessed* is about violent government crackdown on dissent that sparks civil unrest and revolution marked by public violence.[41] *Fire in the Minds of Men* is also the title historian James H. Billington chose for his famous book on the history of revolutions, including the origin of occult Freemasonry and its influence in the American Revolution. In his closing comments, Bush himself tied the inaugural crypticisms to the Masonic involvement in the American Revolution, saying, "When our Founders declared a new order of the ages, they were acting on an ancient hope that is meant to be fulfilled." The phrase, "a new order of the ages," is taken from the Masonically designed Great Seal (*novus ordo seclorum*), and Bush further acknowledged that the secret society members were acting on an "ancient" hope that is "meant to be fulfilled."

To the illumined elite and a handful of historians and scholars, the inaugural addresses by the president were important editions in a larger series of carefully crafted speeches in which line-by-line analysis of his public references uncovered what appeared to be coded language designed to convey shrouded messages at regular intervals to select members of his global audience. Biblical scholar Bruce Lincoln's examination of a speech delivered by Bush to the nation on October 7, 2001 announcing the US attack on Afghanistan repeatedly verified this practice, producing redundant, hidden references from apocalyptic books of the Bible concerning the end times.[42] Lincoln concluded that the word-crafting was a strategy of "double coding" to secretly appeal to people who saw Bush as divinely called to stand up to the enemies of God in an unfolding event in the Middle East, which they believed was foretold in the books of Revelation, Isaiah, and other ancient texts. In this instance, Lincoln asserted that Bush was mirroring the dualistic conflict Osama bin Laden had used in speeches to pit his worldview against the West as a struggle between good and evil, and thus to appeal to religious sentiments and traditions. United States officials were clearly uncomfortable with anything that allowed bin Laden to be cast in a sympathetic light through propaganda and the transmission of veiled messages; therefore, according to Lincoln, Bush joined Osama in constructing public perception of "a Manichaean struggle, where Sons of Light confront Sons of Darkness, and all must enlist on one side or another, without possibility of neutrality, hesitation, or middle ground."[43]

In his book, *American Dynasty*, Kevin Phillips confirms this practice of message-coding by Bush, pointing out the ever-present references in the president's speeches to words such as "evil" and "evil ones."[44] At the top of Phillips' list is reference again to the use of the metaphysical phrase "whirlwind," which he interprets as "a medium for the voice of God in the books of Job and Ezekiel." From an esoteric point of view, Phillips is either unaware of or unwilling to discuss the deeper, contemporary meaning of this language and its importance to secret societies. But such phrasing in the president's public speeches assuredly did not go unnoticed by the appropriate members of his audience. Lincoln comes closest to acknowledging this when he writes:

> Enlisting the specialized reading/listening and hermeneutical skills they cultivate, he encouraged them to probe beneath the surface of his text. There, *sotto voce* ["under voice"], he told them he understands and sympathizes with their views, even if requirements of his office constrain him from giving full-throated voice.[45]

Of course, Bush was not the first president to use the language of the divine to cast himself as "defender of the faith" in order to win support for public policy. Who can forget Ronald Reagan's view of the Soviet Union as the "Evil Empire" and his feeling that war in the Middle East might draw "Gog" into nuclear war and fulfill biblical prophecy? In his 1984 debate with Walter Mondale, Reagan admitted, "No one knows whether those prophecies mean that Armageddon is a thousand years away or the day after tomorrow."

Yet few would argue that, with George W. Bush, the language of godlike appointment went disturbingly deeper. Even members of his own Methodist denomination saw a change in him after he took office. He seemed, to them, to have become a man on a mission, somebody who believed he was "chosen" by God to initiate a prophetic "master plan." And until the 2006 midterm elections unseated Republican control of Congress and effectively stopped the juggernaut of his administration's changes to domestic and foreign policy, the presidency of Bush was believably on a path toward an apocalyptic vision led by inspiration from the angel in the whirlwind. Whether the president fully understood the ramifications of his words and actions, he and others around him had: 1) acknowledged; 2) prayed to; and 3) welcomed supernatural agents to guide and influence the future machine of national sovereignty in a way oddly familiar to end-times prophecy and Dostoyevsky's novel.

We allow that the president might have been unaware of parts of his abstruse actions because he was not the author of his speeches in the conventional sense; members of his staff, with input from unnamed guides, crafted most of these words. Bush nevertheless delivered these speeches after reviewing them, contemplating them, practicing them, and making personal margin notes. More importantly, "He spoke in his official capacity as head of state, representing the state and beyond that the nation," notes Lincoln. So whether

Bush was aware of his actions or was puppeted by dominionist allegiances that he and his father had nurtured (or at a deeper level spoke for fraternal societies), occultists in and behind government knew exactly what they were doing. Their choice of words and actions—from the president's speeches to the counsel he received from members of an elite, top-secret cell of spiritual authorities in Washington (note: this is not a reference to the Christian groups or faith councils that meet with US presidents)—reveal subtle but informing truths: Words were placed in the president's mouth to be spoken in mystic harmony of a sacred craft, an otherworldly discourse, which the men behind the president, the "voices behind the voice," believed would invoke the arrival of a spiritual "kingdom on earth" led by an embodied theocratic representative if these words were uttered at the right moment in history and from chosen men of God. For this "Angel in the Whirlwind," wrote Christopher Findlay, "also carries unsettling connotations of a day of vengeance and judgment…a notion that appeals to…the apocalyptic frame of mind…reminiscent of Winthrop's 'shining city on a hill' image, coupled with the fear of being expelled from this earthly paradise if the new society should fail to fulfill its role in the divine plan."[46]

Later, when some in the public were taking courage that the midterm backlash of November 2006 had sufficiently restrained the administration's dreams of playing a vital role in initiating Armageddon, behind the scenes in Washington, DC, this influential group of powerful men retained faith in their paranormal forces. Setting their eyes on the timeframe of 2009–2012, they were not for the moment concerned if Congress or even the executive branch changed hands now and again. They had received what they wanted—official invitation to supernaturalism by the nation's leaders and, for sufficient time, conformity by the majority of uninitiated Americans. An angel from the whirlwind spread its powerful wings, and a new epoch in American history was ushered in, a time when the government of the US was intentionally brought under influence to dark angelic power.

The statement above may seem daring. But the connection between the president's speeches, signals to "the family" of spiritual advisors as well as to the leaders of the Craft (discussed later), the Bush administration's subsequent actions, and coalescence of Congress—and, for a while, the majority of Americans—set in motion the rules for cosmic game play as defined in the sacred texts of all major religions, including the Bible. Invitation to angels by elected officials, combined with passive civilian conformity, is key to opening doorways for supernatural agents to engage social governance. This is a classic tenet of demonology. Spirits go where they are invited, whether to possess an individual or to take dominion over a region. One could contend, therefore, that starting in 2001, the United States became so disposed in following and not challenging unprecedented changes to longstanding US policies, including the Christian rules for just war, that a powerful force known to the Illuminati as the "Moriah Conquering Wind," a.k.a. "the angel in the whirlwind," accepted the administration's invitation and enthroned itself in the nation's Capitol. Immediately after, it cast its eyes on the ancient home of the Bab-Illi, Babylon, where the coveted "Gate of the Illi" had opened once before.

Into the Home of Bab-Illi

Despite a series of ever-changing explanations as to why George W. Bush was stubbornly resolved to take the US into Iraq/Babylon even though Iraq was not connected to the events of September

11, 2001, years later, if you asked twenty analysts to define the true nature behind the US entering that war, they would probably give you twenty different answers.

Some say it was strategic placement of US military resources against what the administration saw as a growing threat from Islamic radicals. Some say it was an effort to seize and maintain control of Iraqi oil reserves. Others contend that 9/11 was itself either a convenient or orchestrated event (false flag) allowing the Bush administration to extend a global domination project. Still others believe something unusual connected to biblical sites in Babylon had been uncovered during Saddam Hussein's reconstruction of the ancient city, and that the administration went there to capture it. But according to the British press, Bush let his real reasons slip during a meeting with Palestinian leaders in June 2003, when he admitted he had committed the United States to enter Babylon because "God told me to invade Iraq." [47] The same year, while lobbying nations to join his "Coalition of the Willing," Bush startled France's president, Jacques Chirac, by telling him that supernatural forces known as "Gog and Magog" were rising in the Middle East and that his administration had been "willed by God…to use this conflict to erase his people's enemies before a New Age [novus ordo seclorum] begins." [48] In 2009, it emerged that not only was this Bush's state of mind, but that Donald Rumsfeld, as defense secretary, had followed up by routinely adorning top-secret memos concerning the Iraq war for cabinet members and the president, using prophetic quotations from the Bible.

Did a voice from God instruct the leader of the world's most powerful nation to begin what quickly resulted in, at least on the surface, a debacle? One disturbing possibility is that the president was delusional. On the other hand, if God did tell Bush to invade Iraq, given other "signs of the times," we tune our ears to the prophets who foretold an end-of-days event when Babylon would be overthrown by a foreign invader, followed by the release of apocalyptic forces—powers known by the prophets as the descendants of fallen angels who went into hell "in full battle dress."[49] When the prophet Jeremiah prophesied the future of Babylon, he specifically foresaw the catalyst for its destruction as happening when the God of the angel-armies (LORD of hosts) sends a warning that "evil" (*ra* in Hebrew) is to be unleashed upon the nations of the world by "a great whirlwind" that is raised up from the coasts of the earth (Jeremiah 25:32). The people of earth are afterward viewed as hopeless and in need of a savior.

Forebodingly, the end of Bush's second term witnessed such civil clamor for renewed "hope" amidst widespread messianic fervor surrounding the election of America's current president, Barack Hussein Obama. Bush's angel in the whirlwind administration was indeed prophetic in that it accomplished exactly what elite occultists wanted: a fire burning in the minds of men, fanned by multinational chaos and desperation, resulting in universal entreaty for an inspirational and political demigod—a savior—to arise on the global scene promising a New World Order.

Did Bush Know What He Was Doing?

It is entirely possible that Bush's understanding of his calling as the catalyst of these end-times events was a revelation that grew on him over time. In the beginning, many of his ties to evangelical Christianity appear to have been simply for the purpose of producing political advantages. While still in his second term as governor, Bush actually hired influence-peddler Karl Rove to help strategize how he might endear himself to the fundamentalist base in anticipation of a presidential run. Not long after, the highest-ranking members of the nation's politically enthused church leaders were summoned to the governor's mansion, where the hand-picked movers and shakers, selected for their proven power to sway religious voters, were encouraged to conduct a "laying on of hands" to anoint the future president. As the executive mantle was vicariously conferred on Bush, he surprised the group by suddenly evoking the prophetic commissions of the prophets, telling the attendees that he had been "called" (by God) to become the presidential candidate.

Following Bush's consecration by the holy men of 1999, only a brief period transpired in which public religious rhetoric surrounding him was no more unusual than the historiography of other American presidents. Then came the election, followed by 9/11, and the "calling" Bush believed he had received started defining itself in unsettling ways.

Author Bob Woodward noted in his book, *Bush at War,* that just three days after 9/11, during the National Day of Prayer and Remembrance at the National Cathedral in Washington, DC, the president seemed to assume a divinatory role, as if suddenly he had accepted a fantastic cosmic destiny, declaring that the nation's responsibility to history was already clear: "to answer these attacks and rid the world of evil."[50] By taking up the language of "good vs. evil," Woodward viewed the president "casting his vision and that of the country in the grand vision of God's master plan."[51]

Immediately, the dialect of Armageddon theology began surfacing in presidential briefings. Even religious publications were startled by it. Some reacted right away, calling on the president to plainly set out his views. Kevin Phillips recorded how, in March 2003, "The editors of *Christian Century* insisted that 'the American people have a right to know how the president's faith is informing his public policies, not least his design on Iraq.'"[52] Phillips further stated,

More than Bush's earlier religious phraseology, his Scripture-flavored preparation for war against Iraq—the latter-day Babylon of biblical notoriety—stirred scrutiny. Those who followed Bush's religiosity had seen a change, in one pundit's words, "from talking about a Wesleyan theology of 'personal transformation' to describing a Calvinist 'divine plan' laid out by a sovereign God for the country and himself."[53]

So alarming was the president's change in demeanor that even leaders of his own denomination registered dissent. Robin Lovin, Southern Methodist University professor of religion and political thought, cautioned that, "All sorts of warning signals ought to go off when a sense of personal chosen-ness and calling gets transplanted into a sense of calling and mission for a nation."[54]

Ultimately, the prophetic context for war in the very land associated with future Armageddon (and against Saddam Hussein, no less, the man who claimed to be the reincarnated Nebuchadnezzar) held for Bush the language of moral dualism necessary to play out a "divine mission" while earning him admiration from Dominionists, Neocons, Bonesmen, and the guardians of the Craft.

Perhaps more than anyone else, it was precisely for these members of the "family" and their comrades in secrecy that the most startling coded language was drafted at regular cycle. For them, the phrase "fire in the minds of men" from the second inaugural was not only a call for societal upheaval to usher in a New World Order, but a reference to the Promethean faith. That neoconservativism and Prometheanism could be married in this way is keen, as both doctrines are occult visions of a kingdom of God (or gods) on earth established through human endeavor and enlightenment. Prometheus was the Greek Titan who stole fire from the gods and gave it to man. When Prometheus is incarnated in the human mind as the mystical longing for illumination (a "fire in the mind"), the latter produces what James Billington called "the revolutionary faith" or "Promethean faith," a Gnostic doctrine whose origin was solidified in occult Freemasonry and "scientific" Marxism.

Thus, in view of recent history, a "fire in the minds of men," plus two references to "the angel in the whirlwind," were perfect choices for George Bush's inaugurals. This was also key for those who understood it at the time to unlocking what researcher and academic Peter Dale Scott describes as "deep politics"—those below-surface realities that may for political reasons be hidden from the radar of civilians while at the same time signaling the appropriate brokers of power concerning the real or "deep" political and/or spiritual agenda at play. By twice referring to the "angel in the whirlwind," Bush also certified confirmation from God for his actions ("For God speaks once, yea twice" [Job 22:13]; "In the mouth of two…witnesses" [2 Corinthians 13:1]). In occult theology, the number two is also the Zoroastrian math for dualism, and it extended the Manichaean prose necessary for Bush to cast himself as the "son of light" at war with "sons of darkness." For the Illuminatist, this light is derived from Lucifer, the light-bearer, and, as we shall discover, the angel in the whirlwind is key to such dark forces.

Chapter 2

WHAT THE FIRST SYMBOLS COMMUNICATED, AND TO WHOM

Some of the techniques that they use in this psychic dictatorship are words, symbols, colors, rhythms, light, movement, and mudras which have been used for aeons as means of spiritualization, used by cults, infused with mysticism, are now being used on us. —Michael Tsarion

To play those millions of minds, to watch them slowly respond to an unseen stimulas, to guide their aspirations without their knowledge—all this whether in high capacities or in humble—is a big and endless game of chess, of ever extraordinary excitement. —Sidney Webb, founder of the Fabian Society

When contemplating Bush's "angel in the whirlwind" inaugural references and how this was used to set the stage in the American psyche for allegorical cosmic conflict between the forces of good versus evil—the good United States against the evil spirit of Babylon—I recalled how, in 1992, former MI6 British intelligence officer, Dr. John Coleman, wrote a book titled *The Committee of 300*, in which he claimed inside knowledge concerning world manipulation by an occult Illuminati elite. According to Coleman, the angel in the whirlwind, or "Moriah Conquering Wind," is actually one of the names the society members signal each other by. He states:

> Included in the membership are the old families of the European Black Nobility, the American Eastern Liberal Establishment (in Freemason hierarchy and the Order of Skull and Bone), the Illuminati, or, as it is known by the Committee, "MORIAH CONQUERING WIND".... In the Committee of 300, which has a 150-year history, we have some of the most brilliant intellects assembled to form a completely totalitarian, absolutely controlled "new" society—only it isn't new, having drawn most of its ideas from the Clubs of Cultus Diabolicus. It strives toward a one world government rather well described by one of its late members, H. G. Wells, in his work commissioned by the Committee which Wells boldly called: "THE OPEN CONSPIRACY—PLANS FOR A WORLD REVOLUTION."[55]

Dr. Coleman went on to warn about the devotion that the occult oligarchists have toward implementing a one-world order through emerging uniformed codes and laws by which everybody on the planet will be enslaved to the desires of the ruling elite. The connection between Freemasonry, Skull and Bones (in which George W. Bush is also a member), and the knowledge that "Moriah Conquering Wind" is a title by which the occult insiders identify themselves, is notable. "Moriah" is an ancient term, and its connection to "divine wind" as a vehicle for God and angelic war is important to Jewish apocalyptic and mystical literature, as well as to mainstream religious and esoteric-minded peoples for different reasons.

On the surface, Moriah is the sacred mountain on which Abraham nearly sacrificed his son, Isaac, before the angel of God called out of the sky and stopped him. Moriah is also the location of the original Temple Mount in Jerusalem, according to some scholars. The Foundation Stone at the heart of the Dome of the Rock in modern Jerusalem is believed to mark the exact location of Araunah's threshing floor "in mount Moriah" over which the temple of Solomon was built (see 2 Chronicles 3:1). In addition to the significance of the geography, the role that Mt. Moriah (Hebrew: *Mowriyah*, "chosen by Yahweh") plays in "illuminated" mysticism, the relationship between God and man, heaven and earth, and angelology is deeper than most comprehend. Both the physical location of Moriah as the Temple Mount and the associated spiritual concepts of angelic intervention are central to hidden doctrines among the occult hierarchy that will become frighteningly clearer to readers as they move through this book.

In related midrashic discussions of the Abraham/Isaac narrative, the perspective is changed from the Genesis account on Mt. Moriah to heaven, where God watches and ultimately signals the angel to stop the sacrifice of Isaac. The pseudepigraphal *Book of Jubilees* is used in such renderings, as the story from *Jubilees* offers the account from the angel's viewpoint, in the language of the first person from heaven. Similar information about the angel who spoke to Abraham is included in the Zohar, Kabballa, Babylonian Talmud, and the Pseudepigrapha, as well as classic texts by some members of Christianity and Islam who ultimately identify him as "Metatron," the most powerful of all angels, according to these noncanonical works. For illuminatists, the third book of *Enoch* is among the most important of the mystical literature, as it offers the genesis of Metatron by claiming that Enoch himself is the one who ascends into heaven to be transformed into Metatron.

An extract from 3 Enoch reads:

This Enoch, whose flesh was turned to flame, his veins to fire, his eyelashes to flashes of lightning, his eyeballs to flaming torches, and whom God placed on a throne next to the throne of glory, received after this heavenly transformation the name Metatron.[56]

As Metatron, Enoch becomes the "angel in the whirlwind" and master over other angels of wind and whirlwind (including Ruhiel, Ra'miel, and Ra'shiel, et al).

Sparks emanated from him, and storms, whirlwind, and thunder encircled his form. The angels dressed him in magnificent garments, including a crown, and arranged his throne. A heavenly herald proclaimed that from then on his name would no longer be Enoch, but Metatron, and that all angels must obey him, as second only to God.[57]

Because Enoch as Metatron can control all other angels—good and evil—he is thus "a critical figure in Masonry as well as being heavily identified with ritual magic and Qabala [Kabbalah] through his association with—or rather transformation into—Metatron," writes Mark Stavish in his book, *Freemasonry: Rituals, Symbols and History of the Secret Society*.[58] Invoking the "angel in the whirlwind" thus calls upon Metatron (according to belief of the mystical orders) to involve himself as this persona on behalf of the petitioners.

The extra-biblical legend concerning Enoch's transformation into Metatron and the angel's connection with the test of Abraham and Isaac on Mt. Moriah are also deeply encoded within several of the occultist's rituals. In some instances, the formalities combine elements of the Moriah story with other mythologies for the express purpose of aligning the exalted members of the society with the forces behind the conquering wind. Thanks to radio host Alex Jones, the public has seen one such ritual on film. A few years ago, Jones and a British filmmaker slipped into the Bohemian Grove thirty miles west of Santa Rosa, California, where they recorded what is now known as the "Cremation of Care" ceremony. What Jones caught on camera is like something out of a Stanley Kubrick film. Hooded figures of some of the world's wealthiest, most powerful men, including acting and former US presidents such as George W. Bush, George H. W. Bush, Vice President Dick Cheney, and other participants gathered beneath a forty-foot-tall stone owl surrounded by water. A child (or effigy) dubbed "Dull Care" was delivered by a ferryman on a small boat and placed on the altar before the owl, where it was burned as an offering for the purpose of magically alleviating the cares and concerns of those elitists making the sacrifice. Before Jones captured this astonishing ritual on film, American citizens were not even aware that such occultism is carried out under the cover of darkness by the world's most powerful and respected leaders. Does this not cause reasonable people to question what other sorcery is occurring behind the veil?

On his website, Jones says: "This is like something out of a Hollywood movie, where teenagers are out camping in the wilderness and come over a hill and witness some devil cult in black and red garb sacrificing some poor soul on a bloody altar." Jones has written about the similarity between the "Cremation of Care" rite and the ancient Canaanite worship of the owl god Molech, where children were sacrificed for nearly identical reasons. Scholars have debated whether the child sacrifices made to Molech were burned alive, or were slain elsewhere and then drained of blood and offered as food to the deity. If the former, a comparison is made between Molech and Kronos, from whose brazen arms children were rolled alive into an oven of fire. Like the Bohemian ritual, the ancient Baals Molech and Kronos were usually called upon to relieve the ones making the sacrifice of their earthly cares, and people who sought material prosperity believed their lives could be improved by offering the child as a sacrifice to the deity.

Three hundred years before Christ, the Greek author Kleitarchos recorded the dastardly process of sacrificing infants in "Cremations of Care" to Kronos:

> Out of reverence for Kronos, the Phoenicians, and especially the Carthaginians, whenever they seek to obtain some great favor, vow one of their children, burning it as a sacrifice to the deity, if they are especially eager to gain success. There stands in their midst a bronze statue of Kronos, its hands extended over a bronze brazier, the flames of which engulf the child. When the flames fall on the body, the limbs contract and the open mouth seems almost to be laughing [such areas of child sacrifice were often called "the place of laughing"], until the contracted body slips quietly into the brazier.[59]

The sacrifice of children in this way was widespread in antiquity and was practiced by the children of Israel under the reign of King Ahab and Queen Jezebel. A recent archeological find illustrated how far-reaching such offerings were when it unearthed the remains of more than twenty thousand infants who had been sacrificed to a single Baal.

For some, a better candidate than Molech for the deity represented at Bohemian Grove is the Mesopotamian storm demon Lilith, whose giant, horned statues once formed the highest competition to Yahweh. In Hebrew folklore, Lilith is "the dark wind of the storm" who takes the form of an owl (still worshipped in modern Beltane/Mayday rituals) and, among other things, overshadows the sacrifice of children. She is a powerful seductress who, before Eve's creation, was Adam's wife and lover, according to myth. The "Cremation of Care" ceremony conducted by US presidents and other elitists for her (or Molech) at Bohemian Grove is evidently especially seductive, given that metaphysicians among them believe the biblical version of Abraham's test on Moriah was sanitized by Moses in the Genesis account in an attempt to cover up the actual practice of human sacrifice among ancient Hebrews. Perhaps at places like Bohemian Grove they see magic in a "corrected" version of the story—a heretical retelling—where Isaac is extinguished beneath the dark-winged one who rides in the whirlwind and heals her power-hungry and seduced worshippers of their cares. Some claim the same occultists even hid the image of the owl in the Masonically designed US dollar bill for very important and related magical reasons.

Whether Molech or Lilith is the deity represented in the annual Bohemian rituals, a greater legend involving the appropriate semiotic figures—Enoch, Moriah, Metatron, Shekinah, and the Temple Mount in Jerusalem—is captured in higher occult representation pointing directly to the reasoning behind recent changes to US foreign and domestic policy, hidden doctrine of the supranational power elite, and their aspiration for a final earthly kingdom and New World Order ruled by "the one" who has reached apotheosis—the status of a god.

Enter Enoch's Antediluvian Pillars

An important narrative is told from Masonic legend based partly on Talmudist and other traditions including Josephus (indirectly in the first book of *Antiquities*) wherein Enoch, here considered a father of Freemasonry and before he is translated into Metatron, is visited by his female counterpart—the Shekinah of God—and is given a vision of the end of the world. Because of his devotion to God, Enoch constructs nine hidden vaults underground at Mt. Moriah. The vaults are perpendicular, one atop the other, in which he deposits the most important ancient knowledge. In the deepest vault (the ninth), he places a triangular plate of gold, measuring a cubit long on each side, bearing the secret and ineffable name of God. When the vaults of knowledge are complete, Enoch covers them over with soil and erects two pillars on the site—one on which he inscribes the history, arts and sciences, and "doctrines of Speculative Masonry" according to Masonic historian Albert Mackey, and one on which he places hieroglyphic information pointing to the precious treasure in the vaults nearby. The pillars are nearly destroyed in the Great Flood and the vaults lost until the building of Solomon's temple.

Maverick Freemason writers Christopher Knight and Robert Lomas, in their book, *The Second Messiah: Templars, the Turin Shroud, and the Great Secret of Freemasonry*, admit that the legend of Enoch's pillars, as well as the Solomon pillars constructed afterward, are very much a "*pesher*" of Masonic rituals. The term "*pesher*" is a

Hebrew word discovered in the Dead Sea Scrolls that implies that double meanings or "ciphers" occupy certain ancient texts. Thus, "surface interpretation" of particular writings is for common persons of general mental capacity, while deeper concealed truths lay hidden for the initiated persons of higher degree. Knight and Lomas connect this with the legend of Enoch and the illuminated Masonic rites:

> The 13th degree [of the Ancient Scottish Rite of Freemasonry] is "The Royal Arch of Enoch" or "The Master of the Ninth Arch" and it is set at the time of the building of Solomon's Temple three thousand years ago. It is very much a "pesher" of the Holy Royal Arch Degree, which is the story of the Knights Templar removing a keystone in the ruins of Herod's Temple and lowering themselves down into a subterranean vault that contains an ancient scroll.
>
> The degree tells how, in times long before Moses and Abraham, the ancient figure of Enoch foresees that the world will be overwhelmed by an apocalyptic disaster through flood or fire, and he determines to preserve at least some of the knowledge then known to man, that it may be passed on to future civilizations of survivors. He therefore engraves in hieroglyphics the great secrets of science and building onto two pillars: one made of brick and the other of stone.
>
> The Masonic legend goes on to tell how these pillars were almost destroyed, but sections survived the Flood and were subsequently discovered—one by the Jews, the other by the Egyptians—so that civilization could be rebuilt from the secrets that had been engraved on to them. Fragments of one pillar were found by workmen during the excavations for

the foundations of King Solomon's Temple. Whilst preparing the site in Jerusalem three thousand years ago the top of a vault or arch was uncovered, and one of the Masons was lowered into the vault where he found relics of the great pillar of knowledge....

The next degree, "Scotch Knight of Perfection," is set in a room which has at its centre the reassembled fragments of Enoch's pillar, inscribed with hieroglyphics. It is claimed that King Solomon created a "Lodge of Perfection" to rule over the thirteen lower degrees, and its members held their first secret meeting in the sacred vault of Enoch beneath the partly constructed Temple of Solomon.[60]

Consequently in Masonic mysticism, Enoch/Metatron is not only controller of "divine wind," but key to the secrets of illumination. Rituals within Freemasonry related to this legend of Enoch on Moriah, his preservation of the arts and sciences in the underground repositories, and the rediscovery of such during the building of the temple of Solomon are twofold: those based on Enoch's hidden vaults, including the two pillars representing secret knowledge from antiquity, and those based on the pillars in the temple of Solomon representing *the passageway that initiates must move through en route to the guarded knowledge.* The rituals based on these legends are separated for the primitive and higher degrees, with those related to the Enochian pillars being "preserved exclusively to the higher and more modern degrees" of the Craft, while the "only pillars that are alluded to in the primitive degrees are those of Solomon's temple," according to MacKey and Singleton.[61] In *Morals and Dogma*, the late Sovereign Grand Commander of the Scottish Rite Albert Pike adds that Enoch's name in Hebrew signifies "initiate" or "initiator," and hence the columns of knowledge erected by him and those of the temple of Solomon parodied in the Craft and rituals (including the Royal Arch Degree) are symbolic of the Mason's procession from uninitiated to illumined. When a person joins the Order, he passes between the twin columns during initiation, beyond which awaits the mysteries "of which Masonry is the...custodian and depository of the great philosophical and religious truths, unknown to the world at large, and handed down from age to age by an unbroken current of tradition, embodied in symbols, emblems, and allegories."[62] Freemason writers have acknowledged that the two pillars erected at the great temple of Jerusalem are mirrored in the Masonic lodges as sentinels to the entrance "of the inner sanctum, where the Ark and the Divine Shekina resided." The pillars in the Masonic lodges thus represent a "portal the initiate passes through during his admission into Freemasonry" toward the esoteric knowledge represented by and beyond the pillars, available only to those who "traverse this threshold and participate in the mysteries of the Brotherhood." While the original scriptural symbolism (see 1 Kings 7:21) of the pillars in the porch of Solomon's temple suggest by their titles the sustaining power of God (*Jachin*—the right pillar, meaning "he will establish," and *Boaz*— the left pillar, meaning "strength"), the symbolic passage between the pillars in the Masonic lodge establishes, among other things, the goal of passing through the "guardians and gates" in order to reach the presence of the Great Architect of the Universe and the inner sanctum or *sanctum sanctorum*, where "the Ark and the Divine *Shekina*" in Masonic spiritualism hold high occult understanding. Passing through and beyond "twin pillars" is also necessary in occult magical tradition to advance from one epoch to another, as in order to reach the Masonic/Rosicrucian "New Atlantis," which Francis Bacon depicted as lying just beyond the twin pillars of Hercules.

The legend of Hiram Abiff, the Tyrian "First Grand Master" of the Order of Masons and chief architect of the temple of Solomon (whose legend is impersonated every time an initiate reaches the level of Master Mason), is said to have been the only man at the time of the temple's construction who knew, and therefore could pass down, the Enochian secrets. Every Freemason of third degree and higher thus understands what researchers of the Order know as well, that the temple of Solomon is central to the origin, buildings, layout, and rituals of Freemasonry. Each lodge is a representation of the Jewish temple, every lower-degree Mason a depiction of the Jewish workmen who built the temple, and "every Master in the chair a representation of the Jewish King." Significant reasons why this is the case include belief by particular Masons that under the bowels of Moriah, where the temple was built and near the place where Christ was crucified, is Enoch's buried, arched vault that held (or holds) the mysteries of angelic knowledge and the ineffable name of God. In Cryptic (concealed or subterranean) Rites of Freemasonry, the Council of Royal and Select Masters actually ritualizes this concept by playing out the discovery of the concealed vaults wherein the hidden name of God—which some report to be *Jahbulon* (representing the Masonic trinity Yahweh/Baal/Osiris) is bestowed. But there is another name we will unveil later in this book, also related to Baal and Osiris, actually hidden in plain sight. Occultists prefer to keep shrouded why knowing this hidden name is so important. According to ancient ritual magic, it is because one can capture, control, or manipulate the power of the "god" if one possesses his oracular name. This is, of course, a demonization of a biblical tenet that conveys that names have power, such as evil spirits being cast out "in Jesus' name" and Jesus having "a name which is above every name" (see Mark 9:38–40, 16:17; Matthew 7:22–23; Acts 19:13–17; Philippians 2:9–11).

Hebrews, as well as other Old Testament peoples, ascribed great significance to naming their children, believing the name held power to determine the outcome of an individual's life. In occultism, this belief is echoed in the mythos of many magical ceremonies, including those of one of the most important deities from mythology, Isis, who was venerated by the Egyptians, Greeks, and Romans as the undisputed queen of magical skills due to being the "goddess of a thousand names." Her enchantments were so powerful that she even forced the high god Ra to reveal his most secret name to her. She accomplished this by conjuring a magic serpent that bit the sun god—a reptile whose venom was so potent that it brought Ra to the point of death, forcing him to surrender his hidden and powerful name. When Ra succumbed, Isis uttered different secret words, which drove the serpent's poison from his body. Afterward, the victorious goddess added Ra's powerful and hidden name to her archive of divine words. Such magic words were considered by the Egyptians to be of the highest importance for the navigation of physical and spiritual dimensions. This was because Isis not only possessed secret words, but she instructed her followers as to how, when, and with what vocal tones they were to be uttered. If the proper words were pronounced correctly—at the right time of the day and with proper ceremony—they would have the effect of altering reality, manipulating the laws of physics, and forcing the being or object to which they were directed into compliance—including people, spirits, and gods. Interestingly, Freemasonic scholars admit that the legend of Hiram Abiff—their original Grand Master and architect of Solomon's temple—is but a retelling of this legend of Isis and Osiris, a fact that the reader will find significant later and that may also play into why the name "angel in the whirlwind" was uttered by America's president in the year of its tipping-point—2001.

Before ending this chapter I should point out that, due to the occult value or sacredness of the numerous elements surrounding these mythologies and the occultist's version of Solomon's temple, there has been an idea for some time that groups from among the Freemasons and illuminated fraternities intend to rebuild or to participate in the rebuilding of a glorious new temple in Jerusalem fashioned after the one built by Solomon. Disclosure of this has occasionally reached the public's ear. *The Illustrated London News*, August 28, 1909, ran a spectacular supplement detailing this goal. The article was titled, "The Freemason's Plan to Rebuild Solomon's Temple at Jerusalem." Three years later, September 22, 1912, *The New York Times* published an outline by Freemasons to rebuild the temple under the title, "Solomon's Temple: Scheme of Freemasons and Opinions of Jews on Rebuilding." By 1914, some publishers had begun adding unprecedented details, including a report that the land on which the Dome of the Rock now stands had been secretly purchased and that plans were already under design for the construction of the third and final temple. Researchers since have produced intelligence that a hushed collaboration is firmly in place, held back only against the right time, opportunity, and circumstances when exalted Freemasons and their associates will move with haste to reconstruct a new temple, from which their "earthly representative" will reign.

In addition to occultists, groups including the Temple Mount Faithful and the Temple Institute in Jerusalem are busy restoring and constructing the sacred vessels and vestments that will be used for service in the new temple at the arrival of their "Messiah" (see http://www.templeinstitute.org). Students of Bible prophecy recognize the importance of such plans as signaling the coming of Antichrist. Old and New Testament Scriptures explain that a false Jewish messiah will appear, enthroning himself as God in the temple in Jerusalem, but afterward he will defile the holy place by setting up a sacrilegious object in the temple and ordering the sacrifices and offerings to cease (see Daniel 9:27; 2 Thessalonians 2:3–4). For any of this to occur, it is necessary for the temple to be rebuilt, thus making claims by Free-masons or other groups interested in fulfilling this monumental task highly suspect with regard to unfolding end-times events.

A major obstacle that arises when discussing the rebuilding of the temple in Jerusalem is the present-day existence of the Islamic shrines known as the Dome of the Rock and the Al-Aqsa Mosque on the Temple Mount, an issue that may also be resolved in Bible prophecy. A fault line near Jerusalem has been the cause of a half-dozen major earthquakes over the last thousand years, and may be strategically located to utterly destroy the Islamic shrines at any point in time. Zechariah 14:3–4 reads:

Then the LORD will go out and fight against those nations, as he fights in the day of battle. On that day his feet will stand on the Mount of Olives, east of Jerusalem, and the Mount of Olives will be split in two from east to west, form-ing a great valley, with half of the mountain moving north and half moving south.

Such a catastrophic event could wipe out the Muslim compound and provide a catalyst for rebuilding Solomon's temple. Reports in recent years have featured scientific evidence and geological surveys warning that buildings in this area could be severely damaged if not utterly demolished by an earthquake. The Associated Press, in what sounded particularly prophetic in this regard, reported:

Most at risk…is the Old City and the eleven-acre elevated plaza housing two major mosques, including the gold-capped

Dome of the Rock. The site is known to Muslims as the Al Aqsa Mosque compound and to Jews as the Temple Mount— once home to the biblical Temples.[63]

It is also entirely possible that an event such as an earthquake would not be required to bring about the dream of a new temple in Jerusalem. The Middle East is a powder keg, and war, with its missiles and bombs, could take out the Islamic shrines in a single hour. Some claim the Muslim structures could even be intentionally targeted during a conflict as a way of facilitating the construction of a new temple. Some writers and researchers in this field of study predict that a Masonic version of the prophesied third temple (see 2 Thessalonians 2) will be built on the very spot from where the debris of the Muslim structures are cleared following some calamity, and then a new messiah will pass through the golden Masonic portals of the temple, announcing to the world that the universal savior of mankind has come.

On June 18, 2009, a third possibility was announced in Jerusalem as a result of theological research that would allow for an extension of the Temple Mount to be made on which the third Jewish temple could be constructed. In an article called "A New Vision for God's Holy Mountain," Ohr Margalit, rabbinical studies professor at Bar-Ilan University in Israel, wrote that "The scenario of a holy revelation given to an authentic prophet that the temple be rebuilt on the current or an extended Temple Mount in peaceful proximity to the Dome, Al Aqsa Mosque, and nearby Christian shrines" is all it would take to approve such a plan.

According to Jewish law...such a prophetic mandate would then be binding. It would also be in keeping with the words of the twelfth-century Jewish sage Maimonides that Christianity and Islam are part of God's ultimate plan "to direct the entire world to worship God together." Interestingly, Theodore Herzl, the preeminent secular Zionist, detailed the same vision for a rebuilt temple in peaceful proximity to Islamic and Christian shrines on what he called "the holy region of mankind."[64]

Whether or not circumstances will be sufficient to build the new temple before America elects its next president in 2016, what started in 2001 may well have laid the foundation upon which the Man of Sin shall reign.

Chapter 3

SIGNS OF A CONSPIRACY

Mystical Numbers, Contagious Ideas

What was the original visionary imprint of what became the United States of America? It came actually from Francis Bacon, who was one of the great mystics of the late sixteenth and early seventeenth centuries. He wrote a book right before he died… called *New Atlantis*.… It's also worth remembering that the founding fathers of the United States, George Washington, Benjamin Franklin, James Madison, etc., were all Masons and Rosicrucians. They were all students of Bacon. They believed that what they were creating was the new Atlantis, the new Israel, the new Rome, the new Athens, and they consciously set forth to build a nation around light and power. Look on the back of a dollar bill and see the pyramid and the all-seeing Eye of Horus. It's important for Americans to understand that we were born out of a mystical vision of human perfection that was basically Atlantean in its impulse. —Jim Garrison, founder of the Gorbachev Foundation

I n the previous chapter, the Akedah, the account of the binding of Isaac on Moriah, proved enlightening when viewed within the distorted importance the story holds for the occultists and their plans. A second important lesson from the Moriah narrative related to phenomena before and after 9/11 involves how nation-influencing angels—both good and evil—can be "loosed" or "bound" above countries based on decisions made by and allowed of national leaders. In the Moriah example, Abraham's obedience not only resulted in an angel staying the sacrifice of Isaac, but according to the *Genesis Rabbah* from Judaism's classical period (a collection of rabbinical homilies on the book of Genesis), Abraham's submission directly affected the angelic "princes of the heathens" as well.

From *Genesis Rabbah* 56:5, we read:

> Here God immediately rewards Israel when Abraham binds Isaac to the altar by binding the princes of the heathens—the angels who served as guardians to the heathen nations—thus making them subservient to Israel. But this fettering only lasts while Israel upholds its part of the covenant with God. When Israel fails to do so, God unfetters the princes, and the heathen nations take their revenge on Israel.[65]

In view of recent history, and given scriptural support for the idea that supernatural forces can be set in motion or "loosed and bound" above nations in response to government conduct, speeches, symbols, rituals, and gestures, we note with special interest not only the "angel in the whirlwind" that Bush invoked for America's favor, but also the "evil" angel that rules the very territory Bush joined the United States in conflict with—Ahriman, the most powerful of all dark angels. In the tenth chapter of Daniel, Ahriman is indirectly referred to as the "prince" over Iraq/Babylon, where the prophet had been fasting and praying for twenty-one days, hoping the God of Israel would see his fast and grant him revelation of Israel's future. On the twenty-first day of his fast, the angel Gabriel appeared and informed Daniel, "From the first day thou didst set thine heart to understand, and to chasten thyself before thy God, thy words were heard, and I am come for thy words" (Daniel 10:12). If an angel had been dispatched from heaven from the first day, why did it take twenty-one days before he arrived? Gabriel provided the answer by explaining that a supernatural Persian "prince" had opposed him for twenty-one days. Not until Michael, the archangel, came to assist in this conflict was Gabriel free to continue his journey (Daniel 10:13).

In Persian theology, the spirit that opposed Gabriel is identified as Ahriman—enemy of Ahura Mazda. According to Zoroastrianism, he was the powerful and self-existing evil spirit from whom war and all other evils had their origin, and he was the chief of the cacodaemons, or fallen angels, expelled from heaven for their sins. The Bible identifies him specifically as "the prince of the kingdom of Persia" (Iraq/Iran), the same area that George W. Bush, like his father before him, viewed as integral to the launching of a New World Order. In this regard, the Bushes fulfilled prophecy, as the beginning of Babylon was the Tower of Babel, where at the macro level Satan's strategy to formulate a one-world system was initiated. Thereafter, Babylon is viewed as equivalent to a satanic world system at enmity with God and the final "kingdom-spirit" against which God will do battle (Revelation 14:8; 17:5). The Bushes are learned men and members of more than one esoteric order, implying that they may have known exactly what they were doing, and why.

Given widespread doctrine among various religious orders concerning this cause-and-effect relationship between "binding and loosing" of geopolitical supernaturalism, a question arises: During the American invasion of Iraq, was the Bush administration or a multinational power elite operating behind US political machinations trying to "bind" something in or above Babylon through "loosing" the angel in the whirlwind? In other words, was an intentional effort made to magically limit interference from Ahriman by summoning the power of Metatron and Shekinah? Mystical language used by officials during this time frame did seem to be summoning appropriate forces connected to these entities, including the "angel in the whirlwind," the "mother of all bombs" (MOAB), and even the title by which the US battle plan was launched—"Shekinah," pronounced "Shock-n-Awe."

The specifically chosen words, gesticulations, and emblems so employed by key members of the US administration following 9/11 were in fact stunning in their parallel to the deeper destiny for which occultists believe America was designed, and which illuminated fraternities know is graphically depicted in the history, mottoes, layout, and architecture of the nation's Capitol. When the esoteric statements employed by the Bush era involving a New World Order rising from the ashes of chaos is reflected against the "prophetic" design of Washington, DC, even the hardiest skeptic is drawn to consider that an occult hand had been at work beginning well over two hundred years ago and up through this century in the "symbols and emblems" associated with the US cities, buildings, monuments, numbers, and official seals that played a role before, on, and after 9/11. As David Flynn, author of the best-selling book, *Temple at the Center of Time*, emailed me to say:

> The combined occultic numbers, places, people and timing involved in the "terrorist attack" is so consistent with the goals of the Mystery organizations concerning "the secret destiny of America," that it goes beyond the agency of mere humans alone.

Researcher David Bay, director of Cutting Edge Ministries (www.CuttingEdge.org) agreed, interpreting the events surrounding 9/11 as a catalyst for the last stage in the Masonic Baconian New

Atlantis. Bay pointed out that even the street design in Government Center in Washington, DC:

> ...has been cunningly laid out in such a manner that certain Luciferic symbols are depicted by the streets, cul-de-sacs and rotaries...[which demonstrate] that the American continent was to [rise from the ashes of chaos] as the new "Atlantis," and its destiny was to assume the global leadership of the drive to the New World Order. From the beginning, the United States of America was chosen to lead the world into this kingdom of Antichrist, and Washington, DC was to be its Capitol.[66]

Ordo Ab Chao: Through the Twin Towers Toward Atlantis

The antediluvian Atlantis, which Bacon utilized as metaphor and which remains so important to the occultists, was mentioned by Plato in his dialogues *Timaeus* and *Critias* as lying beyond the Pillars of Hercules (the Straits of Gibraltar). In a drawing on the title page of his *Instauratio Magna* ("Great Instauration"), Bacon depicted the Pillars of Hercules (using classic Greek pillars) with a ship sailing through them to conceptualize movement past the limitations of existing scholarship into the area of unlimited scientific and anomalous knowledge, represented in his Rosicrucian utopia, *The New Atlantis*. Bacon, like other medieval thinkers, including Descartes and John Dee, was interested in occult and mystical sciences, practicing alchemy and exhibiting an enduring interest in the philosophy and rituals of secret societies, especially as it involved ciphers, symbols, and cryptic communication. Bacon employed geometry, mathematics, and poetic language as tools for concealing "in plain sight" archetypes that only metaphysicians would be able to decipher in order to find what he had enticingly hidden. History connects these works of Bacon to the founding American Freemasons and Rosicrucians, some of whom believed he was an Ascended Master of Wisdom (Mahatmas), or reincarnated, "spiritually enlightened being" of the theosophical concept who had come to bestow hidden knowledge. Notably, Bacon's use of pillars and specifically the Pillars of Hercules advanced the popularity of figurative portals beyond which await the treasure of lost knowledge, paranormal power, and a *novus ordo seclorum*. Metaphors related to such pillar mysticism also led to the combination of not two, but three pairs of pillars known today as the "Three Great Pillars of Freemasonry." The ritualistic importance of these three sets of pillars is commented on by David Stevenson in the Cambridge University book, *The Origins of Freemasonry*:

> Assuming the pillars were (as in later masonic practice) regarded as flanking the entrance to the lodge, then the mason would be seen when he passed between them as simultaneously entering a holy place (the Temple); acquiring lost knowledge or secrets (as they were also the [Enochian] pillars of knowledge); and venturing from the known to the unknown in search of new worlds (as they were also the Pillars of Hercules).... [This] would have been immensely satisfying in an age that believed that the more complex a symbol was the more powerful and valuable it became.[67]

Symbolically, the Twin Towers in New York (as pillars) echoed the Masonic archetype where the Pillars of Hercules, Enoch, and Solomon likewise represented passageways beyond which one could travel to reclaim what Masons believe was lost in Atlantis, a time known to the Greeks as the "Golden Age of Osiris" and to the Egyptians as "Zep Tepi." Accordingly, if before 9/11 leaders of truly dark powers determined that the ascendancy for the New Atlantis had arrived, occult magical tradition suggests they might have triggered an "event" surrounding a mega-ritual-offering (the people who died on 9/11?) powerful enough to compel the supernatural forces over the nation to move their invisible empire beyond the symbolic pillars in New York—which represented American industrial and financial institutions—by igniting global changes accompanied with appropriate symbolism within the context of ultra-national alchemical transformation. This not only would have been to facilitate a universal call for "order out of chaos," but also to: 1) embed subtle images in the minds of uninitiated citizens for the purpose of creating contagious memes in support of a "war on terror" and tolerance of diminishing Domestic freedoms; and 2) communicate to initiates around the world that the oracular date for the culmination of their New Atlantis had arrived. If what happened on 9/11 was thus meant to signal these objectives, it would necessarily be accompanied by appropriate and redundant symbolism communicating to the members of the Order that, to reach the New Atlantis, movement beyond the Pillars (in this case, the Twin Towers in New York and what they represented) was occurring.

Regardless of how fantastic it seems, a thorough examination of the events happening on and following 9/11 affirm what linguistic specialists and semioticians I consulted called "persuasive evidence of an open conspiracy," or, as one flatly stated, "an undeniable occult signature linked to 9/11." Some pointed out how the number eleven—a number known as the "eleventh hour," or last opportunity to stop an emergency—turns up repeatedly as a "marker" tied to 9/11. The phone number called during the emergency (9-1-1) likewise matches the date on which the Twin Towers were attacked.

But in occult numerology, the number eleven means much more than this. It is the first Master Number and represents a *dark vision*. When doubled to twenty-two (22), the vision is combined with *action*. When tripled to thirty-three (33)—the signal of the highest and most important action in Freemasonry—it means *vision* and *action* have combined to produce *accomplishment* in the world.

Is it therefore mere coincidence that exactly *eleven* years to the date following George H. W. Bush's "New World Order" speech (and *eleven* years before 2012), on September *11*, 2001, Flight *11* crashed into the Twin Towers, whose appearance side by side not only formed a Masonic-like, pillared gateway, but also architecturally depicted the number *eleven*? Also consider that Flight *11* hit the Twin Towers first, and Flight *11* had *eleven* crew members; New York was the *eleventh* state added to the Union; the words, "New York City" have *eleven* letters; *Afghanistan*, the first nation the US attacked following 9/11, has *eleven* letters; the name *George W. Bush* has *eleven* letters; the words, "*The Pentagon*," which was also attacked on 9/11, have *eleven* letters; and Flight 77—an additional twin Master Number—hit the Pentagon, which is located on the seventy-seventh (77th) meridian, and the foundation stone for the Pentagon was laid in 1941 on September *11 in a Masonic ceremony.*

While numerous additional references to the number eleven exist in connection with the events of 9/11, other important dates, equally marked by the number eleven, also changed the course of history. For instance, the end of World War I in 1918 occurred on the eleventh day of the eleventh month at exactly the eleventh hour, when the armistice agreement with Germany came into effect. Another example is the assassination of John F. Kennedy in the Masonic Dealey Plaza on the eleventh month, the twenty-second day, and on the thirty-third parallel (note the occult numerological equation again—11-22-33—for "vision, action, accomplishment"). More importantly, the Bible connects the number eleven with the coming of Antichrist in the book of Daniel. When referring to the beast with ten horns (Roman Empire), the prophet, as he was considering these horns, said, "there came up among them another little horn" (Daniel 7:8). According to scholars, this eleventh horn is the Antichrist, who will derive power from a revived Roman Empire and New World Order, which some believe was earnestly set in motion on 9/11. Lastly, in Jewish mysticism and esoteric numerology, the number eleven is considered "the essence of all that is sinful, harmful, and imperfect."[68]

One of the more fascinating correlations between the number eleven, the Pillars of Hercules, Bacon's New Atlantis, and what happened in New York on 9/11 is the arcane symbolism based on the eleventh labor of Hercules, also important to Kabbalah and Masonic rituals.

In mythology, Hercules was driven mad by Hera and killed his own children. To atone for his sins, he was required by Eurystheus to carry out ten labors, which he did. But Eurystheus, an enemy who had ascended the throne in Hercules' place, would not accept labor number two (killing the nine-headed Lernaean Hydra) or labor number five (cleansing the Augean stables) because Hercules had allowed his nephew, Lolaus, to help him burn the heads of the chthonic Hydra—plus, he had accepted payment for the Augean stables work. Eurystheus therefore assigned two new labors: number eleven—steal the golden apples of the Hesperides that had been hidden by the Titan Atlas, and number twelve—capture Cerberus, the three-headed guard dog of Hades.

In Greek mythology, the garden of the Hesperides (the nymphs who tended Hera's garden) was located in Libya near the Atlas Mountains. Depending on the version of the story, either a single tree or grove of trees yielded golden apples there, which, when eaten, produced immortality. Because Hera was suspicious that the nymphs would eat the apples, she placed a hundred-headed dragon there named Ladon to guard it. To get past the dragon, Hercules tricked Atlas, the first king of Atlantis (whose name means "pillar" and who was burdened with holding the heavens and earth upon his shoulders) into retrieving some of the apples for him, as the beast would not attack him. The Greek scholar Apollodorus, who lived more than one hundred years before Christ, tells what happened next:

> But when Atlas had received three apples from the Hesperides, he came to Hercules, and not wishing to support the sphere he said that he would himself carry the apples to Eurystheus, and bade Hercules hold up the sky in his stead. Hercules promised to do so, but succeeded by craft in putting it on Atlas instead. For at the advice of Prometheus he begged Atlas to hold up the sky till he should put a pad on his head. When Atlas heard that, he laid the apples down on the ground and took the sphere from Hercules. And so Hercules picked up the apples and departed. But some say that he did not get them from Atlas, but that he plucked the apples himself after killing the guardian snake.[69]

Numerous elements from the eleventh labor of Hercules stand out as important to occultists when appreciating the message of 9/11. First is the obvious number eleven, which marked the attack on the Twin Towers in New York as a work of destructive forces. Second, the arch villain in this case was played by Osama bin Laden, whose last name is remarkable in that "bin Laden" means "son of Laden" or, alternatively, "Ladon," the mystical, hundred-headed dragon that Hercules had to avoid or destroy. Third, in Masonic mysticism, Jesus Christ is Hercules. In *Morals and Dogma of the Ancient and Accepted Scottish Rite of Freemasonry*, Albert Pike wrote, "'God,' says Maximus Tyrius, 'did not spare His own Son [Hercules], or exempt Him from the calamities incidental to humanity. The Theban progeny of Jove had his share of pain and trial.'"[70] Fourth, Atlas was the first king of Atlantis, important to both the antediluvian and Baconian Atlantis. Fifth, the Golden Apples of the Hesperides reminds one of the nickname of New York City, where the Twin Towers were attacked: "The Big Apple." Sixth, immediately after retrieving the Golden Apples, Hercules freed Prometheus from the Caucasus Mountains, where Zeus had him chained. Recall the point made earlier in this book that Prometheus was the Greek Titan who stole fire from the gods and gave it to man. When he is incarnated in the human mind as the mystical longing for illumination (a "fire in the mind"), the latter produces what James Billington called "the Promethean faith," a Gnostic doctrine whose origin was solidified in occult Freemasonry. And seventh, the eleventh labor of Hercules centers where the three Pillars of Atlas stood, emphasizing again the role of the Three Pillars of Freemasonry as integral to the events of 9/11 and the metaphor of Hercules.

If the eleventh labor of Hercules was intended as symbolic during 9/11, the ancient story was corrected in the New York version to reveal an interesting interpretation of the allegory. In the retelling, revengeful power (number eleven) was released by the dragon (bin Laden, son of Ladon, the Devil of Revelation 12 and 13) where the Golden Apple Garden (NYC, the Big Apple, where the promise of gold dominated) existed, and overpowered Jesus Christ (Hercules). The result created a fire in the minds of men (the release of Prometheus), which moved through and then beyond the Twin Towers/pillars of New York (the pillars of Atlas-Freemasonry-Enoch-Solomon-Atlantis), quickly resulting in universal appeal for a New World Order (culmination of the New Atlantis).

In addition to the eleventh labor of Hercules, at least two other oddities stand out as evidence of a bizarre and occult synchronicity at work during the events of 9/11. On this date, the Pentagon—located on the seventy-seventh meridian West, and whose foundation stone was laid during a Masonic ceremony on 9/11, 1941—was also attacked. The number seventy-seven happens to be the fire department's "ten code" ("10-77") for a high-rise, multiple-dwelling fire. More importantly, the number seventy-seven, like the number eleven, is a powerful Master Number that occultists believe represents the ascension of a New Age Christ "consciousness." The Islamic radicals who attacked the United States on 9/11 would have known that the number seventy-seven is prominent in the religion of Islam, partly due to a statement by their prophet Muhammad, which is interpreted as faith having "seventy-seven branches." In Luke 3:23–38, there were seventy-seven generations from Adam to Jesus Christ. There were seventy-seven generations from Enoch to Christ, according to one account. In some versions of the Bible, such as the International Standard Version, seventy-seven is the number of times to forgive offenses (most versions read "seventy times seven"). Conversely, St. Augustine thought the number seventy-seven represented the ultimate measure of sin because it was a product of the "sin" number (eleven) times the number of divinity or "perfection" (seven), thus 11 x 7 = 77. Perhaps this is also why Satanists have seventy-seven names for the Devil.

Over and above these generalizations, an enlightening observation is discovered when the number seventy-seven is understood as an "illuminated signal" for the Masonic "Revenge of Lamech." This is drawn from Genesis 4:23–24, which says, "And Lamech said unto his wives, Adah and Zillah, Hear my voice: ye wives of Lamech, hearken unto my speech: for I have slain a man to my wounding, and a young man to my hurt. If Cain shall be avenged sevenfold, truly Lamech seventy and sevenfold [seventy-seven]."

Lamech was a descendant of Cain, the first murderer in the Bible, and the father of Tubal-Cain, a master craftsman. In Masonic tradition, the lineage of Lamech is very important because he is considered the forefather of Hiram Abiff, the First Grand Master of the order of Masons and chief architect of the temple of Solomon. The name of Lamech's son, Tubal-Cain, is used as the title for a secret handgrip in Masonic ritual, which bestows passage of the 33rd-Degree Master Mason. This is more than superficially important, as handgrips in Freemasonry form a luciferian antithesis to the biblical concept of virtuous power-transference or "blessings" through greetings or "laying on of hands." The Mason is actually instructed to "follow in the footsteps of his forefather, Tubal-Cain" in order to master the "seething energies of Lucifer [that] *are in his hands.*"

Celebrated 33rd-Degree Freemason Manly P. Hall explains:

> When the Mason learns that the key to the warrior on the block is the proper application of the dynamo of living power, he has learned the mystery of his Craft. The seething energies of Lucifer are in his hands, and before he may step onward and upward, he must prove his ability to properly apply energy. He must follow in the footsteps of his forefather, Tubal-Cain, who with the mighty strength of the war god hammered his sword into a plowshare.[71]

The relationship between Lucifer and possessing "the mighty strength of the war god" is explained by various Masonic sources as a reference to the Roman god Vulcan, the son of Jupiter and Juno—a sun deity associated with lightning and volcanic fire to which human sacrifices were made. His connection with "the seething energies of Lucifer" thus makes sense given that the myth of Vulcan closely resembles the fall of Lucifer and his subsequent position on earth. Various works have provided evidence that Vulcan is actually identical to or related to the biblical Satan. "According to Diel, he bears a family relationship to the Christian devil," writes J. C. Cirlot in the *Dictionary of Symbols.*[72]

If the number seventy-seven on September 11, 2001, pointed to "revenge" upon the United States by the royal bloodline descendents of Lamech, they were following the footsteps of Tubal-Cain indeed, releasing "the seething energies of Lucifer" and the "strength" of Vulcan (Satan) to whom "human sacrifices" must be made.

Another curious fact related to numerology and cryptic symbolism that may contribute to the mounting evidence that preternatural foreknowledge of 9/11 existed for some time is, for want of a better term, what we call the "US Currency Origami Prophecy." It may be nothing more than a fantastic coincidence, but following the attack on the Twin Towers of the World Trade Center in New York City and the Pentagon in Arlington County, Virginia, it was discovered that by folding the new US twenty-dollar bill three times in a specific way, what appears to be an image of the Twin Towers hit and smoking on one side, and the Pentagon on fire on the opposite side, emerges. Producing both images simultaneously on opposite sides with three folds is curious, as a "mirror three" message equals the high mystical value, thirty-three. That the specific images of the Twin Towers and the Pentagon appear in this way is exceptional when one further learns that by using the exact same folding pattern with concurrent US denominations of five-, ten-, twenty-, fifty-, and one-hundred-dollar bills, the complete template of the attack on 9/11 is illustrated. When the five-dollar bill is folded in this way, it portrays the Twin Towers standing unharmed. Advancing to the ten-dollar bill produces the Twin Towers after the first strike. The twenty-dollar bill folded accordingly then produces the towers burned further, and on the opposite side, the Pentagon has just been struck. The US fifty-dollar bill illustrates the sides of the Twin Towers starting to crumble, and the one-hundred-dollar bill depicts the aftermath with nothing but smoke rising into the air. The fact that the exact same folding pattern in concurrent denominations produces the stages of 9/11 in this way is very curious. Is this, like other documentation in this chapter, evidence of an unseen hand? Or is it nothing more than an incredible coincidence? (To see illustrations of the US currency "Origami Prophecy" illustrations and more, visit www.ApollyonRising2012.com.)

A final, astonishing "coincidence" related to Freemasonry and foreknowledge of what happened on 9/11 can be viewed at the Cathedral of St. John the Divine in New York City. Funded by Freemasons and celebrated on the front page of *Masonic World* in March 1925, the Cathedral is bathed in Masonic symbols, including the pyramid and the all-seeing eye. But in 1997, four years before the destruction of the twin towers, stonemasons added a chilling depiction to the western façade of the Cathedral. Called the Apocalyptic Pillar, it clearly prophesied the destruction and collapse of the Twin Towers. What did these Freemasons know?

The Apocalyptic Pillar, image credit vigilantcitizen.com

Chapter 4

MANUFACTURING THE MAN OF SIN'S NEW WORLD ORDER

Last weekend, speaking in Prague, Barack Obama took the New World Order rhetoric to soaring new heights. "All nations must come together to build a stronger, global regime," he said…. Obama's choice of words leaves little doubt about what he means…. Few freedom-minded people would choose to live under any kind of "regime." —Joseph Farah, editor and chief executive officer, www.WorldNetDaily.com

We have operating within our government and political system, another body representing another form of government, a bureaucratic elite which believes our Constitution is outmoded. —Senator William Jenner, 1954

I t's been assumed for centuries that a prerequisite for the coming of Antichrist would be a "revived" world order—an umbrella under which national boundaries dissolve and ethnic groups, ideologies, religions, and economics from around the world orchestrate a single and dominant sovereignty. At the head of the utopian administration, a single personality will surface. He will appear to be a man of distinguished character, but will ultimately become "a king of fierce countenance" (Daniel 8:23).

With imperious decree, he will facilitate a One-World Government, universal religion, and global socialism. Those who refuse his New World Order will inevitably be imprisoned or destroyed until at last he exalts himself "above all that is called God, or that is worshiped, so that he, as God, sitteth in the temple of God, showing himself that he is God" (2 Thessalonians 2:4).

For many years, the notion of an Orwellian society where One World Government oversees the smallest details of our lives and in which human liberties are abandoned was considered anathema. The idea that rugged individualism would somehow be sacrificed for an anesthetized universal harmony was repudiated by America's greatest minds. Then, in the 1970s, things began to change. Following a call by Nelson Rockefeller for the creation of a "New World Order," presidential candidate Jimmy Carter campaigned, saying, "We must replace balance of power politics with world order politics." This struck a chord with international leaders, including President George Herbert Walker Bush, who in the 1980s began championing the one-world dirge, announcing over national television that the time for a "New World Order" had arrived. The invasion into Kuwait by Iraq/Babylon provided perfect cover for allied forces to engage the Babylonian "prince" by launching Desert Storm against Saddam Hussein's forces, an effort Bush made clear was "to forge for ourselves and for future generations a New World Order...in which a credible United Nations can use its...role to fulfill the promise and vision of the U.N.'s founders." Following this initial statement, Bush addressed the Congress, adding:

> What is at stake is more than one small country [Kuwait], it is a big idea—a New World Order, where diverse nations are drawn together in common cause to achieve the universal

aspirations of mankind.... Such is a world worthy of our struggle, and worthy of our children's future…the long-held promise of a New World Order.[73]

Ever since the president's astonishing newscast, the parade of political and religious leaders in the United States and abroad pushing for a New World Order has multiplied. Britain's Prime Minister Tony Blair, in a speech delivered in Chicago, April 22, 1999, said frankly, "We are all internationalists now, whether we like it or not." Blair could barely have imagined how quickly his doctrine would catch on. By December 9, 2008, respected chief foreign affairs columnist for *The Financial Times*, Gideon Rachman (who attended the 2003 and 2004 Bilderberg meetings at Versailles, France, and Stresa, Italy), admitted, "I have never believed that there is a secret United Nations plot to take over the US. I have never seen black helicopters hovering in the sky above Montana. But, for the first time in my life, I think the formation of some sort of world government is plausible." The United Kingdom's Gordon Brown not only agreed, but in an article for *The Sunday Times*, March 1, 2009, said it was time "for all countries of the world" to renounce "protectionism" and to participate in a new "international" system of banking and regulations "to shape the twenty-first century as the first century of a truly global society." On January 1, 2009, Mikhail Gorbachev, the former head of state of the USSR, said the global clamor for change and the election of Barack Obama was the catalyst that might finally convince the world of the need for global government. In an article for the *International Herald Tribune*, he said:

Throughout the world, there is a clamor for change. That desire was evident in November, in an event that could become both a symbol of this need for change and a real catalyst for that change. Given the special role the United States continues to play in the world, the election of Barack Obama could have consequences that go far beyond that country....

If current ideas for reforming the world's financial and economic institutions are consistently implemented, that would suggest we are finally beginning to understand the important of global governance.

Four days later, on January 5, 2009, the chorus call for a New World Order was ramped up by former Secretary of State Henry Kissinger while on the floor of the New York Stock Exchange. A reporter for CNBC asked Kissinger what he thought Barack Obama's first actions as president should be in light of the global financial crises. He answered, "I think that his task will be to develop an overall strategy for America in this period, when really a New World Order can be created." Kissinger followed on January 13 with an opinion piece distributed by Tribune Media Services titled "The Chance for a New World Order." Addressing the international financial crises inherited by Barack Obama, Kissinger discussed the need for an international political order (world government) to arise and govern a new international monetary and trade system. "The nadir of the existing international financial system coincides with simultaneous political crises around the globe," he wrote. "The alternative to a new international order is chaos." Kissinger went on to highlight Obama's extraordinary impact on the "imagination of humanity," calling it "an important element in shaping a New World Order."[74] Kissinger—a Rockefeller functionary and member of the Bilderberg group and Trilateral Commission who routinely turns up in lists among senior members of the Illuminati—peppered his article with key phrases from Masonic dogma, including the comment about the "alternative to a new international order is chaos," a clear reference to "*ordo ab chao*" from ancient Craft Masonry, a reference to the doctrine of "order out of chaos." Like the mythical phoenix firebird, Kissinger visualized the opportunity for a New World Order to be engineered from the ashes of current global chaos, exactly the point he had made years earlier at the Bilderberger meeting in Evian, France, on May 21, 1991, when describing how the world could be manipulated into willingly embracing global government. He said:

> Today Americans would be outraged if UN troops entered Los Angeles to restore order; tomorrow they will be grateful! This is especially true if they were told there was an outside threat from beyond, whether real or promulgated, that threatened our very existence. It is then that all peoples of the world will plead with world leaders to deliver them from this evil. The one thing every man fears is the unknown. When presented with this scenario, individual rights will be willingly relinquished for the guarantee of their well being granted to them by their world government.[75]

During his second inaugural address, US President George W. Bush likewise envisioned the specter of a Babylonian-like, one-world government. With an almost religious tone, he cited Masonic script, saying, "When our Founders declared a new order of the ages...they were acting on an ancient hope that is meant to be fulfilled."[76] New Age guru Benjamin Creme was clearer still on how the marriage of politics and religion would epitomize the New World Order when he said some years ago, "What is the plan? It includes the installation of a new world government and a new world religion under Maitreia" (Maitreia is a New Age "messiah").[77] Five-time United States senator from Arizona and Republican presidential nominee in 1964, Barry Goldwater, likewise foresaw the union of politics and religion as a catalyst for global government. In writing of the efforts of behind-the-scenes groups, including international bankers, to bring about a New World Order, he said it would occur through consolidating "the four centers of power—political, monetary, intellectual, and ecclesiastical." As the managers and creators of the new (prophetic) system, this power elite would "rule the future" of mankind, he believed.[78] So concerned was Goldwater with the consolidation of government policy and religious creed that on September 16, 1981, he took the unique position of warning political preachers from the floor of the US Senate that he would "fight them every step of the way if they [tried] to dictate their [religious ideas] to all Americans in the name of conservatism." The increasing influence of the Religious Right on the Republican Party was bothersome to Goldwater in particular because of his libertarian views. It should have concerned theologians as well, and I say this as a man often associated with the Religious Right. Combining religious faith with politics as a legislative system of governance hearkens the formula upon which Antichrist will come to power. (Note how in the book of Revelation, chapter 13, the *political* figure of Antichrist derives ultra-national dominance from the world's *religious* faithful through the influence of an ecclesiastical leader known as the False Prophet.) Neither Jesus nor His disciples (who turned the world upside down through preaching the gospel of Christ, the true "power of God," according to Paul) ever imagined the goal of changing the world through supplanting secular government with an authoritarian theocracy. In fact, Jesus made it clear that His followers would not fight earthly authorities purely because His kingdom was "not of this world" (John 18:36). While every modern citizen—religious and non-religious—has responsibility to lobby for moral good, combining the mission of the church with political aspirations is not only unprecedented in New Testament theology—including the life of Christ and the pattern of the New Testament church—but, as Goldwater may have feared, a tragic scheme concocted by sinister forces to defer the church from its true power while enriching insincere bureaucrats, a disastrous fact that only now some are beginning to understand.

Behind these scenes and beyond view of the world's uninitiated members, the alchemy and rituals of the occult masters—Illuminatists, Masons, Bonesmen, Bilderbergers, and Bohemians—have combined to harmonize so completely within recent US foreign and domestic policies as to clearly point to a terrifying Sibyl's conjure, a near-future horizon upon which a leader of indescribable brutality will appear. Although this false prince of peace will seem at first to hold unique answers to life's most challenging questions, ultimately he will make the combined depravities of Antiochus Epiphanes, Hitler, Stalin, and Genghis Khan, all of whom were types of the Antichrist, look like child's play. He will raise his fist, "speaking great things…in blasphemy against God, to blaspheme his name, and his tabernacle, and them that dwell in heaven" (Revelation 13:5–6). He will champion worship of the "old gods" and "cause that as many as would not worship the image of the beast should be killed" (Revelation 13:15), and he will revive an ancient mystery religion that is "the habitation of devils, and the hold of every foul spirit, and a cage of every unclean and hateful bird" (Revelation 18:2).

Nevertheless, the world is readied—indeed, hungry for—a political savior to arise now with a plan to deliver mankind from upheaval.

Enter the Era of Obama

Should the world continue, historians will undoubtedly record how the messianic fervor surrounding the election of the forty-fourth president of the United States reflected not only widespread disapproval for Bush administration policies, but how, in the aftermath of September 11, 2001, the American psyche was primed to accept expansive alterations in political and financial policy with an overarching scheme for salvation from chaos. Among these historians, a few will undoubtedly also argue that, as National German Socialists did in the years following World War I, Barack Hussein Obama appealed to the increasingly disenfranchised voters among American society by playing on their understandable fears in order to posture himself as the essential agent of change. What most of these historians are not likely to record, however, is the involvement before and after the 2008 US presidential election by unseen shapers of the New World Order. If they did, the vast numbers of people would not believe it anyway, the idea that behind the global chaos that gave rise to Obama's popularity was a secret network, a transnational hand directing the course of civilization. Yet no account of history including recent times is complete or even sincere without at least acknowledging the behind-the-scenes masters who manipulate international policy, banking and finance, securities and exchange, trade, commodities, and energy resources. Numerous works, including scholarly ones, have connected the dots between this ruling "superclass" and the integration of policy handed down to governing bodies of nation-states and supra-national organizations.

   The Economist newspaper in the year of Obama's first election as President of the United States pointed to research by academic David Rothkopf, whose book, *Superclass: The Global Power Elite and the World They Are Making*, documented how only a few thousand people worldwide actually dictate the majority of policies operating at a global scale. *The Economist* described this comparatively small number of elites as being "groomed" in "world-spanning institutions...[who] meet at global events such as the World Economic Forum at Davos and the Trilateral Commission or...the Bilderberg meetings or the Bohemian Grove seminars that take place every July in California."[79] More recently, a 2011 Swiss Federal Institute (SFI) study showed less than one-hundred and fifty technocratic "Super Entities"—mainly banks and the families that own them—control 40% of the world's wealth. Long-time radio host and author of *Brotherhood of Darkness*, Stanley Monteith, says such persons are part of an "occult hierarchy" that rules the world and directs the course of human events. "The movement is led by powerful men who reject Christianity, embrace the 'dark side,' and are dedicated to the formation of a world government and a world religion," he writes. "They control the government, the media...many corporations, and both [US] political parties."[80]

Interestingly, Emeritus Pope Benedict XVI may have referred to the same group when, in 2008, he warned United Nations diplomats that multilateral consensus needed to solve global difficulties was "in crisis" because answers to the problems were being "subordinated to the decisions of the few." His predecessor, Pope John Paul II, may have acknowledged the same, believing a One-World Government beneath the guidance of a ruling superclass was inevitable. Before his death, it was prominent American political scientist Samuel P. Huntington who brought the uber-echelon behind the push for global government up from "conspiracy theory" to academic acceptability when he established that they "have little need for national loyalty, view national boundaries as obstacles that thankfully are vanishing, and see national governments as residues from the past whose only useful function is to facilitate the elite's global operations."[81] In other words, according to experts, international affairs, foreign and domestic politics, and taxpayer-funded investment economics are being largely decided by a privileged cadre of families who are dedicated to a New World Order and One-World Government.

I have to admit that, when writing the first edition of this book in 2009, it was difficult to resist the temptation to compile at length the names, dates, and organizations that form the goals of the ruling elite. Having accumulated thousands of pages of research material concerning the CFR, the Trilateral Commission, the Bohemians, the Masons, the Bilderbergers, and other Illuminatus subgroups, my original intention included several chapters on the memberships past and present of the largely unknown powers working behind public affairs. In the end, I determined that enough of this type material is already available to the public, and that this book would be better served in raising awareness—beyond the machinations of financiers and occult ideologues who direct global institutions—by showing that behind their matrix of illusion—which most citizens perceive as reality—is an arena of evil supernaturalism under which these human "conduits" are willingly organized. In more than thirty important biblical texts, the Greek New Testament employs the term *kosmos*, which describes an invisible order or "government behind government." It is here that human ego, separated from God, becomes hostile to the service of mankind while viewing people as commodities to be manipulated in the ministration of fiendish ambition. To some, the origins of this phenomenon began in the distant past, when a "fire in the minds" of angels caused Lucifer to exalt himself above the good of God's creation. The once-glorified spirit was driven mad by an unequivocal thirst to rule, conquer, and dominate. His fall spawned similar lust between his followers, which continues today among human agents of dark power who guard a privileged "cause-and-effect" relationship between diabolical forces and the opportunity for lordship over societies.

The objectives of the secret orders and the very real forces they serve are seldom perceived by citizens of democratic societies who choose to believe national officials actually rule their countries and represent their interests. Yet according to sacred texts, not only does an active collaboration exist between unregenerate social architects and fallen angels, but politicians in particular are vulnerable to "principalities and powers." According to well-known exorcist Gabriele Amorth, who has performed more than seventy thousand official exorcisms, "Evil exists in politics, quite often in fact. The devil loves to take over...those who hold political office."[82] As a result, it is not difficult to see how "fleshy gloves" such as US presidents may be unaware of their role as chess pieces on a terrestrial game board sliding in and out of position as they are moved by "the god of this world" toward the phantasmogoric end game (see 2 Corinthians 4:4). If researchers like Dr. Monteith are correct, and world governments are to this day influenced by such dark angelic powers, the elite who head the current push to establish a New World Order are directly connected with an antichrist system whether they know it or not. With vivid testimony to this, Satan offered to Jesus all the power and glory of the kingdoms of this world. He said, "All this power [control] will I give thee, and the glory of them [earthly cities]: for that is delivered unto me: and to whomsoever I will I give it. If thou therefore wilt worship me, all shall be thine" (Luke 4:6–7).

Signs and evidence of such supernatural involvement in the current move towards worldwide totalitarian government have been increasing in political commentary, occult symbolism, and numerological "coincidences" over the past decade. As public opinion is engineered toward final acceptance of the international subordination, we would expect to see these "mirrors of occult involvement" continue. Recently, there have been so many semiotic messages (visible signs and audible references that communicate subliminal ideas) in the open that it is starting to feel as if the "gods" are mocking us, challenging whether or not we will willingly admit their involvement. This has been exponentially true since the election of US President Barack Hussein Obama, the "President of the World," according to news services around the planet in 2008. While the grandiose title "President of the World"—granted Obama by euphoric crowds on that election night—remains to be prophetic, the glorified ideal behind it reflects the global hunger for and movement toward the arrival of "the one" who represents the invisible agencies mentioned above and who, for a while, will appear to be the world's answer man.

First Public Recognition of Obama as Messiah

Going back to 2008, consider the unprecedented messianic rhetoric that reporters, politicians, celebrities, and even preachers first used in celebrating the "spiritual nature" of Obama's meteoric rise from near obscurity to US president, and how this reflected people's strong desire for the coming of an earthly savoir. *San Francisco Chronicle* columnist Mark Morford characterized it as "a sort of powerful luminosity." In Morford's opinion, this was because Obama is "a Lightworker, that rare kind of attuned being who has the ability to…help usher in a new way of being on the planet."[83] The dean of the Martin Luther King Jr. International Chapel, Lawrence Carter, went further, comparing Obama to the coming of Jesus Christ: "It is powerful and significant on a spiritual level that there is the emergence of Barack Obama.... No one saw him coming, and Christians believe God comes at us from strange angles and places we don't expect, like Jesus being born in a manger."[84] Dinesh Sharma, a marketing science consultant with a PhD in psychology from Harvard, appraised Obama likewise: "Many...see in Obama a messiah-like figure, a great soul, and some affectionately call him Mahatma Obama."[85] It would have been easy to dismiss such commentary as the New Age quiverings of loons had it not been for similar passion on the lips of so many people. The following is a brief list of like expressions from a variety of news sources:

Barack's appeal is actually messianic...he...communicates God-like energy.... What if God decided to incarnate as men preaching "hope and change"? And what if we...let them slip away, not availing ourselves...to be led by God! —Steve Davis, *Journal Gazette*[86]

This is bigger than Kennedy.... This is the New Testament! I felt this thrill going up my leg. I mean, I don't have that too often. No, seriously. It's a dramatic event. —Chris Matthews, *MSNBC*[87]

Does it not feel as if some special hand is guiding Obama on his journey, I mean, as he has said, the utter improbability of it all? —*Daily Kos*[88]

Obama, to me, must be not just an ordinary human being but indeed an Advanced Soul, come to lead America out of this mess. —Lynn Sweet, *Chicago Sun Times*[89]

He is not operating on the same plane as ordinary politicians...the agent of transformation in an age of revolution, as a figure uniquely qualified to open the door to the twenty-first century. —Former US Senator Gary Hart, *Huffington Post*[90]

He is not the Word made flesh [Jesus], but the triumph of word over flesh [better than Jesus?].... Obama is, at his best, able to call us back to our highest selves. —Ezra Klein, *Prospect*[91]

Obama has the capacity to summon heroic forces from the spiritual depths of ordinary citizens and to unleash therefrom a symphonic chorus of unique creative acts whose common purpose is to tame the soul and alleviate the great challenges facing mankind. —Gerald Campbell, *First Things First*[92]

Obama was...blessed and highly favored.... I think that... his election...was divinely ordered.... I'm a preacher and a pastor; I know that that was God's plan.... I think he is being used for some purpose. —Janny Scott, *New York Times*[93]

He won't just heal our city-states and souls. He won't just bring the Heavenly Kingdom—dreamt of in both Platonism and Christianity—to earth. He will heal the earth itself. —Micah Tillman, *The Free Liberal*[94]

The event itself is so extraordinary that another chapter could be added to the Bible to chronicle its significance. —Rep. Jesse Jackson Jr., *Politico*[95]

Though he tried to keep it subtle himself, Obama encouraged such public perception of him as an "anointed" one whose time had come. Officially produced Obama campaign advertising consistently used such words as "faith," "hope," and "change." Republican nominee John McCain picked up on this during his run for office and put out a cynical video called *The One*. Using some of Obama's own words against him, the video mocked Obama's play as a Christ-like figure, showing him in New Hampshire saying, "A light beam will shine through, will light you up, and you will experience an epiphany, and you will suddenly realize that you must go to the polls and vote for Barack!" The video failed to mention that having an "epiphany" actually means the sudden realization or comprehension of an appearance of deity to man. Another part of the video included Obama during his nomination victory speech in St. Paul, Minnesota, saying, "This was the moment when the rise of the oceans began to slow and our planet began to heal." Anybody who followed the presidential campaign would have picked up the same nuances: angelic children organized to sing about Obama; logos depicting rays of sunlight beaming out from his O-shaped hand sign (a gesticulation Hitler used as well); books such as Nikki Grimes' *Barack Obama: Son of Promise, Child of Hope* (Simon & Schuster); comparisons to Plato's "Philosopher King," without whom our souls will remain broken; comparisons to the "spiritually enlightened" Mahatma Gandhi; comparisons to the solar hero Perseus; comparisons to Jesus Christ; and even comparisons to God Himself.

The world is "looking for a superstar," wrote *Prophecy in the News* founder J. R. Church. It wants a man, he said:

...who can solve the problems of our planet. That elusive dream of a world without war, poverty, and disease has always been just beyond our reach. Most politicians are perplexed—overwhelmed by the magnitude of the problem. They are convinced that the dilemma cannot be solved by commerce or systems, be it democracy or socialism. Most believe they can only be solved by a man—a superhuman superstar![96]

Will Obama become the superhuman superstar the world has been waiting for? If symbolic gestures are any indication, there certainly were plenty of religious folks during his march into the White House that thought he was, or that at least he was a forerunner of, "The One." Dozens of churches and faith groups, including mainline Protestants, organized activities to mark Obama's inauguration as a "spiritual" event. Randall Balmer, professor of religion in American history at Columbia University, admitted he had never seen anything like it before.[97] CNN went so far as to compare Obama's inauguration to the Hajj—the journey by Muslims to the holy city of Mecca, an obligatory pilgrimage that demonstrates their dedication to Allah.[98] In Des Moines, Iowa, an inaugural parade for Obama included a simulation of the triumphant entry of Christ in which a facsimile of Obama rode upon a donkey. As the reproduction made its way down the streets, palm branches were handed out to onlookers so that they could wave them like Christ's adorers did in the twenty-first chapter of Matthew.[99] Several ministries, including the Christian Defense Coalition and Faith and Action, came together to perform what was heralded as a first for US presidential inaugurations—applying anointing oil to the doorposts of the arched doorway that Obama passed through as he moved to the platform on the West Front of the Capitol to be sworn in. Congressman Paul Broun (Georgia) was part of the ritual, joining Rev. Rob Schenck, who said, "Anointing with oil is a rich tradition in the Bible and…symbolizes consecration, or setting something apart for God's use."[100] Not content with just using sacred anointing oil to consecrate Obama for God's use, approximately two thousand New Agers, Wiccans, and Shamans gathered at Dupont Circle—chosen because it is considered the gay center of Washington, DC, as well as being the point of the left ear of the Masonic street Pentagram north of the White House—to participate in a cleansing ceremony to purge the White House of evil spirits (which they said were brought there by Bush) for Obama. A Shaman officiated the event, lighting bundles of sage, which smoldered and gave off thick, blue aromatic smoke. "Saging," as it is called, is believed by Wiccan tradition to drive away evil spirits.[101] Even the conventional inaugural prayers, which have been historically offered during US presidential installation ceremonies, carried an unparalleled New Age flavor this time around. Rick Warren, considered America's Christian pastor, rendered a blessing in the name of the Muslim version of Jesus (Isa), while the bishop of New Hampshire, Gene Robinson, invoked the "God of our many understandings."

While all this was highly unusual, even unprecedented, it was not surprising. Obama had spent significant time during the campaign distancing himself from conservative Christians, evangelicals, and especially the Religious Right (which had held prominent sway over Republicans since Ronald Reagan held office), countering that his faith was more universalist and unconvinced of Bible inerrancy. In a five-minute video available on YouTube (see endnotes for address), a pre-election speech by Obama was highly cynical of Bible authority and even derided specific Old and New Testament Scriptures. "Whatever we once were," Obama says on the video, "we're no longer a Christian nation." He added, "Democracy demands that the religiously motivated translate their concerns into universal, rather than religion-specific values.... This is going to be difficult for some who believe in the inerrancy of the Bible, as many evangelicals do."[102] Consequently, the conscious effort by Obama to reorient America away from conventional Christianity was widely embraced by people who identified with the man known to sport Masonic emblems, a ring that says "There Is No God Except Allah," and a tiny idol of the Hindu god Hanuman in his pocket—whose blessings he sought in the race to the White House—a deity about whom Rudyard Kipling wrote the short story "The Mark of the Beast." For Obama, who grew up in a household where the Bible, the Koran, and the Bhagvat Gita sat on a shelf side by side, organized religion was best defined as "closed-mindedness dressed in the garb of piety," but a useful political tool nonetheless. And so he used it masterfully, and earned a cult following while doing so. By February 2009, Obama had replaced Jesus Christ as America's number-one hero according to a Harris poll, and dedication to his come-one, come-all mysticism has continued to spread in esoteric circles, with evangelists of the new religion calling for the "tired" faith of our fathers to be replaced with a global new one. Terry Neal, writing for the *Hamilton Spectator*, is such a disciple, and proclaims boldly: "The faiths of our fathers are tired now...only a global world view will suffice. The marriage of a believable faith with the husbandry of government is the union that must be contracted." This has to occur under Obama, Neal concludes, for only then will there be "peace on earth and goodwill toward all."[103]

Although it is more difficult to understand the broad appeal of Obama's New Age philosophy to the many evangelical and Catholic voters who supported him, the phenomenon can be explained to some degree as the result of a changing culture. Over the past fifty years, and especially as baby boomers listened attentively to pastors telling them to focus on human potential and the "god within us all," eastern philosophies of monism, pantheism, Hinduism, and self-realization grew, providing Americans with an alluring opportunity to throw off the "outdated ideas" of fundamental Christianity and to espouse a more "enlightened," monistic worldview (all is one). Aimed at accomplishing what the builders of the Tower of Babel failed to do (unify the masses of the world under a single religious umbrella), God was viewed as pantheistic, and humans were finally understood to be divine members of the whole "that God is." Pagans argue this principle of inner divinity is older than Christianity, which is true. The gospel according to such New Age concepts—a gospel of "becoming god"—is as old as the fall of man. It began when the serpent said to the woman "ye shall be as gods" (Genesis 3:5), and it will zenith during the reign of the anti-Christian god-king.

Second Term Obama-Messianism Continues

So many including this author were absolutely astonished that Barack Hussein Obama was reelected in 2012 instead of being assigned to the dust bin of a failed one-term presidency. Given his beyond-dismal record of governance (the worst in American history) and the horrific state of the economy under his leadership (also the worst in history), most businessmen and political conservatives were convinced that even an orangutan would trump his chances among the electorate in 2012. Not only were we were wrong but we soon rediscovered that the longing among those who wish to receive him as God remains strong. This includes Oscar-winning actor Jamie Foxx at the Soul Train Awards admonishing the audience to give honor to "our Lord and savior, Barak Obama" as well as street vendors across

Washington, DC selling posters of Obama as the second coming of Jesus Christ. Newsweek Magazine followed with a clear reference to the return of Jesus Christ in their cover of Obama and the headline "The Second Coming," while university professor Barbara A. Thompson released her new book *The Gospel According to Apostle Barack* in which she detailed her divine vision of Obama as equal or superior to the mission of Jesus Christ. "To contemplate ways to assist Barack in his 2012 re-election bid something miraculous happened," she writes. "I felt God's (His) Spirit beckoning me in my dreams at night. Listening, cautiously, I learned that Jesus walked the earth to create a more civilized society, Martin (Luther King) walked the earth to create a more justified society, but, Apostle Barack, the name he was called in my dreams, would walk the earth to create a more equalized society…"[104] We could continue, pointing to such examples as Michael D' Antuono's painting "The Truth," featuring Obama wearing a crown of thorns with his arms stretched out as if on a cross, Democratic National Convention prayer garments with the president's name and a calendar declaring him "heaven sent" (with the month of November depicting the president with people's hands on his back and the phrase "The Lord is my Shepherd, I shall not want") and photographs of Obama with the Bible verse from John 3:16: "For God so loved the world, that He gave His only begotten Son, that whosoever believeth in him should not perish, but have everlasting life." A month after the election, Obama messianism continued as people across the globe celebrated Christmas with nativity scenes hosting figurines of Obama as the prophesied King of kings. This could go on and on, but you probably get the point. Much of the world is ready now, even hungry for the arrival of the Man of Sin.

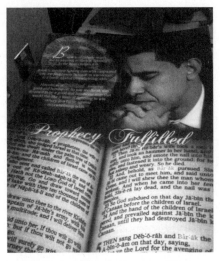

Inauguration Poster Depicts Obama
as Jesus, Prophecy Fulfilled

Conversely, this is where contrasting social feedback becomes equally interesting especially as a Public Policy Poll released in April 2013 reveals that one in four Americans now think Obama may actually be the Antichrist. I myself have taken the position that Obama is _an_ antichrist but probably not _the_ final one described in the book of Revelation (unless something dramatic or otherworldly were to happen with his mental acuity and/or genetics such as described in Chapter Eight of this book wherein Nimrod conceivably transformed from a rebel human to *gibborim*) not the least of which reasons is that he is not, so far as I know, a Roman as identified by the prophet Daniel (chapter 9:26). Nevertheless, as a result of the April, 2013 polling, I decided to find out what other scholars believe in this regard. Some, such as legendary broadcaster Noah Hutchings, believe there is a small chance Obama could be the evil one. In response to my query, Noah emailed, "Tom, concerning Obama being the Antichrist, we know from 1 John 2:18, that in the last days, many Antichrists would arise. From the signs of our time it is evident we are in the last days, and it is evident that Mr. Obama is an antichrist. Could he be THE Antichrist? Possibly. He is the one person who has made this nation more like Sodom and Gomorrah than any other man, president or otherwise. He has dealings with a strange god and people all over the world worship his image on television." Other experts I contacted—men like Dr. Chuck Missler, Jonathan Cahn, Texas megachurch pastor Robert Jeffress, pastor Mark Biltz and others—felt Obama is too much of a "lightweight" to be the final Antichrist, though they did point out some profound comparisons between Obama and the coming Man of Sin. For instance, one noted how Obama is "packaged goods" as in a person devoid of any achievements, about whom the public knows virtually nothing, and has "come out of nowhere" to usurp the most powerful chair (throne) in the world. Another pointed out how Obama echoes the activities of antichrist figures throughout history including raising taxes (see Daniel 11:20), pushing for bigger and bigger government, and pressuring Israel to surrender land given to them by God. This latter point was on the minds of many as President Obama arrived in Israel March 20, 2013 (which, again, was meant to reflect Obama messianism as at sunset on this day Nisan 10 began, the day Jesus made his triumphal entry into Jerusalem as "Messiah" in advance of Passover) under the Netanyahu government code-name "Operation: Brit Amim." This modern-Hebrew term is translated into English as "Unbreakable Alliance" and echoes the ancient prophecy in the book of Daniel (9:27) wherein the Antichrist forms a "firm covenant" with Israel that ultimately allows them to erect their third Temple and to commence their priestly activities, an agreement Antichrist breaks "in the midst of the week" (the seven year tribulation period) when he causes the sacrifices to cease and desecrates the temple.

But the most penetrating response I received on the question of whether Obama could be the Antichrist came from Douglas W. Krieger, Dene McGriff, and S. Douglas Woodward when I learned of their scholarly argument (due out in book form in 2013 under the title "The Final Babylon"), which draws upon historical comparisons between the current administration's rise to power and that of the Third Reich. The following excerpt is used by permission and should be required reading by Christians in particular:

We begin by proposing a troubling issue for the reader's consideration: If Antichrist were to be revealed in America, would the faithful recognize him? Would Americans committed to spiritual values miss the same clues disclosing Antichrist's true nature as did the Germans with Hitler?

There is little doubt that if a figure paraded himself in front of the American people resembling an easily stereotyped leader of the Third Reich—with a mousy moustache, an armband, and wearing a brown shirt—his character and agenda would be obvious to almost everyone. Mounting the podium with an emotional appeal to our national loyalty, the adamant display of venom and vitriol against the enemies of the State, the promise of the restoration of our American "empire" through a continuing buildup of military might, the stark name calling identifying an appropriate scapegoat to fault for our problems—all of these factors would, at best, betray a would-be antichrist figure as a false messiah—or at worst, spotlight an artless actor who undoubtedly took us for fools.

However, we can be certain the apocalypse of (that is,

the revealing of) Antichrist in America, an event we believe
will transpire in the years just ahead, will be a one-of-a-kind
challenge requiring spiritual discernment worthy of only the
most circumspect and attuned "code breakers" whose spe-
cialty is exposing wolves in sheep's clothing.

Remember Hitler achieved a meteoric rise to promi-
nence and power because he understood the soul of his
people. He could relate. He knew what made them tick.
He realized how to couch his message in the context of the
political situation and how to engage those who would be
but mere spectators, by relating to their financial pain and
anxiety over the future. Hitler understood crowd psychology
and how to manipulate it. To mesmerize his audience, he
learned the power of emphatic facial expressions and energetic hand gestures. He compelled unquestioning allegiance
by conveying solutions plainly and confidently no matter
how oversimplified or extreme his answers might be. In fact,
the more oversimplified and uncompromising his solutions
were—the better to persuade the people of their usefulness.

What is the lesson for us? If the Antichrist were to
arise in America at this moment, we would be foolish to
expect him to be anything but a consummate American.
He would look like us. He would talk like us. He would
think—for the most part—like us. And with a straight face
he might even assert a profession of Christian faith—and
why he believes the teaching of Jesus Christ is so well suited
for society. Following Adolf Hitler's lead, he would appeal
to the most devout class of Christian—the Evangelical. He
would offer opportunities to bring biblically-based believers "out front"—to escape the shadows of social disdain and
distance themselves from the hackneyed portrait affirmed

by the intelligentsia and showcased by the media (supposing that those who call themselves Evangelical are intellectually bankrupt). He would convince Bible-believing conservatives that they should no longer see themselves as simple plebeians (the common folk). Their self-image should be elevated so they regard their value no less in status than the progressive patricians of sophisticated national institutions.[105] Not that he would identify himself with the elite nor propose that the common man should be ashamed of his laborer status. Rather, he would argue he remains a man "of the people" yet holds himself sufficiently apart to sanctify his status as our formidable if not fearless leader.

This positioning reflects the example of Herr Hitler in many respects. Likewise, the tone and substance coming from the mouth of the Führer, although etched in the zeitgeist of that age, begs for comparison to what we hear today from select political leaders promoting the American version of The New World Order;[106] especially those who were, are, or would be our President. However, the sham to fool Evangelicals will make use of more than patronizing remarks. It will turn the words of our most popular preachers against us. The ideology that should prohibit the arising of Antichrist—the Christian religion and its worldview—will be a powerful tool co-opted to capture the "believing" masses and to encourage, through a moral veneer and political resolution, an agenda resonating within the heart of the "folks" in these United States. Indeed, the future philosophy of Antichrist will convince us we should resolve to be nothing less than what our most prominent spiritual leaders teach us to be—successful, healthy, and committed to classic American ideals (although our most noble notions of individual liberty, a la Henry David Thoreau and Thomas Jefferson, have long since quietly departed for destinations unknown).

In like manner, Antichrist would deftly implore citizens to follow his lead. He would criticize Christians for failure to follow the most "positive" aspects of our faith. He would call us to be the best Americans we can be. The health of our nation, he would argue, depends upon living productive lives that contribute to economic prosperity for all. Morality, like ethics, should be shaped to improve our communities in light of standards established by the majority. Religion, true religion, will instill these values. It will not conflict with political objectives because positive faith goes hand-in-hand with constructive political ideology. The manifesto of "the public good" will brand any substantial opposition worthy of elimination. True believers will be activists—but for causes that comply with the will of the many.

On the surface, the nature of these ideals will seem consistent with the Bible. After all, who would argue that the spiritually inclined should be unproductive, immoral, unethical, a burden on the public's well-being, and incapable of contributing to the community's economic health? And yet, upon a more cautious objective inspection, there will emerge a thin but distinctive line between a laudable social compact (built upon beneficial principles for both the individual and the nation) with a overreaching "State" that demands unquestioned obedience—commanding allegiance above all other causes no matter how worthy.

Moreover, the challenge to discern the agenda of the Antichrist will be difficult for many reasons, not just intellectual. Social pressure to conform will be "maxed out." The path to achieve clarity will be a lonely path, for our peers will be only too ready to encourage complicity. Any complaint and disparagement will be interpreted as unpatriotic, a threat to social order, and harmful not only to our own health, but to those we love and care about. One's consciousness raising must be done in stealth to not draw attention to an expressed awareness that the enemy of Christ speaks profanely in our presence. It will not be easy to resist even if we come to the realization we have been asked to serve Antichrist. Our peers will plead with us not to rock the boat, not to question falling in line, not to label the State as anything but what is best for one and all. To be "the best Christian one can be" will appear synonymous with being the perfect US citizen.

As a harbinger of the evil one to come, study the words of Hitler below. Consider just how difficult our task to discern the voice of Antichrist when it reverberates in America:

> "We demand liberty for all religious denominations in the State, so far as they are not a danger to it and do not militate against the morality and moral sense of the German race. The Party, as such, stands for *positive* Christianity, but does not bind itself in the matter of creed to any particular confession."[107] [emphasis added]

> "The National Government regards the two Christian Confessions as the weightiest factors for the maintenance of our nationality. They will respect the agreements concluded between them and the federal States. Their rights are not to be infringed... It will be the Government's care to maintain honest

co-operation between Church and State; the struggle against materialistic views and for a real national community is just as much in the interest of the German nation as in that of the welfare of our Christian faith. The Government of the Reich, who regard Christianity as the unshakable foundation of the morals and moral code of the nation, attach the greatest value to friendly relations with the Holy See and are endeavoring to develop them."[108]

A "Nod" from the Craft and the Altar of Zeus

When Obama's new CIA director John Brennan was sworn in at the White House's Roosevelt Room March 8, 2013, he chose to follow an example first made by Obama himself—rejecting the Bible to instead place his hand on a copy of the Constitution for the ceremony. This wasn't just any version of the founding document either, mind you, but an older one *before it included the Bill of Rights!*[109] It would be pleasant to think that such ceremonies and the use of the Bible especially during the US presidential oath of office actually means something to those who place their hand on it and swear to "faithfully execute the office of president of the United States... so help me God." But Obama, who had to repeat his swearing-in ceremony after the word "faithfully" was garbled by Chief Justice John Roberts during the first inauguration, did so the following day in the Map Room of the White House before a press pool and a small group of aides. This time, just like his CIA director John Brennan would later do, the oath was administered without the use of a Bible, insinuating to some that the Good Book was only public "eye-candy" in the first instance, and also that the oath of Barack

Hussein Obama was biblically invalid. While this may seem trivial to the average person, what it means to secret orders is consequential. Groups such as Masons (who honored Obama with their first-ever inaugural ball in Washington, DC, January 20, 2009) esteem rituals, gestures, the use of books such as the Bible, and oaths taken by heads of state to be of the highest mystical importance. This is why everything they do is administered through appropriate rituals, initiations, and incitations. Ethereal power—including supernatural agents—can be manipulated, bound, and released to execute blessings or curses as a result of proper oaths. Breaking an oath can likewise result in dire repercussion, in their opinion. Because this is not taken lightly by occultists, members of the Craft would have a difficult time believing the oath of office of the president of the US—one of the most hallowed American traditions—was so easily flubbed at the start of his presidency. The very beginning of the oath, "I do solemnly swear," is a spiritual petition. The word "solemn" means "an invocation of a religious sanction" or entreaty before deity to witness, sanction, and bless the binding nature of the ceremony to carry out the office or duty. The oath also binds the individual before "God" to faithfully execute the covenant. Thus, government representatives make an oath before taking public office, and witnesses in a court of law take an oath to "swear to tell the truth" before offering testimony. These principles are deeply rooted in the Judeo-Christian faith as well as most other religions. Though there is no way of knowing what the presidential oath of office deeply means to Obama, or whether the blunder and redo of the swearing-in ceremony was anything more than an accident, the unprecedented gaffe was suspicious to some as possibly representing important hidden meaning. Misgivings over it were additionally compounded when reflected against other curious activities and declarations by Barack Obama, which most of the media missed, downplayed, or simply refused to report on, that strongly connected his emergence with occult mythology identified in the Bible as both *prophetic* and *demonic*.

An extraordinary example of this was when Obama gave his speech titled "The World that Stands as One" in Berlin, Germany, on July 24, 2008. More than a few students of occult history took notice of the symbolism and location of the event, even causing some who until then had rejected any "antichrist" labels hurled at Obama to reconsider their position. This included respected Catholic writer Michael O'Brien, best known for his apocalyptic novel, *Father Elijah*. O'Brien had received numerous letters and emails from subscribers and visitors to his website wondering if Obama was the Antichrist. At first, O'Brien wrote that this was not possible. Then a friend who had seen Obama's speech in Berlin called him, talking about how mesmerizing the speech was, and stating that an announcer over German radio had said: "We have just heard the next president of the United States…and the future President of the World." By now, Obama was conveying an unusual likeness to the Antichrist character of his novel. After watching the Berlin speech several times for himself, O'Brien sent out a newsletter in which he admitted that while he still doubted Obama was the prophesied ruler of the end times, he had come to believe he was "a carrier of a deadly moral virus, indeed a kind of anti-apostle spreading concepts and agendas that are not only anti-Christ but anti-human as well." O'Brien finally conceded Obama could be instrumental in ushering in the dreaded Great Tribulation period, and worse, that he was "of the spirit of Antichrist."[110] After Obama's term of office was underway, O'Brien pointed out the numerous foreign and domestic problems Obama was facing, including wars in Afghanistan and Iraq, the possibility of a new war with Iran, and issues related to the crumbling financial systems, saying these obstacles could overshadow Obama and lead to his defeat in the next presidential election. O'Brien then added in what was a clear reference to the coming of Antichrist, "Alternatively, he could become the 'Great Facilitator,' negotiator, peacemaker, working marvels throughout the world as he moves from one seemingly unsolvable problem to another."[111] Because it is true that any significant public political event requires both forethought and symbolic meaning, the location where Obama gave his Berlin speech in front of Berlin's Victory Column contributed to O'Brien's conclusions. The site was offensive to educated Germans as well as to Christians and Jews because of its ties to Adolf Hitler and the Nazis. It was nevertheless oddly appropriate, for it was upon this exact location that Hitler had planned to enthrone himself in the Welthauptstadt Germania—the new "World Capitol" upon winning World War II.

During the 1930s, Hitler commissioned Albert Speer, "the first architect of the Third Reich," to design the new Capitol. As part of the plans, the "Siegessäule," or Berlin Victory Column—a 226-foot monument topped by a golden-winged figure representing Borussia, the female personification of Prussia, and Victoria, the cult goddess of military victory—was removed from its location in front of the Reichstag building in 1939 and relocated to its current location in the Tiergarten, a 495-acre park in the middle of Berlin where Obama gave his speech in front of the Nazi symbol.

Rainer Brüderle, deputy leader of the liberal political party Free Democrats in Germany, complained to the newspaper *Bild am Sonntag*: "The Siegessäule in Berlin was moved to where it is now by Adolf Hitler. He saw it as a symbol of German superiority and of the victorious wars against Denmark, Austria and France." This represented a serious question In Brüderle's mind as to "whether Barack Obama was advised correctly in his choice of the Siegessäule as the site to hold a speech on his vision for a more cooperative world."[112] Another German politician named Andreas Schockenhoff was equally disturbed, saying, "It is a problematic symbol."[113]

Evidently it was not problematic for Obama, who stood in front of it and saluted the German audience in a way eerily similar to what Adolf Hitler used to do, followed by thousands returning the salute, which is against German law. When Obama ended his speech in front of the war goddess, he said, "With an eye toward the future, with resolve in our hearts, let us remember this history, and answer our destiny, and remake the world once again." This is exactly what Hitler had promised to do and exactly where he had planned to memorialize it.

Of greater significance and not far from where Obama delivered his rousing speech is the Great Altar of Zeus in the Pergamon Museum. According to several reports, Obama visited the Great Altar while in Berlin, which is especially important, given what he did on returning to the United States. Before we examine Obama's revealing actions, consider carefully what the Bible says about the Altar of Zeus in the letter to the church in Pergamos (also Pergamum; Pergamon):

> And to the angel of the church in Pergamos write; These things saith he which hath the sharp sword with two edges; I know thy works, and where thou dwellest, even where Satan's seat is: and thou holdest fast my name, and has not denied my faith, even in those days wherein Antipas was my faithful martyr, who was slain among you, where Satan dwelleth. (Revelation 2:12–13)

In the Greek, the phrase, "where Satan's seat is," literally means, "where a throne to Satan is." Scholars identify this throne or "seat" as the Great Altar of Zeus that existed in Pergamos at that time. So important was the worship of Zeus in ancient Pergamos that perpetual sacrifices were offered to him upon the towering and famous forty-foot-high altar. Antipas, the first leader and martyr of the early Christian church, is believed to have been slain on this altar, slowly roasting to death inside the statue of a bull, the symbol and companion of Zeus. The phrase in Revelation 2:13, "wherein Antipas was my faithful martyr, who was slain among you, where Satan dwelleth," is considered a citation of this event.

Approximately two thousand years after Revelation 2:13 was written, German archeologists removed the massive altar of Zeus from the ruins of Pergamos and took it to Berlin, where it was restored as the centerpiece of the Pergamon Museum. It is here that Hitler first adored it, later building an outdoor replica of it from which he gave a series of speeches that mesmerized many Germans.

"Fast forward about another seventy-five years," says blogger El Gallo. "Another charismatic young politician mesmerizes huge German crowds with a rousing speech in Berlin. Barack Hussein Obama…[and] did Barack Obama visit…the Great Altar of Zeus…? Presumably he did."[114]

Whether Obama received inspiration from the throne of Satan while in Berlin or not, what he did next was astonishing. Upon returning to the United States, he immediately commissioned the construction of a Greek-columned stage from which he made his acceptance speech for his party's nomination. Because Greek temples such as those built to honor Zeus were thought to house the patron deity, the GOP ridiculed Obama, mocking him as playing Zeus of "Mount Olympus" and accusing his supporters of "kneeling" before the "Temple of Obama." *The New York Post* ran an enlightening "Convention Special" supplement on August 28, 2008, with the telling headline: "'O' My God: Dems Erect Obama Temple" blazoned across the front cover. But it was not until blogger Joel Richardson pointed out how the design of Obama's stage was a dead ringer for the Great Altar of Zeus[115] that Obama's campaign managers tried to explain away the design as being a conglomeration representing the portico of the White House with the US capitol building. "But experts agreed with Richardson," Gallo wrote. "It was a replica of the Great Altar of Pergamum."[116]

Thus incredibly, like Hitler, Obama honored the goddess Victoria with his presence before ordering a replica of the biblical throne of Satan, upon which he accepted his date with destiny.

Following this, Barack Hussein Obama on June 4, 2009 gave an unprecedented speech to the Muslim world from Cairo, Egypt, declaring that he was launching a new era between the United States and the Muslim world. For the first time, Obama was forthright about his Muslim heritage and stated that the United States—which he is on record as saying is "no longer a Christian nation"—is now "one of the largest Muslim countries in the world." *Newsweek* editor Evan Thomas followed the president's speech with a declaration, reflected in the opinion of many, that "Obama is standing above the country, above the world, he is a sort of God."[117]

Now imagine—if such sentiments as illustrated above were afforded to a man like Obama—what would America and people around the world be willing to accept if a truly amazing, even "otherworldly" man stepped forward in 2016 with seemingly all of the answers to mankind's woes?

Chapter 5

WAS THE UNITED STATES DESIGNED TO GENERATE THE ANTICHRIST?

America was designated as the New Atlantis that would lead the world to the Antichrist. The original national bird envisioned by our Masonic leadership in the late 1700s was not the American Eagle, but the Phoenix Bird. This historic fact strongly suggests that, at the right moment in world history, with the world entering through the portals of the Kingdom of Antichrist, America might suddenly be immolated in fiery flames, burning to the ashes; out of these ashes, the New World Order would arise. —David Bay, Cutting Edge Ministries

The rise of the Christian church broke up the intellectual pattern of the classical pagan world. By persecution of this pattern's ideologies it drove the secret societies into greater secrecy; the pagan intellectuals then reclothed their original ideas in a garment of Christian phraseology, but bestowed the keys of the symbolism only upon those duly initiated and bound to secrecy by their vows. —Manly P. Hall, 33rd-Degree Freemason, *The Secret Destiny of America*

When US Representative Nancy Pelosi, on January 4, 2007, assumed her role as Speaker of the House at the opening of the 110th Congress, she followed the pattern set by George W. Bush and his old man, infusing a loaded statement concerning the founding fathers, saying they were so confident in "the America they were advancing, they put on the seal, the great seal of the United States, '*novus ordo seclorum*'—a new order for the centuries." Pelosi did not go into detail as to why she considered the phrase *novus ordo seclorum* important dialectic during the momentous changeover of the control of congress, nor did she add why this expression exists beneath the unfinished pyramid and the all-seeing eye (eye of Horus/Osiris/Apollo) in the Great Seal of the United States in the first place. But her allusion to it was not coincidental, and the origins of the motto and the importance behind the increase in references to the cryptic passage by government insiders in recent years will become evident soon enough.

Undoubtedly upon reading the next two chapters, low-level Masons who are intentionally kept in the dark by their superiors will write to complain about the stereotype of them as members in a secret plot toward global domination. Truth is, most Masons are moral people who know nothing about the goals of the uber echelon above them. Yet respected historians, including some Masonic writers, admit to what Gary Lachman, in his book, *Politics and the Occult*, called the most sensational historical association between Freemasons and American occult politics. Citing the works of professors like Robert Hieronimus, Lachman says, "The United States is—or at least was originally planned to be—the kind of utopia aimed at by the Rosicrucians." Furthermore, Lachman writes, Washington, DC was laid out according to the precepts of sacred geometry "associated with Freemasonry."[118]

That a Rosicrucian-Masonic brotherhood was involved in the American and French, as well as European, revolutions is indisputable today. As many as forty-four (though probably a lower number) of the fifty-six signers of the Declaration of Independence were Freemasons. Numerous US presidents were also part of the Craft, including Washington, Monroe, Jackson, Polk, Buchanan, A. Johnson, Garfield, McKinley, T. Roosevelt, Taft, Harding, F. Roosevelt, Truman, L.B. Johnson, and Ford. Additional elites in the Order included Benjamin Franklin, Paul Revere, Edmund Burke, John Hancock, and more, while John Adams, Alexander Hamilton, Thomas Jefferson, and numerous others were accounted friends of the brotherhood.

Besides membership, the question of whether the Order of Freemasons engineered the US city named after America's first president according to an occult grand design is something that a growing body of historians and researchers are coming around to. David Ovason, who became a Mason after writing *The Secret Architecture of our Nation's Capitol: The Masons and the Building of Washington, D.C.*, argues effectively that the city's layout intentionally incorporated the esoteric belief system of Freemasonry, especially as it involved astrologically aligning the Capitol with the constellation Virgo (Isis). In 1793, when George Washington sanctioned the laying of the capitol building's cornerstone, he did so wearing a Masonic apron emblazoned with the brotherhood's symbols. For occult expert Manly P. Hall, this made perfect sense. "Was Francis Bacon's vision of the 'New Atlantis' a prophetic dream of the great civilization, which was so soon to rise upon the soil of the New World?" he asked in *The Secret Teachings of All Ages*. "It cannot be doubted that the secret societies…conspired to establish [such] upon the American continent." Hall continued that historical incidents in the early development of the United States clearly bore "the influence of that secret body, which has so long guided the destinies of peoples and religions. By them nations are created as vehicles for the promulgation of ideals, and while nations are true to these ideals they survive; when they vary from them, they vanish like the Atlantis of old which had ceased to 'know the gods.'"[119]

For those unfamiliar with this secret American-Masonic history or who do not have time to dedicate to the study, I cannot recommend highly enough an award-winning film series on the subject from Adullam Films now available on DVD. The three films in *The Secret Mysteries of America's Beginnings* are a perfect primer for understanding the fascinating history behind the founding of America as the fulfillment of Bacon's Rosicrucian New Atlantis and what this portends for humanity today. The three-DVD series (available at www.SurvivorMall.com) includes: Volume 1—*Secret Mysteries of America's Beginnings: The New Atlantis*; Volume 2—*Riddles in Stone: The Secret Architecture of Washington, D.C.*; and Volume 3—*Eye of the Phoenix: Secrets of the Dollar Bill*. Filmmaker Christian J. Pinto, who wrote the preface to this book, also kindly provided the Washington, DC street map included in this chapter.

Involvement by Freemasons in the development of early America and the symbolic layout of Washington, DC as the Capitol for the New Atlantis has been so well documented over the last two decades that even many Masons have ceased denying the affiliation. Daily Masonic tours through services devoted to this history are now offered of the city's landmarks to illustrate the connection. For a fee, a guide will help you visit locations such as the George Washington Masonic National Memorial or the House of the Temple, the headquarters building of the Scottish Rite of Freemasonry. Designed in 1911 (note the connection again between Masons and the numerological value 9-11), the House of the Temple hosts the Freemason

Hall of Fame, an enormous collection of Freemason memorabilia including various artworks important to Masons, a library of two hundred fifty thousand books, and is the location for the Rite's Supreme Council 33rd-degree meetings. Upon leaving, you can exit the House of the Temple, walk down the street, and take pictures of the enormous Masonic Obelisk (phallic Egyptian symbol of fertility) in the distance known as the Washington Monument.

For obvious reasons, while modern Masons may openly admit these days to involvement by their Jacobite ancestors toward establishing the foundation for a utopian New World Order in Washington, DC, most vigorously deny that the talisman-like layout of the streets, government buildings, and Masonic monuments were meant for what researcher David Bay calls an "electric-type grid" that pulsates "with Luciferic power twenty-four hours a day, seven days a week."

Notwithstanding this denial, the government's own records explain otherwise, clearly stating that the capital city's design was "shepherded" by those who wanted it to reflect dedication to "pagan gods." For instance, the article, "The Most Approved Plan: The Competition for the Capitol's Design," on the Library of Congress' website tells how, after advertising a competition for the design of Government Center in DC, "Washington, Jefferson, and the Commissioners of the District of Colombia" were disappointed by the entries, and a design based on "The Roman Pantheon—the circular domed rotunda *dedicated to all pagan gods*—was suggested by Jefferson, who later shepherded it through several transformations [emphasis added]."[120] Freemason David Ovason adds that when the cornerstone of the US Capitol building was laid, it was done through Masonic ritual meant to procure *approval of the pagan gods.* As recorded in two bronze panels on the Senate doors of the Capitol, George Washington is seen standing in front of a Mason who holds two versions of the Masonic square, while he himself uses a Masonic trowel on the cornerstone.

George Washington's Masonic Apron

It is the apron Washington so famously wore that day that bears specific Masonic symbolism, which Ovason explains as designed to please the "invisible agencies" who watched over the event. "Undoubtedly, invisible agencies were present at the cornerstone ceremony," he says, "but they were made visible in the apron's symbolism. The radiant eye represented the invisible presence of the Great Architect—the high Spiritual Being who had been invited by prayer and ritual to oversee the ceremonial. The radiant eye was…the 'sun-eye,' or Spiritual Sun [Horus/Osiris/Apollo]."

Acknowledgment to such pagan gods through the use of images and symbols by Masons is interesting, given their avowed consecration of the Bible, a book that clearly forbids this type activity as devotion to demons. Acts 7:41–42 explains that when men serve idols, they are worshipping the host or "army" of heaven. Psalms 96:5 adds, "For all the gods of the nations are idols" ("*elilim*," LXX "*daimonia*" [demons]). Other references conclude that idols of stone or relevant imagery, such as permeates Washington, DC, are *elilim* ("empty," "nothing," "vanity"); but that behind these images exist the true dynamic of idolatry—demons. The apostle Paul confirmed this in 1 Corinthians 10:20, saying, "The things which the Gentiles sacrifice, they sacrifice to devils, and not to God: and I would not that ye should have fellowship with devils."

Metaphysicians who do not rely solely on the Bible for authority often agree that powerful non-human energies, including evil ones, can emanate from symbols and, once released, take on a mind of their own. Writing about the Masonic involvement in the French Revolution, Gary Lachman makes an extraordinary and important observation about immaterial destructive forces—which had unseen plans of their own— released as a result of occult politics:

Cazotte himself was aware of the dangerous energies unleashed by the Revolution.… Although Cazotte didn't use the term, he would no doubt have agreed that, whatever started it, the Revolution soon took on a life of its own, coming under the power of an *egregore*, Greek for "watcher," a kind of immaterial entity that is created by and presides over a human activity or collective. According to the anonymous author of the fascinating *Meditations on the Tarot*, there are no "good" *egregores*, only "negative" ones.… True or not, *egregores* can nevertheless be "engendered by the collective will and imagination of nations." As Joscelyn Godwin points out, "an *egregore* is augmented by human belief, ritual and especially by sacrifice. If it is sufficiently nourished by such energies, the *egregore* can take on a life of its own and appear to be an independent, personal divinity, with a limited power on behalf of its devotees and an unlimited appetite for their future devotion." If, as some esotericists believe, human conflicts are the result of spiritual forces for spiritual ends, and these forces are not all "good," then collective catastrophes like the French Revolution take on a different significance.[121]

In addition to *egregores,* or demons by any other name, being drawn—like flies to a light bulb—to men and energized through symbols, statues, and rituals, Ovason says the dedication of the US Capitol building cornerstone in particular had to be done at a certain astrological time related to the zodiacal constellation Virgo (Isis), while Jupiter was rising in Scorpio, because "the cornerstone ceremonial was designed not only to gain the approval of the spiritual beings, but also to ensure that these were content that the building was being brought into the world at the right time."[122] Ovason later adds more directly, "Whoever arranged for Virgo to be so consistently operative during foundation and cornerstone ceremonies, must have been alert to the fact that *they were inviting some archetype, or spiritual being, to direct the destiny of the city*" (italics in the original).[123] Finally, Ovason hints who the "spiritual being" governing the Capitol of the United States is: "A medieval esotericist…would have said that Washington, DC, was governed by the intelligency Hamaliel, the spiritual entity which ruled Virgo, and which worked hand in hand with Mercury."[124] Hamaliel is an evil adversary of the cherubim of God, serving under Lilith, whom earlier we wrote about concerning her devotees, who gather annually to honor her at the Bohemian Grove.

EAs a result of this alignment of the Capitol buildings and streets in Washington, DC with this constellation, every August 10, an astrological event reoccurs in the sky above Washington, tying the city to the pagan Virgo—known in ancient Egypt as the goddess Isis. "At dusk, as golden light turns brick facades a dusty rose, the shimmering sun floats a few degrees just to the left of Pennsylvania Avenue, gradually inching to the right until it sets directly over the famous street," writes Julie Duin. "If the horizon remains cloudless, three stars are visible in a straight line from the Capitol to the White House to the skies in the west. Known as Regulus, Arcturus and Spica, the stars form a right-angled triangle framing the constellation of Virgo."[125] Such mysticism incorporated into the design of Washington, DC by Freemasons for summoning the timing, presence, and approval of these "invisible agents" was a formula perfected in pagan Rome. John Fellows explains why:

> They consulted the gods, to know if the enterprise would
> be acceptable to them, and if they approved of the day

chosen to begin the work…they invoked, besides the gods of the country, the gods to whose protection the new city was recommended, which was done secretly, because it was necessary that the tutelary gods should be unknown to the vulgar.[126]

It may come as little surprise then that when George W. Bush, in a speech the day before his second inaugural, said the United States had "a calling from beyond the stars" (a disturbing statement taken directly from the satanic *Necronomicon* fiction concerning alien creator gods) that the Capitol building had been intentionally set in the head of a Masonic owl figure, which in turn stands atop the White House, located on the chin of the pentagramic goat of Mendes. The upside-down pentagram, or "baphomet," clearly visible in the DC street layout, represents the goat's head and is considered the most powerful symbol in Satanism, while the owl figure is a well-known representative of the Masonic, Illuminati, Bohemian owl of wisdom incarnation of Athene, Minerva, Lilith, and Hecate.

Occultists around the world understand the power of these DC symbols and rituals, and realize they are not only for conveying psychological concepts, but actually to coerce the mysterious and potent supernaturalism invited to take residence there. This belief is deeply preserved in all of the Babylonian, Egyptian, Greek, Roman, and Kabalistic symbolism that is a part of Masonic history, and according to famous Freemason Foster Bailey, these symbols intentionally hide "a secret…which veils mysterious forces. These energies when released can have a potent effect."[127] Scottish philosopher Thomas Carlyle once famously added: "By symbols, accordingly, is man guided and commanded, made happy, made wretched." Masons, as a result, are under oath never to reveal the true meaning of their symbols, and when somehow they are compelled to offer explanation, they falsify the statement, even to lower-degree Masons, as explained by Sovereign Grand Commander Albert Pike in the Masonic handbook *Morals and Dogma*:

> Masonry, like all the Religions, all the Mysteries, Hermetic, and Alchemy, conceals its secrets from all except the Adepts and Sages, or the Elect, and uses false explanations and misinterpretations of its symbols to mislead those who deserve only to be misled; to conceal the Truth, which it calls Light, from them, and to draw them away from it.[128]

Substantial reasons exist for why the designers of Washington's Government Center would have wanted to obscure the meaning behind the occultic layout of America's Capitol. If the public in general had been prematurely convinced of the end-game prophesied in the DC symbolism, it would have been beyond the acceptance of prior generations who likely would have demanded change in leaders and facilities. But as time has moved forward and increasingly it has become necessary for public understanding of America's heritage and intended purpose, little by little—either by providence, promotion, or even resistance—a clearer picture has emerged of what Manly P. Hall called "the secret destiny of America."

According to the symbolism in Washington, DC, the secret destiny of America includes future national and global subservience to the god of Freemasonry, a deity most Americans would not imagine when reciting the pledge of allegiance to "one nation under *God*." In fact, the idea by some that the United States was established as a monotheistic, "Christian nation" by those who designed Washington, DC, and that the "God" referred to on American currency is a Judeo-Christian one, is a puzzling conclusion when reflected against the deistic beliefs of so many of the founding fathers (as perpetually viewed in the "Supreme Architect" deism of Freemasons and in the "Supreme Judge of the world" and "Divine Providence" notations in the Declaration of Independence) and the countless pagan icons that dominate the symbols, statues, buildings, and seals carefully drafted under official government auspices. The Great Seal of the United States, which Hall rightly called "the signature" of that exalted body of Masons who designed America for a "peculiar and particular purpose," bears rich symbolism forecasting anything but Christianity. In fact, when Christians in the 1800s argued that a hypothetical annihilation of the United States would lead to "antiquaries of succeeding centuries" concluding that America had been a heathen nation based on symbolism of the Great Seal, Congress was pushed to create something reflecting the Christian faith of so many of its citizens. US President and Freemason Theodore Roosevelt strongly opposed this idea, while other Masons were not as frustrated with the plan. Given the ambivalence of the term "God" and the axiom that, interpreted within the context of the Great Seal symbolism, this would certainly not infer a traditional Christian God, the slogan "IN GOD WE TRUST" (whomever you believe that is) was accommodated by Masons and other illuminatus and so approved as the official US motto.

To illustrate the point that one would not determine the "God" in America's official motto refers to the Father of Jesus Christ or a biblical Trinity, imagine yourself as a space traveler who visits earth in a fictional, post-apocalyptic world. Digging through the rubble of the once-thriving planet, you come across a copy of a US one-dollar bill with the two-sided Great Seal of the United States joined in the middle by the phrase, "IN GOD WE TRUST."

Upon consideration, you ask yourself, "What *god* did this refer to?" With no preconceptions, you allow the symbolism on the seal to speak for itself, from which you quickly determine that this had been a great culture who worshipped Egyptian and Greek deities, especially a particular solar one whose all-seeing eye glared from atop an unfinished Egyptian pyramid. Upon further investigation into the specific beliefs of the strange group whose members had influenced the Great Seal, you discover from their highest masters, including one "illustrious" Albert Pike, that the sun god they venerated so highly had been known to them at various times in history by the names *Apollo, Osiris,* and *Nimrod.*

Then, you decode something even more important—a hidden divination in the Great Seal that prophesied a time when this "god" would return to earth in a physical body. His coming, according to the information you gleaned from the draftsmen of the Great Seal, would herald a New World Order. In retrospect, you wonder: *Was this prophesied advent on this Great Seal the fomenter of destruction that annihilated what at once was so beautiful a world?*

Chapter 6

THE FIRST PART OF THE FINAL
MYSTERY OF THE GREAT SEAL

Not only were many of the founders of the United States
Government Masons, but they received aid from a secret and
august body existing in Europe, which helped them to establish this country for a peculiar and particular purpose known
only to the initiated few. The Great Seal is the signature of this
exalted body—unseen and for the most part unknown—and
the unfinished pyramid upon its reverse side is a trestleboard
setting forth symbolically the task to the accomplishment of
which the United States Government was dedicated from the
day of its inception. —Manly P. Hall, 33rd-Degree Freemason

O f all the Masonic symbols associated with the founding
of America, Manly Hall viewed the design of the Great
Seal of the United States as the highest signature of
occult planning by Freemasons. This was not only due
to the repetition of the number thirteen, the pentagram shapes,
the uncapped pyramid, or the phoenix-eagle, but Hall, like other
experts in mystical literature and Western esoteric tradition, understood the "mass of occult and Masonic symbols" on the Great Seal
represented both the tangible ambitions of a new society and a
metaphysical concept attributed to Hermes Trismegistus, which

means that visible matter is mirrored by unseen reality, or, "as above, so below." Hall believed what this meant practically was that only students of archaic or esoteric symbolism would be able to decipher the true meaning hidden within the subterfuge of the seal's design, and that the symbolism was thus intended to convey two sets of meaning—the first for non-illuminates having to do with certain natural or historical issues perceived to be important to society; and the second, deeper occult truisms meant for comprehension by members of the exalted Order.

While examining the mountains of literature publicly available on the Great Seal, including its history from the original resolution in 1776 to its final approval in 1782, it is important to note that general harmony exists among researchers concerning the superficial interpretation of the primary symbols. For instance, the obverse side of the Great Seal portrays a bald eagle clutching a bundle of arrows in its left talon, while its right claw grips an olive branch. The eagle is looking to the right, indicating that while the United States prefers peace, it is always ready to go to war if necessary.

The original thirteen colonies are said to be represented in the thirteen leaves of the olive branch, thirteen olives on the branch, thirteen bars and stripes in the shield, thirteen arrows in the phrase, "*E Pluribus Unum*," and the thirteen stars above the eagle's head (which, as researchers point out, forms a hexagram). On the reverse of the seal, the number thirteen continues in the stone layers of the pyramid and the thirteen letters of the words "*Annuit Coeptis.*"

But according to esotericists like Hall, the extraordinary truth about the number thirteen so affixed to the Great Seal was actually more than representation of the original colonies. It was a marker for those who understood it as a Masonic "power number," sacred to the moon and representative of the head of Isis, while the eagle, Hall wrote, was a shrewd masquerade for the mythical phoenix so important to Masonic mysticism. Hall partly came to this conclusion based on the early seal prototype of William Barton showing a phoenix in its nest of flames.

"Most of the designs originally submitted had the Phoenix bird on its nest of flames as the central motif," Hall said, continuing:

Its selection would of course have been appropriate…
[because] the Phoenix is one sign of the secret orders of the
ancient world and of the initiate of those orders, for it was
common to refer to one who had been accepted into the
temples as a man twice-born, or re-born. Wisdom confers a
new life, and those who become wise are born again.

Hall went on in *The Secret Destiny of America*:

The Phoenix symbol is important in another way, as an
emblem among nearly all civilized nations of royalty, power,
superiority, and immortality. The Phoenix of China is identical in meaning with the Phoenix of Egypt; and the Phoenix of the Greeks is the same as the Thunder Bird of the
American Indians.…

It is immediately evident that the bird on the original
seal is not an eagle…but the Phoenix.… The beak is of a
different shape, the neck is much longer, and the small tuft
of hair at the back of the head leaves no doubt as to the artist's intention.[129]

Hall then acknowledged that if the design "on the obverse side
of the seal is stamped with the signature" of the Masons, the design
on the reverse was even more related to the Order's "mysteries," casting the United States within the society's secret scheme to fulfill the
Baconian dream of a New Atlantis by establishing America as the
capital of the New World Order.

Hall continued:

Here is represented the great pyramid of Gizah, composed
of thirteen rows of masonry, showing seventy-two stones.

The pyramid is without a cap stone, and above its upper platform floats a triangle containing the all-seeing eye surrounded by rays of light....

The Pyramid of Gizah was believed by the ancient Egyptians to be the shrine tomb of the god Hermes, or Thot, the personification of universal wisdom.

No trace has ever been found of the cap of the great pyramid. A flat platform about thirty feet square gives no indication that this part of the structure was ever otherwise finished; and this is appropriate, as the Pyramid represents human society itself, imperfect and incomplete. The structure's ascending converging angles and faces represent the common aspiration of humankind; above floats the symbol of the esoteric orders, the radiant triangle with its all-seeing eye....

There is a legend that in the lost Atlantis stood a great university in which originated most of the arts and sciences of the present race. The University was in the form of an immense pyramid with many galleries and corridors, and on the top was an observatory for the study of the stars. This temple to the sciences in the old Atlantis is shadowed forth in the seal of the new Atlantis. Was it the society of the unknown philosophers who scaled the new nation with the eternal emblems, that all the nations might know the purpose for which the new country had been founded?

...The combination of the Phoenix, the pyramid, and the all-seeing eye is more than chance or coincidence. There is nothing about the early struggles of the colonists to suggest such a selection to farmers, shopkeepers, and country gentlemen. There is only one possible origin for these symbols, and that is the secret societies which came to this country 150 years before the Revolutionary War. Most of the patriots who achieved American independence belonged to these societies, and derived their inspiration, courage, and high purpose from the ancient teaching. There can be no question that the great seal was directly inspired by these orders of the human quest, and that it set forth the purpose for this nation as that purpose was seen and known to the Founding Fathers.

The monogram of the new Atlantis reveals this continent as set apart for the accomplishment of the great work— here is to arise the pyramid of human aspiration, the school of the secret sciences.[130]

Besides Manly Hall, late scholars who recognized the occult symbolism of the Great Seal as pointing to this "secret destiny of America" included Rhodes Scholar James H. Billington and Harvard professor Charles Eliot Norton, who described the Great Seal as hardly other than an "emblem of a Masonic Fraternity." In 1846, 33rd-Degree Freemason and noted author James D. Carter inadvertently confirmed this as well when *he admitted the Masonic symbolism is clearly known whenever "an informed Mason examines the Great Seal."*

Yet for all the volumes written in the early years about the arcane meaning behind the symbols and mottoes of the Great Seal, it was not until the 1940s that, perhaps by providence, the significance of the seal started finding its defining moment.

It happened when during the summer of 1940, two-term President Franklin D. Roosevelt decided to run for an unprecedented third term and chose as his running mate for the Vice-Presidency, secretary of agriculture and 32nd-Degree Mason, Henry Wallace. Among other things, Roosevelt needed an unyielding supporter for the fading New Deal and saw in Wallace a farm-bred intellectual whose scrubbed Midwestern looks would appeal to a cross section of Americans—from ranchers to big-city unionists. Democratic National Committee Chairman Jim Farley couldn't have disagreed more, and made his opinion known not only to Roosevelt but to his wife, Eleanor, a strong and respected civil rights activist who, after discussing the liberalism and mysticism of Wallace, phoned her husband and told him, "I've been talking with Jim Farley and I agree with him. Henry Wallace won't do." But FDR was determined to have his Masonic brother as his second in command and drafted a speech in which he would refuse the party's nomination unless Wallace was designated for VP. The first lady followed by giving a speech of her own—a first time in which a woman addressed the Democratic National Convention—asking the delegates to respect her husband's reasoning. Wallace went on to become thirty-third vice president of the United States under the thirty-second president, Franklin D. Roosevelt—himself a 32nd-Degree Mason and Knight of Pythias (Shriner) with an equal thirst for mysticism. Of course, at the time, the delegates could hardly have imagined such weird instruments as a 1938 White House interoffice memo from Wallace to Roosevelt that illustrated how deeply mysticism was already a part of the two men's relationship. It read in part:

> I feel for a short time yet that we must deal with the "strong ones," the "turbulent ones," the "fervent ones," and perhaps even with a temporary resurgence, with the "flameless ones," who with the last dying gasp will strive to reanimate their dying giant "Capitalism." Mr. President, you can be the "flaming one," the one with an ever-upsurging spirit to lead into the time when the children of men can sing again.[131]

If at first this strange language befuddles the reader, it becomes much clearer when the history of Wallace, who openly referred to himself as a "practical mystic," is brought to light, including his veneration of Agni Yoga Society founder and theosophist Nicholas Roerich. Known in his native land as Nicolai Rerikh, Roerich and his wife had migrated from the Soviet Union to the United States in the 1920s where they made a name for themselves on the New York scene as teachers of Madam Blavatsky's theosophical *Secret Doctrine*. Roerich's particular devotion to mysticism was, however, increasingly focused on apocalyptic themes surrounding the coming of a new earthly order, which struck a chord with Wallace. This came to light later when Wallace began the VP race and was threatened with embarrassment by the Republicans, who had come into possession of a series of letters written by Wallace in the 1930s. Some of the communications were addressed to Roerich as "Dear Guru," and described the anticipation Wallace felt for "the breaking of the New Day," a time when a mythical kingdom would arrive on earth accompanied by a special breed of people. Earlier letters by Wallace simply addressed the mystic as "Dear Prof. R," and reflected the yearning Wallace felt to become Roerich's disciple and to make contact with those supernatural masters who populated Blavatsky's spiritual universe. In early 1934, Wallace wrote Roerich:

> ...Long have I been aware of the occasional fragrance from that other world which is the real world. But now I must live in the outer world and at the same time make over my mind and body to serve as fit instruments for the Lord of Justice. The changes in awareness must come as a result of steady, earnest recollectedness. I shall strive to grow as rapidly as possible.... Yes, the Chalice is filling.[132]

The phrase by Wallace "I must…make over my mind and body to serve as fit instruments for the Lord of Justice" is a direct reference to Helena Blavatsky's *Secret Doctrine* to which Wallace and Roerich were dedicated. On page 332 of her related work, Blavatsky explains that "Osiris" is this Lord of Justice who rules over the "Seven Luminous Ones" or seven stars that Wallace would later speak of and under which the United States would serve following the inauguration of the New World Order and the resurrection of Osiris/Apollo.[133] The other phrase, "Yes, the Chalice is filling" corresponds to Holy Grail teachings by Roerich concerning a mystical cup, called the "Chalice of Buddha" or sometimes "the Blessed One" which was (at least metaphorically) a vessel of knowledge to those who honored the messianic figure and which would be filled by the appearance of the King of the New World Order—Osiris/Apollo to Masons. Though in the 1930s and 40s such coded letters gave Wallace an air of mystery as well as space for criticism in his political life; Roosevelt, too, was more than a casual acquaintance of Roerich. John C. Culver and John Hyde in their biography *American Dreamer: The Life and Times of Henry A. Wallace* note how:

> Roosevelt, perhaps influenced by his mother's enthusiasm for Eastern art and mysticism, took a personal interest in the Roerichs' causes. Roosevelt met Roerich at least once, met with Roerich's associates on several occasions, and between 1934 and 1936 personally corresponded with Helena Roerich several times. "Mr. President," she wrote in a typical letter, "Your message was transmitted to me. I am happy that your great heart has so beautifully accepted the Message and Your lightbearing mind was free from prejudice."
>
> Indeed, it was Roosevelt who suggested to Wallace that

he read an allegory by Arthur Hopkins called *The Glory Road*, which served as the basis for the coded language in the guru letters.[134]

Behind the Guru Letters:
Belief in the Great Seal Prophecy

Although Roosevelt would be the one to set in motion the push to place the Great Seal of the United States on the US one-dollar bill, Wallace claimed it was he who first brought the seal's oracular significance to Roosevelt, believing the symbolism of the emblems carried inference to Roosevelt's "New Deal," and, more important, a Masonic prophecy toward a New World Order. Wallace describes the meeting he had with Roosevelt:

> Roosevelt as he looked at the colored reproduction of the Seal was first struck with the representation of the All-Seeing Eye—a Masonic representation of the Great Architect of the Universe. Next, he was impressed with the idea that the foundation for the new order of the ages had been laid in 1776 but that it would be completed only under the eye of the Great Architect. Roosevelt, like myself, was a 32nd-degree Mason. He suggested that the Seal be put on the dollar bill…and took the matter up with the Secretary of the Treasury [also a Freemason].… He brought it up in a Cabinet meeting and asked James Farley [Postmaster General and a Roman Catholic] if he thought the Catholics would have any objection to the "all-seeing Eye," which he as a Mason looked on as a Masonic symbol of Deity. Farley said, "No, there would be no objection."[135]

Regardless of who between Roosevelt and Wallace first perceived the seal's Masonic prophetic significance, surviving records clearly show it was Roosevelt (and in his own handwriting no less) who instructed that the obverse side of the seal be placed on the right back of the dollar and the reverse side of the seal with the pyramid and all-seeing eye be put on the left so that it would be the first thing a person saw when reading the back of the dollar from left to right. Thus, most Americans "were left with the impression that the mysterious pyramid and its heralding of a 'new order' were the foremost symbols of the American republic," notes Mitch Horowitz in *Occult America.*[136] It is natural to thus assume Wallace and Roosevelt also pondered the eagle on the Great Seal with its thirty-two feathers on the right wing and thirty-three on the left, representing the 32nd and 33rd degrees of Freemasonry, because in addition to being 32nd-Degree Masons, Roosevelt was the thirty-second president and Wallace the thirty-third vice president, an especially remarkable numerological "coincidence" given that Roosevelt was succeeded by Harry Truman, the thirty-third president of the United States and a 33rd-Degree Freemason! Additionally, in a 1991 hardcover book on American presidents by the Smithsonian Institution (the world's largest research complex, founded by Freemason James Smithson) titled *The Smithsonian Treasury: Presidents*, it says on page 72 that when Franklin Roosevelt died during the closing days of World War II, the responsibility "to formulate policies for a new world order" fell to Freemason Harry Truman.[137] A painting on the same page depicts Truman standing over four other Masons—Joint Chiefs of Staff Admiral William D. Leahy; Army Air Force General Henry H. Arnold; Army Chief of Staff George C. Marshall; and Navy Commander in Chief Ernest J. King—a fitting diagram given that all this is depicted on page 72 of a Smithsonian work, an intriguing choice for a statement on the vision for a new world order given what the number seventy-two means within Masonic Gnosticism regarding the seventy-two fallen angels or "kosmokrators" that currently administer the affairs of earth and who are magically bound within the US Capitol Dome to bring about a New World Order (discussed elsewhere).

As a mystic and Mason, Wallace (like we do) undoubtedly believed these numerologies were not coincidence. Furthermore, what is now known is that Wallace viewed the unfinished pyramid with the all-seeing eye hovering above it on the Great Seal as a prophecy about the dawn of a new world with America at its head. Whenever the United States assumed its position as the new capital of the world, Wallace wrote, the Grand Architect would return and metaphorically the all-seeing eye would be fitted atop the Great Seal pyramid as the finished "apex stone." For that to happen, Wallace penned in 1934, "It will take a more definite recognition of the Grand Architect of the Universe before the apex stone [capstone of the pyramid] is finally fitted into place and this nation in the full strength of its power is in position to assume leadership among the nations in inaugurating 'the New Order of the Ages.'"[138]

Finding or making "a more definite recognition" of this messianic figure appears to have secretly obsessed Wallace (as well as Roosevelt) while also playing a key role in the decision to include the Great Seal on the US dollar. Both men were fascinated with the concept of a new breed of people—new Atlantians for the New Atlantis similar to Hitler's contemporaneous exploration for the Aryan supermen—led by an earthly messiah. Incredibly, if this supernatural leader were to be a magical reincarnation or resurrection of deity, the body or DNA of this savior may have been kept in or represented by a coffin (echoing the coffin symbolism on Masonic aprons), cryptically mentioned in correspondence between Wallace and Nicholas Roerich. On March 12, 1933, Wallace wrote Roerich:

> Dear Guru,
>
> I have been thinking of you holding the casket—the sacred most precious casket. And I have thought of the New Country going forward to meet the seven stars [Blavatsky's "Seven Luminous Ones" that serve under "Osiris," the Lord of Justice, and under which the US would serve at the fulfillment of the Sibyl's *novus ordo seclorum* prophecy on the Great Seal] under the sign of the three stars [possibly the three belt stars of Orion, related in myth to Osiris]. And I have thought of the admonition "Await the Stone."
>
> We await the Stone and we welcome you again to this glorious land of destiny, clouded though it may be with strange fumbling fears. Who shall hold up the compelling vision to those who wander in darkness? In answer to this question we again welcome you. To drive out depression. To drive out fear.... And so I await your convenience prepared to do what I am to do.[139]

Investigative mythologist William Henry says this letter from Wallace made it clear that Roosevelt, Nicholas Roerich, and Henry Wallace "were in search of this Divine Child...and his secret... Stone...[and that] they awaited...in the 'New Country' [America as the New Atlantis]."[140] Central to the fulfillment of this scheme was the "sacred casket" that Wallace mentioned in his letter to Roerich, considered in esoteric circles to be the same as the casket or "coffin" of Osiris, and the Chintamani "Stone" or magical meteorite and holy relic believed to have been left by "missionaries" to Earth from the region of the star Sirius in the constellation Canis Major (The Great Dog). The "Stone" supposedly held properties that could give eternal life and was believed by devotees to be the true Cup of Christ. This mythology is also connected with Shambhala (which Roerich was looking for), a legendary kingdom in Tibet where supposedly enlightened immortals secretly live and who currently are guiding human evolution toward a one-world order. In fact, a portion of the Chintamani Stone was reportedly carried by Roerich as an emissary in 1935 to the founders of the now defunct League of Nations, whose goal also was to create a one-world order.

Whatever the case for Wallace, like Manly Hall had, he and Roosevelt viewed the all-seeing eye above the unfinished pyramid as pointing to the return (or reincarnation) of this coming savior, whose arrival would cap the pyramid and launch the New World Order. The all-seeing eye on the Great Seal is fashioned after the Eye of Horus, the offspring of Osiris (or Osiris resurrected), as both men surely understood. Aliester Crowley, 33rd-Degree Freemason (the "wickedest man on earth") and a Roerich occult contemporary, often spoke of this as the "New Age of Horus" and the breaking dawn of the rebirth of Osiris. That such mystics and Freemasons simultaneously used such identical language is telling, given that the Great Seal's mottoes and symbolism relate to both Osiris and Apollo specifically, yet as one. Osiris is the dominant theme of the Egyptian symbols, his resurrection and return, while the *mottoes* of the seal point directly to Apollo, and the eagle, a pagan emblem of Jupiter, to Apollo's father. For instance, the motto *annuit coeptis* is from Virgil's *Aeneid*, in which Ascanius, the son of Aeneas from conquered Troy, prays to Apollo's father, Jupiter [Zeus]. Charles Thompson, designer of the Great Seal's final version, condensed line 625 of book IX of Virgil's *Aeneid*, which reads, *Juppiter omnipotes, audacibus annue coeptis* ("All-powerful Jupiter favors [the] daring undertakings"), to

Annuit coeptis ("He approves [our] undertakings"), while the phrase *novus ordo seclorum* ("a new order of the ages") was adapted in 1782 from inspiration Thompson found in a prophetic line in Virgil's Eclogue IV: *Magnus ab integro seclorum nascitur ordo* (Virgil's *Eclogue IV*, line 5), the interpretation of the original Latin being, "And the majestic roll of circling centuries begins anew." This phrase is from the Cumaean Sibyl (a pagan prophetess of Apollo, identified in the Bible as a demonic deceiver) and involves the future birth of a divine son, spawned of "a new breed of men sent down from heaven" (what Roosevelt, Wallace, and Roerich were looking for) when he receives "the life of gods, and sees Heroes with gods commingling." According to the prophecy, this is Apollo, son of Jupiter (Zeus), who returns to Earth through mystical "life" given to him from the gods when the deity Saturn (Saturn is the Roman version of the biblical *Satan*) returns to reign over the Earth in a new Pagan Golden Age.

From the beginning of the prophecy we read:

Now the last age by Cumae's Sibyl sung Has come and gone, and the majestic roll Of circling centuries begins anew: Justice returns, returns old Saturn's reign, With a new breed of men sent down from heaven. Only do thou, at the boy's birth in whom The iron shall cease, the golden race arise, Befriend him, chaste Lucina; 'tis thine own Apollo reigns.

He shall receive the life of gods, and see Heroes with gods commingling, and himself Be seen of them, and with his father's worth Reign o'er a world....

Assume thy greatness, for the time draws nigh, Dear child of gods, great progeny of Jove [Jupiter/Zeus]! See how it totters—the world's orbed might, Earth, and wide ocean, and the vault profound, All, see, enraptured of the coming time![141]

According to Virgil and the Cumaean Sibyl, whose prophecy formed the *novus ordo seclorum* of the Great Seal of the United States, the New World Order begins during a time of chaos when the earth and oceans are tottering—a time like today. This is when the "son" of promise arrives on earth—Apollo incarnate—a pagan savior born of "a new breed of men sent down from heaven" when "heroes" and "gods" are blended together. This sounds eerily similar to what the Watchers did during the creation of the Nephilim and to what scientists are doing this century through genetic engineering of human-animal chimeras. But to understand why such a fanciful prophecy about Apollo, son of Jupiter, returning to Earth should be important to you: In ancient literature, Jupiter was the Roman replacement of Yahweh as the greatest of the gods—a "counter-Yahweh." His son Apollo is a replacement of Jesus, a "counter-Jesus." This Apollo comes to rule the final New World Order, when "Justice returns, returns old Saturn's [Satan's] reign." The ancient goddess Justice, who returns Satan's reign (*Saturnia regna*, the pagan golden age), was known to the Egyptians as Ma'at and to the Greeks as Themis, while to the Romans she was Lustitia. Statues and reliefs of her adorn thousands of government buildings and courts around the world, especially in Washington, DC, as familiar Lady Justice, blindfolded and holding scales and a sword. She represents the enforcement of secular law and is, according to the Sibyl's conjure, the authority that will require global compliance to the zenith of Satan's dominion concurrent with the coming of Apollo. What's more, the Bible's accuracy concerning this subject is alarming, including the idea that "pagan justice" will require surrender to a satanic system in a final world order under the rule of Jupiter's son.

In the New Testament, the identity of the god Apollo, repeat-coded in the Great Seal of the United States as the Masonic "messiah" who returns to rule the earth, is the same spirit—verified by the *same name*—that will inhabit the political leader of the end-times New World Order. According to key Bible prophecies, the Antichrist will be the progeny or incarnation of the ancient spirit, *Apollo*. Second Thessalonians 2:3 warns: "Let no man deceive you by any means: for that day shall not come, except there come a falling away first, and that man of sin be revealed, the son of *perdition* [*Apoleia*; Apollyon, Apollo]" (emphasis added). Numerous scholarly and classical works identify "Apollyon" as the god "Apollo"—the Greek deity "of death and pestilence," and Webster's Dictionary points out that "Apollyon" was a common variant of "Apollo" throughout history. An example of this is found in the classical play by the ancient Greek playwright Aeschylus, *The Agamemnon of Aeschylus*, in which Cassandra repeats more than once, "Apollo, thou destroyer, O Apollo, Lord of fair streets, Apollyon to me."[142] Accordingly, the name Apollo turns up in ancient literature with the verb *apollymi* or *apollyo* (destroy), and scholars including W. R. F. Browning believe apostle Paul may have identified the god Apollo as the "spirit of Antichrist" operating behind the persecuting Roman emperor, Domitian, who wanted to be recognized as "Apollo incarnate" in his day. Such identifying of Apollo with despots and "the spirit of Antichrist" is consistent even in modern history. For instance, note how Napoleon's name literally translates to "the true Apollo."

Revelation 17:8 likewise ties the coming of Antichrist with Apollo, revealing that the Beast shall ascend from the bottomless pit and enter him:

The Beast that thou sawest was, and is not; and shall ascend out of the Bottomless Pit, and go into *perdition* [*Apolia*, Apollo]: and they that dwell on the Earth shall wonder, whose names were not written in the Book of Life from the foundation of the world, when they behold the Beast that was, and is not, and yet is. (emphasis added)

Among other things, this means the Great Seal of the United States is a prophecy, hidden in plain sight by the Founding Fathers and devotees of Bacon's New Atlantis for more than two hundred years, foretelling the return of a terrifying demonic god who seizes control of Earth in the new order of the ages. This supernatural entity was known and feared in ancient times by different names: Apollo, Osiris, and even farther back as Nimrod, whom Masons consider to be the father of their institution.

We are willing to bet, however, few people know how Washington, DC's mirror city, the Vatican, also believes in the Cumaean Sibyl's *novus ordo seclorum* prophecy, so much so in fact that they even had Michelangelo gloriously encode it on the ceiling of the Sistine Chapel.

Pythians, Romanists, and the Sign of the 6th Knuckle

According to the Greeks, the greatest outcome of the love affair between Zeus and Leto was the birth of the most beloved—and soon to reappear oracle gods—Apollo. More than any other deity in ancient history, Apollo represented the passion for prophetic inquiry among the nations. Though mostly associated with classical Greece, scholars agree that Apollo existed before the Olympian pantheon and some even claim that he was at first the god of the Hyperboreans—an ancient and legendary people to the north. Herodotus came to this conclusion and recorded how the Hyperboreans continued in worship of Apollo even after his induction into the Greek pantheon, making an annual pilgrimage to the land of Delos, where they participated in the famous Greek festivals of Apollo. Lycia—a small country in southwest Turkey—also had an early connection with Apollo, where he was known as *Lykeios*, which some have joined to the Greek *Lykos* or "wolf," thus making one of his ancient titles, "the wolf slayer."

Apollo, with his twin sister Artemis, was said by the Greeks to have been born in the land of Delos—the children of Zeus (Jupiter) and of the Titaness Leto. While an important oracle existed there and played a role in the festivals of the god, it was the famous oracle at Delphi that became the celebrated mouthpiece of the Olympian. Located on the mainland of Greece, the *omphalos* of Delphi (the stone the Greeks believed marked the center of the earth) can still be found among the ruins of Apollo's Delphic temple. So important was Apollo's oracle at Delphi that wherever Hellenism existed, its citizens and kings, including some from as far away as Spain, ordered their lives, colonies, and wars by its sacred communications. It was here that the Olympian gods spoke to mortal men through the use of a priesthood, which interpreted the trance-induced utterances of the Pythoness or Pythia. She was a middle-aged woman who sat on a copper-and-gold tripod, or, much earlier, on the "rock of the sibyl" (medium), and crouched over a fire while inhaling the smoke of burning laurel leaves, barley, marijuana, and oil, until a sufficient intoxication for her prophecies had been produced. While the use of the laurel leaves may have referred to the nymph Daphne (Greek for "laurel"), who escaped from Apollo's sexual intentions by transforming herself into a laurel tree, the leaves also served the practical purpose of supplying the necessary amounts of hydrocyanic acid and complex alkaloids which, when combined with hemp, created powerful hallucinogenic visions. Another drug possibly used by the

Pythia is known as DMT [dimethyltryptamine]. This chemical—naturally produced in the pineal gland and present in some wild plants—has been used for thousands of years by shamans to contact the spirit world. Others suggest that the Pythia may have employed a version of the psychoactive drug "absinthe" to induce a spirit-traversing mental gateway—a practice also employed throughout Greek paganism as well as by shamans of other cultures but condemned in the Scriptures (Galatians 5:20; Revelation 9:21 and 18:23) as *pharmakeia*—the administering of drugs for sorcery or magical arts in connection with demonic contact. The book, *Forbidden Gates: How Genetics, Robotics, Artificial Intelligence, Synthetic Biology, Nanotechnology, and Human Enhancement Herald the Dawn of TechoDimensional Spiritual Warfare*, discusses this phenomenon in more recent times, saying of absinthe in particular:

> This unique, distinctive distilled liquid of pale green color was known in the late nineteenth and early twentieth centuries as the "green fairy." Although its consumption almost became an obsession across Europe and more mystical cosmopolitan centers in America like New Orleans, it was most closely associated with the bohemian artistic culture thriving at the time. It was a favorite of eclectic artists such as the painter Salvador Dali and writer Oscar Wilde, due to its reliable propensity to facilitate their contact directly with their inspirational spirit "muses." Occult magician Aleister Crowley was so devoted to absinthe for its spiritual invocation capabilities that he wrote his famous lengthy poem, "The Green Goddess," in its honor. It was the only alcoholic beverage banned across Europe (as well as North America) because the diagnosed "absinthism" addiction and effects were deemed much worse than regular alcohol. *The curious*

matter about absinthe is that it is distilled from the wormwood plant, which has the official name of Artemis absinthium. Artemis was a Greek and Roman goddess who was (a) considered a "huntress"; (b) associated with fire and keys; and (c) the sister of Apollo. She was associated with the goddess Hecate, who was known as a "luminal" god who controlled the access to portals in the spirit world.[143] (emphasis added)

Whatever the case may have been for the ancient Pythian or Sibyl, it was under the influence of such "forces" that she prophesied in an unfamiliar voice thought to be that of Apollo, himself. During the Pythian trance, the medium's personality often changed, becoming melancholic, defiant, or even animal-like, exhibiting a "possession" psychosis that may have been the source of the werewolf myth, or *lycanthropy*, as the Pythia reacted to an encounter with Apollo/Lykeios—the wolf god. Delphic "women of python" prophesied in this way for nearly a thousand years and were considered to be a vital part of the pagan order and local economy of every Hellenistic community.

The Cumaean Sibyl (also known as Amalthaea), whose prophecy about the return of the god Apollo is encoded in the Great Seal of the United States, was the oldest of these Sibyls and the seer of the underworld who, in the *Aeneid*, gave Aeneas a tour of the infernal region. This adds to a mystery of adoption of the Pythians and Sibyls by the Vatican as "vessels of truth." These seers, whose lives were dedicated to channeling from frenzied lips the messages of gods and goddesses, turn up in Catholic art, from altars to illustrated books and even upon the ceiling of the Sistine Chapel, where five Sibyls including the Delphic (like Paul cast a demon out of) join the Old Testament prophets in places of sacred honor. Yet it is the Cumaean who not only sits so prominently inside Catholicism's most celebrated chapel, but who's painting, on close examination, unveils a secret—a magnificent clue—which her Italian Renaissance artist left concerning her, and her returning Lord's, origin and identity. For upon consideration, the portrait reveals "the sign of the 6th knuckle." The Cumaean's left thumb is inside the book and the fingers of her left hand wrapped outside in standard book-holding fashion. A clearly visible extra knuckle is portrayed, secreted perhaps by Michelangelo to depict a sixth digit bent under the palm, or to illustrate that a sixth finger had been lost or cut off at the knuckle. Either meaning is deeply occultic, and as students of history and the Bible clearly know, this ties both the Sibyl and her prophesied savior Apollo to the offspring of the fallen Watchers, the Nephilim (see 2 Samuel 21:20), of which Apollo/Osiris/Nimrod was chief.

This is the tip of the iceberg. What it has to do with Petrus Romanus and his Apollonian master continues in the following chapter.

The Sign of the Sixth Knuckle in the Sistine Chapel

Also at the Vatican—Petrus Romanus and the Number 13

As this book goes into a new expanded edition, the election of Pope Francis necessitates a response. To say some of the sanctified speculations in this book and the companion works *Petrus Romanus: The Final Pope Is Here* (Defender Publishing, 2012) and *Exo-Vaticana: Petrus Romanus, Project LUCIFER, and the Vatican's Astonishing Exo-Theological Plan for the Arrival of an Alien Savior* (Defender Publishing, 2013) have been confirmed is an understatement. Pope Benedict XVI's February 11, 2013 announcement—as forecast a year in advance in *Petrus Romanus*—was unprecedented because the last pope to resign was Gregory XII in 1415, nearly six hundred years ago. We did not venture this hypothesis uninformed. In his book, *Light of the World: The Pope, the Church, and the Signs of the Times*, when asked if he thought it appropriate for a pope to retire, Pope Benedict XVI responded, "If a pope clearly realizes that he is no longer physically, psychologically and spiritually capable of handling the duties of his office, then he has a right and, under some circumstances, also an obligation to resign."[144] Thus, based on a conflation of prophecy and current events we went out on a limb, taking a risky position on pages 57–58 of *Petrus Romanus* by asserting that Benedict XVI would step down for reasons related to health concerns. Indeed, it came to pass and many former skeptics picked up our book in earnest.

As the reader may be aware, we correlated Pope Benedict's predisposition to retire with the work of the Jesuit scholar, René Thibaut, who predicted that the door would be opened for the arrival of the final pope on the famous "Prophecy of the Popes" list in 2012. Of course, the year 2012 came and went with seemingly no fulfillment. Consequently, we were a little disappointed when it seemed like Thibaut was mistaken. All the same, Thibaut's code-breaking work was a relatively small portion of our book's content, so we never felt our work was made irrelevant. However, as it turns out, Thiabaut was far more correct—astoundingly so—than anyone would ever imagine until February 2013! According to the *New York Times*:

> That the resignation was long in the planning was confirmed by Giovanni Maria Vian, the editor of the Vatican newspaper, *L'Osservatore Romano*, who wrote on Monday that the pope's decision "was taken many months ago," after his trip to Mexico and Cuba in March 2012, "and kept with a reserve that no one could violate."[145]

In other words, Pope Benedict officially and secretly resigned right when Thibaut—and we—speculated he would in 2012, and then his February 11, 2013 public affirmation was quickly punctuated by two dramatic lightning bolts striking St. Peter's Basilica.[146] Most people including perhaps Pope Benedict XVI himself, were blissfully unaware of the ancient signature the dual lightning strikes atop St. Peter's Basilica represented, especially as it involved the looming papal inauguration of Petrus Romanus (Pope Francis). For a few adepts of history and secret orders, the sign from heaven was deliciously staged. The term "inaugurate" is from the Latin "inauguratio," and refers to the archaic ceremony by which the Roman augurs (soothsayers) approved a king or ruler (or other action) through omens as being "sanctioned by the gods." As for Petrus Romanus, his "inauguration" was sealed by the same omen the ancient augurs used in determining the will of the gods for a king—thunder and lightning as the most important auspice and sign that Jupiter— the father of Apollo—was watching. In either case, credit must be given to Rene Thibaut who accurately predicted this changing of the guard over sixty years prior. Pope Benedict's South American tour was ongoing as the first edition of our book *Petrus Romanus* went to print and it is now evident that he decided to step down simultane-ous with its release exactly when the Belgian Jesuit said he would—decades before. This is also evidenced by the fact that renovations to a property hosting Benedict's retirement home ensued in 2012 as well.[147] Thus, with two living *Pontificus Maximi,* we have entered into *terra incognita* as far as the modern papacy is concerned. This brings us to the new pope.

According to the prophecy of St. Malachy, Peter the Roman has arrived. Pope Francis, formerly known as Jorge Mario Bergoglio the son of Italian immigrants to Argentina, has assumed the 112th posi-tion on Malachy's famous list. While shallow skeptics were quick to point out that "his name is not Peter," their complaint betrays ignorance of the way the Malachy prophecy works. We had stated from the beginning that the title "Peter the Roman" was symbolic. All popes claim apostolic succession from Peter and, for this reason, it is called the *Petrine* office. They claim to sit on the chair of St. Peter and in this way all popes are Peters and are often referred to by knowledgeable Catholic churchmen as "the latest Peter in the line." On this, in an interview with World Net Daily prior to the Pope Francis election, Tom Horn was quoted thus:

> Regardless, Horn said he's always maintained that it doesn't take someone whose Christian name is Peter to fulfill the prophecy. "In fact, if any Italian is elected, that would be a fairly transparent fulfillment," he said. Moreover, he argued, "in a very general sense, every pope could be regarded as 'Peter the Roman,' and in that sense, this could be the last one."[148]

Scholars who have studied the prophecy down through time unanimously come to a similar conclusion—that the title *Petrus Romanus* ("Peter the Roman") was symbolic and not indicative of a birth name any more than *Gloria Olivae* (the 111th line in the prophecy of the popes, the one for Pope Benedict XVI) was Cardinal Ratzinger's given name before he became Pope Benedict XVI, naming himself after the founder of the Benedictine Order, of which the Olivetans are one branch (in order to fulfill his place in the prophecy). Over sixty years ago, Thibaut similarly rejected the possibility of a pope literally named Peter and wrote that the name symbolized the totality of the papacy:

> We therefore reject the Roman appointed Peter as the impossible Peter II. There is only one Peter, the first of the Roman pontiffs, and he saw in his many successors. He still to serve in the final as in the first persecution. We believe Petrus Romanus represents all the Roman Pontiffs from St. Peter to the recipient Gloria Olivae.[149]

In Thibaut's reckoning, the meaning of "Petrus" is that all the ambitions and pretensions of the papal dynasty are now encompassed in one man, Pope Francis. This was our position as well, but we were more than a little astounded recently when the Archpriest of St. Peter's Basilica, Cardinal Angelo Comastri acknowledged how Petrus Romanus is in fact incarnate now in Pope Francis. In discussing details of the new Pope's April 1, 2013 visit to St. Peter's tomb in the necropolis under the basilica, Comastri said:

> We then made a second stop before the funerary stele of a man called Istatilio. He was certainly Christian: on his grave is the monogram [chi-rho] of Christ. On the stele is inscribed: "He was at peace with everyone and never caused strife." The Pope, after reading the phrase, looked at us and

said, "That is a beautiful program of life." Climbing back up the stairs and having reached the Clementine Chapel, Pope Francis became absorbed in prayer and repeated with a loud voice the three professions of Peter: "Lord, You are the Christ, Son of the Living God"; "Lord, to whom do we go? You have the words of eternal life"; "Lord, You know all things! You know that I love you!" *At that moment, we had the distinct impression that the life of Peter rose out of centuries past and became present and living in the current Successor of the Apostle Peter.* (emphasis added)[150]

In addition to this incredible fulfillment of the Malachy prophecy, many scholars of various schools of thought see Bible prophecy in general near its climax. In fact, events in Israel also fell in place just as the first edition of the book Petrus Romanus forecast a year prior. In chapter 16, "The Burdensome Stone," we wrote about an obscure, under-the-table deal concerning the Hall of the Last Supper on Mount Zion, and it seems that deal has been consummated. Reporter Shlomo Cesana broke the story in the Israel Hayom newsletter on January 30, 2013:

A historical agreement has been signed between Israel and the Vatican, ending a 20 year dispute. Israel has granted the pope an official seat in the room where the Last Supper is believed to have taken place, on Mount Zion in Jerusalem.[151]

Even though it is being ignored by the mainstream media, this is momentous because end-time prophecy plays out in Jerusalem and now, for the first time since the reformation of Israel in 1948, *the Roman Pontiff has an official seat on Mount Zion.* Watch for Pope

Francis to visit Israel and pay attention to the details. Accordingly, Hal Lindsey agrees with us that exegesis of Revelation 13:11–18 implies the final pope is likely the false prophet:

> The Apostle John in the Book of the Revelation describes very plainly how the leader of the world religious system (based in Rome) will pave the way for the rise of the man who will be the Antichrist. Unfortunately for that churchman, the Antichrist and the False Prophet will later turn on him and destroy the religious system and the city.[152]

Another interesting and possibly noteworthy aspect of the Final Pope is the timing of his arrival. While we ourselves don't put a lot of stock in numerology, mystics do and the great biblical scholar and Anglican theologian, Ethelbert W. Bullinger, wrote an exhaustive treatise in the nineteenth century which has yielded some interesting connections to the new pontiff and the Masonic beliefs discussed earlier in this chapter. Just like on the Great Seal of the United States, the numbers surrounding Pope Francis' election kept coming up *thirteen*. White smoke at 7:06 p.m.: 7 + 6 = 13; he is 76 years old: 7 + 6 = 13; he was elected on the calendar date 3/13/13, which sports two thirteens of its own; 3/13/2013 also yields 3 + 1 + 3 + 2 + 0 + 1 + 3 = 13; he was announced at precisely 8:13 p.m. Vatican time, or, in military and European time 20:13, making for an astounding 3/13/2013 at 20:13. According to Bullinger:

> As to the significance of *thirteen*, all are aware that it has come down to us as a number of ill-omen. Many superstitions cluster around it, and various explanations are current concerning them.
>
> Unfortunately, those who go backwards to find a reason

seldom go back far enough. The popular explanations do not, so far as we are aware, go further back than the Apostles. But we must go back to *the first occurrence* of the number *thirteen* in order to discover the key to its significance. It occurs first in Genesis 14:4, where we read "*Twelve* years they served Chedorlaomer, and the *thirteenth* year they REBELLED."

Hence every occurrence of the number *thirteen*, and likewise of *every multiple* of it, stamps that with which it stands in connection with *rebellion, apostasy, defection, corruption, disintegration, revolution*, or some kindred idea.[153]

This ill omen suggests the apostasy prophesied by Paul (2 Thessalonians 2:3) and the many Revelation judgments along with the "many tribulations" and destruction of Rome predicted by the Malachy prophecy. Bullinger goes on to cite these remarkably suggestive numerical concurrences:

θηρίον (*theerion*), beast = 247 (x19)
"He had two horns" = 1521 (^{2}x9)
"And he had two horns like a lamb" = 2704 (^{2}x16)
Revelation 13:11, The whole verse = 6318 (x486)[154]

"And I beheld another beast coming up out of the earth; and he had two horns like a lamb, and he spake as a dragon" (Revelation 13:11). Indeed this second beast—the false prophet—is predicted to be viewed "like a lamb" and the accolades afforded the new pontiff on 3/13/2013 at 20:13 support that notion. As Protestants, we feel well within our rights to assert all claimants to Pontifex Maximus Vicar of Christ as false prophets.[155] Please do not be fooled by the media's unwitting accolades concerning Pope Francis' feigned humility, this man believes he is literally Christ on Earth, or he would not accept the title of Vicar of Christ. All the same, if the predictions of St. Malachy are truly at their fruition, then the second beast, the one from the Earth called the "false prophet" (Revelation 16:13; 19:20; 20:10) may well be Pope Francis in the role of *Petrus Romanus* who, unwittingly or not, will lead the world to worship the dragon. Interestingly, his namesake St. Francis of Assisi would agree.

The Argentine Cardinal Jorge Mario Bergoglio has chosen Francis as his papal name, a first in tribute to Francis of Assisi. It is noteworthy that St. Francis of Assisi's long Italian name is Francesco di Bernardone, a title that can accurately be viewed as "Peter the Roman" from the final line in the Prophecy of the Popes. Since the phrase that supplanted the birth name Giovanni is Francesco di, and that by sainthood, it is safe to say that by choosing Francis of Assisi's name, he in effect chose Francesco di Pietro, and he is unlikely to prefer truncation of the Pietro element since Catholicism esteems Peter as the rock of the church and spuriously maintains he was the first pope. Rome was an empire and a city so Bergoglio's Italian ancestry arguably meets the Roman aspect in a similar way. Accordingly, many argue that Bergoglio has fulfilled the Peter the Roman title with his choice of papal name.

As the 2013 conclave concluded, Bergoglio said he chose the original papal name Francis after St. Francis of Assisi when Cardinal Claudio Hummes exhorted him to "remember the poor."[156] The reader might recall that the book you are now holding mentions an apocalyptic prediction by Pope Francis' namesake, which he made soon after St. Malachy's prophecy concerning a Final Pope:

> At the time of this tribulation a man, not canonically elected, will be raised to the Pontificate, who, by his cunning, will

endeavor to draw many into error and death... Some preachers will keep silence about the truth, and others will trample it under foot and deny it...for in those days Jesus Christ will send them not a true Pastor, but a destroyer.[157]

Was there something non-canonic about the election of Pope Francis? Well for starters, Pope Benedict XVI's retirement makes for an unprecedented situation. When a pope is elected, the Church expects that he will remain in office until his death. Before now, only five popes unambiguously resigned with historical certainty, all between the tenth and fifteenth centuries. Arguably, that makes Bergoglio's election suspect but, apparently, not a violation of canon law. In 1294, Celestine V issued a decree declaring it permissible for a pope to resign, and then resigned himself after only five months as pope. He lived a few more years as a hermit and then as a prisoner of his tyrannical successor, Boniface VIII. Because his decree was never repealed, canon law experts allow that a pope can resign, albeit it is discouraged. Others have objected that the fifteen-day rule between the vacancy of the office and the start of the conclave was circumvented in order to speed up the process. This was done by Pope Benedict's final decree but the urgency to seat his successor seems suspicious. While Pope Francis represents many firsts, overall, the most interesting aspect is his status as the first ever *Jesuit pope*.

The sitting pontiff's background has great prophetic significance as the Jesuit order was formed to specifically combat the Protestant reformation and assert papal supremacy over the entire world. According to a historian, "The Jesuits were the soldiers of the pope: they knew no law but the will of their general, no mode of worship but the pope's dictate no church but themselves."[158] Because of this, the Jesuit order was suppressed and disbanded for its pernicious skullduggery by Pope Clement XIV in 1773, and by the mid-eighteenth century, the Jesuits had earned a bad reputation in Europe for political maneuvering and economic exploitation bar-none. The order was reinstated in the early nineteenth century with the mission to conquer by scholarship and infiltration of the education system. Interestingly, Pope Benedict XVI addressed the Jesuit order in 2008, encouraging them to reinvigorate the *fourth vow*. He said, "For this very reason I have invited you and also invite you today to reflect in order to rediscover the fullest meaning of your characteristic 'fourth vow' of obedience to the Successor of Peter."[159]

Church historians record that the fourth vow of obedience is one of "absolute subservience to the pope; to do whatever he enjoined, and go on any service he wished, and into any quarter of the globe."[160] A few ex-Jesuit whistle-blowers have called this a blood oath involving pagan rites which were laid bare in the suppressed document, "Jesuit Extreme Oath of Induction," which was once recorded in records of the US Congress, but was suspiciously expunged. According to this document, they are indoctrinated into the principle of *Iustum, Necar, Reges, Impious*, meaning, "It is just to exterminate or annihilate impious or heretical Kings, Governments, or Rulers."[161] The Jesuit modernists of today prefer more subtle methods like infiltrating the education system and promoting biblical higher criticism that undermines biblical authority.

Protestants and Catholics have written about a clandestine war that has been playing out for some time behind the scenes between the papacy and the Jesuit order. For example, the Reverend Ian Paisley has observed, "Since their restitution in 1814, the Jesuits have sought to control the papacy."[162] Yet, it is the insider, Malachi Martin, former Jesuit and advisor to three popes, who wrote a bestselling exposé, *The Jesuits: The Society of Jesus and the Betrayal of the Roman*

Catholic Church, accusing the order of systematically undermining Church teachings and replacing them with *new world order* doctrines. The first lines of the book state:

> A state of war exists between the papacy and the Religious Order of the Jesuits—the Society of Jesus, to give the Order its official name. That war signals the most lethal change to take place within the ranks of the professional Roman clergy over the last thousand years. And, as with all important events in the Roman Catholic Church, it involves the interests, the lives, and the destinies of ordinary men and women in their millions.[163]

It seems rather obvious that the first Jesuit pope (Pope Francis) indicates the Jesuits won that war and to the victors go the spoils. What might this mean? Most probably a new level of ecumenism that will culminate in the one-world religion, after all, the word "Catholic" means "universal." This has far-reaching implications, further than one might think—as in *astronomical.* We address the Jesuits who make up the Vatican Observatory Research Group in some detail in our new book, *Exo-Vaticana: Petrus Romanus, Project L.U.C.I.F.E.R., and the Vatican's Astonishing Plan for the Arrival of an Alien Savior,* and offer some surprising revelations as to what might entice the entire world to unite under the new pontiff. This new investigative work documents the Vatican Observatory Research Group's (VORG) endorsement of the astrobiological project and theological revisionsim in expectation of extraterrestrial contact. In light of *Exo-Vaticana's* extraordinary exposé of the Vatican's plans for the arrival of an alien savior, the unexpected election of Pope Francis comes into a brilliant new focus. The sequel was already written and sent to the printer when Francis ascended the papacy, but now, astonishing facts connect these three books. Pope Francis is uniquely positioned as an insider to be the extraterrestrial disclosure pontiff.

As a young adult, Bergoglio earned a master's degree in chemistry from the University of Buenos Aires and had scientific ambitions prior to entering the Jesuit order.[164] When the current leader of the VORG, José Gabriel Funes, S. J. (also from Argentina), entered the Jesuit order, one of the three examiners was Bergoglio. As it turns out, fantastically, even the papal name of Francis connects to Funes and the ET issue! Funes, who astounded the world with his essay, *The Extraterrestrial Is My Brother*, is infamous for invoking the new pope's namesake St. Francis of Assisi as an apologetic for accepting ET: "To say it with St. Francis, if we can consider some earthly creatures as 'brothers' or 'sisters', why could we not speak of a 'brother alien'? He would also belong to the creation."[165] In other words, Funes and the VORG are leading the charge to accept extraterrestrials at face value even arguing they could be morally superior to humans. Funes believes the first Jesuit pope will soon turn his attention to issues like astrobiology once his papacy is established:

> One Jesuit who shares the pope's Argentine roots and has known him since his own days as a novice, said the election of the man he first knew as Father Bergoglio is "a joy for the country."
>
> Father Jose Funes, head of the Vatican Observatory, told *Catholic News Service* that the election of an Argentine Jesuit with a background in science (he studied chemistry at a trade school before entering the Jesuits) can only be good for all those interests. However, he said, "I think the pope will be focused on other priorities first."[166]

Pope Francis' intimate and personal association with the VORG leader implies a surprising new relevance to his election in the role of Petrus Romanus. The Pontifical Academy of Science's 2009 Astrobiology Conference key note speaker, Dr. Chris Impey, predicted a forthcoming extraterrestrial disclosure, saying, "The first discovery is only a few years away."[167] Impey's few years are now upon us and recent exoplanet discoveries seem to offer promise. Thus, it appears that Pope Francis will indeed be the sitting pontiff when that disclosure event occurs. In *Exo-Vaticana*, we offer evidence and arguments that this entails the strong delusion that leads the world to believe the lie that the Apostle Paul warned us to expect (2 Thessalonians 2: 11) and which appears to be playing out on a grandiose scale.

Chapter 7

THE COMING GODS OF THE NEW WORLD ORDER

In the E at Delphoi, although the sun represents God.... Plutarch here associates this supreme god with the Apollon of religion, while in the essay on Isis religion, he is associated with Osiris. Both Apollo(n) and Osiris are sun gods [who]...turns out to be (not to our surprise) the Delphic Apollo (A-pollon). —Frederick E. Brank, *Relighting the Souls: Studies in Plutarch, in Greek Literature, Religion, and Philosophy, and in the New Testament Background*

The Solar Eye [on the Great Seal of the United States] was called the eye of...Apollo...the sacred and mysterious Eye of the Most High of the gods.... Thus it is held in the highest estimation by all Royal Arch Masons. —Charles A. L. Totten, *Our Inheritance in the Great Seal of Manasseh, the United States of America*

This is he...who shall again set up the Golden Age amid the fields where Saturn once reigned. —Virgil, *Aeneid* 6.790

I n the study of the Divine Council—the pantheon of divine beings or angels who currently administer the affairs of heaven and earth—experts typically agree that, beginning at the Tower of Babel, the world and its inhabitants were disinherited by the sovereign God of Israel and placed under the authority of lesser divine beings that became corrupt and disloyal to God in their administration of those nations (Psalm 82). According to the theory, these beings quickly became worshipped on earth as gods following Babel, and because these angels, unlike their human admirers, would continue on earth until the end of time, each "spirit" behind the pagan attributions was known at miscellaneous times in history and to various cultures by different names. This certainly agrees with the biblical definition of idolatry as the worship of fallen angels, and means the characterization of such spirits as Jupiter, Justice, Osiris, and Isis can be correctly understood to be titles ascribed to distinct and individual supernaturalism. The spirit behind Apollo was thus a real personality; Osiris actually lived, and still does. Yet Osiris could have been the same entity known elsewhere as Apollo or Dionysus. Numerous Greek historians, including Plutarch, Herodotus, and Diodorus Siculus, observed Osiris of the Egyptians and Dionysus of the Greeks as the same god, while others found Apollo and Dionysus to be one and the same. Since the designers of the Great Seal of the United States incorporated the appropriate Egyptian symbols and Roman-Greek mottoes into the seal's scheme to cipher a prophecy about the return of this god—Apollo-Osiris (a.k.a. Nimrod)—it seems reasonable that the occultists also perceived the two gods as representing a singular unseen agency. As a result, readers will benefit from understanding the mythos behind these deities. In the mythological records, trace-nuances, which communicate specific traits having to do with the nature of the entity, can be found. This is helpful in understanding the nature of the "god" that is prophesied to return.

The Beginning of Organized Mythology Dawns in Sumeria

It was the year 3500 BC, and the alluvial desert of the Middle East was alive with spiritual and physical activity. In a valley forged between the twin rivers of the Tigris and the Euphrates, magnificent walled cities awoke to the chatter of busy streets and marketplaces. In what the Greeks would later call "Mesopotamia" ("between the rivers"), the world's first great trade center and civilization had developed. The opulent Sumerian cities of Ur—the home of Abram, Uruk and Lagash—formed the economic machines of the ancient Middle East, while industries from as far away as Jericho near the Mediterranean Sea and Catal Huyuk in Asia Minor competed for the trade opportunities they provided. Laborers from the biblical city of Jericho exported salt into Sumer, and miners from Catal Huyuk prepared obsidian, used in making mirrors, for shipment into the ancient metropolis. But while the prehistoric people of the East looked to the Sumerians for their supply of daily bread, the Sumerians themselves gazed heavenward to the early rising of Utu (Shamash), the all-providing sun god, as he prepared once again to ride across the sky in his chariot. In 3500 BC, Utu was not alone among the gods. By now, the Sumerian pantheon provided the earliest-known description of organized mythology consisting of a complex system of more than three thousand deities covering nearly every detail of nature and human enterprise. There were gods of sunshine and of rain. There were vegetation gods, fertility gods, river gods, animal gods, and gods of the afterlife. There were great gods—Enlil (prince of the air), Anu (ruler of the heavens), Enki, (the god of water), and so on. Under these existed a second level of deities, including Nannar, the moon god; Utu, the sun god; and Inanna, the "Queen of Heaven."

A significant question that has puzzled scholars and historians for more than a millennium is where the Sumerian deities come from. Since the religion of Sumeria was the first-known organized mythology, and would greatly influence the foundational beliefs of Assyria, Egypt, Greece, Rome, and others, where does one find the beginning of its many gods? Were the Sumerian deities the product of human imagination, or the distortion of some earlier prehistoric revelation? Were they the "mythologizing" of certain ancient heroes, or, as some New Age followers suggest, the result of an extraterrestrial "alien" visitation whose appearance gave birth to the legends and mythological gods? More importantly, did the gods of Sumeria reflect the emergence of an unknown *power* operating through pagan dynamics, or were the gods purely the creation of primitive imaginations?

These questions are both fascinating and difficult since the gods and goddesses of ancient Sumeria/Mesopotamia continue to be shrouded in a history of unknown origins. It was as though from out of nowhere the Sumerians sprang onto the scene thousands of years ago, bringing with them the first written language and a corpus of progressive knowledge—from complicated religious concepts to an advanced understanding of astrology, chemistry, and mathematics. The questionable origin of the Sumerian culture has caused more than a few orthodox theorists to conclude that these gods, and the subsequent mythologies that grew out of them (Assyrian, Egyptian, etc.), were the diabolical scheme of a regressive and evil supernatural presence. If this is true, does the ancient power continue to work within our world? Do primordial and living entities, once worshipped as "gods," coexist with modern man?

The biblical view of the origin of the pagan gods begins with what in my second book I coined "the original revelation." This means there was a perfect revelation from God to man at the time of creation. The first man, Adam, was at one with God, and perceived divine knowledge from the mind of God. The human was "in tune" with the mental processes of God, and understood, therefore, what God knew about science, astronomy, cosmogony, geology, eschatology, and so on. After the fall of man, Adam was "detached" from the mind of God, but retained an imperfect memory of the divine revelation, including knowledge of God's plan of redemption from the time of the Fall through the end of time and everything in between, including Noah's Flood, the coming of Messiah, and the final world empire. Two things began to occur in the decades after the Fall: 1) Information from the original revelation became distant and distorted as it was dispersed among the nations and passed from generation to generation; and 2) The realm of Satan seized upon this opportunity to receive worship, and to turn people away from Yahweh, by distorting and counterfeiting the original revelation with pagan ideas and "gods." This point of view seems reasonable when one considers that the earliest historical and archeological records from civilizations around the world consistently point back to and repeat portions of the original story.

In their startling book, *The Discovery of Genesis*, Rev. C. H. Kang and Dr. Ethel R. Nelson confirm that prehistoric Chinese ideographic pictures (used in very ancient Chinese writing) report the story of Genesis, including the creation of the man and woman, the Garden, the temptation and fall, Noah's Flood, and the Tower of Babel. In his book, *The Real Meaning of the Zodiac*, the late Dr. James Kennedy claimed that the ancient signs of the zodiac also indicate a singular and original revelation—a kind of gospel in the stars—and that the message of the stars, though demonized and converted into astrology after the fall of man, originally recorded the gospel of God. He wrote:

> There exists in the writings of virtually all civilized nations a description of the major stars in the heavens—something which might be called their "Constellations of the Zodiac" or the "Signs of the Zodiac," of which there are twelve. If you go back in time to Rome, or beyond that to Greece, or before that to Egypt, Persia, Assyria, or Babylonia—regardless of how far back you go, there is a remarkable phenomenon: Nearly all nations had the same twelve signs, representing the same twelve things, placed in the same order.… The book of Job, which is thought by many to be the oldest book of the Bible, goes back to approximately 2150 B.C., which is 650 years before Moses came upon the scene to write the Pentateuch; over1,100 years before Homer wrote the *Odyssey* and the *Illiad*; and 1,500 years before Thales, the first of the philosophers, was born. In chapter 38, God finally breaks in and speaks to Job and to his false comforters. As He is questioning Job, showing him and his companions their ignorance, God says to them: "Canst thou bind the sweet influences of Pleiades, or loose the bands of Orion? Canst thou bring forth Mazzaroth in his season? Or canst thou guide Arcturus with his sons?" (Job 38:31, 32). We see here reference to the constellations of Orion and Pleiades, and the star Arcturus. Also in the book of Job there is reference to *Cetus,* the *Sea Monster,* and to *Draco, the Great Dragon.* I would call your attention to Job 38:32a: "Canst thou bring forth Mazzaroth in his season?" *Mazzaroth* is a Hebrew word which means "The Constellations of the Zodiac." In what may be the oldest book in all of human

history, we find that the constellations of the zodiac were already clearly known and understood.... Having made it clear that the Bible expressly, explicitly, and repeatedly condemns what is now known as astrology, the fact remains that there was a God-given Gospel in the stars which lays beyond and behind that which has now been corrupted.[168]

In his book, Kennedy condemned the practice of astrology, while asserting his view that the constellations of the zodiac were likely given by God to the first man as "record-keepers" of the original revelation of God.

If the primary assumption of this view is correct—that an original revelation was corrupted after the Fall of man and subsequently degenerated into mythologies of the pagan gods—one should be able to find numerous examples of such corruption from as far back as the beginning of history and within various civilizations around the world. Since the myths behind the gods would thus be "borrowed" ideas, the corrupted texts would be similar to the original truth, and, in that sense, evidence *of* a singular and original revelation. If the distortions of the original revelation were in fact energized by evil supernaturalism, the goal of the alterations would be to draw people away from the worship of Yahweh. In certain ancient legends—such as the *Enuma Elish*, the *Adapa Epic*, and the *Epic of Gilgamesh*—we discover early traces of the kaleidoscope of the original revelation plagiarized for the purpose of constructing the mythologies of the pagan gods.

Early Traces of Corruption

Evidence suggests that the earliest legends of mythology were preceded by a belief in "the God" (*Yahweh* or YHWH to the Hebrews) as the Creator of all things and the "ruler of heaven." Later, Satan was described as "the god of this world" (2 Corinthians 4:4), and the prince of the "air" (Ephesians 2:2). A fascinating struggle between the "ruler of the heavens" versus the "power of the air" occurred in early Sumerian mythology after Enki, the god of wisdom and water, created the human race out of clay. It appears that Anu, who was at first the most powerful of the Sumerian gods and the "ruler of the heavens," was superseded in power and popularity by Enlil, the "god of the air." To the Christian mind, this is perceived as nothing less than Satan, the god of the air, continuing his pretense to the throne of God, and his usurpation of Yahweh—"the Lord of the heavens." It also indicates a corruption of the original revelation and perhaps an effort on the part of Satan to trick the Sumerians into perceiving him as the "supreme" god (above the God of heaven) and therefore worthy of adoration. Correspondingly, in the *Enuma Elish* (a Babylonian epic), Marduk, the great god of the city of Babylon, was exalted above the benevolent gods and extolled as the creator of the world. Marduk was symbolized as a dragon (as is Satan in Revelation 12:9) called the *Muscrussu*, and his legend appears to contain several distortions of the important elements of the biblical account of creation. The *Adapa Epic* tells of another Babylonian legend also roughly equivalent to the Genesis account of creation. In it, Adapa, like Adam, underwent a test on food consumption, failed the test, and forfeited his opportunity for immortality. As a result of the failure, suffering and death were passed along to humanity. Finally, the *Epic of Gilgamesh* is a Sumerian poem, which, like the *Adapa Epic*, is deeply rooted in ancient Assyrian and Babylonian mythology. In 1872, George Smith discovered the Gilgamesh tablets while doing research on the Assyrian library of Ashurbanipal at the British Museum. Because of the strong similarity to the biblical account of Noah and the Great Flood, Bible scholars have viewed the Gilgamesh epic with interest since its discovery. As the legend goes,

Gilgamesh, the king of the city of Uruk, was told about the flood from his immortal friend, Utnapishtim (the Sumerian equivalent of Noah). Utnapishtim described for Gilgamesh how the great god Enlil decided to destroy all of mankind because of its "noisy" sins. A plague was sent, but failed to persuade mankind of better behavior, and, consequently, the gods determined a complete extermination of the human race. Enki, the lord of the waters, was not happy with the other gods for this decision and warned Utnapishtim of the coming deluge, instructing him to tear down his house and build a great boat. Utnapishtim obeyed Enki, built a great vessel, and sealed it with pitch and bitumen. The family of Utnapishtim loaded onto the boat together with various beasts and fowl. When the rains came, the doors were closed and the vessel rose up above the waters. Like Noah, Utnapishtim sent out a dove, and later a swallow, to search for dry land. They both returned. Later, a raven was released and it never came back. After several more days, the boat came to rest on the top of a mountain where Utnapishtim built an altar and offered a sacrifice of thanksgiving to the gods. As the gods smelled the sweet offering, all but Enlil repented for sending the flood.

In my first book, *Spiritual Warfare—The Invisible Invasion*, I described another interesting example of the original revelation of God as distorted or plagiarized by Satan in order to draw men away from the worship of Yahweh. Concerning Asclepius, the Greek god of healing, I wrote:

> At the base of Pergamum's hill stood the shrine of Asclepius, equipped with its own library, theater, sleeping chambers used in healing rituals, and long underground tunnels joining various other shrines to which pagans journeyed to receive the healing powers of Apollo's favorite son. The Christian Church considered these mystical powers as demonic,

for the worship of Asclepius focused on the image of a serpent, sometimes called Glycon, an enormous serpent-figure some historians see as the origin for the modern symbol of healing—a serpent winding about a pole. Asclepius carried the lofty title, the hero god of healing.

In Numbers 21, Moses designed the brazen serpent on a pole that was used of God as an oracle of healing. Seven hundred forty-three years later, in 2 Kings 18:4, we find that Israel had begun to worship the brazen serpent with offerings and incense. From here the image was adopted into Greek mythology where it became the symbol of Asclepius, the Greek god of healing.

Asclepius was reported to have cured untold numbers from every conceivable disease—even raising a man from the dead. This caused Apollo through his Oracle at Delphi to declare, "Oh Asclepius! thou who art born a great joy to all mortals, whom lovely Coronis bare to me, the child of love, at rocky Epidaurus." Such a healer was he reported to be, that Pluto, god of Hades, complained to Zeus that hardly anyone was dying anymore, and so Zeus destroyed Asclepius with a thunderbolt. Afterward, Apollo pleaded with Zeus to restore his son and this intercession so moved Zeus that he not only brought Asclepius back to life, but immortalized him as the god of medicine. First at Thessaly, and finally throughout the Greek and Roman world, Asclepius was worshiped as the saviour god of healing.[169]

Besides the entwined serpent symbolism, plagiarism of the *Original Revelation* is found in Greek mythology where Asclepius has the power to heal the sick and to bring the dead back to life by drawing blood out from the side of the goddess of justice, the same deity who "returns" old Satan's reign during the *novus ordo seclorum*. Asclepius was symbolized by a serpent winding about a pole, and was called the great "Physician." The obvious intention of the serpent on a pole in Numbers 21 was to focus mankind on the coming Messiah, the true Great Physician, Jesus Christ, who would hang upon a pole to deliver His followers from sickness and from death by the blood that ran out from His side.

The Rise of Osiris

As the centuries passed by, the god and goddess-worshipping cities of the Sumerians faded away. The flourishing fields of agriculture that once provided the underpinnings of the great Sumerian economy were depleted of fertility through over-irrigation, and residues of salt buildup appeared to chaff the surface of the land. The city-states of Sumeria—Kish, Ur, Lagash, and Umma—damaged by a millennium of ruthless infighting among the Sumerians, finally succumbed to militant external forces. The barbarian armies of the Elamites (Persians) invaded and destroyed the city of Ur, and Amorites from the West overran the northern province of Sumer and subsequently established the hitherto little-known town of Babylon as their capital. By 1840 BC, Hammurabi, the sixth king of Babylon, conquered the remaining cities of Sumeria and forged northern Mesopotamia and Sumeria into a single nation. Yet the ultimate demise of the Sumerian people did not vanquish their ideas. Sumerian art, language, literature, and especially religion, had been forever absorbed into the cultures and social academics of the nations surrounding Mesopotamia, including the Hittite nation, the Babylonians, and the ancient Assyrians. Ultimately a principal benefactor of Sumeria's ideas, and a people who would make their own contributions to the ancient mythologies, was an old and flourishing population of agrarians known as the Egyptians.

By the year 1350 BC, Egyptian dominance had spread from Syria and Palestine into the farthest corners of the Fertile Crescent. From northern Mesopotamia to the Baltic Sea, the pharaohs of Egypt had established themselves as the social and economic leaders of the civilized world, ruling an area more than two thousand miles in length. The military superiority of the Egyptian army demonstrated the ability to subdue the threat of resistance, maintaining a hegemony that extended from the Nubians to the Hyksos. Even so, in the final analysis, it was the influence of the gods of Egypt—with their magic, myths, and rituals—that provided the Egyptians a lasting place in history and led succeeding generations into an immense, enlightening description of the ancient mythologies, including a wealth of information regarding the dynamics and supernatural possibilities of paganism. Prehistoric Egyptians believed in the same fundamental idea that most evolutionists subscribe to today—the premise that the oceans both preceded and in some way contributed to the creation of the living cosmos. From the Fifth Dynasty *Pyramid Texts*, the Heliopolitan theory of creation stated that Atum (the sun god Ra) independently created himself from a singular expression of self will—an act visualized by the Egyptians as a divine egg that appeared upon the primordial waters of the all-filling ocean called Nun, out of which Atum (meaning "he who created himself") emerged. According to myth, a second act of creation developed around a divine masturbation when Atum, the great "He-She," orally copulated himself and afterward regurgitated his children—Shu and Tefnut— who assumed the positions of god and goddess of air and moisture. Later, when Shu and Tefnut became lost in the universal ocean of

Nun, Atum exhibited his paternal care by sending out his eye, which had the curious habit of detaching itself from Atum and of thinking independent thoughts, to look for them. The eye of Atum succeeded in finding the child gods and eventually returned to discover that Atum had grown impatient during the wait and had created a second eye. In order to placate the hostility that soon developed between the two divine eyes, Atum affixed the first eye upon his forehead, where it was to oversee and rule the forthcoming world of creation. Thus the eye of Atum became the jealous, destructive aspect of the sun god Ra.

To avoid getting lost again in the all-filling waters of Nun, Shu, and Tefnut procreated Geb (the earth), and Nut (the sky), and thus provided the more stable elements of earth, nature, and the seasons. Later, Geb was conceptualized as cohabiting with Nut and producing four children of his own: Seth, Osiris, Isis, and Nephthys. Of these, Osiris and Isis grew into such powerful cult deities that Osiris, with the help of his sister-wife Isis, nearly overthrew Ra as the most powerful of the gods—an action that so enraged his brother Seth that the hateful and jealous sibling killed him. Seth's murderous act was followed by the jackal-headed god, Anubis, assisting Isis with the embalming of her slain husband-brother Osiris, an act through which Anubis secured his position as "the god of embalming." Then, while still in mourning, Isis summoned the wisdom of Thoth, which she combined with her own proficient magical skills, and produced a resurrected Osiris, who, in turn, impregnated her with Horus, the god of daylight. Horus promptly avenged his father's death by killing the evil brother Seth.

Another version of the myth claims that Horus was born to Isis only after she impregnated herself with semen that she had taken from the corpse of Osiris (activity that sounds suspiciously like advanced science, artificial insemination, or cloning). The god Seth was angry and sought to destroy Horus, and Ufologists may note with interest how Isis seeks help from Thoth, who comes in a flying craft—the Boat of the Celestial Disc—as recorded in the *Metternich Stela*:

> Then Isis sent forth a cry to heaven and addressed her appeal to the Boat of Millions of Years. And the Celestial Disc stood still, and moved not from the place where it was. And Thoth came down, and he was provided with magical powers, and possessed the great power.... And he said: "O Isis, thou goddess, thou glorious one.... I have come this day in the Boat of the Celestial Disc from the place where it was yesterday.... I have come from the skies to save the child for his mother."

Yet another story claims that Seth persuaded his brother Osiris to climb into a box, which he quickly shut and threw into the Nile. Osiris drowned, and his body floated down the Nile River, where it snagged on the limbs of a tamarisk tree. In Byblos, Isis recovered the body from the river bank and took it into her care. In her absence, Seth stole the body again and chopped it into fourteen pieces, which he threw into the Nile. Isis searched the river bank until she recovered every piece, except for the genitals, which had been swallowed by a fish (Plutarch says a crocodile). Isis simply replaced the missing organ with a facsimile and was somehow able to reconstruct Osiris and impregnate herself with the ithyphallic corpse.

From this time forward, Osiris was considered the chief god of the deceased and the judge of the *netherworld*—the dark and dreary underworld region of the dead. In human form, Osiris was perceived as a mummy and, paradoxically, while he was loved as the guarantor of life after death, he was feared as the demonic presence that decayed the bodies of the dead. Such necromantic worship of Osiris grew to become an important part of several Mediterranean religions, with his most famous cult center being at Abydos in Upper Egypt, where an annual festival reenacted his death and resurrection. In Abydos, Osiris was called the god of the setting sun—the mysterious "force" that ruled the region of the dead just beneath the western horizon. He was venerated in this way primarily because death, and specifically the fear of one's estate after death, grew to constitute so much of Egyptian concern.

In the funerary texts known as the *Book of the Dead*, the most elaborate magical steps were developed around the Osiris myth to assist the Egyptians with their journey into the afterlife. It was believed that every person had a *ka*—a spiritual and invisible duplicate—and that the ka accompanied them throughout eternity. Since the ka provided each person with a resurrected body in the kingdom of the dead, yet could not exist without the maintenance of the earthly body, every effort was made to preserve the human corpse. The body was therefore mummified according to the elaborate magic rituals passed down from Isis, who, according to legend, singularly perfected the rituals of mummification through her work on Osiris. Wooden replicas of the body were also placed in the tomb as a kind of substitute in case the mummy was accidently destroyed, and additional protection for the corpse was provided through the construction of ingenious burial tombs specifically designed to hide and preserve the human body for all of eternity. Finally, curses were placed throughout the tomb as a warning to intruders.

At death, the Egyptian ka departed the human body and, accompanied by the hymns and prayers of the living, used the formulas memorized from the funerary texts to outsmart the horrible demons seeking to impede the ka's progress into the kingdom (or hall) of Osiris. Arriving at the judgment hall, the heart of the ka was "weighed in the balance" by Osiris and his forty-two demons. If they found the deceased lacking in virtue, he was condemned to an eternity of hunger and thirst. If the ka was determined to have belonged to an outright "sinner," it was cut to pieces and fed to Ammit—the miserable little goddess and "eater of souls." But if the deceased was judged to have lived a virtuous life, the ka was granted admittance to the heavenly fields of Yaru, where foods were abundant and pleasures unending. The only toil in this heaven was to serve in the grain fields of Osiris, and even this could be obviated by placing substitutionary statues, called shawabty, into the tomb.

There is some evidence that the forty-two demons or "judges" of Osiris were in some way related to the prehistoric *Watchers*—the mysterious angelic beings who first appeared in the early cultures of the Middle East (discussed in the next chapter). The early Egyptian scribes viewed the leaders from among these fallen Watchers as the underworld demons of Osiris whose "terrible knives" exacted judgment upon the ka of the wicked. The Egyptians were desperately afraid of the netherworld Watchers, and a significant amount of time was spent determining how to placate the judgment of Osiris and his forty-two demons. The worship of Isis—the sister-wife of Osiris—thus became integral. As pointed out earlier, Isis was one of the most important goddesses of ancient mythology and was venerated by the Egyptians, Greeks, and Romans as the "goddess of a thousand names" and the undisputed queen of magical skills. An example of her form of magic is found in the *Theban Recension* of the *Book of the Dead* and depicts Isis providing a spell for controlling the forty-two demons of Osiris. The formula consisted of an amulet made of carnelian that had been soaked in the water of ankhami flowers. It was supposed to be placed around the neck of the dead person in combination with the spoken words of magic. If performed properly, it would empower the ka of the individual to enter into the region of the dead under the protection of Isis, where the ka would thereafter move about wherever it wanted without fear of the forty-two demons of Osiris. The only Egyptian who did not benefit from this particular spell was the Pharaoh, and for a very good reason. Although Pharaoh was considered to be the "son of the sun god" (Ra) and the incarnation of the falcon god Horus during his lifetime, at death he became the Osiris—the divine judge of the netherworld. On earth, Pharaoh's son and predecessor would take his place as the newly anointed manifestation of Horus, and thus each new generation of the pharaohs provided the gods with a divine spokesman for the present world and for the afterlife.

The observant reader may wonder, "Was there something more to the Pharaoh's deification than meets the eye?" The cult center of Amun-Ra at Thebes may hold the answer, as it was the site of the largest religious structure ever built—the temple of Amun-Ra at Karnak—and the location of many extraordinary magical rituals. The great temple with its one hundred miles of walls and gardens (the primary object of fascination and worship by the nemesis of Moses—the Pharaoh of the Exodus, Ramses II) was the place where each pharaoh reconciled his divinity in the company of Amun-Ra during the festival of Opet. The festival was held at the temple of Luxor and included a procession of gods carried on barges up the Nile River from Karnak to the temple. The royal family accompanied the gods on boats while the Egyptian laity walked along the shore, calling aloud and making requests of the gods. Once at Luxor, the Pharaoh and his entourage entered the holy of holies, where the king joined his ka (the mysterious science or ritual is unknown) and transmogrified into a living deity, the son of Amun-Ra. Outside, large groups of dancers and musicians waited anxiously. When the king emerged "transformed," the crowd erupted in gaiety. From that day forward, the Pharaoh was considered to be—just as the god ciphered in the Great Seal of the United States will be—the son and spiritual incarnation of the Supreme Deity. The all-seeing eye of Horus/Apollo/Osiris above the unfinished pyramid on the Great Seal represents this spirit.

From Ancient Egypt to Greece:
'Tis Thine Own Apollo Reigns

According to the Greeks, the greatest outcome of the love affair between Zeus and Leto was the birth of the most beloved of the oracle gods—Apollo. More than any other god in ancient history, Apollo represented the passion for prophetic inquiry among the nations. Though mostly associated with classical Greece, scholars agree that Apollo existed before the Olympian pantheon and some even claim that he was at first the god of the Hyperboreans—an ancient and legendary people to the north. Herodotus came to this conclusion and recorded how the Hyperboreans continued in worship of Apollo even after his induction into the Greek pantheon, making an annual pilgrimage to the land of Delos, where they participated in the famous Greek festivals of Apollo. Lycia—a small country in southwest Turkey—also had an early connection with Apollo, where he was known as *Lykeios*, which some have joined to the Greek *Lykos* or "wolf," thus making one of his ancient titles, "the wolf slayer."

Apollo, with his twin sister Artemis, was said by the Greeks to have been born in the land of Delos—the children of Zeus (Jupiter) and of the Titaness Leto. While an important oracle existed there and played a role in the festivals of the god, it was the famous oracle at Delphi that became the celebrated mouthpiece of the Olympian. Located on the mainland of Greece, the *omphalos* of Delphi (the stone the Greeks believed marked the center of the earth) can still be found among the ruins of Apollo's Delphic temple. So important was Apollo's oracle at Delphi that wherever Hellenism existed, its citizens and kings, including some from as far away as Spain, ordered their lives, colonies, and wars by its sacred communications. It was here that the Olympian gods spoke to mortal men through the use of a priesthood, which interpreted the trance-induced utterances of the Pythoness or Pythia. She was a middle-aged woman who sat on a copper-and-gold tripod, or, much earlier, on the "rock of the sibyl" (medium), and crouched over a fire while inhaling the smoke of burning laurel leaves, barley, marijuana, and oil, until a sufficient intoxication for her prophecies had been produced. While the use of the laurel leaves may have referred to the nymph Daphne (Greek for "laurel"), who escaped from Apollo's sexual intentions by transforming herself into a laurel tree, the leaves also served the practical purpose of supplying the necessary amounts of hydrocyanic acid and complex alkaloids which, when combined with hemp, created powerful hallucinogenic visions. An alternative version of the oracle myth claims that the Pythia sat over a fissure breathing in magic vapors that rose up from a deep crevice within the earth. The vapors "became magic" as they were mingled with the "smells" of the rotting carcass of the dragon Python, which had been slain and thrown down into the crevice by Apollo as a youth. In either case, it was under the influence of such "forces" that the Pythia prophesied in an unfamiliar voice thought to be that of Apollo himself. During the Pythian trance, the medium's personality often changed, becoming melancholic, defiant, or even animal-like, exhibiting a psychosis that may have been the source of the werewolf myth, or *lycanthropy*, as the Pythia reacted to an encounter with Apollo/Lykeios—the wolf god. Delphic "women of python" prophesied in this way for nearly a thousand years and were considered to be a vital part of the pagan order and local economy of every Hellenistic community. This adds to the mystery of adoption of the Pythians and Sibyls by certain quarters of Christianity as "vessels of truth." These women, whose lives were dedicated to channeling from frenzied lips the messages of gods and goddesses, turn up especially in Catholic art, from altars to illustrated books and even upon the ceiling of the Sistine Chapel, where five Sibyls join the Old Testament prophets in places of sacred honor. The Cumaean Sibyl (also known as Amalthaea), whose prophecy about the return of the god Apollo is encoded in the Great Seal of the United States, was the oldest of the Sibyls and the seer of the underworld who in the *Aeneid* gave Aeneas a tour of the infernal region.

Whether by trickery or occult power, the prophecies of the Sibyls were sometimes amazingly accurate. The Greek historian Herodotus (considered the father of history) recorded an interesting example of this. Croesus, the king of Lydia, had expressed doubt regarding the accuracy of Apollo's oracle at Delphi. To test the oracle, Croesus sent messengers to inquire of the Pythian prophetess as to what he, the king, was doing on a certain day. The priestess surprised the king's messengers by visualizing the question and by formulating the answer before they arrived. A portion of the historian's account says:

> The moment that the Lydians (the messengers of Croesus) entered the sanctuary, and before they put their questions, the Pythoness thus answered them in hexameter verse: "...Lo! on my sense there striketh the smell of a shell-covered tortoise, Boiling now on a fire, with the flesh of a lamb, in a cauldron. Brass is the vessel below, and brass the cover above it." These

words the Lydians wrote down at the mouth of the Pythoness as she prophesied, and then set off on their return to Sar-
dis.... [When] Croesus undid the rolls...[he] instantly made
an act of adoration...declaring that the Delphic was the only
really oracular shrine.... For on the departure of his messengers he had set himself to think what was most impossible
for any one to conceive of his doing, and then, waiting till
the day agreed on came, he acted as he had determined. He
took a tortoise and a lamb, and cutting them in pieces with
his own hands, boiled them together in a brazen cauldron,
covered over with a lid which was also of brass. (Herodotus,
Book 1: 47)

Another interesting example of spiritual insight by an Apollonian Sibyl is found in the New Testament book of Acts. Here the
demonic resource that energized the Sibyls is revealed.

And it came to pass, as we went to prayer, a certain damsel
possessed with a spirit of divination [*of python*, a seeress of
Delphi] met us, which brought her masters much gain by
soothsaying: The same followed Paul and us, and cried, saying, These men are the servants of the most high God, which
shew unto us the way of salvation. And this did she many
days. But Paul, being grieved, turned and said to the spirit,
I command thee in the name of Jesus Christ to come out of
her. And he came out the same hour. And when her masters saw that the hope of their gains was gone, they caught
Paul and Silas.... And brought them to the magistrates, saying, These men, being Jews, do exceedingly trouble our city.
(Acts 16:16–20)

The story in Acts is interesting because it illustrates the level of culture and economy that had been built around the oracle worship of Apollo. It cost the average Athenian more than two days' wages for an oracular inquiry, and the average cost to a lawmaker or military official seeking important state information was charged at ten times that rate. This is why, in some ways, the action of the woman in the book of Acts is difficult to understand. She undoubtedly grasped the damage Paul's preaching could do to her industry. Furthermore, the Pythia of Delphi had a historically unfriendly relationship with the Jews and was considered a pawn of demonic power. Quoting again from *Spiritual Warfare—The Invisible Invasion*, we read:

> Delphi with its surrounding area, in which the famous oracle ordained and approved the worship of Asclepius, was earlier known by the name Pytho, a chief city of Phocis. In Greek mythology, Python—the namesake of the city of Pytho—was the great serpent who dwelt in the mountains of Parnassus.... In Acts 16:16, the demonic woman who troubled Paul was possessed with a spirit of divination. In Greek this means a spirit of python (a seeress of Delphi, a pythoness)... [and] reflects...the accepted Jewish belief...that the worship of Asclepius [Apollo's son] and other such idolatries were, as Paul would later articulate in 1 Corinthians 10:20, the worship of demons.[170]

It could be said that the Pythia of Acts 16 simply prophesied the inevitable. That is, the spirit that possessed her knew the time of Apollo's reign was over for the moment, and that the spread of Christianity would lead to the demise of the Delphic oracle. This is possible, as demons are sometimes aware of changing dispensations.

(Compare the pleas of the demons in Matthew 8:29, "What have we to do with thee, Jesus, thou Son of God? art thou come hither to torment us *before the time?*"). The last recorded utterance of the oracle at Delphi seems to indicate the spirit of the Olympians understood this.

From *Man, Myth, and Magic*, we read: [Vol 1, 160]

> Apollo…delivered his last oracle in the year 362 AD, to the physician of the Emperor Julian, the Byzantine ruler who tried to restore paganism after Christianity had become the official religion of the Byzantine Empire. "Tell the King," said the oracle, "that the curiously built temple has fallen to the ground, that bright Apollo no longer has a roof over his head, or prophetic laurel, or babbling spring. Yes, even the murmuring water has dried up."[171]

As the oracle at Delphi slowly diminished, Apollo secured his final and most durable ancient characterization through the influence of his favorite son—Asclepius. Beginning at Thessaly and spreading throughout the whole of Asia Minor, the cult of Asclepius—the Greek god of healing—became the chief competitor of early Christianity. Asclepius was even believed by many pagan converts of Christianity to be a living presence who possessed the power of healing. Major shrines were erected to Asclepius at Epidaurus and at Pergamum, and for a long time he enjoyed a strong cult following in Rome, where he was known as *Aesculapius*. Usually depicted in Greek and Roman art carrying a snake wound around a pole, Asclepius was often accompanied by Telesphoros, the Greek god of convalescence. He was credited with healing a variety of incurable diseases, including raising a man from the dead, a miracle that later caused Hades to complain to Zeus who responded by killing Asclepius with a thunderbolt. When Apollo argued that his son had done nothing worthy of death, Zeus repented and restored Asclepius to life, immortalizing him as the god of medicine.

Dionysus: The Psychotic Aspect of the Demon Apollo/Osiris

Around the first century BC, historians began using the term "Osiris-Dionysus" to commonly refer to dying-and-resurrecting deities, often part-human and born of "virgins" who were worshipped in the years before the emergence of Jesus Christ. In the fifth century BC, Herodotus spoke in particular of the syncretic relationship between Osiris and Dionysus, the thirteenth god of the Greeks. By adding Dionysus to what we have already written about Osiris and Apollo, one can imagine a kind of demonic trinity—a single spirit represented in three manifestations, each of which illustrates a different side of the entity's makeup. As Osiris, this spirit is the god of death and the underworld, and as Apollo he is an oracular sun deity and destroyer demon. As Dionysus, he is superficially depicted as the inventor of wine, abandon, and revelry, a description that seems inadequate in that it refers only to the basic elements of intoxication and enthusiasm, which was used of the *Bacchae* (the female participants of the Dionystic mysteries; also known as Maenads and Bacchantes) in their rituals to experience Dionysus, the intoxicating god of unbridled human desire.

Ancient followers of Dionysus believed he was the *presence* that is otherwise defined as the craving within man that longs to "let itself go" and to "give itself over" to baser, earthly desires. What a Christian might resist as the lustful wants of the carnal man, the followers of

Dionysus embraced as the incarnate power that would, in the next life, liberate the souls of mankind from the constraints of this present world and from the customs that sought to define respectability through a person's obedience to moral law. Until that day arrives, the worshippers of Dionysus attempted to bring themselves into union with the god through a ritual casting off of the bonds of sexual denial and primal constraint by seeking to attain a higher state of ecstasy. The uninhibited rituals of *ecstasy* (Greek for "outside the body") were believed to bring the followers of Dionysus into a supernatural condition that enabled them to escape the temporary limitations of the body and mind and to achieve a state of *enthousiasmos*, or, "outside the body" and "inside the god." In this sense, Dionysus represented a dichotomy within the Greek religion, as the primary maxim of the Greek culture was one of moderation, or "nothing too extreme." But Dionysus embodied the absolute extreme in that he sought to inflame the forbidden passions of human desire. Interestingly, as most students of psychology will understand, this gave Dionysus a stronger allure among the Greeks who otherwise tried in so many ways to suppress and control the wild and secret lusts of the human heart. Dionysus resisted every such effort, and, according to myth, visited a terrible madness upon those who tried to deny him free expression. This Dionystic idea of mental disease resulting from the suppression of secret inner desires, especially aberrant sexual desires, was later reflected in the atheistic teachings of Sigmund Freud. Freudianism might therefore be called the grandchild of the cult of Dionysus. Conversely, the person who gave himself over to the will of Dionysus was rewarded with unlimited psychological and physical delights. These mythical systems of mental punishments and physical rewards based on resistance and/or submission to Dionysus were both symbolically and literally illustrated in the cult rituals of the Bacchae, as the Bacchae women (married and unmarried Greek women had the "right" to participate in the mysteries of Dionysus) migrated in frenzied hillside groups, dressed transvestite in fawn skins and accompanied by screaming, music, dancing, and licentious behavior. When, for instance, a baby animal was too young and lacking in instinct to sense the danger and run away from the revelers, it was picked up and suckled by nursing mothers who participated in the hillside rituals. On the other hand, when older animals sought to escape the marauding Bacchae, they were considered "resistant" to the will of Dionysus and were torn apart and eaten alive as a part of the fevered ritual. Human participants were sometimes subjected to the same orgiastic cruelty, as the rule of the cult was "anything goes," including lesbianism, bestiality, etc. Later versions of the ritual (Bacchanalia) expanded to include pedophilia and male revelers, and perversions of sexual behavior were often worse between men than they were between men and women. Any creature that dared to resist such perversion of Dionysus was subjected to *sparagmos* ("torn apart") and *omophagia* ("consumed raw").

In 410 BC, Euripides wrote of the bloody rituals of the Bacchae in his famous play, *The Bacchantes*:

> The Bacchantes…with hands that bore no weapon of steel, attacked our cattle as they browsed. Then wouldst thou have seen Agave mastering some sleek lowing calf, while others rent the heifers limb from limb. Before thy eyes there would have been hurling of ribs and hoofs this way and that, and strips of flesh, all blood be-dabbled, dripped as they hung from the pine branches. Wild bulls, that glared but now with rage along their horns, found themselves tripped up, dragged down to earth by countless maidens hands.[172]

Euripedes went on to describe how Pentheus, the King of Thebes, was torn apart and eaten alive by his own mother as, according to the play, she fell under the spell of Dionysus. Tearing apart and eating alive of a sacrificial victim may refer to the earliest history of the cult of Dionysus. An ancient and violent cult ritual existing since the dawn of paganism stipulated that, by eating alive, or by drinking the blood of, an enemy or an animal, a person might somehow capture the essence or "soul-strength" of the victim. The earliest Norwegian huntsmen believed in this idea and drank the blood of bears in an effort to capture their physical strength. East African Masai warriors also practiced omophagia and sought to gain the strength of the wild by drinking the blood of lions. Human victims were treated in this way by Arabs before Mohammed, and headhunters of the East Indies practiced omophagia in an effort to capture the essence of their enemies.

Today, omophagia is practiced by certain voodoo sects as well as by cult Satanists, possibly illustrating an ongoing effort on the part of Satan to distort the *original revelation* of God, as eating human flesh and drinking human blood to "become one" with the devoured is a demonization of the Eucharist or Holy Communion. While the goal of the Satanist is to profane the holy, sparagmos and omophagia, as practiced by the followers of Dionysus, was neither an attempt at sacrilege or of *transubstantiation* (as in the Catholic Eucharist), *consubstantiation* (as in the Lutheran communion), nor yet of a symbolic ordinance (as in evangelical circles), all of which have as a common goal elevating the worshipper into sacramental communion with God. The goal of the Bacchae was the opposite—the frenzied dance, the thunderous song, the licentious behavior, the tearing apart and eating alive: all were efforts on the part of the Bacchae to capture the essence of the god (Dionysus) and bring him down into incarnated rage within man. The idea was not one of Holy Communion, but of possession by the spirit of Dionysus. When one recalls the horrific rituals of the followers of Dionysus, it's easy to believe demonic possession actually occurred. A Christian should find this idea plausible, and, it would seem, so did the Hebrews.

The Hebrew people considered Hades (the Greek god of the underworld) to be equal with hell and/or the Devil, and many ancient writers likewise saw no difference between Hades (in this sense the Devil) and Dionysus. Euripedes echoed this sentiment in the *Hecuba*, and referred to the followers of Dionysus as the "Bacchants of Hades." In Syracuse, Dionysus was known as *Dionysus Morychos* ("the dark one") a fiendish creature, roughly equivalent to the biblical Satan, who wore goatskins and dwelt in the regions of the underworld. In the scholarly book, *Dionysus Myth and Cult*, Walter F. Otto likewise connected Dionysus with the prince of the underworld. He wrote:

> The similarity and relationship which Dionysus has with the prince of the underworld (and this is revealed by a large number of comparisons) is not only confirmed by an authority of the first rank, but he says the two deities are actually the same. Heraclitus says, "...Hades and Dionysus, for whom they go mad and rage, are one and the same."[173]

Some Hebrews considered the magic (witchcraft) of the Bacchae to be the best evidence of Dionysus' satanic connection, and while most of the details are no longer available because Dionysus was a mystery god and his rituals were revealed to the initiated only, the Hebrew prophet Ezekiel made an important statement about the "magic bands" (*kesatot*) of the Bacchae, which, as in the omophagia, were used to capture (magically imprison) the souls of men. We read, "Wherefore thus saith the Lord God; Behold I am against your pillows [*kesatot*, "magic bands"] wherewith ye there hunt the souls to make them fly, and I will tear them from your arms and will let the souls go, even the souls that ye hunt to make them fly" (Ezekiel 13:20). The kesatot was a magic arm band used in connection with a container called the *kiste*. Wherever the kiste is inscribed on sarcophagi and on Bacchic scenes, it is depicted as a sacred vessel (a soul prison?) with a snake peering through an open lid. How the magic worked and in what way a soul was imprisoned is still a mystery. Pan, the half-man/half-goat god (later relegated to devildom) is sometimes pictured kicking the lid open and letting the snake (soul?) out. Such loose snakes were then depicted as being enslaved around the limbs, and bound in the hair, of the Bacchae women. Whatever this imagery of Pan, the serpents, the imprisoned souls, and the magic kesatot and kiste actually represented, a noteworthy verification of the magical properties represented by them is discussed in the scholarly book *Scripture and Other Artifacts* by Phillip King and Michael David:

> In the closing verses of Ezekiel 13 the prophet turns his attention to magic practices whose details remain obscure. Two key terms are *kesatot* and *mispabot*.... The *kesatot* are "sewn" on the arms, while the *mispabot* are made "on the head of every height" (?), which has been understood to mean "on the heads of persons of every height" [including those of *great* height; giants, offspring of the Watchers]....
>
> In modern times archaeological discoveries and texts from Babylonia in particular have shed further light on what

might be involved: G. A. Cooke cited Hellenistic figurines from Tell Sandahannah (Mareshah) in Palestine with wire twisted around their arms and ankles…and a magical text from Babylonia that speaks of white and black wool being bound to a person or to someone's bed.… J. Herrmann [notes] that both words can be related to Akkadian verbs, *kasu* and *sapabu*, which mean respectively "to bind" and "to loose."… Herrmann also drew attention to texts in which these verbs were used in a specifically magical sense.… This indicates that, whatever the objects were, their function was to act as "binders" and "loosers" in a magical sense, in other words as means of attack and defense in sorcery.[174]

The text in Ezekiel is believed to specifically refer to Dionysian or Bacchanalian magic, which is important in the context of this book when combined with a related two-part "binding" and "loosing" question from God in Job 38:31: "Canst thou bind the sweet influences of Pleiades, or loose the bands of Orion?" The first part of God's challenge to Job here involves the star cluster Pleiades, which in mythology represented the seven sisters or teachers of the infant Dionysus, the very priestesses of whom used the *kesatot* and *kiste* to magically "bind" those souls that Ezekiel said God would "loose." The second part of God's proposition to Job is equally meaningful, "Can you…loose the bands of Orion?" Studies in recent years have made intriguing findings that suggest the Giza Plateau—which according to Zahi Hawass (current secretary general of Egypt's Supreme Council of Antiquities) was known to ancient Egyptians as the "House of Osiris, Lord of the Underground Tunnels"—was designed to reflect the constellation Orion. The three pyramids of Giza do appear to be laid out in a pattern reflecting the three stars of Orion, which is none other than the heavenly representation of Osiris.

In Greek mythology, the god Orion (Osiris) fell in love with Apollo's sister, Diana (Artemis). Apollo did not like this arrangement and tricked Diana into shooting an arrow into Orion's head. When she saw what she had done, Diana placed the dead Osiris among the stars and transformed him into the constellation Orion. Thereafter, Orion was thought to be the "Soul of Osiris."

Earlier history connects the constellation Orion to the Sumerian legend of Gilgamesh, identified in the Bible as Nimrod—the giant "mighty hunter" before the Lord—a fantastic personality who in later mythology was also called Osiris and Apollo. If Job 38:31 is therefore interpreted according to these ancient astrological and mythological renderings, it would have God asking Job if he could bind the magic bands (*kesatot?*) of Osiris-Dionysus or loose the bindings (*mispabot?*) of the mighty hunter, the giant Orion/Gilgamesh/Nimrod/Osiris/Apollo. What is potentially more explosive is the deep possible implication from this text that not only can God do this—that is, loose the forces bound at Giza and the constellation Orion—but that, when the correct time comes, He *will*.

When the star systems Pleiades and Orion are compared to Henry Wallace's letter to Nicholas Roerich, in which he said, "Dear Guru, I have been thinking of you holding the casket—the sacred most precious casket. And I have thought of the New Country going forward to meet the *seven stars* under the sign of the *three stars* [emphasis added]," the mystery may unfold that Wallace was referring to the Pleiades and Orion specifically and to the deity, and earthly location, they represent. This is an excellent possibility, as these star systems—the *seven stars* of the Pleiades and the *three stars* of Orion—relate to one another in mythology as well as in the Bible:

Seek him that maketh the seven stars [of the Pleiades] and
[the three stars of] Orion. (Amos 5:8)

Which maketh Arcturus, Orion, and Pleiades, and the
chambers of the South. (Job 9:9)

Further, both star systems represent the god encoded in the
Great Seal, the central fascination of Wallace and Roosevelt. The
Pleiades points to Apollo-Dionysus while the Orion system points
to the soul of Osiris in heaven and, on earth, to his speculative tomb
location in Giza. If Wallace was referring to these star systems by
his cryptic phrase "going forward to meet the *seven stars* under the
sign of the *three stars*," Roerich and Wallace may have believed the
New Country (America as the New Atlantis) was destined to meet
Apollo-Dionysus under the sign of the three stars (on the Giza Plateau), where the most precious casket or "coffin" of Osiris-Apollo-
Dionysus held the material remains of the god.

Belief that these gods—or, more accurately, the single entity represented by these many names—would return to rule the earth one
day is not limited to Masonic mystics or the divine manifestation
from the apostle Paul to the Thessalonians (2 Thessalonians 2:3).
The return of these gods "to an active and outward position as rulers
of mankind is predicted in the *Asclepius*," notes Peter Goodgame,
"which is predicted to come after the long period of spiritual decline
in Egypt."

The prophecy Goodgame refers to from the ancient Asclepius
says: "Those gods who rule the earth will be restored, and they will
be installed in a city at the furthest threshold of Egypt, which will be
founded towards the setting sun and to which all human kind will
hasten by land and by sea."

Goodgame notes the physical whereabouts of the "city" in this prophecy is the Giza Plateau, as located by Garth Fowden in his book, *The Egyptian Hermes*:

> In answer to Asclepius enquiry where these gods are at the moment, Trismegistus replies (at *Ascl. 27*): "In a very great city, in the mountains of Libya (*in monte Libyco*)," by which is meant the edge of the desert plateau to the west of the Nile valley. A subsequent reference (*Ascl. 37*) to the temple and tomb of Asclepius (Imhotep) in *monte Libyae* establishes that the allusion at *Ascl. 27* is to the ancient and holy Memphite necropolis, which lay on the desert *jabal* to the west of Memphis itself.

"The 'mountains of Libya,'" Goodgame concludes, "is simply a reference to the plateau that rises above the desert on the west bank of the Nile, west of the ancient city of Memphis. In other words, according to this Hermetic prediction, when the Kosmokrators are 'restored' they will be 'installed in a city' on or near the Giza Plateau."[175] Will the ancient superman, Apollo-Osiris, rise from a hidden tomb at the Giza Plateau, as Goodgame believes may be the case? If so, the *Asclepius* could have been more than a pagan prophecy. It may have been a record pointing to where the body of the "god" was stored in times past. Do the occult masters already know this, and is this why an unfinished pyramid adorns the Great Seal of the United States, over which the portentous eye of Apollo-Osiris glares from the ancient past? Has DNA been recovered from Giza that is needed for the return of this god? Will a forbidden "science" that once allowed incarnation and "deity" status to powerful fallen beings be restored in this modern age? Prophecy suggests exactly this, and for the immediate future, I believe.

Chapter 8

THE LUCIFERIAN SCIENCE OF DEITY RESURRECTION

Osiris will rise in splendor from the dead and rule the world through those sages and philosophers in whom wisdom has become incarnate. —Manly P. Hall, 33rd-Degree Freemason

The World will soon come to us for its Sovereigns and Pontiffs. We shall constitute the equilibrium of the Universe, and be rulers over the Masters of the World. —Albert Pike, Sovereign Grand Commander of the Scottish Rite Freemasonry

I am Yesterday and I am Today; and I have the power to be born a second time. —Statement of Osiris from the *Egyptian Book of the Dead*

To understand how the pagan god of death and destruction so cleverly hidden in the Great Seal of the United States could fulfill the Sibyl's conjure and return with "the life of gods," with "heroes and gods commingling," we gaze into the distant past when the forbidden science was initially used, and to the powerful beings that first developed it—and that, in my opinion, intend to use it again.

As far back as the beginning of time and within every major culture of the ancient world, the astonishingly consistent story is told of "gods" that descended from heaven and materialized in bodies of flesh. From Rome to Greece—and before that, to Egypt, Persia, Assyria, Babylonia, and Sumer—the earliest records of civilization tell of the era when powerful beings known to the Hebrews as *Watchers* and in the book of Genesis as the *benei ha-elohim* (sons of God) mingled themselves with humans, giving birth to part-celestial, part-terrestrial hybrids known as *nephilim*. The Bible says this happened when men began to increase on earth and daughters were born to them. When the sons of God saw the women's beauty, they took wives from among them to sire their unusual offspring. In Genesis 6:4 we read the following account: "There were giants in the earth in those days; and also after that, when the sons of God came in unto the daughters of men, and they bare children to them, the same became mighty men which were of old, men of renown."

When this Scripture is compared with other ancient texts, including Enoch, Jubilees, Baruch, Genesis Apocryphon, Philo, Josephus, Jasher, and others, it unfolds to some that the giants of the Old Testament, such as Goliath, were the part-human, part-animal, part-angelic offspring of a supernatural interruption into the divine order and natural evolution of the species. The apocryphal book of Enoch gives a name to the angels involved in this cosmic conspiracy, calling them "Watchers." We read:

> And I Enoch was blessing the Lord of majesty and the King of the ages, and lo! the Watchers called me—Enoch the scribe—and said to me: "Enoch, thou scribe of righteousness, go, declare to the Watchers of the heaven who have left the high heaven, the holy eternal place, and have defiled

themselves with women, and have done as the children of earth do, and have taken unto themselves wives: Ye have wrought great destruction on the earth: And ye shall have no peace nor forgiveness of sin: and inasmuch as they delight themselves in their children [the Nephilim], The murder of their beloved ones shall they see, and over the destruction of their children shall they lament, and shall make supplication unto eternity, but mercy and peace shall ye not attain." (1 Enoch 10:3–8)

According to Enoch, two hundred of these powerful angels departed "high heaven" and used women (among other things) to extend their progeny into mankind's plane of existence. The Interlinear Hebrew Bible offers an interesting interpretation of Genesis 6:2 in this regard. Where the King James Bible says, "The sons of God saw the daughters of men that they [were] fair," the IHN interprets this as, "The benei Elohim saw the daughters of Adam, that they were *fit extensions*" (emphasis added). The term "fit extensions" seems applicable when the whole of the ancient record is understood to mean that the Watchers wanted to leave their proper sphere of existence in order to enter earth's three-dimensional reality. They viewed women—or at least their genetic material—as part of the formula for accomplishing this task. Departing the proper habitation that God had assigned them was grievous to the Lord and led to divine penalization. Jude described it this way: The "angels which kept not their first estate, but left their own habitation, he hath reserved in everlasting chains under darkness unto the judgment of the great day" (Jude 6).

Besides apocryphal, pseudepigraphic, and Jewish traditions

related to the legend of the Watchers and the "mighty men" born of their union with humans, mythologized accounts tell the stories of "gods" using humans to produce heroes or demigods (half-gods). When the ancient Greek version of the Hebrew Old Testament (the LXX or Septuagint) was made, the word *nephilim*—referring to the part-human offspring of the Watchers—was translated *"gegenes,"* a word implying "earth-born." This same terminology was used to describe the Greek Titans and other legendary heroes of partly celestial and partly terrestrial origin, such as Hercules (born of Zeus and the mortal Alcmena), Achilles (the Trojan hero son of Thetis and Peleus), and Gilgamesh (the two-thirds god and one-third human child of Lugalbanda and Ninsun).

These demigods were likewise accompanied in texts and idol representation by half-animal and half-human creatures like centaurs (the part-human, part-horse offspring of Apollo's son, Centaurus), chimeras, furies, satyrs, gorgons, nymphs, Minotaurs, and other genetic aberrations. Historian Andrew Tomas believes these mythological records are "thought-fossils depicting the story of vanished cultures in symbols and allegories," or, as Stephen Quayle, in his book, *Genesis 6 Giants*, explains: "The collective memories in the form of myths, fables and fairy tales from various cultures and ages of mankind are overwhelming evidence that the Nephilim existed."[176] All of this indicates that the Watchers not only modified human DNA during the construction of Nephilim, but animals as well, a point the book of Enoch supports, saying in the seventh chapter that the fallen angels "sinned" against animals as well as humans. Other books such as *Jubilees* add that this interspecies mingling eventually resulted in mutations among normal humans and animals whose "flesh" (genetic makeup) was "corrupted" by the activity, presumably through crossbreeding (see 5:1–5; 7:21–25). Even the Old Testament contains reference to the genetic mutations that developed among humans following this time frame, including "men" of unusual size, physical strength, six fingers, six toes, animal appetite for blood, and even lion-like features (2 Samuel 21:20; 23:20). J. R. Church makes an interesting point that since this activity was satanic in nature, it refers to the "seed of the serpent" that was at enmity with Christ. "The concept of a reptilian race continues throughout the Bible as a metaphoric symbol of the devil," he wrote in his *Prophecy in the News* magazine, February 2009. "Later Scriptures add the term 'dragon,' with the implication that these other-worldly creatures were designed with the DNA code of a reptilian race." Church went on to state how some of these satanic creatures were depicted as "bat-like gargoyles, or winged dragons" in ancient art, and that we should not be surprised that "a humanoid-type reptilian race could cohabit with human women and produce a race of giants."

But of all the ancient records, the most telling extra-biblical script is from the book of Jasher, a mostly forgotten text referred to in the Bible in Joshua 10:13 and 2 Samuel 1:18. Jasher records the familiar story of the fall of the Watchers, then adds an exceptional detail that none of the other texts is as unequivocal about, something that can only be understood in modern language to mean advanced biotechnology, genetic engineering, or "transgenic modification" of species. After the Watchers had instructed humans "in the secrets of heaven," note what Jasher says occurred:

> [Then] the sons of men [began teaching] the mixture of animals of one species with the other, in order therewith to provoke the Lord. (Jasher 4:18)

The phrase "the mixture of animals of one species with the other" does not mean Watchers had taught men hybridization, as this would not have "provoked the Lord." God made like animals of different breeds capable of reproducing. For example, horses can propagate with other mammals of the equidae classification (the taxonomic "horse family"), including donkeys and zebras. It would not have "provoked the Lord" for this type of animal breeding to have taken place, as God Himself made the animals able to do this.

If, on the other hand, the Watchers were crossing species boundaries by mixing incompatible animals *of one species with the other*, such as a horse with a human (a centaur), this would have been a different matter and may cast light on the numerous ancient stories of mythical beings of variant-species manufacturing that fit perfectly within the records of what the Watchers were accomplishing. Understandably, this kind of chimera-making would have "provoked the Lord" and raises the serious question of why the Watchers would have risked eternal damnation by tinkering with God's creation in this way. Yahweh had placed boundaries between the species and strictly ordered that "each kind" reproduce only after its "own kind." Was the motive of the Watchers to break these rules simply the desire to rebel, to assault God's creative genius through biologically altering what He had made? Or was something of deeper significance behind the activity?

Some believe the corruption of antediluvian DNA by Watchers was an effort to cut off the birth line of the Messiah. This theory posits that Satan understood the protoevangelium—the promise in Genesis 3:15 that a Savior would be born, the seed of the woman, and that He would destroy the fallen angel's power. Satan's followers therefore intermingled with the human race in a conspiracy to stop the birth of Christ. If human DNA could be universally corrupted or "demonized," they reasoned, no Savior would be born and mankind would be lost forever. Those who support this theory believe this is why God ordered His people to maintain a pure bloodline and not to intermarry with the other nations. When Israel breached this command and the mutated DNA began rapidly spreading among men and animals, God instructed Noah to build an ark and to prepare for a flood that would destroy every living thing. That God had to send such a universal fiat like the Flood illustrates how widespread the altered DNA eventually became. In fact, the Bible says in Genesis 6:9 that only Noah and by extension his children were found "perfect" in their generation. The Hebrew word for "perfect" in this case is *tamiym*, which means "without blemish" or "healthy," the same word used in Leviticus to describe an unblemished sacrificial lamb. The meaning was not that Noah was morally perfect, but that his physical makeup—his DNA—had not been contaminated with Nephilim descent, as apparently the rest of the world had become. In order to preserve mankind as He had made them, God destroyed all but Noah's family in the Flood. The ancient records including those of the Bible appear to agree with this theology, consistently describing the cause of the Flood as happening in response to "all flesh" having become "corrupted, both man and beast."

An Alternative Reason the Watchers Blended DNA

While I believe the theory of DNA corruption as an intended method for halting the coming of Christ has merit, an alternative or additional reason the Watchers may have blended living organisms exists. This theory is original with me and grew from my need to incorporate the voluminous historical texts, which described this peculiar history, into a consistent account that corresponds with Scripture.

To harmonize the ancient records, I came to believe that the overriding motive for whatever the Watchers were doing with the DNA of various species had to be understood within the context of their foremost goal, which was to leave their plane of existence and to enter ours. My challenge then became to answer the question of how blending various species would satisfy this goal or provide the Watchers with a method of departure from "high heaven" and incarnation into man's "habitation." While I will not take time here to explain every detail (a five-hour CD set called *As It Was In the Days Of Noah: The Return of the Nephilim* that covers this and related material is available from www.SurvivorMall.com), I eventually hypothesized that the Watchers *had* to blend species in the way they did in order to create a soulless or spiritless body into which they could extend themselves. The rationale is that every creature as it existed originally had its beginning in God, who ordered each creature to reproduce "after its own kind." The phrase "after its own kind" verifies what kind of spirit can enter into an intelligent being at conception. When the sperm of a dog meets ovum of a dog and the life of a dog is formed, at the first spark of life the spirit or personality of a dog enters that embryo and it grows to become a dog in spirit and form. The spirit of a man does not enter it, in the same way that a man is not born with the spirit of a horse or cow. This creature/ spirit integrity is part of the divine order and would have kept the Watchers, who wanted to incarnate within the human realm (not just "possess" creatures), from displacing the spirits of humans or animals and replacing them with their own. How did they overcome this problem? Like scientists are doing today, it appears based on the ancient records that they blended existing DNA of several living creatures and made something that neither the spirit of man or beast would enter at conception, for it was neither man nor beast. As the quarterly online travel guide *Mysterious World*, in its 2003 feature, "Giants in the Earth," noted:

> The Nephilim were genetically manufactured beings created from the genetic material of various pre-existing animal species.... The fallen angels did not personally interbreed with the daughters of men, but used their godlike intellect to delve into the secrets of YHWH's Creation and manipulate it to their own purposes. And the key to creating or recreating man, as we have (re)discovered in the twentieth century, is the human genome—DNA.

This manipulation of living tissue by the fallen angels led to an unusual body made up of human, animal, and plant genetics known as Nephilim, an "earth-born" facsimile or "fit extension" into which they could incarnate. What's more, the long history of demonological phenomenon related to manipulation of biological matter suggests that versions of this curious activity have been ongoing ever since.

Former college professor and BBC correspondent, Dr. I. D. E. Thomas, in his highly recommended book, *The Omega Conspiracy*, chronicled the burgeoning of so-called "alien abduction" activity and tied it to end-time prophecy concerning the return of the Nephilim. Documentation by "abductees" worldwide and the stories of DNA harvesting by "aliens" reminded him of the history of biological misuse by the Watchers, and led Thomas to conclude that the identity of the Watchers and whoever the alien entities are were somehow connected. Dr. Thomas told me personally that the special desire by these unknown agents for human and animal molecular matter "would explain why animals have been killed, mutilated, and stolen by the aliens in UFO flap areas." Respected UFO researcher, Dr. Jacques F. Vallée, raised similar questions.

> In order to materialize and take definite form, these entities seem to require a source of energy…a living thing…a human medium…. Our sciences have not reached a point where they can offer us any kind of working hypothesis for this process. But we can speculate that these beings need living energy which they can reconstruct into physical form. Perhaps that is why dogs and animals tend to vanish in flap areas. Perhaps the living cells of those animals are somehow used by the ultraterrestrials to create forms which we can see and sense with our limited perceptions.[177]

Like Thomas, Vallée connected this activity with the legendary acts of the Watchers.

Are we dealing…with a parallel universe, another dimension, where there are…races only semi-human, so that in order to maintain contact with us, they need cross-breeding with men and woman of our planet? Is this the origin of the many tales and legends where genetics play a great role:… the fairy tales involving human midwives and changelings, the sexual overtones of the flying saucer reports, the Biblical stories of intermarriage between the Lord's angels and terrestrial women, whose offspring were giants?[178]

Whether or not there is a connection between the ancient power behind the Watcher narrative and the modern "alien abduction" activity documented by Vallée and others involving biological harvesting from humans and animals, records from antiquity include mysterious possibilities regarding the ability of the Watchers' deceased offspring to return to "physical form" at particular moments in time. The relationship between the rephaim—the giant occupants of Canaan (of which Og, King of Bashan whose bed was eighteen feet long belonged)—and the Nephilim becomes important here, as the rephaim were associated by the ancients with the "shades of the dead," including Nephilim in Sheol. The meaning of the word "rephaim" is especially germane, as it carries with it the idea "to heal" or "to be healed" as in a "resurrection" from the place of the dead, Sheol-Hades. In Hebrew, the seraphim were powerful angels whose name combined *ser*, meaning "a higher being or angel," and *rapha*, "to heal." This connotes angels of healing or those that can be healed. The rephaim may therefore be considered seraphim, which followed Lucifer in the fall.

In the Ras Shamra texts, the rephaim were described as demigods who worshipped the Amorite god Ba'al, the ruler of the underworld. When rephaim died, their spirits went into the underworld, where they joined Ba'al's acolyte assembly of lesser gods, kings, heroes, and rulers. These beings had the power to return from the dead through reincarnation into bodily form as Nephilim. As *Mysterious World* in "Giants in the Earth" also included, "The Rephaim giants were specifically noted by Moses as being the return of the antediluvian Nephilim, that the Rephaim were in fact the reincarnations of the demonic spirits of the Nephilim giants who had been destroyed in the Flood." A surprise to many Bible students would be to learn that the prophet Isaiah may have considered this Amorite dogma factual, and that he tied the power of these beings to the king of Babylon and Lucifer himself. After prophesying against the Babylonian leader, Isaiah says in parallel to rephaim theology:

> Hell [Sheol-Hades] from beneath is moved for thee to meet thee at thy coming: it stirreth up the dead [rapha, raphaim] for thee, even all the chief ones of the earth; it hath raised up from their thrones all the kings of the nations. And they shall speak and say unto thee, Art thou also become weak as we? Art thou become like unto us? (Isaiah 14:9–10)

Immediately following this statement, Isaiah looked beyond the rephaim at who their Ba'al actually was, identifying him in verse 12, saying, "How art thou fallen from heaven, O Lucifer, son of the morning!"

Other places in the Bible such as Job 26:5 may agree with the idea of a luciferian power that can, under some circumstances, return rephaim from the underworld to physical bodies known as Nephilim. "Dead things are formed from under the waters," Job says. The dead in this text are rapha (rephaim), and the phrase "are formed" is from "*chuwl*," meaning to twist or whirl as in a double helix coil or genetic manufacturing. The startling implication of this and similar texts is that beneath the surface of earth, agents of darkness wait the moment of their return. Before the end of this book, we shall consider several ancient documents and Scriptures that seem to forecast such a terrifying event for the end times.

A Biblical Example of Nephilim Resurrection?

If indeed the activity of Watchers was the use of biotechnology to produce exotic bodies of flesh for beings that have the ability under extraordinary circumstances to reincarnate after physical death, would the method of their returning from the grave likewise be an advanced form of science? I believe this could be the case, and the Bible may actually provide a record of this occurring. The story is doubly important to our book because it centers around Nimrod, the original character who later was mythologized as the god prophesied by the apostle Paul in the New Testament and by the occult elite in the Great Seal of the United States as the ancient spirit that will return to earth to rule the *novus ordo seclorum*—Apollo/Osiris. Earlier we pointed out how Apollo is reanimated on earth in the end times when "the Beast" ascends from the bottomless pit and goes "into perdition" (into *Apolia*, Apollo. See Revelation 17:8). The story of Nimrod (Gilgamesh/Apollo/Osiris) in the book of Genesis may illustrate how this could happen through genetic influence or a retrovirus of demonic design that integrates with a host's genome and rewrites the living specimen's DNA, thus making it a "fit extension" for infection by the entity. Genesis 10:8 says about Nimrod: "And Cush begat Nimrod: he began to be a mighty one in the earth."

Three sections in this unprecedented verse indicate something very peculiar had happened to Nimrod. First, note where the text says, "he *began* to be." In Hebrew, this is *chalal,* which means "to become profaned, defiled, polluted, or desecrated ritually, sexually or genetically." Second, this verse tells us exactly *what* Nimrod began to be—"a mighty one" (gibbowr, gibborim), one of the offspring of Nephilim. As Annette Yoshiko Reed says in the Cambridge University book, *Fallen Angels and the History of Judaism and Christianity,* "The Nephilim of [Genesis] 6:4 are always…grouped together with the gibborim as the progeny of the Watchers and human women."[179] And the third part of this text says the change to Nimrod started while he was on "earth." Therefore, in modern language, this text could accurately be translated to say:

> And Nimrod began to change genetically, becoming a gibborim, the offspring of watchers on earth. To understand how as a mature, living specimen Nimrod could have begun to be a gibborim, it is helpful to imagine this in terms of biology as we know it. For instance, not long ago, I "began to be" a diabetic. Because of poor choices of food, diet, and exercise, my doctor tells me that I triggered a genetic inherent and that it began changing me in powerful, metabolic ways. This change is so powerful that today I have to take drugs to keep it from killing me. Yet just because I had the heritable, disease-related genotype that can lead to diabetes, this did not mean necessarily that I would develop the medical condition. It is entirely possible to be a carrier of a genetic mutation that increases the risk of developing a particular disease without ever actually becoming afflicted with the disorder in the course of a lifetime. Due to my earlier lifestyle, or maybe even certain environmental conditions I was unaware of, the gene mutation involved in the action of insulin "turned on" and I "began to be" a diabetic.

I've often wondered if the record of Nimrod that says he "began to be" a "gibborim" indicated something similar about his genetics, DNA, or bloodline that "turned on" as a result of his decisions, triggering a change in him from one type of being to another. It is also a possibility, I suppose, that Nimrod became afflicted with a retrovirus that integrated with his genome and, in essence, "rewrote" his genetic makeup, fashioning him into a "fit extension" for an underworldly spirit. When I asked Sharon Gilbert, author of *The Armageddon Strain* whose formal education includes molecular biology and genetics, if she thought this was possible, she said:

> Absolutely, Tom. Retroviruses essentially inject single-stranded RNA strands into somatic (body) cells during "infection." These ssRNA strands access nucleotide pools in the host cell and form a double-stranded DNA copy. This dsDNA can then incorporate itself into the host chromosome using a viral enzyme called "integrase." The new "fake gene" then orders the cell to make more mRNA copies of the original virus RNA. These then travel out of the cell and infect the next cell, and so on.

Perhaps this type genetic rewriting is implied in Genesis 10:8, which says, "And Cush begat Nimrod: he began to be a mighty one [gibborim] in the earth."

In addition to such scientific deduction, another reason I believe this story is suspicious is because of what Nimrod did immediately following Genesis chapter 10. As soon as he "began to be a mighty one" in the earth, one chapter later he set out to build a tower whose top would "reach unto heaven" (Genesis 11:4). This was the infamous Tower of Babel, and Nimrod was designing it so that the top of it would extend into *Shamayim* ("heaven"), the abode of God.

The *Jewish Encyclopedia* confirms several historical records that Nimrod, whom it establishes was also identified by various ancient cultures alternatively as Osiris, Orion, Apollo, and Gilgamesh, built the Tower of Babel in an attempt to ascend into the presence of God. Jehovah Himself came down and said of the Tower's design: "Nothing will be restrained from them, which they have imagined to do" (Genesis 11:6). In other words, according to the Lord, Nimrod would have accomplished what he "imagined" to do—to build a tower whose top would reach into the abode of God.

That this section of Scripture could be viewed as a secondary support for the concept of Nimrod having become "revived Watcher offspring" is thus supported by Nimrod seeming to abruptly be aware of *where* and *how tall* to build a tower so that the top of it would penetrate the dwelling place of God. Were his eyes suddenly opened to realities that are outside man's normal mode of perception? As he became *gibborim*, he would have taken on Watchers' propensities, which, as angels, could see into the supernatural realm including where heaven is located and possibly where to enter it. Even the name "Babylon" implies this, meaning the "gate of God" or "gateway *to* God." That there could be sacred locations where those beings that can see into the supernatural realm could literally walk up onto a high place and enter heaven is not as farfetched as it sounds. Numerous records, including from the Bible, appear to substantiate the idea that heaven could be attained on high towers or mountainous locations. Consider Moses meeting with God on Sinai, Jesus returning atop the Mount of Olives, the two hundred Watchers that "descended in the days of Jared on the summit of Mount Hermon" (Enoch 6:6) and other examples, including Jacob's ladder. This could also explain why, in the deep recesses of our psyche, people tend to believe they can draw closer to God when going up onto mountains.

In addition to the possibility of suddenly seeing into the supernatural realm as a result of integration with fallen angels, if Nimrod was genetically modified according to the original Watcher formula, he would have inherited animal characteristics within his new material makeup, and animals, like angels, can perceive "domains" that humans cannot. This includes obvious things, such as wavelengths of the electromagnetic spectrum, but possibly something even more substantial, like the spirit realm. This is important to keep in mind as we consider in the next chapter how the move by modern scientists to revive Watcher technology and to blend humans with animals could set in motion the return of Nephilim and the coming of Apollo.

Chapter 9

WILL MODERN SCIENCE PLAY A ROLE IN THE COMING OF APOLLO?

Joe raised the special container with a heavy sigh. "So, if Apollyon is somehow embodied in Apol, we could actually be carrying the embryo of the Antichrist here?"

"That's correct," Stark said, "According to the Bible, the Antichrist will be 'the son of perdition,' the male progeny of the Greek apoleia, or Apollyon. The implication couldn't be clearer—the Man of Sin will be the physical offspring of the destroyer demon, a transgenic of the highest order." —From the novel, *The Ahriman Gate,* by Thomas and Nita Horn

Stoop not down, therefore, Unto the Darkly Shining World, Where the ABSU lies in Dark Waters, And CUTHALU sleeps and dreams, Stoop not down, therefore, For an Abyss lies beneath the World, Reached by a descending Ladder, That hath Seven Steps, Reached by a descending Pathway, That hath Seven Gates, And therein is established, The Throne, Of an Evil and Fatal Force. For from the Cavities of the World, Leaps forth the Evil Demon, The Evil God, The Evil Genius, The Evil Ensnarer, The Evil Phantom, The Evil Devil, The Evil Larvae, Showing no true Signs, Unto mortal Man. AND THE DEAD WILL RISE AND SMELL THE INCENSE! —The Babylonian creation epic *Enuma Elish* (Magian Version) V n recent years, astonishing technological developments have pushed the frontiers of humanity toward far-reaching morphological transformation that promises in the very near future to redefine what it means to be human. An international, intellectual, and fast-growing cultural movement known as *transhumanism,* whose vision is supported by a growing list of US military advisors, bioethicists, law professors, and academics, intends the use of genetics, robotics, artificial intelligence and nanotechnology (GRIN technologies) as tools that will radically redesign our minds, our memories, our physiology, our offspring, and even perhaps— as Joel Garreau, in his bestselling book *Radical Evolution,* claims—our very souls.

Unfortunately for mankind, the technological and cultural shift now underway not only unapologetically forecasts a future dominated by a new species of unrecognizably superior humans, but an unfathomable war—both physical and spiritual—that the world is not prepared for. It will be fought on land, within the air and sea, and in dimensions as yet incomprehensible. Even now, the synthetic forces that will plot man's wholesale annihilation are quietly under design in leading laboratories, public and private, funded by the most advanced nations on earth, including the official governments of the United States, France, Britain, Australia, and China, to name a few. As a result of progressive deduction, reasoning, and problem solving in fields of neurotechnology and cybernetics, strong artificial intelligence or "artilects" will emerge from this research, godlike, massively intelligent machines that are "trillions of trillions of times smarter than humans" and whose rise will prove profoundly disruptive to human culture, leading to a stark division between philosophical, ideological, and political groups who either support the newly evolved life forms as the next step in human and technological evolution or who view this vastly superior intellect as an incalculable risk and deadly threat to the future of humanity. These diametrically opposed worldviews will ultimately result in a preemptive new world war—what is already being described as *gigadeath,* the bloodiest battle in history with billions of deaths before the end of the twenty-first century.

For those who find the fantastic elements in the statements above implicative of science fiction or even future Armageddon as forecast in the ancient apocalyptic and prophetic books of the Bible, the catastrophic vision is actually derived from near-future scenarios, which leading scientists like Prof. Hugo de Garis, director of the Artificial Brain Lab at Xiamen University in China, outlines in his book, *The Artilect War: Cosmists vs. Terrans: A Bitter Controversy Concerning Whether Humanity Should Build Godlike Massively Intelligent Machines,* as unfolding due to exponential growth and development this century in GRIN technologies.

"I believe that the twenty-first century will be dominated by the question as to whether humanity should or should not build artilects, i.e., machines of godlike intelligence," de Garis says. "I see humanity splitting into two major political groups, which in time will become increasingly bitterly opposed, as the artilect issue becomes more real."

Professor de Garis continues:

> The human group in favor of building artilects, I label the "Cosmists" [to whom] building artilects will be like a religion…something truly magnificent and worthy of worship.…
>
> The second human group, opposed to the building of artilects, I label the "Terrans"…who will argue that allowing the Cosmists to build [artilects] implies accepting the *risk,*

that one day, the artilects might decide…that the human species is a pest. Since the artilects would be so vastly superior to human beings in intelligence, it would be easy for [them] to exterminate the human species.…

Thus to the Terrans, the Cosmists are…far worse than the regimes of Hitler, Stalin, Mao…or any other regime that murdered tens of millions of people in the twentieth century, because [this] time…we are talking about the potential annihilation of the whole human species, billions of people.[180]

Professor de Garis continues in his book to describe how the work to build artilects is proceeding nonetheless with anticipation of its realization potentially close at hand. As a result, he falls asleep at night thinking about the godlike synthetic intelligence he and others are constructing. Sometimes his mind becomes enraptured of his creations with a sense of intellectual and spiritual awe. Then, waking up a few hours later in a cold sweat, he is jolted from bed by a horrific dream in which vivid scenes depict the slaughter of his descendents at the hands of the artificial deities.

Dr. de Garis is not alone in this fear, that what he and other research scientists are feverishly working toward could soon become a nightmarish predicament mankind will not survive. Because it is difficult, if not impossible, to accurately predict how strong artificial intelligence will actually affect the world, it is unclear whether humans will be viewed by the unnatural life forms as serving a purpose in a world dominated by super-intelligent machines or whether they will be weighed as lacking any practical function and therefore be considered expendable. It could be that we won't even see the question coming. In other words, we may already be in the process of being lulled into subservience toward the rise of the machines. As the brilliantly insane Theodore Kaczynski, in his thirty-five-thousand-word paper, "Industrial Society and Its Future" (also called the "Unabomber Manifesto"), wrote:

> As society and the problems that face it become more and more complex and machines become more and more intelligent, people will let machines make more of their decisions for them, simply because machine-made decisions will bring better result than man-made ones. Eventually a stage may be reached at which the decisions necessary to keep the system running will be so complex that human beings will be incapable of making them intelligently. At that stage, the machines will be in effective control. People won't be able to just turn the machines off, because they will be so dependent on them that turning them off would amount to suicide.[181]

Crazy or not, Kaczynski may be right in that man's demise at the hands of machines will happen gradually, during which time we humans will become the proverbial frogs in the kettle set to boil. On the other hand, we are more likely to be reduced any day now in the blink of an enhanced eye to the status of domestic animals in the minds of artificial intelligence, as *Technological Singularity*—that magical future moment that many futurists and tech experts believe could be imminent—gives birth overnight to some version of the artilects, who suddenly come online as conscious, living superminds, immensely more powerful than human beings.

"As a metaphor for mind-boggling social change, the Singularity has been borrowed from math and physics," writes Joel Garreau in *Radical Evolution*. "In those realms, singularities are the point where everything stops making sense. In math it is a point where you are dividing through by zero [and in physics it is] black holes—points in space so dense that even light cannot escape their horrible gravity. If you were to approach one in a spaceship, you would find that even the laws of physics no longer seemed to function. That's what a Singularity is like."[182] Ray Kurzweil, who is credited with groundbreaking work in artificial intelligence and is, among other things, the co-founder of an interdisciplinary graduate studies program backed by NASA known as the Singularity University, appreciates the comparison between the coming Technological Singularity and the physics of black holes:

> Just as a black hole in space dramatically alters the patterns of matter and energy accelerating toward its event horizon, the impending Singularity in our future is [a] period during which the pace of technological change will be so rapid, its impact so deep, that human life will be irreversibly transformed. The key idea underlying the impending Singularity is that the rate of change of our human-created technology is accelerating and its powers are expanding at an exponential pace. Exponential growth is deceptive. It starts out almost imperceptibly and then explodes with unexpected fury.[183]

In plain language, Abou Farman says Kurzweil's work on the Singularity:

> analyzes the curve of technological development from humble flint-knapping to the zippy microchip. The curve he draws rises exponentially, and we are sitting right on the elbow, which means very suddenly this trend toward

smaller and smarter technologies will yield greater-than-human machine intelligence. That sort of superintelligence will proliferate not by self-replication, but by building other agents with even greater intelligence than itself, which will in turn build more superior agents. The result will be an "intelligence explosion" so fast and so vast that the laws and certainties with which we are familiar will no longer apply. That event-horizon is called the Singularity.[184]

Kurzweil elaborates further on what the Singularity will mean:

Our version 1.0 biological bodies are frail and subject to a myriad of failure modes. The Singularity will allow us to transcend these limitations. We will gain power over our fates. Our mortality will be in our own hands [and] the nonbiological portion of our intelligence will be trillions of trillions of times more powerful than unaided human intelligence.

We are now in the early stages of this transition. The acceleration of paradigm shift as well as the exponential growth of the capacity of information technology are both beginning to reach the "knee of the curve," which is the stage at which an exponential trend becomes noticeable. Shortly after this stage, the trend becomes explosive. [Soon] the growth rates of our technology—which will be indistinguishable from ourselves—will be so steep as to appear essentially vertical. That, at least, will be the perspective of unenhanced biological humanity.

The Singularity will represent the culmination of the merger of our biological thinking and existence with our technology, resulting in a world that transcends our biological roots. There will be no distinction, post-Singularity, between human and machine.[185]

In 1993, critical thinking about the timing of the Singularity concerning the emergence of strong artificial intelligence led retired San Diego State University professor and computer scientist Vernor Vinge, in his often-quoted and now-famous lecture, "The Coming Technological Singularity," (delivered at VISION-21 Symposium sponsored by NASA Lewis Research Center and the Ohio Aerospace Institute), to add that when science achieves "the technological means to create superhuman intelligence[,] shortly after, the human era will be ended."[186] In contrast to Vinge, cyborgists like Kevin Warwick, professor of cybernetics at Reading University in England who endorsed de Garis' book, believe Singularity will not so much represent the end of the human era as it will the assimilation of man with machine intelligence, like the Borg of *Star Trek* fame. This is because, according to Warwick, Technological Singularity will not occur as a result of freestanding independent machines, but inside human cyborgs where human-machine integration is realized and enhanced biology is recombined to include living brains that are cybernetic, machine readable, and interfaced with artificial neural networks where transhumans with amplified intelligence become so completely superior to their biological counterparts (normal humans) as to be incomprehensible—ultimately "posthuman." The technology to accomplish this task is already well underway and is considered by researchers like Warwick to be one of the most important scientific utilities currently under employment toward man's posthuman future. As a result of this bridge between technology and human biology being attained this century, nothing less than the wholesale redesign of humans, including genetic inte-

gration with other life-forms—plants, animals, and synthetic creations—will be realized. This vision—the borgification (marriage
between biology and machine) of man—is supported in the latest
"State of the Future" report (2010) by the global think tank, the
Millennium Project, founded after a three-year feasibility study with
the United Nations University, Smithsonian Institution, and the
Futures Group International, where synthetic biologists affirm that
"as computer code is written to create software to augment human
capabilities, so too *genetic code will be written to create life forms to
augment civilization.*"[187] Furthermore, as biotech, infotech, nano-
tech, and cognotech breakthroughs quickly migrate with appropriate synergies to create widespread man-machine adaptation within
society, a "global collective intelligence system [hive supermind] will
be needed to track all these science and technology advances," the
report goes on to say.

I (Tom) have personally debated leading transhumanist, Dr.
James Hughes, concerning this inevitable techno-sapien future on
his weekly syndicated talk show, *Changesurfer Radio*. Hughes is executive director of the Institute for Ethics and Emerging Technologies
and teaches at Trinity College in Hartford, Connecticut. He is the
author of *Citizen Cyborg: Why Democratic Societies Must Respond to
the Redesigned Human of the Future*, a sort of bible for transhumanist
values. Dr. Hughes joins a growing body of academics, bioethicists,
and sociologists who support:

> Large-scale genetic and neurological engineering of our-
> selves…[a] new chapter in evolution [as] the result of accel-
> erating developments in the fields of genomics, stem-cell
> research, genetic enhancement, germ-line engineering,
> neuro-pharmacology, artificial intelligence, robotics, pattern
> recognition technologies, and nanotechnology…at the inter-

section of science and religion [which has begun to question] what it means to be human.[188]

Though the transformation of man to this posthuman condition is in its fledgling state, complete integration of the technology necessary to replace existing Homo sapiens as the dominant life-form on earth is approaching Kurzweil's exponential curve. A *Reuters* article dated November 9, 2009, titled "Scientists Want Debate on Animals with Human Genes," hinted at just how far scientists have come and how far they intend to go. The news piece started out, "A mouse that can speak? A monkey with Down's Syndrome? Dogs with human hands or feet? British scientists want to know if such experiments are acceptable," and it continued with revelations that scientists inside Britain are comfortable now with up to 50/50 animal-human integration. The article implied that not all the research currently under design is kept at the embryonic level, and that fully mature monstrosities (like the creature in the 2010 movie *Splice*) may be under study as "some scientists in some places want to push boundaries." *National Geographic* magazine speculated in 2007 that within ten years, the first of such human-animals would walk the earth, and Vernor Vinge agreed recently that we are entering that period in history when questions like "What is the meaning of life?" will be nothing more than an engineering question.

Most readers may be surprised to learn that in preparation of this posthuman revolution, the United States government, through the National Institute of Health, recently granted Case Law School in Cleveland $773,000 of American taxpayers' money to begin developing the actual guidelines that will be used for setting government policy on the next step in human evolution—"genetic enhancement." Maxwell Mehlman, Arthur E. Petersilge Professor of Law, director

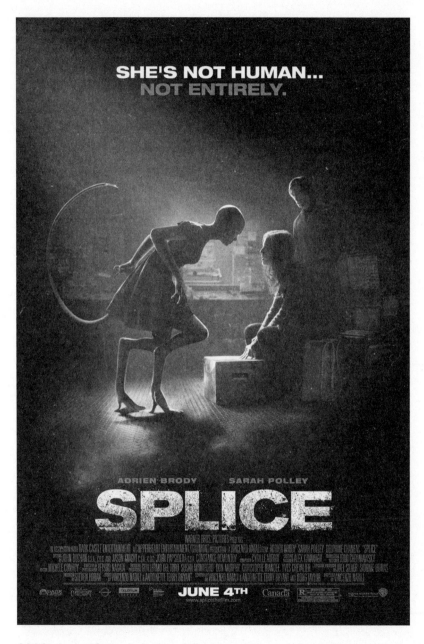

2010 movie "Splice" depicts fully grown human-animal chimera of the Law-Medicine Center at the Case Western Reserve University School of Law, and professor of bioethics in the Case School of Medicine, led the team of law professors, physicians, and bioethicists over the two-year project "to develop standards for tests on human subjects in research that involves the use of genetic technologies to enhance 'normal' individuals."[189] Following the initial study, Mehlman began offering two university lectures: "Directed Evolution: Public Policy and Human Enhancement" and "Transhumanism and the Future of Democracy," addressing the need for society to comprehend how emerging fields of science will, in approaching years, alter what it means to be human, and what this means to democracy, individual rights, free will, eugenics, and equality. Other law schools, including Stanford and Oxford, are now hosting similar annual "Human Enhancement and Technology" conferences, where transhumanists, futurists, bioethicists, and legal scholars are busying themselves with the ethical, legal, and inevitable ramifications of posthumanity.

As the director of the Future of Humanity Institute and a professor of philosophy at Oxford University, Nick Bostrom (www. NickBostrom.com) is a leading advocate of transhumanism who, as a young man, was heavily influenced by the works of Friedrich Nietzsche (from whom the phrase "God is dead" derives) and Goethe, the author of *Faust*. Nietzsche was the originator of the *Übermensch* or "Overman" that Adolf Hitler dreamed of engineering, and the "entity" that man—who is nothing more than a rope "tied between beast and Overman, a rope over an abyss"—according to Nietzsche, will eventually evolve into. Like the ancient Watchers before him (Watchers, remember, were fallen angels that mingled human DNA with animals and their seed to produce Nephilim. More on this will be discussed later), Bostrom envisions giving life to Nietzsche's Overman (posthumans) by remanufacturing men with animals, plants, and other synthetic life-forms through the use of modern sciences including recombinant DNA technology, germ-line engineering, and transgenics (in which the genetic structure of one species is altered by the transfer of genes from another). Given that molecular biologists classify the functions of genes within native species yet remain unsure in most cases how a gene's coding might react from one species to another, one should expect the genetic structure of the modified animal/humans to be changed in physical appearance, sensory modalities, disease propensity, personality, behavior traits, and more as a result of these modifications.

Despite these unknowns, such genetic tinkering as depicted in the movie *Splice* is already taking place in thousands of research laboratories around the world, including the United States, Britain, and Australia, where animal eggs are being used to create hybrid human embryos from which stem-cell lines can be produced for medical research. Not counting synthetic biology, where entirely new forms of life are being brewed, there is no limit to the number of human-animal concoctions currently under development within openly contracted as well as top-secret science facilities. A team at Newcastle and Durham universities in the United Kingdom recently illustrated this when they announced plans to create "hybrid rabbit and human embryos, as well as other 'chimera' embryos mixing human and cow genes." The same researchers more alarmingly have already managed to reanimate tissue "from dead human cells in another breakthrough which was heralded as a way of overcoming ethical dilemmas over using living embryos for medical research."[190] In the United States, similar studies led Irv Weissman, director of Stanford University's Institute of Cancer/Stem Cell Biology and Medicine in California, to create mice with partly human brains, causing some ethicists to raise the issue of "humanized animals" in the future that could become "self-aware" as a result of genetic modification. Even former president of the United States, George W. Bush, in his January 31, 2006, State of the Union address, called for legislation to "prohibit... creating human-animal hybrids, and buying, selling, or patenting human embryos." His words mostly fell on deaf ears, and now "the chimera, or combination of species, is a subject of serious discussion in certain scientific circles," writes senior counsel for the Alliance Defense Fund, Joseph Infranco. "We are well beyond the science fiction of H. G. Wells' tormented hybrids in the *Island of Doctor Moreau*; we are in a time where scientists are seriously contemplating the creation of human-animal hybrids."[191] When describing the benefits of man-with-beast combinations in his online thesis, "Transhumanist Values," Bostrom cites how animals have "sonar, magnetic orientation, or sensors for electricity and vibration," among other extrahuman abilities. He goes on to include how the range of sensory modalities for transhumans would not be limited to those among animals, and that there is "no fundamental block to adding, say, a capacity to see infrared radiation or to perceive radio signals and perhaps to add some kind of telepathic sense by augmenting our brains,"[192] a position verified by the US National Science Foundation and Department of Commerce in the report, *Converging Technologies for Improving Human Performance*.

Bostrom and the US government are correct in that the animal kingdom has levels of perception beyond human. Some animals can "sense" earthquakes and "smell" tumors. Others, like dogs, can hear sounds as high as 40,000 Hz—and dolphins can hear even higher. It is also known that at least some animals see wavelengths beyond normal human capacity. This is where things start getting interesting, perhaps even supernatural, as Bostrom may understand and anticipate. According to the biblical story of Balaam's donkey, certain animals see into the *spirit world*. Contemporary and secular studies likewise indicate animals may at times be reacting to intelligence beyond normal human perception. Will this have peculiar consequences for enhanced humans with animal DNA? Earlier in this book, we described how opening supernatural gateways that exist within the mind can be achieved through altered mental states induced by psychoactive drugs such as DMT and absinthe. Do transhumanists and/or military scientists imagine a more stable pathway or connection with the beyond—the ability to see into other dimensions or the spirit world—as a result of brain enhancement through integrating men with beasts? Do they envision reopening the portions of the mind that some scholars believe were closed off following the fall of man? Late philosopher and scientist Terrance McKenna, originator of "Novelty Theory," speculated that brain enhancement following Technological Singularity might accomplish this very thing—contact with other-dimensional beings. More recently, at Arizona State University (ASU), where the Templeton Foundation has been funding a long series of pro-transhumanist lectures titled "Facing the Challenges of Transhumanism: Religion, Science, Technology,"[193] some of the instructors agree that radical alteration of Homo sapiens could open a door to *unseen intelligence*. Consequently, in 2009, ASU launched another study, this time to explore discovery of—and communication with—"entities." Called the SOPHIA project (after the Greek goddess), the express purpose of this university study is to verify communication "with deceased people, spirit guides, angels, otherworldly entities/extraterrestrials, and/or a Universal Intelligence/God."[194] Imagine what this could mean if government laboratories with unlimited budgets working beyond congressional review were to decode the gene functions that lead animals to have preternatural capabilities of sense, smell, and sight, and then blended them with Homo sapiens. Among other things, something that perhaps DARPA (Defense Advanced Research Projects Agency) has envisioned for years could be created for use against entire populations—genetically engineered "Nephilim agents" that appear to be human but that hypothetically see and even interact with invisible forces. Overnight, the rules for spiritual warfare as well as regular warfare would take on an unprecedented (at least in modern times) dimension.

Enhanced Humans: The New (Nephilim) Arms Race

While the former chairman of the President's Council on Bioethics, Leon Kass, does not elaborate on issues of spiritual warfare, he provided a status report on how real and how imminent the dangers of GRIN technologies could be in the hands of transhumanists. In the introduction to his book, *Life, Liberty and the Defense of Dignity: The Challenges of Bioethics*, Kass warned:

> Human nature itself lies on the operating table, ready for alteration, for eugenic and psychic "enhancement," for wholesale redesign. In leading laboratories, academic and industrial, new creators are confidently amassing their powers and quietly honing their skills, while on the street their evangelists [transhumanists] are zealously prophesying a posthuman future. For anyone who cares about preserving our humanity, the time has come for paying attention.[195]

The warning by Kass of the potential hazards of emerging technologies coupled with transhumanist aspirations is not an overreaction. One law school in the United Kingdom where students are taught crime-scene investigation is already discussing the need to add classes in the future devoted to analyzing crime scenes committed by posthumans. The requirement for such specially trained law enforcement personnel will arise due to part-human, part-animal beings possessing behavior patterns not consistent with present-day profiling or forensics understanding. Add to this other unknowns such as "memory transference" (an entirely new field of study suggesting that complex behavior patterns and even memories can be transferred from donors of large human organs to their recipients), and the potential for tomorrow's human-animal chimera issues multiplies. How would the memories, behavior patterns, and instincts, for instance, of a wolf affect the mind of a human? That such unprecedented questions will have to be dealt with sooner than later has already been illustrated in animal-to-animal experiments, including those conducted by Evan Balaban at McGill University in Montreal, where sections of brain from embryonic quails were transplanted into the brains of chickens, and the resultant chickens exhibited head bobs and vocal trills unique to quail.[196] The implication from this field of study alone proves that complex behavior patterns can be transferred from one species to another, strongly suggesting that transhumans will likely bear unintended behavior and appetite disorders that could literally produce lycanthropes (werewolves) and other nightmarish Nephilim traits.

As troubling as those thoughts are, some in government and science communities believe these dangers could be just the tip of the iceberg. One-on-one, interpersonal malevolence by human-animals might quickly be overshadowed by global acts of swarm violence. The seriousness of this for the conceivable future is significant enough that a recent House Foreign Affairs (HFA) committee chaired by California Democrat Brad Sherman, best known for his expertise on the spread of nuclear weapons and terrorism, is among a number of government panels currently studying the implications of genetic modification and human-transforming technologies related to future terrorism. *Congressional Quarterly* columnist Mark Stencel listened to the HFA committee hearings and wrote in his March 15, 2009, article, "Futurist: Genes without Borders," that the conference "sounded more like a Hollywood pitch for a sci-fi thriller than a sober discussion of scientific reality...with talk of biotech's potential for creating supersoldiers, superintelligence, and superanimals [that could become] agents of unprecedented lethal force."[197] George Annas, Lori Andrews, and Rosario Isasi were even more apocalyptic in their American Journal of Law and Medicine article, "Protecting the Endangered Human: Toward an International Treaty Prohibiting Cloning and Inheritable Alterations," when they wrote:

> The new species, or "posthuman," will likely view the old "normal" humans as inferior, even savages, and fit for slavery or slaughter. The normals, on the other hand, may see the posthumans as a threat and if they can, may engage in a preemptive strike by killing the posthumans before they themselves are killed or enslaved by them. It is ultimately this predictable potential for genocide that makes species-altering experiments potential weapons of mass destruction, and makes the unaccountable genetic engineer a potential bioterrorist.[198]

Observations like those of Annas, Andrews, and Isasi support Prof. Hugo de Garis' nightmarish vision of a near future wherein artilects and posthumans join against "normals" in an incomprehensible war leading to gigadeath. Notwithstanding such warnings, the problem could be unavoidable, as Prof. Gregory Stock, in his well-researched and convincing book, *Redesigning Humans: Our Inevitable Genetic Future,* argues that stopping what we have already started (planned genetic enhancement of humans) is impossible. "We simply cannot find the brakes."[199] Verner Vinge agrees, adding, "Even if all the governments of the world were to understand the 'threat' and be in deadly fear of it, progress toward the goal would continue. In fact, the competitive advantage—economic, military, even artistic—of every advance in automation is so compelling that passing laws, or having customs, that forbid such things merely assures that someone else will get them first."[200] In what the writers of this book found to be a bit unnerving, academic scientists and technical consultants to the US Pentagon have advised the agency that the principal argument by Vinge is correct. As such, the United States could be forced into large-scale species-altering output, including human enhancement for military purposes. This is based on solid military intelligence, which suggests that America's competitors (and potential enemies) are privately seeking to develop the same this century and use it to dominate the US if they can. This worrisome "government think tank" scenario is even shared by the JASONs—the celebrated scientists on the Pentagon's most prestigious scientific advisory panel who now perceive "Mankind 2.0" as the next arms race. Just as the old Soviet Union and the United States with their respective allies competed for supremacy in nuclear arms following the Second World War through the 1980s (what is now commonly known as "the nuclear arms race during the cold war"), the JASONs "are worried about adversaries' ability to exploit advances in Human Performance Modification, and thus create a threat to national security," wrote military analyst Noah Shachtman in "Top Pentagon Scientists Fear Brain-Modified Foes." This recent special for *Wired* magazine was based on a leaked military report in which the JASONs admitted concern over "neuro-pharmaceutical performance enhancement and brain-computer interfaces" technology being developed by other countries ahead of the United States. "The JASONs are recommending that the American military push ahead with its own performance-enhancement research—and monitor foreign studies—to make sure that the US' enemies don't suddenly become smarter, faster, or better able to endure the harsh realities of war than American troops," the article continued. "The JASONs are particularly concerned about [new technologies] that promote 'brain plasticity'—rewiring the mind, essentially, by helping to 'permanently establish new neural pathways, and thus new cognitive capabilities.'"[201] Though it might be tempting to disregard the conclusions by the JASONs as a rush to judgment on the emerging threat of techno-sapiens, it would be a serious mistake to do so. As GRIN technologies continue to race toward an exponential curve, parallel to these advances will be the increasingly sophisticated argument that societies must take control of human biological limitations and move the species—or at least some of its members—into new forms of existence. Prof. Nigel M. de S. Cameron, director for the Council for Biotechnology Policy in Washington, DC, documents this move, concluding that the genie is out of the bottle and that "the federal government's National Nanotechnology Initiative's Web site already gives evidence of this kind of future vision, in which human dignity is undermined by [being transformed into posthumans]."[202] Dr. C. Christopher Hook, a member of the government committee on human genetics who has given testimony before the US Congress, offered similar insight on the state of the situation:

> [The goal of posthumanism] is most evident in the degree to which the U.S. government has formally embraced

transhumanist ideals and is actively supporting the development of transhumanist technologies. The US National Science Foundation, together with the US Department of Commerce, has initiated a major program (NBIC) for converging several technologies (including those from which the acronym is derived—nanotechnology, biotechnologies, information technologies and cognitive technologies, e.g., cybernetics and neurotechnologies) for the express purpose of *enhancing human performance.* The NBIC program director, Mihail Roco, declared at the second public meeting of the project that the expenditure of financial and human capital to pursue the needs of *reengineering humanity* by the US government will be second in equivalent value only to the moon landing program.[203]

The presentation by Mihail Roco to which Dr. Hook refers is contained in the 482-page report, *Converging Technologies for Improving Human Performance,* commissioned by the US National Science Foundation and Department of Commerce. Among other things, the report discusses planned applications of human enhancement technologies in the military (and in rationalization of the human-machine interface in industrial settings) wherein DARPA is devising "Nano, Bio, Info, and Cogno" scenarios "focused on enhancing human performance." The plan echoes a Mephistophelian bargain (a deal with the devil) in which "a golden age" merges technological and human cognition into "a single, distributed and interconnected brain."[204] Just visiting the US Army Research Laboratory's Web site is dizzying in this regard, with its cascading pages of super-soldier technology categories including molecular genetics and genomics; biochemistry, microbiology and biodegradation; and neurophysiology and cognitive neurosciences. If writers like us can so easily discover these facts on the Web, just imagine what is happening in Special Access Programs (SAPs) where, according to the Senate's own Commission on Protecting and Reducing Government Secrecy, there are hundreds of "waived SAPs"—the blackest of black programs—functioning at any given time beyond congressional oversight. Because of this and given the seriousness of weaponized biology and human enhancement technology blossoming so quickly, on May 24, 2010, a wide range of experts from the military, the private sector, and academia gathered in Washington, DC for an important conference titled "Warring Futures: A Future Tense Event: How Biotech and Robotics are Transforming Today's Military—and How That Will Change the Rest of Us." Participants explored how human enhancement and related technologies are unfolding as an emerging battlefield strategy that will inevitably migrate to the broader culture, and what that means for the future of humanity. As the conference Web site noted:

> New technologies are changing warfare as profoundly as did gunpowder. How are everything from flying robots as small as birds to "peak warrior performance" biology [human enhancement] altering the nature of the military as an institution, as well as the ethics and strategy of combat? How will the adoption of emerging technologies by our forces or others affect our understanding of asymmetrical conflict? New technologies are always embraced wherever there is the greatest competition for advantage, but quickly move out to the rest of us not engaged in sport or warfare.[205]

The impressive list of speakers at the DC conference included Vice Admiral Joseph W. Dyer (US Navy, retired), president of the

Government and Industrial Robots Division at iRobot; Major General Robert E. Schmidle Jr., United States Marine Corps lead for the 2010 Quadrennial Defense Review; Robert Wright, author of *The Evolution of God* and a Global Governance Fellow; P. W. Singer, Senior Fellow and director of the Twenty-First Century Defense Initiative at the Brookings Institution; Stephen Tillery from the Harrington Department of Bioengineering at Arizona State University; and Jon Mogford, acting deputy director of the Defense Sciences Office at DARPA.

Having taken the lead in human-enhancement studies as a US military objective decades ago, DARPA saw the writing on the wall and in scenes reminiscent of Saruman the wizard creating monstrous Uruk-Hai to wage unending, merciless war (from J. R. R. Tolkein's *Lord of the Rings*), began investing billions of American tax dollars into the Pentagon's Frankensteinian dream of "super-soldiers" and "extended performance war fighter" programs. Not only has this research led to diagrams of soldiers "with hormonal, neurological, and genetic concoctions; implanting microchips and electrodes in their bodies to control their internal organs and brain functions; and plying them with drugs that deaden some of their normal human tendencies: the need for sleep, the fear of death, [and] the reluctance to kill their fellow human beings," but as Chris Floyd, in an article for *CounterPunch* a while back, continued, "some of the research now underway involves actually altering the genetic code of soldiers, modifying bits of DNA to fashion a new type of human specimen, one that functions like a machine, killing tirelessly for days and nights on end...mutations [that] will 'revolutionize the contemporary order of battle' and guarantee 'operational dominance across the whole range of potential US military employments.'"[206]

Related to these developments and unknown to most Americans

was a series of hushed events following the sacking of Admiral John Poindexter (who served as the director of the DARPA Information Awareness Office from 2002 to 2003) during a series of flaps, which resulted in public interest into the goings-on at the agency and brief discovery of DARPA's advanced human enhancement research. When the ensuing political pressure led the Senate Appropriations Committee to take a deeper look into just how money was flowing through DARPA, the staffers were shocked to find "time-reversal methods" in the special focus area, and unstoppable super-soldiers— enhanced warriors with extra-human physical, physiological, and cognitive abilities that even allowed for "communication by thought alone" on the drawing board. Prof. Joel Garreau, investigative journalist, provides a summary of what happened next:

> The staffers went down the list of DARPA's projects, found the ones with titles that sounded frighteningly as though they involved the creation of a master race of superhumans, and zeroed out their budgets from the defense appropriations bill. There is scant evidence they knew much, if anything, about these projects. But we will probably never know the details, because significant people are determined that the whole affair be forever shrouded in mystery. The levels of secrecy were remarkable even for DARPA; they were astounding by the standards of the notoriously leaky Senate. Even insiders said it was hard to get a feel for what the facts really were. It took months of reporting and questioning, poking, and prodding even to get a formal "no comment" either from the leadership of the Senate Appropriations Committee or from Anthony J. Tether, the director of DARPA.
>
> A careful study of DARPA's programs a year later, how-

ever, showed little change. Considerable creative budgetary maneuvering ensued. The peas of quite a few programs now reside under new, and much better camouflaged, shells. "They're saying, 'Okay, this is the second strike. Do we have to go three strikes?'" one manager said. "It doesn't stop anything. We'll be smarter about how we position things." Meanwhile, he said, new human enhancement programs are in the pipeline, "as bold or bolder" than the ones that preceded them.[207]

Recent hints at DARPA's "bold or bolder" investment in human enhancement as part of an emerging arms race is reflected in two of its newest projects (launched July 2010), titled "Biochronicity and Temporal Mechanisms Arising in Nature" and "Robustness of Biologically-Inspired Networks," in which the express intention of transforming "biology from a descriptive to a predictive field of science" in order to boost "biological design principles" in troop performance is made.[208] DARPA's Department of Defense Fiscal Year 2011 President's Budget also includes funding for science that will lead to "editing a soldier's DNA"[209] while more exotically providing millions of dollars for the creation of "BioDesign," a mysterious artificial life project with military applications in which DARPA plans to eliminate the randomness of natural evolution "by advanced genetic engineering and molecular biology technologies," the budget report states. The language in this section of the document actually speaks of eliminating "cell death" through creation of "a new generation of regenerative cells that could ultimately be programmed to live indefinitely." In other words, whatever this synthetic life application is (*Wired* magazine described it as "living, breathing creatures"), the plan is to make *it* immortal.[210] To this end, the authors of this book believe the "it" that man may soon uncover through its species-barrier-crossing technologies dates back to ancient times, and that the science of human enhancement and transhumanism is unwittingly playing into the hands of powerful supernaturalism toward a Luciferian endgame—something "it" tried once before, and which "it" was prophesied to attempt again just before the end of time.

From Jurassic Park to the Tomb of Apollo/Osiris/Nimrod

Could the same technology described above or some variation lead to the resurrection of the pagan deity Apollo/Osiris/Nimrod, who returns to rule the *novus order seclorum*? Is material from the deity's "body" concealed in a tomb at Giza…or in Washington, DC…or in the "sacred casket" that former US Vice President Henry Wallace mentioned in his letter to Nicholas Roerich, considered in esoteric circles to be the same as the casket or "coffin" of Osiris? If so, is it conceivable that plans to revive the Apollonian tissue using biotechnology have already been made—or worse, have already been accomplished and the pagan god waits the moment of its unveiling?

People not familiar with biblical eschatology may find this idea fantastic, that the being who becomes the Antichrist was once alive, then was dead, and returns from the grave to rule the *novus ordo seclorum*. But this is exactly what Revelation 17:8 appears to say will happen: "The beast that thou sawest was, and is not; and shall ascend out of the bottomless pit, and go into perdition [*Apoleia*, Apollo]: and they that dwell on the earth shall wonder…when they behold the beast that was, and is not, and yet is."

Further, the mythos of the Eye of Horus on the Great Seal, which so fascinated Wallace and company, represents this very concept of deity incarnation into the "king" that is to rule. As mentioned in chapter seven of this book, in ancient Egypt where this Great Seal symbol originated, each Pharaoh "became" the incarnation of the falcon god Horus during his lifetime, and at death, the Osiris—the divine judge of the netherworld.

As biotechnology and synthetic biology advance to the degree that we can now realistically anticipate reviving long-dead species, I have been able to convince a few scholarly minds that the man of sin could in fact be the return of a deceased Apollo/Osiris/Nimrod who arrives via biotech resurrection. Even Chuck Missler, though not with the same details, raised the appropriate question not long ago in an online article about the Antichrist. He asked, "Could it be that this final world dictator will be, in some sense, a return of Nimrod?"[211] In my opinion, this is more than a possibility, and I remember with curiosity how in 1998, Zahi Hawass, the current secretary general of Egypt's Supreme Council of Antiquities, claimed to have found the burial tomb of the god Osiris (Apollo/Nimrod) at the Giza Plateau. In the article, "Sandpit of Royalty," from the newspaper *Extra Bladet* (Copenhagen), January 31, 1999, Hawass was quoted saying:

> I have found a shaft, going twenty-nine meters vertically down into the ground, exactly halfway between the Chefren Pyramid and the Sphinx. At the bottom, which was filled with water, we have found a burial chamber with four pillars. In the middle is a large granite sarcophagus, which I expect to be the grave of Osiris, the god.... I have been digging in Egypt's sand for more than thirty years, and up to date this is the most exciting discovery I have made.... We found the shaft in November and began pumping up the water recently. So several years will pass before we have finished investigating the find.[212]

As far as we know, this discovery did not ultimately provide the physical remains of the deity. Of course, that is *as far as we know*. But what it did illustrate is that at least some very powerful Egyptologists believe Osiris was a historical figure, and that his body was stored somewhere at or near the Great Pyramid. Manly P. Hall, who knew the Masonic legend of Hiram Abiff was a thinly veiled prophecy of the resurrection of Osiris, may have understood what Zahi Hawass was looking for, and why. Consider that he wrote in *The Secret Teachings of All Ages*:

> The Dying God shall rise again! The secret room in the House of the Hidden Places shall be rediscovered. The Pyramid again shall stand as the ideal emblem of solidarity, inspiration, aspiration, resurrection, and regeneration.[213]

Over the years, biblical scholar Gary Stearman has written extensively about Nimrod (Apollo/Osiris/Gilgamesh) and the connection this historical figure has with Babylonian Mystery Religion, Watchers, Nephilim (including their resurrection), the spirit of the end-times Antichrist, and revival of paganism. It appears he, too, believes the coming of Antichrist represents a return of Nimrod. "But who is this Assyrian[?]" he asked in the July 2001 *Prophecy in the News Magazine*. "He is none other than the spiritual inheritor of the first great post-Flood religious apostasy. He is the keeper of the great heritage that began at the Assyrian capital, Nineveh. Its founder was Nimrod.... He is the Antichrist, the future despot who comes in the name of the ancient mystery religion."

A year earlier, in June of 2000, Stearman had written in *Prophecy in the News* concerning Nimrod:

He was a rebel who allowed himself to be worshipped as a god. After the Flood, his rebellion became the foundation of mankind's greatest religious apostasy. Down through the generations, this system of false worship became known simply as the "Babylonian Mystery Religion." Its basis is quite clear. *It attempts to channel the power of the ancient gods through the figure of one, powerful man. Nimrod became that god.* (emphasis added)

Alexander Hislop, in his classic text, *The Two Babylons*, substantiates Stearman's thesis that the Babylonian Mystery Religion was based on the worship of Nimrod. "It was to glorify Nimrod that the whole Chaldean system of iniquity was formed," he wrote.[214] Yet Stearman sees that the Mystery Religion continued secretly through the ages, shrouded in hiding by adepts of the occult in anticipation of a final moment when the ancient spirit should be awakened:

Corrupt priesthoods have flourished, carrying with them the shadow of Nimrod and his ancient mysteries. Their inner secrets have been known by various names, including alchemy, magic, sorcery, conjuring, soothsaying and so forth.... waiting for the prophesied day when it would rise once again. This movement will result in the reign of the Antichrist.

In addition to the supernatural aspects biotechnology could provide the luciferian technology to resurrect the Nimrod/Apollo/Osiris character in the person of the last-days Man of Sin, the ramifications of using the same science to revive extinct animals or Nephilim, or to create newly engineered versions of demigods and mythological animals, may also play a key role in the kingdom of Antichrist. This is because as interbreeding begins between transgenic animals, genetically modified humans, and species as God made them, the altered DNA will quickly migrate into the natural environment, and when that happens (as is already occurring among genetically modified plants and animals), "alien" and/or animal characteristics will be introduced to the human gene pool and spread through intermarriage, altering the human genetic code and eventually eliminating humanity as we know it. This is what happened before the Great Flood, according to many theologians, and perhaps that has been the whole idea for the end times as well—to create a generation of genetically altered "Nimrods" to serve as "fit extensions" for the resurrection of underworld Nephilim-hordes in preparation of Armageddon.

Does a curious verse in the book of Daniel hint at this? Speaking of the last days of human government, Daniel said:

> They shall mingle themselves with the seed of men: but they shall not cleave one to another, even as iron is not mixed with clay. (Daniel 2:43)

While Daniel does not explain who "they" that "mingle themselves with the seed of men" are, the personal pronoun "they" caused Chuck Missler and Mark Eastman, in their book, *Alien Encounters*, to ask: "Just what (or who) are 'mingling with the seed of men?' Who are these Non-seed? It staggers the mind to contemplate the potential significance of Daniel's passage and its implications for the future global governance."[215]

Daniel's verse troubled Missler and Eastman because it seemed to indicate that the same phenomenon that occurred in Genesis chapter 6, where non-human species or "non-seed" mingled with human seed and produced Nephilim, would happen again in the end times. When this verse from Daniel is coupled with Genesis 3:15, which says, "And I will put enmity between thee and the woman, and between thy *seed* [*zera*, meaning "offspring," "descendents," or "children"] and her *seed*," an incredible tenet emerges—that Satan has seed, and that it is at enmity with Christ.

To "mingle" non-human seed with Homo sapiens through altering human DNA while simultaneously returning Nephilim to earth has been the inspiration of the spirit of antichrist ever since God halted the practice during the Great Flood. According to Louis Pauwells and Jacques Bergier in *The Dawn of Magic*, this was certainly the goal of the antichrist Adolf Hitler:

> Hitler's aim was neither the founding of a race of supermen, nor the conquest of the world; these were only means towards the realization of the great work he dreamed of. His real aim was to perform an act of creation, a divine operation, the goal of a biological mutation which would result in an unprecedented exaltation of the human race and the "apparition of a new race of heroes and demigods and god-men."[216]

One cannot read the conclusion by Pauwells and Bergier regarding Hitler's antichrist ambition without seeing how it corresponds perfectly with the Cumaean Sibyl's prophecy pertaining to the coming of Apollo, who receives "the life of gods, and sees Heroes with gods commingling." This calls to mind that from the Middle Ages forward, church leaders have believed the Antichrist would ultimately represent the return of the Nephilim—the reunion of demons with humans. St. Augustine himself wrote of such demoniality in the *City of God*,[217] and in the *De Daemonialitate, et Incubis, et Succubi,* Fr. Ludovicus Maria Sinistrari de Ameno (1622–1701) also perceived the coming of Antichrist as representing the biological hybridization of demons with humans. "To theologians and philosophers," he wrote, "it is a fact, that from the copulation of humans with the demon…Antichrist must be born."[218]

The English theologian George Hawkins Pember also agreed with this premise, and in his 1876 masterpiece, *Earth's Earliest Ages,* he analyzed the prophecy of Christ that says the end times would be a repeat of "the days of Noah." Pember outlined the seven great causes of the antediluvian destruction and documented their developmental beginnings in his lifetime. The seventh and most fearful sign, Pember wrote, would be the return of the Nephilim, "The appearance upon earth of beings from the Principality of the Air, and their unlawful intercourse with the human race."

Consequently, if the Antichrist is the reincarnation of the demon Apollo as prophesied by the apostle Paul, not only will he be the exact opposite of Jesus (Son of God), but the forerunner of the return of the Nephilim. The prophet Isaiah (chapters 13 and 14) likewise spoke of the return of these beings, and tied the advent to the destruction of the city of Babylon in the final age. The following verse should give us pause in light of the ongoing presence of US armed forces in Iraq/Babylon and the powder keg surrounding it. From the Septuagint, we read:

> The vision which Esaias son of Amos saw against Babylon. Lift up a standard on the mountain of the plain, exalt the voice to them, beckon with the hand, open the gates, ye ruler. I give command and I bring them: giants are coming to fulfill my wrath.… For behold! The day of the Lord

is coming which cannot be escaped, a day of wrath and anger, to make the world desolate.... And Babylon…shall be as when God overthrew Sodom and Gomorrah.... It shall never be inhabited…and monsters shall rest there, and devils shall dance there and satyrs shall dwell there. (Isaiah 13:1–3, 9, 19–22)

One can only speculate if something more than is casually perceived is meant by Isaiah when he says, "open the gates, ye ruler," but whoever this ruler is, he opens "gates" in Iraq/Babylon through which end-times giants (gibborim) return to the surface of earth as agents of God's wrath. Noting that Isaiah ties the destruction of Iraq/Babylon with the reappearance of gibborim in this way, we recall how thousands of US troops on invading Iraq during the Bush administration admittedly filled US containers with archaeological materials, including what some have speculated to be cuneiform tablets pointing to the location of pure-blooded Nephilim buried in underground caves. This is exactly where Enoch said the antediluvian Nephilim are, and it raises fascinating questions: Would agencies like DARPA have interest in studying or cloning the extinct beings if they were, or have been, found? Could man in his arrogance revive ancient DNA, revitalizing or blending it with other living organisms in a way similar to what the Watchers did in making the first Nephilim? Is this how the rephaim (dead Nephilim) who are viewed as squirming beneath the surface of the earth arise to challenge the armies of God during Armageddon? Is the factual reappearance on earth of legendary beings verified by Isaiah, who foresaw creatures such as *satyrs* (transgenic half-men, half-goats) accompanying the return of giants in the end times, or why other apocryphal books like 2 Esdras 5:8 prophesy the birth of "monsters" for the same period of time? Some may be shocked to learn that in addition to the citations above, the Bible actually describes an end-times confrontation between the "mythological gods" and Christ. "The Lord will be terrible unto them: for he will famish all the gods of the earth" says Zephaniah 2:11. "The Lord of hosts, the God of Israel, saith; Behold, I will punish the...gods" (Jeremiah 46:25). Human followers of the pagan deities will also join the conflict, calling upon their "idols of gold, and silver, and brass, and stone, and of wood" (Revelation 9:20) to convene their powers against the Christian God, uniting with "unclean spirits like frogs...the spirits of devils working miracles, which go forth unto the kings of the earth...to gather them to the battle of that great day...[to] a place called in the Hebrew tongue Armageddon [Megiddo]" (Revelation 16:13–14, 16).

Given that the prophets foretold a day when mythical characters and "gods" would return to earth to conduct war against the God of the Bible, it is more than a little disturbing that man has, for the first time since before the Great Flood, intentionally set course to repeat what ancient records say the Watchers did. The accelerated pace by scientific exploration against God's divine order, and the subsequent revival of Watcher technology leading to transhuman or revived forms of Nephilim, has without doubt pushed the end-times clock closer to midnight than most comprehend.

Enoch's Seventy Generations:
Is that the Ground I Feel Rumbling?

Enoch was the son of Jared, father of Methuselah, and great-grandfather of Noah whose writings provide the most detailed account of the fall of the Watchers, the angels who fathered the infamous Nephilim. While the book of Enoch is no longer included in most versions of the Bible, Enoch's writings are quoted in the New Testament in at least two places, and he is mentioned by name in both the Old and New Testaments, including Jude 14–15, where one of his prophecies is cited. During the discovery of the Dead Sea Scrolls, pre-Maccabean fragments of the book of Enoch were found, helping scholars verify the book's antiquity while also illustrating that the ancients held these texts to be inspired. Many early church fathers likewise considered the book of Enoch to be sacred, including Tertullian, Justin Martyr, Irenaeus, Origen, and Clement of Alexandria. This is an important fact because if Enoch was truly a prophet, then the world may be in for an unfathomable surprise concerning the return of Nephilim, and soon.

The tenth chapter of the book of Enoch says the Watchers who were judged during the Flood would be bound beneath the hills of the earth for seventy generations, until the day of their final judgment, when they will be released from those confines and thrown into an abyss of fire, "to the torment and the prison in which they shall be confined for ever."

But in the fifteenth chapter, Enoch writes about the deceased offspring of the Watchers, the giants, or Nephilim, and describes them as being released at the same time to bring slaughter and destruction upon man: "The spirits of the giants…shall be concealed, and shall not rise up against the sons of men, and against women; until they come forth during the days of slaughter and destruction" (Enoch 15:9–10).

This particular prophecy mirrors those of Isaiah and other apocryphal works, which indicate a future date in which Watchers will rise for judgment while their giant offspring resurrect "from beneath the hills of the earth" to wreak havoc upon earth. According to Enoch, this unparalleled event is scheduled to occur after seventy generations have passed from the time of the Flood.

This could be troubling.

Although traditional scholarship places the time of the Great Flood between 2500 and 2300 BC, modern dating by some researchers has roughly estimated the Flood to have actually transpired between 2900 and 2800 BC. For instance, this is the dating given by a group of scientists from the USA, Russia, Australia, France, and Ireland, known as the Holocene Impact Working Group, who hypothesizes the Great Flood resulted from a comet striking the Indian Ocean between 2800–2900 BC, resulting in a mega-tsunami. Because a prophetic generation is seventy years based on Psalm 90:10 ("The days of our *years* are threescore *years* and ten"), Enoch's seventy generations times seventy years equals exactly 4,900 years forward from the Flood. If the Flood took place between 2800 and 2900 BC, this brings the return of the Nephilim to the immediate hour. In other words, if this 2800 to 2900 BC dating is correct, mankind is on the threshold of Watchers being raised from their underground prisons and thrown into an abyss of fire, while their giant offspring return to the surface of earth in violent fulfillment of multiple prophecies.

We have no idea whether the modern time frame for the Great Flood is reasonable, but the book of *Jubilees*—another apocryphal text—seems to verify this frightening scenario, prophesying Nephilim on earth in the last days. Again, the familiar word "corruption" turns up in association with these beings, insinuating an end-times repeat of what the Watchers did by corrupting human DNA and blending it with animals to retrofit human bodies for Nephilim incarnation. Note that this happens just before Satan is judged:

> The malignant evil ones [spirits of Nephilim destroyed in the flood] were bound in the place of condemnation, but a tenth part of them were left that they might be subject before Satan on the earth. These are for corruption [corrup-

tion of DNA as in days of old?] and leading astray men before Satan's judgment. (Jubilees 10:7–12)

Finally, a prophecy in the second chapter of the book of Joel could refer to the same end-times volcano of resurrected Nephilim. While some expositors say Joel was probably describing an army of locusts, with phrases like "[They are] a great people and a strong" and "they shall run like *mighty men* [gibborim]," it is hard to believe these verses are talking about grasshoppers.

> [They are] a great people and a strong; there hath not been ever the like, neither shall be any more after it…and nothing shall escape them. The appearance of them is as the appearance of horses; and as horsemen, so shall they run…. They shall run like mighty men [gibbowr, gibborim]; they shall climb the wall like men of war…. They shall run to and fro in the city; they shall run upon the wall, they shall climb up upon the houses; they shall enter in at the windows like a thief. The earth shall quake before them…. And the LORD shall utter his voice before his army: for his camp is very great: for he is strong that executeth his word: for the day of the LORD is great and very terrible; and who can abide it? (Joel 2:2–11)

When the numerous ancient texts, from inerrant Scriptures to extra-biblical sources, are added up, there is persuasive evidence that Joel's army could indeed be more than simple grasshoppers, and that this massive gibborim army that runs upon the wall from which nobody can escape could be the result of man's willingness to play "god" in reviving forbidden science and opening "gates" to what lurks beyond.

Chapter 10

OTHER USEFUL BIOTECH TOOLS FOR ANTICHRIST

By responsible use of science, technology, and other rational means we shall eventually manage to become posthuman.
—Professor Nick Bostrom

We can devise ways of at least trying to manage the enormous powers of nanotechnology, but superintelligence by its nature cannot be controlled. The nano/robotic revolution will force us to reconsider the very definition of human. —Ray Kurzweil

The spirit one discerns in pondering the ruminations of the Transhumanists causes one to conclude that what these thinkers propose is developmental progressing towards something along the lines of the Borg from Star Trek or the Cybermen or Darleks from Doctor Who. —Frederick B. Meekins

Not long ago, a writer for *Wired* magazine named Elizabeth Svoboda contacted me (Tom) to let me know she was writing an article about "research advances using transgenic animals to produce pharmaceutical compounds." She had come across an editorial by me raising caution about this kind of experimentation and wondered if I might be willing to provide points for her article, elaborating in areas where I saw producing transgenic human-animals as potentially harmful. She stated that most of the scientists she planned to quote were "pretty gung-ho about the practice," and said she thought it would be important to provide some balance. I thanked her for the invitation and sent a short summary of some, though not all, of the areas where concerns about this science could be raised.

When the article was finally published by *Wired*, I was surprised that none of my notes had made it into the story. I contacted Elizabeth and asked why, and she replied that they had originally been included in her article, "Pharm Animals Crank Out Drugs," but in order to create a positive spin on the story, the editors had censored my cautionary notes during the editing process. Elizabeth apologized and said she hoped the experience had not soured me on dealing with the magazine.

"It doesn't sour me," I assured her. "I just think the reporting by most agencies is lopsided and missing the opportunity to thoroughly engage such an important issue." The fact was, *Wired* magazine deprived the public of balanced treatment on an important subject and concluded instead with a scientist by the name of Marie Cecile Van de Lavoir saying that potential human health benefits from transgenic research "justify tinkering" with nature's plan. "If a transgenic animal produces a great cancer therapy," she said, "I won't hear anyone saying, 'You shouldn't do that.'" Van de Lavoir's comments were undoubtedly in response to some of my observations before they were pulled, because in offering caution, I had specifically used the phrase "tinkering with nature's plan." Van de Lavoir's short-sighted approach, like too many bioethicists engaged in the current debate, is as scary as the science, in our opinion. We wanted to contact her to suggest that she watch the film *I Am Legend* starring Will Smith, which opens appropriately enough with a scientist announcing the cure to cancer using a genetically engineered vaccine that blends animal and human genetics. If you've seen the film, you know the "cure" results in a human form of rabies that wipes out most life on earth—a real possibility, given the scenario.

Because any attempt at covering each potential GRIN-tech, catastrophic, *I-Am-Legend* possibility in this book would be impractical, we summarize below a few of the most important areas in which conservatives, bioethicists, regulators, and especially Christians could become informed and involved in the public dialogue over the potential benefits and threats represented by these emerging fields of science.

Genetically Modified Food

Besides potential problems with transgenic animals, we have cited laboratory results in the past that were first reported by Dr. Árpád Pusztai, repeat verified by scientist Irina Ermakova, and later substantiated by the *International Journal of Biological Sciences* that showed genetically modified (GM) food had surprisingly ill effects on the health of test rats, including the deterioration of every animal organ, atrophied livers, altered cells, testicular damage, altered sperm counts, shortened life spans, and cancer development. The laboratory findings led to the biotech industry suppressing the data and an eight-year court battle with monster corporations that did not want these results made public. Over the last year, the silenced information has been in the news again as Greenpeace activists published evidence from the Russian trials verifying the ramifications of the negative health issues related to genetically modified foods. The wider ramifications from these and similar controlled experiments suggest that as current technology inserts pesticides, insect genes, animal DNA, and other modified organisms directly into crops, the threat of hybrid viruses, prion contamination and new disease strains—which man can neither anticipate or prepare for—may arise. The prospects of this having an impact on mammalian health is almost certain to be a "when," not "if," concern, because, as Momma always said, "you are what you eat," and the fact that the food you consumed this week most likely contained genetically modified ingredients is a current reality. For example, a large portion of the soybean, corn, cottonseed, and canola in today's human food supply and sold in most developed countries including the United States now has genes spliced in from foreign species—including bacteria and viruses—in its genetic makeup. These genetically modified organisms (GMOs) have not only been linked to sickness, sterility, allergies, and even death among animals, but the Institute for Responsible Technology (IRT) documents how the functioning genetically modified genes from these foods linger inside the human body, which could be future-catastrophic. "The only published human feeding experiment verified that genetic material inserted into GM soy transfers into the DNA of intestinal bacteria and continues to function," IRT published. "This means that long after we stop eating GM foods, we may still have their GM proteins produced continuously inside us."[219]

Among other things, IRT says this means that: 1) If the antibiotic gene inserted into most GM crops were to transfer, it could create super diseases resistant to antibiotics; 2) If the gene that creates Bt toxin in GM corn were to transfer, it might turn our intestinal flora into living pesticide factories; and 3) Animal studies show that DNA in food can travel into organs throughout the body, even into the fetus. Add to this the growing secrecy over the use of nanoparticles (eighty-four food-related uses are already on the market and in numerous consumer products such as sunscreens and cosmetics), which as a result of their size behave fundamentally different than other particles, and the possibility of health-related complications increases exponentially. Due to the large corporations (that stand to make billions of dollars from these products) having co-opted the FDA into not requiring food labeling or package warnings on GMO foods and health products, you and I are now the biggest lab rats of all time in a "wait-and-see" experiment that will, feasibly within the decade, illustrate whether Pusztai and Ermakova's rodent findings apply to us and our children.

Synthetic Biology

Synthetic biology is one of the newest areas of biological research that seeks to design new forms of life and biological functions not found in nature. The concept began emerging in 1974, when Polish geneticist Waclaw Szybalski speculated about how scientists and engineers would soon enter "the synthetic biology phase of research in our field. We will then devise new control elements and add these new modules to the existing genomes or build up wholly new genomes. This would be a field with the unlimited expansion [of] building new 'synthetic' organisms, like a 'new better mouse.'"[222] Following Szybalski's speculation, the field of synthetic biology reached its first major milestone in 2010 with the announcement that researchers at the J. Craig Venter Institute (JCVI) had created an entirely new form of life nicknamed "Synthia" by inserting artificial genetic material, which had been chemically synthesized, into cells that were then able to grow. The JCVI Web site explains:

> Genomic science has greatly enhanced our understanding of the biological world. It is enabling researchers to "read" the genetic code of organisms from all branches of life by

sequencing the four letters that make up DNA. Sequencing genomes has now become routine, giving rise to thousands of genomes in the public databases. In essence, scientists are digitizing biology by converting the A, C, T, and G's of the chemical makeup of DNA into 1's and 0's in a computer. But can one reverse the process and start with 1's and 0's in a computer to define the characteristics of a living cell? We set out to answer this question [and] now, this scientific team headed by Drs. Craig Venter, Hamilton Smith, and Clyde Hutchison have achieved the final step in their quest to create the first synthetic genome [which] has been "booted up" in a cell to create the first cell controlled completely by a synthetic genome.[221]

The JCVI site goes on to explain how the ability to routinely write the software of life will usher in a new era in science, and with it, unnatural "living" products like Szybalski's "new better mouse." Better mice, dogs, horses, cows, or humans that grow from this science will be unlike any of the versions God made. In fact, researchers at the University of Copenhagen may look at what Venter has accomplished as amateur hour compared to their posthuman plans. They're working on a third Peptide Nucleic Acid (PNA) strand—a synthetic hybrid of protein and DNA—to upgrade humanity's two existing DNA strands from double helix to triple. In so doing, these scientists "dream of synthesizing life that is utterly alien to this world—both to better understand the minimum components required for life (as part of the quest to uncover the essence of life and how life originated on earth) and, frankly, to see if they can do it. That is, they hope to put together a novel combination of molecules that can self-organize, metabolize (make use of an energy source), grow, reproduce and evolve."[222] Our good friend Gary Stearman of *Proph-*

ecy in the News and other biblical scholars are raising red flags over Synthia technology, warning that any biotech life application leading to modification of the human genotype for "improved" humans will be an inconceivable affront to God and could result in divine repercussions.

Patenting New Life-Forms

Questions are evolving now over "patenting" of transgenic seeds, animals, plants, and synthetic life-forms by large corporations, which at a minimum has already begun to impact the economy of rural workers and farmers through such products as Monsanto's "terminator" seeds. Patenting of human genes will escalate these issues, as best-selling author Michael Crichton pointed out a while back in a piece for the *New York Times* titled, "Gene Patents Aren't Benign and Never Will Be," in which he claimed that people could die in the future from not being able to afford medical treatment as a result of medicines owned by patent holders of specific genes related to the genetic makeup of those persons. Former special counsel for President Richard Nixon, Charles Colson, added, "The patenting of genes and other human tissue has already begun to turn human nature into property. The misuse of genetic information will enable insurers and employers to exercise the ultimate form of discrimination. Meanwhile, advances in nanotechnology and cybernetics threaten to 'enhance' and one day perhaps rival or replace human nature itself—in what some thinkers are already calling 'transhumanism.'"[223]

Animal Rights

Animal-rights activists have raised similar questions having to do with the ethics of altering animals in ways that could be demeaning to them—for instance, creating zombielike creatures that grow in feeder labs and gaze off into space from birth until death. Militarized animals that behave in unnatural, unpredictable ways. Humanized animals that become "self-aware," or animals that produce human sperm and eggs, which then are used for in vitro fertilization to produce a human child. Who would the parents be? A pair of mice?

Human Cloning

The prospect of human cloning was raised in the nineties immediately after the creation of the much-celebrated "Dolly," a female domestic sheep clone. Dolly was the first mammal to be cloned using "somatic cell nuclear transfer," which involves removing the DNA from an unfertilized egg and replacing the nucleus of it with the DNA that is to be cloned. Today, a version of this science is common practice in genetics engineering labs worldwide, where "therapeutic cloning" of human and human-animal embryos is employed for stem-cell harvesting (the stem cells, in turn, are used to generate virtually any type of specialized cell in the human body). This type of cloning was in the news during the writing of this book when it emerged from William J. Clinton Presidential Center documents that the newest member of the Supreme Court, Elena Kagan, had opposed during the Clinton White House any effort by Congress to prevent humans from being cloned specifically for experimental purposes, then killed. A second form of human cloning is called "reproductive cloning" and is the technology that could be used to create a person who is genetically identical with a current or previously existing human. While Dolly was created by this type of cloning technology, the American Medical Association and the American Association for the Advancement of Science have raised caution on using this approach to create human clones, at least at this stage. Government bodies including the US Congress have considered legislation to ban mature human cloning, and though a few states have implemented restrictions, contrary to public perception and except where institutions receive federal funding, no federal laws exist at this time in the United States to prohibit the cloning of humans. The United Nations, the European Union, and Australia likewise considered and failed to approve a comprehensive ban on human cloning technology, leaving the door open to perfect the science should society, government, or the military come to believe that duplicate or replacement humans hold intrinsic value.

Redefining Humans and Human Rights

Where biotechnology is ultimately headed includes not only redefining what it means to be human, but redefining subsequent human rights as well. For instance, Dr. James Hughes wants transgenic chimps and great apes uplifted genetically so that they achieve "personhood." The underlying goal behind this theory would be to establish that basic cognitive aptitude should equal "personhood" and that this "cognitive standard" and not "human-ness" should be the key to constitutional protections and privileges. Among other things, this would lead to nonhuman "persons" and "nonperson" humans, unhinging the existing argument behind intrinsic sanctity of human life and paving the way for such things as harvesting organs from people like Terry Schiavo whenever the loss of cognitive ability equals the dispossession of "personhood." These would be the first victims of transhumanism, according to Prof. Francis Fukuyama, concerning who does or does not qualify as fully human and is thus represented by the founding concept that "all men are created equal." Most would argue that *any* human fits this bill, but women and blacks were not included in these rights in 1776 when Thomas Jefferson wrote the Declaration of Independence. So who is to say what protections can be automatically assumed in an age when human biology is altered and when personhood theory challenges what bioethicists like Wesley J. Smith champion as "human exceptionalism": the idea that human beings carry special moral status in nature and special rights, such as the right to life, plus unique responsibilities, such as stewardship of the environment. Some, but not all, believers in human exceptionalism arrive at this concept from a biblical worldview based on Genesis 1:26, which says, "And God said, 'Let us make man in our image, after our likeness: and let them have dominion over the fish of the sea, and over the fowl of the air, and over the cattle, and over all the earth, and over every creeping thing that creepeth upon the earth.'"

Nanotechnology and Cybernetics

As discussed in the previous chapter, technology to merge human brains with machines is progressing at a fantastic rate. Nanotechnology—the science of engineering materials or devices on an atomic and molecular scale between 1 to 100 nanometers (a nanometer is one billionth of a meter) in size—is poised to take the development between brain-machine interfaces and cybernetic devices to a whole new adaptive level for human modification. This will happen because, as Dr. C. Christopher Hook points out:

> Engineering or manipulating matter and life at nanometer scale [foresees] that the structures of our bodies and our current tools could be significantly altered. In recent years, many

governments around the world, including the United States with its National Nanotechnology Initiative, and scores of academic centers and corporations have committed increasing support for developing nanotechnology programs. The military, which has a significant interest in nanotechnology, has created the Center for Soldier Nanotechnologies (CSN) [which is] interested in the use of such technology to help create the seamless interface of electronic devices with the human nervous system, engineering the cyborg soldier.[224]

Transhuman Eugenics

In the early part of the twentieth century, the study and practice of selective human breeding known as *eugenics* sought to counter dysgenic aspects within the human gene pool and to improve overall human "genetic qualities." Researchers in the United States, Britain, Canada, and Germany (where, under Adolf Hitler, eugenics operated under the banner of "racial hygiene" and allowed Josef Mengele, Otmar von Verschuer, and others to perform horrific experiments on live human beings in concentration camps to test their genetic theories) were interested in weeding out "inferior" human bloodlines and used studies to insinuate heritability between certain families and illnesses such as schizophrenia, blindness, deafness, dwarfism, bipolar disorder, and depression. Their published reports fueled the eugenics movement to develop state laws in the 1800s and 1900s that forcefully sterilized persons considered unhealthy or mentally ill in order to prevent them from "passing on" their genetic inferiority to future generations. Such laws were not abolished in the US until the mid-twentieth century, leading to more than sixty thousand sterilized Americans in the meantime. Between 1934 and 1937, the

Nazis likewise sterilized an estimated four hundred thousand people they deemed of inferior genetic stock while also setting forth to selectively exterminate the Jews as "genetic aberrations" under the same program. Transhumanist goals of using biotechnology, nanotechnology, mind-interfacing, and related sciences to create a superior man and thus classifications of persons—the enhanced and the unenhanced—opens the door for a new form of eugenics and social Darwinism.

Germ-Line Genetic Engineering

Germ-line genetic engineering has the potential to actually achieve the goals of the early eugenics movement (which sought to create superior humans via improving genetics through selective breeding) through genetically modifying human genes in very early embryos, sperm, and eggs. As a result, germ-line engineering is considered by some conservative bioethicists to be the most dangerous of human-enhancement technology, as it has the power to truly reassemble the very nature of humanity into posthuman, altering an embryo's every cell and leading to inheritable modifications extending to all succeeding generations. Debate over germ-line engineering is therefore most critical, because as changes to "downline" genetic offspring are set in motion, the nature and physical makeup of mankind will be altered with no hope of reversal, thereby permanently reshaping humanity's future. A respected proponent of germ-line technology is Dr. Gregory Stock, who, like cyborgist Kevin Warwick, departs from Kurzweil's version of Humans 2.0 first arriving as a result of computer Singularity. Stock believes man can choose to transcend existing biological limitations in the nearer future (at or before computers reach strong artificial intelligence) through germ-line engineering. If we can make better humans by adding new genes to their DNA, he asks, why shouldn't we? "We have spent billions to unravel our biology, not out of idle curiosity, but in the hope of bettering our lives. We are not about to turn away from this," he says, before admitting elsewhere that this could lead to "clusters of genetically enhanced superhumans who will dominate if not enslave us."[225] The titles to Stock's books speak for themselves concerning what germ-line engineering would do to the human race. The name of one is *Redesigning Humans: Our Inevitable Genetic Future* and another is *Metaman: The Merging of Humans and Machines into a Global Superorganism.*

Besides the short list above, additional areas of concern where readers may wish to become well advised on the pros and cons of enhancement technology include immortalism, postgenderism, augmented reality, cryonics, designer babies, neurohacking, mind uploading, neural implants, xenotransplantation, reprogenetics, rejuvenation, radical life extension, and more.

Heaven and Hell Scenarios

While positive advances either already have been or will come from some of the science and technology fields we have discussed, learned men like Prof. Francis Fukuyama, in his book, *Our Posthuman Future: Consequences of the Biotechnology Revolution,* warn that unintended consequences resulting from what mankind has now set in motion represents the most dangerous time in earth's history, a period when exotic technology in the hands of transhumanist ambitions could forever alter what it means to be human. To those who would engineer a transhuman future, Fukuyama warns of a dehumanized "hell scenario" in which we "no longer struggle, aspire, love, feel pain, make difficult moral choices, have families, or do any of the things that we traditionally associate with being human." In this ultimate identity crisis, we would "no longer have the characteristics that give us human dignity" because, for one thing, "people dehumanized à la *Brave New World* don't know that they are dehumanized, and, what is worse, would not care if they knew. They are, indeed, happy slaves with a slavish happiness."[226] The "hell scenario" envisioned by Fukuyama is but a beginning to what other intelligent thinkers believe could go wrong.

On the other end of the spectrum and diametrically opposed to Fukuyama's conclusions is an equally energetic crowd that subscribes to a form of technological utopianism called the "heaven scenario." Among this group, a "who's who" of transhumansist evangelists such as Ray Kurzweil, James Hughes, Nick Bostrom, and Gregory Stock see the dawn of a new Age of Enlightenment arriving as a result of the accelerating pace of GRIN technologies. As with the eighteenth-century Enlightenment in which intellectual and scientific reason elevated the authority of scientists over priests, techno-utopians believe they will triumph over prophets of doom by "stealing fire from the gods, breathing life into inert matter, and gaining immortality. Our efforts to become something more than human have a long and distinguished genealogy. Tracing the history of those efforts illuminates human nature. In every civilization, in every era, we have given the gods no peace."[227] Such men are joined in their quest for godlike constitutions by a growing list of official US departments that dole out hundreds of millions of dollars each year for science and technology research. The National Science Foundation and the United States Department of Commerce anticipated this development over a decade ago, publishing the government report *Converging Technologies for Improving Human Performance*—complete with diagrams and bullet points—to lay out the blueprint for the radical evolution of man and machine. Their vision imagined that, starting around the year 2012, the "heaven scenario" would begin to be manifested and quickly result in (among other things):

- The transhuman body being "more durable, healthy, energetic, easier to repair, and resistant to many kinds of stress, biological threats, and aging processes."
- Brain-machine interfacing that will "transform work in factories, control automobiles, ensure military superiority, and enable new sports, art forms and modes of interaction between people."
- "Engineers, artists, architects, and designers will experience tremendously expanded creative abilities," in part through "improved understanding of the wellspring of human creativity."
- "Average persons, as well as policymakers, will have a vastly improved awareness of the cognitive, social, and biological forces operating their lives, enabling far better adjustment, creativity, and daily decision making…"
- "Factories of tomorrow will be organized" around "increased human-machine capabilities."[228]

Beyond how human augmentation and biological reinvention would spread into the wider culture following 2012 (the same date former counter-terrorism czar, Richard Clark, in his book, *Breakpoint*, predicted serious GRIN rollout), the government report detailed the *especially* important global and economic aspects of genetically superior humans acting in superior ways, offering how, as a result of GRIN leading to techno-sapien DNA upgrading, brain-to-brain interaction, human-machine interfaces, personal sensory device interfaces, and biological war fighting systems, "The twenty-first century could end in world peace, universal prosperity, and evolution to a higher level [as] humanity become[s] like a single, transcendent nervous system, an interconnected 'brain' based in new core pathways of society." The first version of the government's report asserted that the only real roadblock to this "heaven scenario" would be the "catastrophe" that would be unleashed if society fails to employ the technological opportunities available to us now. "We may not have the luxury of delay, because the remarkable economic, political and even violent turmoil of recent years implies that the world system is unstable. If we fail to chart the direction of change boldly, we may become the victims of unpredictable catastrophe."[229] This argument parallels what is currently echoed in military corridors, where sentiments hold that failure to commit resources to develop GRIN as the next step in human and technological evolution will only lead to others doing so ahead of us and using it for global domination.

Not everybody likes the "heaven scenario" imperative, and from the dreamy fantasies of Star Trek to the dismal vision of Aldous Huxley's Brave New World, some have come to believe there are demons hiding inside transhumanism's mystical (or mythical?) "Shangri-la."

"Many of the writers [of the government report cited above] share a faith in technology which borders on religiosity, boasting of miracles once thought to be the province of the Almighty," write the editors of *The New Atlantis: A Journal of Technology and Society*. "[But] without any serious reflection about the hazards of technically manipulating our brains and our consciousnessa different sort of catastrophe is nearer at hand. Without honestly and seriously assessing the consequences associated with these powerful new [GRIN] technologies, we are certain, in our enthusiasm and fantasy and pride, to rush headlong into disaster."[230]

Few people would be more qualified than computer scientist Bill Joy to annunciate these dangers, or to outline the "hell scenario" that could unfold as a result of GRIN. Yet it must have come as a real surprise to some of those who remembered him as the level-headed Silicon Valley scientist and co-founder of Sun Microsystems (SM) when, as chief scientist for the corporation, he released a vast and now-famous essay, "Why the Future Doesn't Need Us," arguing how GRIN would threaten in the very near future to obliterate mankind. What was extraordinary about Joy's prophecy was how he saw himself—and people like him—as responsible for building the very machines that "will enable the construction of the technology that may replace our species."

"From the very moment I became involved in the creation of new technologies, their ethical dimensions have concerned me," he begins. But it was not until the autumn of 1998 that he became "anxiously aware of how great are the dangers facing us in the twenty-first century." Joy dates his "awakening" to a chance meeting with Ray Kurzweil, whom he talked with in a hotel bar during a conference at which they both spoke. Kurzweil was finishing his manuscript for *The Age of Spiritual Machines* and the powerful descriptions of sentient robots and near-term enhanced humans left Joy taken aback, "especially given Ray's proven ability to imagine and create the future," Joy wrote. "I already knew that new technologies like genetic engineering and nanotechnology were giving us the power to remake the world, but a realistic and imminent scenario for intelligent robots surprised me."

Over the weeks and months following the hotel conversation, Joy puzzled over Kurzweil's vision of the future until finally it dawned on him that genetic engineering, robotics, artificial intelligence, and nanotechnology posed "a different threat than the technologies that have come before. Specifically, robots, engineered organisms, and nanobots share a dangerous amplifying factor: They can self-replicate. A bomb is blown up only once—but one bot can become many, and quickly get out of control." The unprecedented threat of self-replication particularly burdened Joy because, as a computer scientist, he thoroughly understood the concept of out-of-control replication or viruses leading to machine systems or computer networks being disabled. Uncontrolled self-replication of nanobots or engineered organisms would run "a much greater risk of substantial damage in the physical world," Joy concluded before adding his deeper fear:

> What was different in the twentieth century? Certainly, the technologies underlying the weapons of mass destruction (WMD)—nuclear, biological, and chemical (NBC)—were powerful, and the weapons an enormous threat. But building nuclear weapons required highly protected information; biological and chemical weapons programs also tended to require large-scale activities.
>
> The twenty-first-century technologies—genetics, nanotechnology, and robotics are so powerful that they can spawn whole new classes of accidents and abuses. Most dangerously, for the first time, these accidents and abuses are widely within the reach of individuals or small groups. They will not require large facilities or rare raw materials. Knowledge alone will enable the use of them.
>
> Thus we have the possibility not just of weapons of mass destruction but of knowledge-enabled mass destruction (KMD), this destructiveness hugely amplified by the power of self-replication.

I think it is no exaggeration to say we are on the cusp of *the further perfection of extreme evil, an evil whose possibility spreads well beyond that which weapons of mass destruction bequeathed to the nation states, on to a surprising and terrible empowerment.*[231]

Joy's prophecy about self-replicating "extreme evil" as an imminent and enormous transformative power that threatens to rewrite the laws of nature and permanently alter the course of life as we know it was frighteningly revived this year in the creation of Venter's "self-replicating" Synthia species (Venter's description). Parasites such as the mycoplasma mycoides that Venter modified to create Synthia can be resistant to antibiotics and acquire and smuggle DNA from one species to another, causing a variety of diseases. The dangers represented by Synthia's self-replicating parasitism has thus refueled Joy's opus and given experts in the field of counter-terrorism sleepless nights over how extremists could use open-source information to create a Frankenstein version of Synthia in fulfillment of Carl Sagan's *Pale Blue Dot*, which Joy quoted as, "the first moment in the history of our planet when any species, by its own voluntary actions, has become a danger to itself." As a dire example of the possibilities this represents, a genetically modified version of mouse pox was created not long ago that immediately reached 100 percent lethality. If such pathogens were unleashed into population centers, the results would be catastrophic. This is why Joy and others were hoping a few years ago that a universal moratorium or voluntary relinquishment of GRIN developments would be initiated by national laboratories and governments. But the genie is so far out of the bottle today that even college students are attending annual synthetic biology contests (such as the International Genetically Engineered Machine

Competition, or iGEM) where nature-altering witches' brews are being concocted by the scores, splicing and dicing DNA into task-fulfilling living entities. For instance, the iGEM 2009 winners built "E. chromi"—a programmable version of the bacteria that often leads to food poisoning, *Escherichia coli* (commonly abbreviated *E. coli*). A growing list of similar DNA sequences are readily available over the Internet, exasperating security experts who see the absence of universal rules for controlling what is increasingly available through information networks as threatening to unleash a "runaway sorcerer's apprentice" with unavoidable biological fallout. Venter and his collaborators say they recognize this danger—that self-replicating biological systems like the ones they are building—hold peril as well as hope, and they have joined in calling on Congress to enact laws to attempt to control the flow of information and synthetic "recipes" that could provide lethal new pathogens for terrorists. The problem, as always, is getting all of the governments in the world to voluntarily follow a firm set of ethics or rules. This is wishful thinking at best. It is far more likely the world is racing toward what Joel Garreau was first to call the "hell scenario"—a moment in which human-driven GRIN technologies place earth and all its inhabitants on course to self-eradication.

Ironically, some advocates of posthumanity are now using the same threat scenario to advocate *for* transhumanism as the best way to deal with the inevitable extinction of mankind via GRIN. At the global interdisciplinary institute Metanexus (www.metanexus.net/), Mark Walker, assistant professor at New Mexico State University (who holds the Richard L. Hedden of Advanced Philosophical Studies Chair) concludes like Bill Joy that "technological advances mean that there is a high probability that a human-only future will end in extinction." From this he makes a paradoxical argument:

In a nutshell, the argument is that even though creating posthumans may be a very dangerous social experiment, it is even more dangerous not to attempt it.

I suspect that those who think the transhumanist future is risky often have something like the following reasoning in mind: (1) If we alter human nature then we will be conducting an experiment whose outcome we cannot be sure of. (2) We should not conduct experiments of great magnitude if we do not know the outcome. (3) We do not know the outcome of the transhumanist experiment. (4) So, we ought not to alter human nature.

The problem with the argument is. Because genetic engineering is already with us, and it has the potential to destroy civilization and create posthumans, we are already entering uncharted waters, so we must experiment. The question is not whether to experiment, but only the residual question of which social experiment will we conduct. Will we try relinquishment? This would be an unparalleled social experiment to eradicate knowledge and technology. Will it be the steady-as-she-goes experiment where for the first time governments, organizations and private citizens will have access to knowledge and technology that (accidently or intentionally) could be turned to civilization ending purposes? Or finally, will it be the transhumanist social experiment where we attempt to make beings brighter and more virtuous to deal with these powerful technologies?

I have tried to make at least a *prima facie* case that transhumanism promises the safest passage through twenty-first century technologies.[232]

The authors of this book believe the "brighter and more virtuous beings" Professor Walker and others are arguing for possess
supernatural elements and that the *spirit* behind the transhumanist
nightmare will put the "hell" in the "hell scenario" sooner than most
comprehend.

Additionally, besides potentially being a mechanism that unseen
forces could use to incarnate the man of sin and raise from Sheol-
Hades his army of extinct Nephilim in time for Armageddon,
biotechnology could provide a number of other useful tools for
facilitating the empire of Antichrist, including eugenics, food con-
tagions, hybrid viruses, prion contamination, exotic new diseases,
and plagues of biblical proportions, just to name a few. Because we
cannot take time in this book to properly cover each of these risks,
we present two aspects of biotech (in addition to Apollonian and
Nephilim resurrection) that could eventually stand out as related to
the book of Revelation and the advent of Antichrist. These would
be: 1) end-time plagues and 2) the mark of the Beast. Credit must
be given to my perfect wife, Nita, who first brought to my attention
the unique idea of biotech and the mark of the Beast, and two of
my favorite writers—Sharon Gilbert and Sue Bradley—who offered
their expertise in defining the following two points.

1) Modern Watcher Science and Opening Pandora's Box

In 1818, Mary Shelley, the author of *Frankenstein*, first described her
expedition into "murky subterranean passages" within the trapezoid
cavern of Cumaean Sibyl near Naples, Italy. It was here, in the cave
so frequently described in Virgil's first-century *Eclogues* and *Æneid*,
that Shelley asserts she discovered the ancient apocalyptic writings
of the Roman prophetess Cumaean Sybil, recorded on oak leaves.

Translating and editing the Sibylline Prophecies, Mary Shelley published *The Last Man* in 1826.

Described as "a memory at the end of history," *The Last Man* begins, *"Let me fancy myself as I was in 2094,"* and continues to describe a horrific plague that destroys mankind as a species. *The Last Man* would become the first modern account of an apocalyptic pandemic, and disturbingly, would be written as a nihilist narrative in a posthuman era.

Contagion, the transmission of disease, has always been a unique entity, surpassing all potential cataclysms with its singular characteristic of being entirely sovereign and nondiscriminatory. Borderless, apolitical, and smugly defiant, disease has spread, multiplied, and mutated—and has historically shown deference to no one.

Though mortality estimates of pandemics throughout history are often unreliable (if not entirely unknown), their impact has often been measured only by these statistics, with less examination of concurrent societal disruption. With the exception of medical and scientific study, epidemics were understood mostly within their literary and classical context. Children's songs, nursery rhymes, and colloquialisms would hint of their impact, but nothing in recent memory would demand the serious attention of many in western society. The sustained scourge of AIDS is familiar in concept, but easily dismissed unless there is direct involvement. Ebola, cholera, plague, Marburg, SARS, and anthrax are serious sounding, but largely irrelevant to the generations raised in a society of "eradication" vaccines and fix-'em-fast antibiotics.

Nonetheless, there has been growing concern among modern experts of the fast-rising density of human populations and the immediate need to strategize to avoid high death tolls in inevitable natural disasters. Similarly, public health experts warn that vigilance and speed in tracking and responding to disease outbreaks is vital to limit the chances of a pandemic.

Every age in history has had its plagues, wars, and disasters. What is different about our world today is the enormous potential of a catastrophic pandemic situation. A public health emergency at this level would be far more catastrophic than any other type of naturally occurring, accidental, or other instigated event the world has experienced.

While Hollywood has steadily inoculated the comfortably preoccupied masses with remarkably prescient bio-threat scenarios, including *I Am Legend*, *Outbreak*, *The Stand*, and *V for Vendetta*, the very real and prolific research programs began to notice that life forms confined to the microscopic realm were changing: rapidly, sometimes predictably, oftentimes unpredictably, and in some instances, chillingly purposefully.

Add to this the unpleasant reality of biological warfare, which begins in its ancient past and ends in a time yet forward. From poisoning enemy wells, hurling dead corpses over city walls, or giving smallpox ridden blankets to American Indians, it is difficult to grasp the concept of being assaulted by a living, albeit microscopic, enemy.

But the plagues of history past bear little resemblance to their emergent constructs.

As science continued its quest for unlocking DNA, a parallel priority—with a far more sinister agenda—was already growing, and on the loose. Designed for maximum casualties and high emotional impact, this nano-army can be crafted for ethnic specific targeting. Despite warnings and flags, these unseen warriors are eager to meet their new hosts and are prepared to launch a new campaign, promising to reveal themselves in all of their horror, in an unprecedented, spectacular finale.

In *Plague Wars: The Terrifying Reality of Biological Warfare*, authors Tom Mangold and Jeff Goldberg assert:

> Biological weapons are both more immoral and more lethal than their pestilential cohorts in the nuclear and chemical armoury, for infecting the enemy aggressor can infect his own side; the pathogens blur the lines between peace and war as they silently spread through the ranks of families and non-combatants....
>
> But for some who wore cloaks and broke the rules, exotic bugs and toxins were preferable to daggers.
>
> ...To contemplate their use is to wink at evil, for pestilence and poison are afflictions as much as weapons.[233]

Creations on the drawing board that promise exotic delivery systems for dispersing the biological materials are no less startling. Recently, the Israeli newspaper *Yedioth Ahronoth* reported that Israel is using nanotechnology to create a robot no bigger than a hornet that would be able to chase, corner, photograph, and deliver lethal agents to kill its targets. The flying robot, nicknamed the "bionic hornet," would be able to navigate its way down narrow alleyways to target otherwise unreachable enemies. Similar biomechanic developments in the United States are being funded by DARPA, where cyborg-insect interfaces envision warbots no bigger than a bug that can take to the battlefield one at a time as spies or in swarms powerful enough to bring down fighter jets. The same micro-mechanical insect sentinels could serve up biological weapons, delivering viruses, bacteria, toxins, or microorganisms that afflict or destroy people, animals, and agriculture.

While such stratagems obviously appeal to the highest levels of

US military intelligence, theologians will be troubled by glaring similarities between this technology and biblical predictions of an end-time spiral by mankind into a cataclysmic war in which locust-sized weapons are "given power, as the scorpions of the earth have power" (Revelation 9:3).

In describing the activity of the Antichrist demon Apollo, Revelation 9:1–11 says this "king" of transgenic locusts opens the bottomless pit and releases synthesized insectoids to torment mankind. Some scholars believe when John the Revelator made these recordings, he was actually describing future technologies and that he simply referred to the bio-mechanized hybrids in terms he understood—i.e., swarms of Israel's "bionic hornets" were perceived as locusts whose wings sounded like "many horses running to battle" (Revelation 9:9).

Are the locust hordes of Revelation chapter 9 created in human laboratories that employ the same Watchers technology we believe could give rise to Apollo's return? Could be, and these less glamorous and decidedly more dramatic bio products seek a more pernicious and indelible glow than the cutesy biologic "novelties" the public has seen so far—genetically engineered puppies that glow in the dark, fish, and plants.

Plum Island and NEST

Located off the Northeast coast of Long Island, New York, beyond Montauk, the Plum Island Animal Disease Center (PIADC) is a Level 3 Biosafety Agriculture facility. Transferred in 2002 from the US Department of Agriculture to the US Department of Homeland Security, Plum Island is a federal facility for the research and investigation of foreign and Domestic animal pathogens. Plum Island's offshore status allows the study of forbidden mainland organisms including the housing of freezers that contain samples of polio and other microbial diseases that can be transferred from animals to humans.

NEST (Nuclear Emergency Support Team), on the other hand, is one of seven emergency response branches of the US Department of Energy's Nuclear Safety Administration. Information from the *Bulletin of Atomic Scientists* indicates that NEST has the ability to deploy up to six hundred experts in the event of an "incident" alongside the Federal Bureau of Investigation's Domestic Emergency Support Team or the State Department's Foreign Emergency Support Team.

In February, 2004, *Popular Mechanics* magazine featured a cover story, "When UFOs Arrive," that described such an "incident" scenario in which NEST would be activated. Within the seemingly whimsical text, story author Jim Wilson wrote:

> State Of Emergency: If ET turns up at NASA's doorstep bearing that invitation, it is in for a surprise. Instead of getting a handshake from the head of NASA, it will be handcuffed by an FBI agent dressed in a Biosafety Level 4 suit. Instead of sleeping in the Lincoln Bedroom at the White House, the alien will be whisked away to the Department of Agriculture's Animal Disease Center on Plum Island, off the coast of New York's Long Island. Here it will be poked and probed by doctors from the National Institutes of Health. A Department of Energy (DOE) Nuclear Emergency Search Team (NEST) will tow away its spacecraft.
>
> Unfriendly as this welcome may seem, it is the chain of events that most likely will follow the visitor's arrival.

Unique as the appearance of an alien-piloted spacecraft may be, the event incorporates elements of three situations familiar to federal emergency response workers: a plane crash, the release of radioactive material, and the capture of an animal suspected of harboring a contagious disease. Responsibilities in these situations are spelled out in Presidential Executive Orders.[234]

All of the prophets, including Jesus Christ, predicted that the last days would witness NEST-like "incidents" of unexpected nuclear and/or biological "pestilences" (Matthew 24:7) washing upon earth. Zechariah the prophet provided a vivid description of one such plague, saying:

Their flesh shall consume away while they stand upon their feet, and their eyes shall consume away in their holes, and their tongue shall consume away in their mouth. (Zechariah 14:12)

Though Mary Shelley's apocalyptic pandemic in *The Last Man* does not sit authoritatively on the same shelf as Scripture, it is worth remembering her insistence that this work is a translation of the nine ancient Sibylline Books as recorded by the priestess Cumaean Sibyl while presiding over the Apollonian oracle—the same prophetess whose *novus ordo seclorum* rests upon the Great Seal of the United States, pointing to the arrival of the deity that Scripture and occultists agree comes to rule the final pagan empire. Will biotech play a role in the fulfillment of her prophecies by providing the tools to raise her god and the plagues Scripture say will accompany him? People in high places evidently believe so.

2) Modern Watcher Science and the Mark of the Beast

Recently on a drive, my wife Nita brought up a point I had never considered. She asked if the biblical mark of the Beast might be a conspiracy employing biotechnology in the form of a manufactured virus, a bioweapon. Her theory was gripping. An occult elite operating behind the US government devises a virus that is a crossover between human and animal disease—let's say an entirely new and highly contagious influenza mutation—and intentionally releases it into the public. A pandemic ensues, and the period between when a person contracts the virus and death is something like ten days. With tens of thousands dead in a few weeks and the rate of death increasing hourly around the globe, a universal cry for a cure goes out. Seemingly miraculously, the government then steps forward with a vaccine. The only catch, they explain, is that, given the nature of the animal-human strain, the "cure" rewrites one's genetics, so that the person is no longer entirely human. Nita's point was that those who receive this antidote would become part "beast," and thus the title, "mark of the Beast."

No longer "entirely human" would also mean—according to this outline—that the individual could no longer be "saved" or go to heaven, explaining why the book of Revelation says "whosoever receiveth the mark" is damned forever while also explaining why the Nephilim similarly could not be redeemed. If one imagines the global chaos of such a pandemic, the concept of how the Antichrist "causes all," both small and great, to receive this mark becomes clearer. When looking into the eyes of dying children, parents, or a spouse, it would be incredibly difficult to allow oneself to die or to encourage others to do the same. Lastly, this scenario would mean that nobody is allowed to "buy or sell" in the marketplace without the mark-cure due to the need to quarantine all but the inoculated, thus fulfilling all aspects of the mark of the Beast prophecy.

To find out if the science behind this abstract would be as reasonable as it appeared on the surface, I contacted Sharon Gilbert. This was her troubling response:

> Tom, what is human? Until recently, most of us would readily respond that *we* are humans. You and I, we might argue, are *Homo sapiens*: erect, bipedal hominids with twenty-three pairs of matched chromosomes and nifty little thumbs capable of apposition to the palm that enable us to grasp the fine tools that our highly developed, bi-lobed brains devise.
>
> Humans, we might argue, sit as rulers of the earth, gazing down from the pinnacle of a pyramid consisting of all plant and animal species. We would remind the listener that natural selection and evolution have developed mankind into a superior thinker and doer, thereby granting us royal privilege, if not infinite responsibility.
>
> The Bible would take this definition much further, of course, adding that mankind is the only part of God's creation formed by His hands, rather than spoken into existence, and that you and I bear God's unique signature as having been created "in His image" (Genesis 1:27).
>
> Many members of the "illuminated brotherhood of science" would likely demur to the previous statement. These have, in point of fact, redefined *human*. Like Shelley's *Modern Prometheus*, Victor Frankenstein, today's molecular magicians play "god" not by stitching together rotting corpses, but by reforming the very essence of our beings: our DNA.

So-called "Postmodern Man" began as a literary reference but has evolved into an iconic metaphor representing a collective image of perfected humanity beyond the confines of genetic constraints. Transhumanism, also known as the H+ movement (see www.HPlusMagazine.com, for example) envisions a higher lifeform yet, surpassing *Homo sapiens* in favor of *Homo sapiens 2.0*, a bioengineered construct that fuses man's original genome with animal and/or synthetic DNA.

While such claims ring of science fiction, they are indeed science fact. For decades, laboratories have created chimeric combinations of animal, plant, and even human DNA under the guise of medical research. The stated goal is to better man's lot by curing disease, but this benign mask hides an inner, sardonic grin that follows an ancient blueprint to blend God's perfect creature with the seed of fallen angels: "You shall be as gods."

You and Nita speak to the heart of the matter when you warn of a day when true humans may unknowingly receive transhuman instructions via an implant or injection. A seemingly innocuous vaccine or identification "chip" can initiate intracellular changes, not only in somatic or "body" cells but also in germline cells such as ova and sperm. The former alters the recipient only; the latter alters the recipient's doomed descendents as well.

In my second novel, *The Armageddon Strain*, I present a device called the "BioStrain Chip" that employs nanotechnology to induce genetic changes inside the carrier's body. This miracle chip is advertised as a cure for the H5N1/ebola chimera that is released in the prologue to the book. Of course, if you've read the novel, then you know the BioStrain chip does far more than "cure"—it also kills.

Though a work of fiction, *The Armageddon Strain* raises a chilling question: What limitations lie within the payload of a biochip? Can such a tiny device do more than carry digitized information? Could it actually serve as the *mark of the Beast?*

The answer is yes.

DNA (Deoxyribonucleic acid) has become the darling of researchers who specialize in synthetic constructs. The "sticky-end" design of the DNA double-helix makes it ideal for use in computing. Though an infinite number of polyhedra are possible, the most robust and stable of these "building blocks" is called the double crossover (DX). An intriguing name, is it not? The double-cross.

Picture an injectible chip comprised of DNA-DX, containing instructions for a super-soldier. Picture, too, how this DNA framework, if transcribed, might also serve a second, *sinister*, purpose—not only to instruct, but also to *alter*.

Mankind has come perilously far in his search for perfection through chemistry. Although millennia passed with little progress beyond roots, herbs, and alchemical quests for gold from lead, the twentieth century ushered science into the rosy dawn of breathless discovery. Electricity, lighter than air travel, wireless communication, and computing transformed the ponderous pace of the scientific method into a light speed race toward self-destruction.

By the mid-1950s, Watson and Crick had solved the structure of the DNA molecule and the double helix became all the rage. Early gene splicing, and thus transgenics, began in 1952 as a crude, cut-and-paste sort of science cooked up in kitchen blenders and petri dishes—as much accident as inspiration. As knowledge has increased (Daniel 12:4), genetic scientists learned to utilize microbiological "vectors" and sophisticated methods to insert animal or plant genes from one specie into another. It's the ultimate "Mr. Potato Head" game, where interchangeable plastic pieces give rise to an infinite number of combinations; only, in genetic splicing, humanity is the unhappy potato.

Vectors provide the means of transport and integration for this brave new science. Think of these vectors as biological trucks that carry genetic building materials and workers into your body's cells. Such "trucks" could be a microsyringe, a bacterium, or a virion (a virus particle). Any entity that can carry genetic information (the larger the load capacity, the better) and then surreptitiously gain entry into the cell is a potential vector. Viruses, for example, can be stripped of certain innate genes that might harm the cell. Not only does this (supposedly) render the viral delivery truck "harmless," it also clears out space for the cargo.

Once inside the cell, the "workers" take over. Some of these "workers" are enzymes that cut human genes at specific sites, while others integrate—or load—the "cargo" into appropriate reading frames—like microscopic librarians. Once the payload is stored in the cell's nuclear "library stacks," the new genes can be translated, copied, and "read" to produce altered or brand-new, "alien" polymers and proteins.

The resulting hybrid cell is no longer purely human. If a hybridized skin cell, it may now glow, or perhaps form scales rather than hair, claws rather than fingernails. If a brain cell, the new genetic instructions could produce an altered neurotransmitter that reduces or even eliminates the body's need for sleep. Muscle cells may grow larger and more efficient at using low levels of calcium and oxygen. Retina cells may encode for receptors that enable the "posthuman being" to perceive infrared or ultraviolet light frequencies. The hybrid ears may now sense a wider range of sounds, taste buds a greater range of chemicals. Altered brains might even attune to metaphysics and "unseen" gateways, allowing communication with supernatural realms.

Germline alterations, mentioned earlier, form a terrifying picture of generational development and may very well already be a reality. Genetic "enhancement" of sperm-producing cells would change human sperm into tiny infiltrators, and any fertilized ovum a living chimera. Science routinely conducts experiments with transgenic mice, rats, chickens, pigs, cows, horses, and many other species. It is naïve to believe humans have been left out of this transgenic equation.

You and I constantly battle mutagenic assaults from external and internal pressures. Externally, our cells endure daily bombardment by pollution, waveform radiation, and chemicals that can alter the molecular structure of nucleotides (guanine, cytosine, thymine, adenine). Internally, our systems work overtime to filter genetically altered food, impure water, and pharmaceuticals. Our bodies are changing. To paraphrase Shakespeare, humanity "alters when it alteration finds" (Sonnet 116).

If so many scientists (funded by government entities)

believe in the "promise" of genetic alteration and transgenic "enhancement," how then can humanity remain human? We cannot. We will not. Perhaps, *some have not.*

Spiritually, the enemy has ever sought to corrupt God's plan. Originally, fallen angels lay with human women to corrupt the original base pair arrangements. Our genome is filled with "junk DNA" that seemingly encodes for nothing. These "introns" may be the remains of the corrupted genes, and God Himself may have switched them off when fallen angels continued their program, post-Flood. If so, today's scientists might need only to "switch them back on" to resurrect old forms such as gibborim and nephilim.

I should point out that not all "trucks" (vectors) deliver their payload immediately. Some operate on a time delay. Cytomegalovirus (CMV) is a common infective agent resident in the cells of many humans today. It "sleeps" in our systems, waiting for a window of opportunity to strike. Recently, genetic specialists began utilizing CMV vectors in transgenic experiments. In 1997, the Fox television program *Millennium* featured an episode in the second season called "Sense and Antisense" (referring to the two sides of the DNA molecule). In this chilling story, a scientist named Lacuna reveals a genetic truth to Frank Black: "They have the map, the map, they can make us go down any street they want to. Streets that we would never even dream of going down. They flip a switch, we go east. They flip another switch, we go north. And we never know we have been flipped, let alone know how."[235]

In the final days of this current age, humanity may indeed "flip." Paul tells us that Christians will be transformed in a moment (1 Corinthians 15:51–53). Is it possible that the enemy also plans an instantaneous "flip"? Are genetic sleeper agents (idling "trucks") already at work in humanity's DNA, waiting and ready to deploy at the appropriate moment?

Science is ready. Knowledge has been increased. The spiritual players have taken the stage.

All we need is the signal. The sign. The injection. The mark. The moment.

We shall ALL be changed. Some to incorruptible bodies ready to meet the Lord. Others to corrupted genomes ready to serve the Beast.

WHEN APOLLO/OSIRIS/NIMROD, SON OF LUCIFER, SHALL COME

Seek ye where the broken twig lies and the dead stick molds away, where the clouds float together and the stones rest by the hillside, for all these mark the grave of Hiram [Osiris] who has carried my Will with him to the tomb. This eternal quest is yours until ye have found your Builder, until the cup giveth up its secret, until the grave giveth up its ghosts. No more shall I speak until ye have found and raised my beloved Son [Osiris], and have listened to the words of my Messenger and with Him as your guide have finished the temple which I shall then inhabit. Amen. —Manly P. Hall, *The Lost Keys of Freemasonry*, Prologue

Recently on a business trip to Washington, DC, I met with two current members of the Scottish Rite Freemasonry (whose names I cannot reveal), who have unrestricted access to all but the most secret and highest guarded documents of the Order. I joined one of them at The House of the Temple, the headquarters building of the Scottish Rite of Freemasonry, Southern Jurisdiction, where the Rite's Supreme Council, 33rd Degree, have their meetings, and the other at the George Washington Masonic Memorial in Alexandria, Virginia.

While both men were very helpful and informative, they were evasive whenever I probed too deeply into certain areas. I suppose this is not surprising, given that Masons are sworn to secrecy under blood oaths of horrific repercussion, including having their throats slit, eyeballs pierced, tongues torn out, feet flayed, bodies hacked into pieces, and so on if they give up the wrong information. Perhaps this is why at one point, one of the men I conferred with became visibly nervous as soon as I started asking specific questions about Masonic religious practices, which would include secret rituals that are performed in the Temple Room on the third floor at the House of the Temple, and the hidden meaning behind the name of their deity—the Great Architect of the Universe.

What most in the public do not understand is that, in spite of denial by some Masons, theirs is a religious institution with rituals and even prophetic beliefs concerning a human-transforming final world order, founded on and maintained by dozens of doctrines that can be defined by what "Masonry's greatest philosopher," Manly P. Hall, in *The Lost Keys of Freemasonry*,[236] called "the principles of mysticism and the occult rites." The reason lower-degree Masons would deny this is because the Masters of the Craft intentionally mislead them. Speaking of the first three degrees of Freemasonry, Albert Pike admitted in *Morals & Dogma*:

> The Blue Degrees are but the outer court or portico of the Temple. Part of the symbols are displayed there to the initiate, but he is intentionally misled by false interpretations. It is not intended that he shall understand them; but it is intended that he shall imagine he understands them. Their true explication is reserved for the Adepts, the Princes of Masonry.... It is well enough for the mass of those called

Masons to imagine that all is contained in the Blue Degrees; and whoso attempts to undeceive them will labor in vain, and without any true reward violate his obligations as an Adept.[237]

At these lower degrees, most members of Freemasonry belong to what is maintained as a fraternal organization that simply requires belief in a "Supreme Being" while avoiding discussion of politics and religion in the lodge, using metaphors of stonemasons building Solomon's temple to convey what they publically describe as "a system of morality veiled in allegory and illustrated by symbols." I've known several of these type Masons, all of whom were sincere members of society who worked together in a brotherhood for common benefit and to pool resources for charitable goals. None of these lower-degree Masons with whom I have been acquainted would ever, insofar as I know, participate in a conspiracy toward a global world order in which people will be politically and spiritually enslaved. But as one former Freemason friend told me, "This is the veneer of the lower degrees that exists on the Order's public face. What is happening with at least some of the members at the 33rd level, or among the York Rite Knights Templar and the Shriners, is another matter altogether. When I was part of the brotherhood," he continued, "I watched as specific members with the correct disposition and ideology were identified, separated, groomed, and initiated into the higher degrees for reasons you *would* find corresponding with the goals of a New World Order."

Famous Freemason Foster Bailey once described how the Masons not included among this elite are unaware of an "Illuminati" presence among Master Masons, who in turn are the guardians of a secret "Plan":

Little as it may be realised by the unthinking Mason who is interested only in the outer aspects of the Craft work, the whole fabric of Masonry may be regarded as an externalisation of that inner spiritual group whose members, down the ages, have been the Custodians of the Plan.… These Master Masons, to whom TGAOTU [The Great Architect of the Universe] has given the design and Who are familiar with the tracing board of the G.M. [Grand Master] on high, are…sometimes known as and can direct the searchlight of truth wherever its beams are needed to guide the pilgrim on his way. They are the Rishis of the oriental philosophy, the Builders of the occult tradition.[238]

Part of the carefully guarded Illuminati "Plan" Bailey referred to involves the need for each Mason to navigate the meaning behind the various rituals in order to discover the secret doctrine of Masonry involving the true identity of deity and what this means now and for the future (which is unveiled for the first time publically in this book as reflected in the prophecy of the Great Seal of the United States). Manly Hall, who rightly called the Great Seal "the signature" of that exalted body of Masons who designed America for a "peculiar and particular purpose," described these two kinds of Masons as members of a "fraternity within a fraternity," the elect of which are dedicated to a mysterious *arcanum arcandrum* (a "sacred secret") unknown to the rest of the Order:

Freemasonry is a fraternity within a fraternity—an outer organization concealing an inner brotherhood of the elect.

…it is necessary to establish the existence of these two separate yet independent orders, the one visible and the other invisible.

The visible society is a splendid camaraderie of "free and accepted" men enjoined to devote themselves to ethical, educational, fraternal, patriotic, and humanitarian concerns.

The invisible society is a secret and most august fraternity whose members are dedicated to the service of a mysterious arcanum arcandrum.

Those brethren who have essayed to write the history of their craft have not included in their disquisitions the story of that truly secret inner society which is to the body Freemasonic what the heart is to the body human.

In each generation only a few are accepted into the inner sanctuary of the work…the great initiate-philosophers of Freemasonry are…masters of that secret doctrine which forms the invisible foundation of every great theological and rational institution.[239]

Thomas Horn at the Pillars of Charity

Among dedicatories to those who support this "invisible" secret doctrine, there is a memorial alcove in the heart of the House of the Temple called the "Pillars of Charity." Here, between two vaults on either side—one containing the exhumed remains of former Sovereign Grand Commander Albert Pike and the other containing Sovereign Grand Commander John Henry Cowles, marked by busts of each man on marble pedestals—a stained-glass window depicts the all-seeing eye above the words "*Fiat Lux*" emitting thirty-three beams of light downward onto the phrase "*ordo ab chao*" from ancient craft Masonic doctrine, "order out of chaos."

In between meetings with the anonymous Masons who met with me during research for this book, I stepped into this shrine and read the names of those who are hallowed there on reflective golden inscriptions for contributing at least one million dollars to advance the cause of Scottish Rite Freemasonry, including the George Bush family, whose work to initiate the New World Order is universally understood.

At the House of the Temple, like elsewhere, "The Brotherhood of Darkness" (as my friend Dr. Stanley Monteith calls it) intentionally hides in plain sight the occult aspirations of universalism, which ultimately will be conceived in a one-world order and one-world religion under the son of Lucifer—Apollo/Osiris/Nimrod—or, as Manly Hall put it:

> The outcome of the "secret destiny" is a World Order ruled by a King with supernatural powers. This King was descended of a divine race; that is, he belonged to the Order of the Illumined for those who come to a state of wisdom then belong to a family of heroes-perfected human beings.[240]

When Hall offered this astonishingly perceptive commentary about the future Masonic "King" who is "descended of a divine race" of "Illumined" (luciferic) "heroes-perfected" (half-man, half-god) human beings, he nailed exactly what the Watchers had done, and what the Cumaean Sibyl's Great Seal prophecy says will occur concerning the coming of Apollo/Osiris/Nimrod.

Have the keepers of the secret destiny of America also hidden in public view the *timing* of their king's arrival? We believe they did, and that the entire prophecy—who, what, when, and where—is openly encoded within two Masonic artifacts: the national cipher known as the Great Seal of the United States, and the "key" known as the Lost Symbol. The means to understanding when the *novus ordo seclorum* shall enthrone its Apollonian leader may have also been known by Hall, as he correctly noted that the "unfinished pyramid" upon the seal's reverse side is the "trestleboard setting forth symbolically the task to the accomplishment of which the United States Government was dedicated from the day of its inception."[241]

Previously we summarized Hall's comments about the "mass of occult and Masonic symbols" on the Great Seal, which he believed only students of archaic or esoteric symbolism would be able to accurately decipher. This included the obverse side of the Great Seal, where a bald eagle, which he illustrated was a shrewd mythical phoenix so important to Masonic mysticism, clutches a bundle of arrows in its left talon, while its right claw grips an olive branch. "But," Hall then went on to say:

> If this design on the obverse side of the seal is stamped with the signature of the Order of the Quest, the design on the reverse is even more definitely related to the old Mysteries.... Here is represented the great pyramid of Gizah, composed

of thirteen rows of masonry, showing seventy-two stones. The pyramid is without a cap stone, and above its upper platform floats a triangle containing the all-seeing eye surrounded by rays of light.… The combination of the phoenix, the pyramid, and the all-seeing eye is more than chance or coincidence.… There is only one possible origin for these symbols, and that is the secret societies which came to this country 150 years before the Revolutionary War.… There can be no question that the great seal was directly inspired by these orders of the human Quest, and that it set forth the purpose for this nation as that purpose was seen and known to the Founding Fathers.[242]

As Manly Hall did, thirty-third vice president of the United States and 32nd-Degree Mason Henry Wallace also viewed the unfinished pyramid with the all-seeing eye hovering above it on the Great Seal as central to the prophecy of a New World Order. Whenever the United States assumed its position as the capital of the world, he believed, the Grand Architect would return and metaphorically the all-seeing eye would be fitted atop the pyramid as the finished "apex stone."

But Whose All-Seeing Eye Is This, Anyway?

While different versions of the eye of providence or all-seeing eye have appeared throughout time within various cultures, the origin of each can usually be understood within the context of its adjoined symbolism. In the case of the all-seeing eye on the Great Seal of the United States, the connection to the uncapped Egyptian pyramid and to the Osiris-Apollo-related mottoes positively determines the culture to which this specific "eye" refers, and the solar deity represented by it: Osiris/Horus/Apollo/Nimrod.

This is further illustrated by the "numerological values" of the arcane mottoes, which were carefully chosen for the Great Seal due to their connection to the pagan deity. So important was it that the Masonic numbers three (3) and thirteen (13) be reinforced with the multi-named "god" (the numbers three and thirteen are historically connected with the deities Apollo, Osiris, and Nimrod, and this is why, for instance, the American space mission Apollo 13 was named after the deity and had this number), that not only was the original amount of American states intentionally set at thirteen, but Freemason David Ovason, whom Robert Hieronimus (considered one of the world's foremost authorities on the Great Seal) calls "exceptionally well referenced," confirms how a letter was "cut" from the Latin word *saeclorum* (the usual spelling) in order to create the word *seclorum* to contribute to three sets of thirteen on the reverse side of the Great Seal.

After acknowledging that the top motto, *annuit coeptis*, had the obligatory thirteen letters, Ovason pointed out how *saeclorum* was letter-cut to join the bottom motto, *novus ordo seclorum*, so that the phrase would end up being seventeen letters, which when added to the nine numerals in the Roman date would equal a total of twenty-six, or two sets of the number thirteen. Combined with the top motto, these three sets of thirteen were very important to establish, Ovason says, in order to reflect the trinity represented in the Great Seal "Eye of Providence, and in the nominal triangle from which the pyramid is constructed."[243]

Based purely on the Great Seal's symbolism, the trinity these three sets of the number thirteen denote is authoritatively identified as Osiris, Horus, and Isis, the pagan versions of Father, Son, and

Holy Spirit, respectively. The use of the number thirteen in this way also connects the Great Seal to the mythological and astrological significance of the legend of Osiris as the dying and rising god. It was evidently so important to maintain this talisman-like value, thirteen, that other phases of the design and layout of Washington, DC were coordinated accordingly, says Ovason. This includes the laying of the White House cornerstone on October 13, 1792, by Masons, and the Fourth of July signing of the Declaration of Independence thirteen days after summer solstice, so that the sun would be on Sirius. In Egyptian mythology, the sun represented Osiris while the star Sirius symbolized Isis, and thirteen was the number of pieces of Osiris that Isis was able to find after Seth, his evil brother, murdered and threw fourteen pieces of him into the Nile. Isis searched the riverbank until she recovered every piece, except for his genitals, which had been swallowed by a fish. Isis replaced the missing organ with an Obelisk and magically impregnated herself with Horus. Therefore, in Masonic as well as in ancient Egyptian mythology, the number thirteen—used a total of thirteen times on the Great Seal, counting front and back—is the number that represents the return or resurrection of Osiris.

This mythology was so meaningful to the founding of the United States and the construction of its Capitol—including having the missing Osiris genitalia represented by the 6,666-inches-high Egyptian Obelisk known as the Washington Monument—that nearly all of David Ovason's five hundred-plus-page *Secret Architecture of Our Nation's Capital* is dedicated to establishing the singular correlation between Washington, DC and Virgo, the constellation of Isis, or what Ovason calls, "Isis, who was the chief of the feminine mystery deities and the prototype of the steller Virgo."[244]

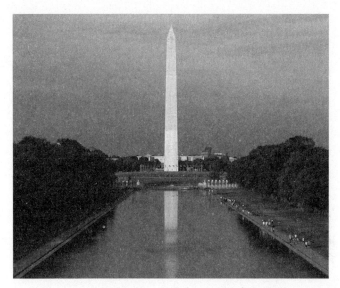

This affiliation existed from the very day Freemasons gathered on April 15, 1791, beginning appropriately at 3:30 PM (reflecting the mystical value, thirty-three) because of the astrological position of Jupiter and Virgo, and what this would mean for the secret destiny of America:

At exactly 3:30 PM, Jupiter…began to rise over the horizon. It was in 23 degrees of Virgo…. By this means, the zodiacal power of Virgo, which was called in later Masonic circles "the Beautiful Virgin," was able to stamp her benign influence on the building of the federal city…. A few of the many Freemasons present at this ceremony would have been only too well aware of the profound implications of what they were doing…. It is quite clear that the ceremonial placing of the stone related to more than merely the founding of the federal district: it was somehow linked to the future destiny of America itself.[245]

By dedicating the United States through its astrological align-ment to the "Virgin" constellation of Isis, the founders had dedicated the "destiny" of America to fulfilling the secret doctrine of Freema-sonry, as also reflected in the Osiris/Apollo symbolism of the Great Seal, concerning subservience—now and upon his return as Anti-christ—to Osiris/Apollo/Nimrod.

Interestingly, the same dedication to Osiris/Isis/Apollo exists in New York where the events of September 11, 2001, initiated the push toward the *novus ordo seclorum*. The Statue of Liberty in New York's Harbor, which holds the Masonic "Torch of Enlightenment," was presented in 1884 as a gift to American Masons by the French Grand Orient Temple Masons.

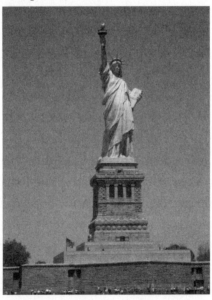

Designed by French Freemason and sculptor Frédéric Auguste Bartholdi and built by another French Freemason, Gustave Eiffel, the statue was originally identified as "the goddess Isis" with the statue's head formed to represent "the Greek Sun-god Apollo…as preserved on an ancient marble tablet (today in the Archaeological Museum of Corinth, Corinth, Greece)—Apollo was represented as a solar deity, dressed in a similar robe and having on its head a 'radiate crown' with the seven spiked rays of the Helios-Apollo's sun rays."[246]

The legend of Osiris and Isis, the connection with Apollo, the magical number thirteen, and the history surrounding their mythos is often openly discussed in Masonic and brotherhood-friendly literature. For instance in *Morals and Dogma*, Albert Pike enumerated the esoteric significance of the Osiris epic at length, adding that lower-level Masons (Blue Masonry) are ignorant of its true meaning, which is only known to those who are "initiated into the Mysteries."[247] Pike also spoke of the star Sirius—connected to Isis and at length to Lucifer/Satan—as "still glittering" in the Masonic lodges as "the Blazing Star." Elsewhere in *Morals and Dogma*, Pike reiterated that the "All-Seeing Eye... was the emblem of Osiris"[248] and that the "Sun was termed by the Greeks the Eye of Jupiter, and the Eye of the World; and his is the All-Seeing Eye in our Lodges."[249]

Once people understand this illuminated Masonic connection to the "trinity" on America's Great Seal, and what the prophetic symbolism, mottoes, and numerology imply, it becomes apparent why so much effort was put forward for so long by those who felt it was necessary to hide this extraordinary destiny. Ovason acknowledges this conspiracy of silence as well:

> The motto at the top of the seal, *Annuit Coeptis*, is from Virgil...from the *Aeneid*.... This is a prayer to the god Jupiter.... We should observe that while the subject matter of the reverse of the seal is undoubtedly pagan—if symbolic of hermetic Egypt—the superior motto is itself a prayer to a

pagan god. Could *this* be the reason why there has been so much reluctance to bring the reverse of the seal into the light of day? Whatever the nature of the god, the prayer directed in this way is a petition that the daring undertaking [the secret destiny of America as symbolized in "finishing" the pyramid] may be completed, and that the new age will find fulfillment.[250]

Ovason, a Mason whose research earned praise from Fred Kleinknecht, Sovereign Grand Commander of the 33rd-Degree Supreme Council of Freemasons in Washington, DC, is to be thanked for inadvertently revealing what the Illuminatus has secretly known for ages—that the Great Seal of the United States is a pagan prophecy and petition to a pagan god (the same entity the Bible identifies by name as the end-times Antichrist) to assist in the conclusion of the great work by his return. "When we have grasped the importance of these New Age expectations," Ovason concludes, "we shall be in a better position to understand why the design for this reverse [side of the Great Seal] has remained so consistently hidden."[251]

The Unfinished Pyramid Beneath the All-Seeing Eye

Where the numerology and astrological signs related to the all-seeing eye add to why certain symbolism on the Great Seal was important to Freemasons, it is the unfinished pyramid upon the seal's reverse side that Manly Hall called the "trestleboard" that set forth symbolically the "task to the accomplishment of which the United States Government was dedicated from the day of its inception." This language, drawn directly from how trestleboards are used and what they represent in both operative and speculative Masonry, is revealing, as the trestleboard is the board upon which the Master Mason draws out the diagrams and geometric figures that are to be used as a blueprint for directing the workers in the construction of the task. In speculative Masonry, the trestleboard also takes on spiritual meaning, which reflects lessons from the Books of Nature and the will of the Great Architect of the Universe. In Masonic rituals, this means a spiritual plan has been put in place and that it is to be carried out on an individual, family, social, national, and international level. The plan includes the timing as to when the project should officially start, as well as generally when it is to be concluded. Thus, if the pyramid on the Great Seal is the trestleboard laying out the "task of which the United States Government was dedicated from the day of its inception," it is the drawing board for the destiny of America and is branded by 1) the identity of the Great Architect to whom the work is dedicated; and 2) the date on which the work was started and is to be completed.

Concerning the first subject matter—the identity of the Great Architect—we have illustrated numerous times how the symbols and mottoes speak for themselves in communicating who this deity is. In the prologue of his book, *The Lost Keys of Freemasonry*, Manly Hall joins in this revelation by recounting the familiar story of Hiram Abiff, the Tyrian "First Grand Master" of the order of Masons and the chief builder who sets out to construct the temple of the Great Architect of the Universe, but is killed by three spectres. This story, impersonated every time an initiate reaches the level of Master Mason, is by admission of Freemasons a retelling of the death-epic of the god Osiris. In *Lost Keys*, Hall narrates how the Great Architect gives Hiram (Osiris) the trestleboard for the construction of the great temple, and when he is killed by three ruffians, the Great Architect bathes him in "a glory celestial," as in the glory surrounding the all-seeing eye of Osisis above the pyramid on the Great Seal. The Great Architect follows this by charging those who would finish the building with the task of finding the body of Hiram (Osiris) and raising him from the dead. When *this* has been accomplished, the great work will conclude and the god will inhabit the temple:

> Seek ye where the broken twig lies and the dead stick molds away, where the clouds float together and the stones rest by the hillside, for all these mark the grave of Hiram [Osiris] who has carried my Will with him to the tomb. This eternal quest is yours until ye have found your Builder, until the cup giveth up its secret, until the grave giveth up its ghosts. No more shall I speak until ye have found and raised my beloved Son [Osiris], and have listened to the words of my Messenger and with Him as your guide have finished the temple which I shall then inhabit. Amen.[252]

"So once again we are brought back to the Great Pyramid of Giza," writes Peter Goodgame, "the first built and last remaining of the Seven Wonders of the ancient world, which is the reputed resting place of Osiris. The Great Pyramid itself is but one structure within a major Necropolis that was designed according to the layout of the constellation Orion, the Great Hunter in the sky [Osiris/Gilgamesh/Nimrod]. As we have endeavored to show, Osiris is none other than the Biblical Nimrod, the 'mighty hunter before the Lord.'"[253]

The *Encyclopedia of Freemasonry* identifies the character Nimrod with this legend of the Brotherhood as well, in the Old Constitutions, where it distinguishes him as a founder of Masonry. "Thus in the York MS., No. 1, we read: 'At ye making of ye toure of Babell there was a Masonrie first much esteemed of, and the King of Babilon yet called Nimrod was a Mason himself and loved well Masons.'"254

Other authorities not only connect the Masonic founder Hiram Abiff with Osiris and Nimrod, but explain that Nimrod plus the building of the Tower of Babel—not the temple of Solomon—was the true origin of Masonic cosmology.

In *Symbols of Freemasonry*, translated from the French *Les Symboles des Francs-Macons*, Daniel Beresniak notes:

> The date of the construction of King Solomon's temple has not always been the key date in the Freemasons' cosmology. This central role was once given to the Tower of Babel. The Regius manuscript, which predates Cooke [1410] by twenty years, cites King Nemrod, the builder of that famous tower, as "the first and most excellent master." He it was, and not King Solomon, who gave the Masons their first "charge," their rules of conduct and professional code....
>
> A Masonic text known as the Thistle manuscript, of 1756, says that Nemrod "created the Masons" and "gave them their signs and terms so that they could distinguish themselves from other people...it was the first time that the Masons were organised as a craft."255

Thus the appearance of the uncapped pyramid of Giza on the Great Seal of the United States echoes the ancient pagan as well as Masonic beliefs concerning the old mysteries, and the prophecy of the return of Osiris/Apollo/Nimrod. In *Rosicrucian and Masonic Origins*, Manly Hall, who had said in *The Secret Teachings of All Ages* that the Great Pyramid was "the tomb of Osiris,"256 explains that Preston, Gould, Mackey, Oliver, Pike, and nearly every other great historian of Freemasonry were aware of this connection between Freemasonry and the ancient mysteries and primitive ceremonials based on Osiris. "These eminent Masonic scholars have all recognized in the legend of Hiram Abiff an adaptation of the Osiris myth; nor do they deny that the major part of the symbolism of the craft is derived from the pagan institutions of antiquity when the gods were venerated in secret places with strange figures and appropriate rituals."[257]

But whereas Freemasons like Manly Hall considered the symbolism and myth related to the pyramid on the Great Seal and the history of Apollo/Osiris/Nimrod to be the working "trestleboard" laying out the secret destiny of America, New Age esotericists like Robert Hieronimus—one of the world's foremost authorities on the reverse of the seal's symbolism—view the circular design and symbolism on the Great Seal to be an "initiatory mandala."

Mandalas, from the Hindu term for "circle," are concentric diagrams, such as is familiar in Tantrism, Buddhism, and Hinduism, having ritual and spiritual use for "focusing" or trance-inducing aspirants and adepts who seek mystical oneness with the cosmos or deeper levels of the unconscious mind. Related to the design of the Great Seal, Hieronimus, as an occultist, views the geometric patterns as representing a type of mandala or microcosm embodying the cosmic or metaphysical divine powers at work in the secret destiny of America, including the god or universal forces represented in the diagram that herald a coming new age of gods and demigods.

Occultists often use mandalas based on the concept of a "protective circle" or variation, which they believe allow certain doorways into the supernatural to be opened or closed, and entities compelled accordingly, as in the magical five-pointed pentagram circle. This is similar to an initiatory mandala used in Hindu and Buddhist Tantrism, in which deities are represented by specific locations in the diagram. In *Yoga: Immortality and Freedom*, scholar Mircea Eliade explains the importance of this part of the mandala design:

> At the periphery of the construction there are four cardinal doors, defended by terrifying images called "guardians of the doors." Their role is twofold. On the one hand, the guardians defend consciousness from the disintegrating forces of the unconscious; on the other, they have an offensive mission— in order to lay hold upon the fluid and mysterious world of the unconscious, consciousness must carry the struggle into the enemy's camp and hence assume the violent and terrible aspect appropriate to the forces to be combated. Indeed, even the divinities inside the *mandala* sometimes have a terrifying appearance; they are the gods whom man will encounter after death, in the state of *bardo*. The guardians of the doors and the terrible divinities emphasize the initiatory character of entrance into a *mandala*.... The typical initiatory ordeal is the "struggle with a monster"...both spiritual (against evil spirits and demons, forces of chaos) and material (against enemies)...who [attempt] to return "forms" to the amorphous state from which they originated.[258]

What makes this interesting is that the arcane symbols and mottoes of the Great Seal represent—as admitted by Masonry's greatest historians, mystics, and philosophers—gods that were known in ancient times alternatively as saviors or demons, creators, and destroyers; spirits that seek entry into the conscious and unconscious world. That such concepts would be related to the uncapped pyramid on the seal is fitting in that the Great Pyramid of Giza is not only thought of as the actual tomb-site of the deity, but as a symbol of Christ by some and of the Antichrist by others. These paradoxical conclusions arrive because of certain mysterious attributes related to the Great Pyramid.

In his wonderful book, *The Great Pyramid: Prophecy in Stone*, Dr. Noah Hutchings is able to show that the Great Pyramid, unlike the other inferior ones on the Giza Plateau whose walls are covered with Egyptian symbols, is devoid of such idolatrous symbolism and defies to this day what methods were employed to manufacture its unparalleled creation. Just how matchless is the Great Pyramid? Hutchings starts out by showing that it is:

- A building so large that all the locomotives in the world today could not pull its weight.
- A building so large that it could hold the cathedrals of Rome, Florence, and Milan and still have room for the Empire State Building, Westminster Abbey, St. Paul's Cathedral, and both houses of the British Parliament.
- A building made up of two and one-half million blocks of stone ranging from three to sixty tons each.
- A building that has not settled, has not shifted, has not budged even one-tenth of an inch in thousands of years—a feat that even modern engineering could not equal.[259]

I've had the privilege of being on the Southwest Radio Ministries broadcast with Dr. Hutchings, and have told him on the air how the first edition of his book, *Prophecy in Stone* (in the 1970s), was an eye-opener for me. I was not aware back then of the intriguing tidbits of information concerning the Great Pyramid that seemed to parallel biblical prophecy—for instance, how some ancient writers referred to the Great Pyramid as "the Pillar of Enoch." This was engaging to me because the so-called "King's Chamber" in the Great Pyramid was found to have never been occupied, and Enoch "was not, for God took him" (Genesis 5:24). When the empty coffer in the King's Chamber was measured, it was discovered that the interior dimensions are the same as the biblical Ark of the Covenant. Besides this, 144,000 polished limestone blocks originally covered the exterior of the Great Pyramid, which were sealed with an adhesive so strong that they would break anywhere but at the seal. This is the same number of the saints who, in the book of Revelation 7:3–8, are sealed with the seal of God.

Yet of all such fascinating findings Dr. Hutchings describes in *The Great Pyramid: Prophecy In Stone*, the sections in his book I found most interesting focus on the missing head cornerstone (apex stone, capstone) of the Great Pyramid, and the curious verses in Psalms 118:22 and Acts 4:11 pertaining to Jesus as the "stone" the builders rejected and that has become the "head cornerstone." As Hutchings points out, the only kind of building in all the world that requires a head cornerstone is a pyramid. Because of this, Hutchings believes the "pillar" that Isaiah (Isaiah 19:19–20) said would stand as a "sign and for a witness unto the Lord" in the end times may be the Great Pyramid on the old border that separated lower and upper Egypt.

Conversely, a few years ago, another friend of mine named Patrick (Paddy) Heron wrote a book entitled *Pyramid of the Apocalypse*, in which he postulated that the Great Pyramid at Giza had been built by the Nephilim, the offspring of Watchers. Besides associated legends, part of his reasoning had to do with the scale of the massive undertaking and the same biblical parallels—the one hundred forty-four thousand, the missing capstone, etc.—which Heron viewed as the Watchers trying to copy, plagiarize, mimic, or borrow from the fame of something known only to the angels, namely, the design of the New Jerusalem in heaven, whose height and width are the same, as in a pyramidal structure (as opposed to those who believe the New Jerusalem will be cube-shaped). Heron and researchers like him further warn that an antichrist who is somehow related to the Great Pyramid—as a resurrected Osiris/Apollo/Nimrod would be, though we could only offer at this point fantastic speculation how this deity, returned to flesh, would be outrightly connected to the Great Pyramid—could use these mysterious attributes of the Great Pyramid, which seem related to biblical prophecy, as a great deception to guide people away from the true Messiah. This theological premise is interesting, as everything about the coming of the False Christ will be an antithetical mirror of Jesus. For example, Jesus has seven stars in His right hand (Revelation 1:20), while the Antichrist Osiris/Apollo/Nimrod is represented by the seven-star Pleiades system. The Great Pyramid capstone is missing, representing temporary vacancy by Apollo according to the mottoes, whose coming will "cap" the pyramid, and yet as we have seen, Jesus is also called the head cornerstone.

Whoever turns out to be correct in the debate above, the design of the Great Seal of the United States makes it clear which side of the discussion America's national cipher points to. There are no biblical verses on the Great Seal heralding the second coming of Jesus Christ. And, unlike the actual Great Pyramid in Giza, whose walls are devoid of idolatrous symbols, the Great Seal is made up entirely of mottoes and prayers to the pagan father of the deity Apollo, to fulfill the Cumaean Sibyl's prophecy and to return to earthly rule the disembodied spirit of the deceased god Apollo/Osiris/Nimrod. Is this what is meant in Psalms 118 and Acts chapter 4 where Jesus is the capstone the builders refused? Was He rejected as the Messiah by "the builders"—a literal reference to "Masons"—because another is coming that will cap their pyramid? A second messiah?

Trestleboard Dates:
The Start and Finish of the Great Work

We have seen over and over that the seal's symbolism leaves no doubts as to the identity of the deity behind the all-seeing eye, or to the prophecy from the mottoes regarding the return of the deity known at various times in history as Apollo, Osiris, and Nimrod. This leaves the second issue that needs to be resolved from the Great Seal's "trestleboard" as to the timing of the work: when it was started and when it is scheduled to be completed.

One key to the starting date of this mystical work is magnificently ciphered in the number 888, the sum of the letters in Greek for the name of Jesus (each Greek letter represents a number). This cipher also confirms the prophecies of Psalms 118 and Acts 4 concerning Jesus as the rejected capstone: This same number—888—is also found in "the riddle" of the *Sibylline Oracles*, ascribed to the Cumaean Sibyl, which J. L. Lightfoot says was hoped by some early Christians to represent Jesus, but was clearly understood by pagans to be a prophecy of the return of Apollo[260] because 888 was Olen's number, the founder of Apollo's oracle and his first prophet, and signified the "spiritual sun" represented in the glory surrounding the all-seeing eye of Apollo/Horus on the Great Seal, and the *novus ordo seclorum* or "new age" that his coming would herald. Gnostics and mystics among the occult hierarchy maintain this interpretation as the true meaning of the Apollonian Sibyl's prophecy. The text in question comes from the Sibylline Oracles:

> Then will come to men the Son of the Great God, coated flesh, similar to mortals on earth.... But I want to tell you the whole [of his] number: eight units [8], so much tens in

addition [80], and eight hundreds [800, or 8+80+800=888], here are what to the friends of incredulity, to men, the Name will reveal; but you, in the spirit, thinks well of the immortal and very high Son of God, to the Christ.[261]

So here we have two "messiahs" represented by the number 888—Jesus, the Christ of the Bible, and Apollo, the Sibyl's messiah of the *novus ordo seclorum*. What is astonishing about this is that adding the number of these two messiahs together (888+888) equals the year 1776—the date chosen for the founding of the United States and reflected in the Roman numerals at the base of the uncapped pyramid on the Great Seal.

Adepts of the mystical order actually go to great lengths to show how this addition of 888+888=1776 is the "cardinal number" of the "great work" also known as the "eagle of eagles" reflected in the well-known Masonic symbol of the two-headed eagle or phoenix, which Masonic dictionaries define as historically representing the "merger" *of two gods* (in this instance, Jesus with Apollo).[262]

Given everything else we have learned from the works of Freemasons like David Ovason and Manly P. Hall, this date, 1776, representing two messiahs—the rejection of one in favor of the other—is not likely a mistake. Thus, the trestleboard's 1776 "beginning" date for the great work of the Craft truly marked the start in history of the secret doctrine of Freemasonic Illuminatus toward establishing a New Atlantis in anticipation of the return of their founder and deity, Apollo/Osiris/Nimrod.

To further verify this part of the cipher pointing to an "alternative capstone" or second messiah, the year 1776 at the base of the pyramid is understood by Masons worldwide to be the year 5776 Anno Lucis ("in the year of light"). This is because Masons of the ancient Craft add four thousand years to the common date, the number of years that conventional theology assumes creation began before Christ: thus, 4,000+1,776=5,776.

Why is this important? Because 5,776 is exactly how many inches high the Great Pyramid in Giza would be when completed with its capstone, a sacred fact to occultists. Completing the pyramid symbolically in this way is central to the rituals and mysticism of Freemasons and numerous Illuminated fraternities. This has been true throughout the ages, and is why this symbolism was encoded on the Great Seal and remains at the core of esoteric ambition today. The year 1776 thus represents 1) the trestleboard date on which the great work and secret destiny began; and 2) is a prophetic marker toward the descent of the eye of Apollo/Osiris/Nimrod upon the uncapped pyramid in accomplishment of the Great Work.

Yet if the year 1776 represents the *starting* date on the trestleboard toward the accomplishment "of which the United States Government was dedicated from the day of its inception," as Manly P. Hall said, what date did the Master Masons envision that the work would be *finished* in order that Hiram Abiff (Osiris/Apollo/Nimrod) could return to inhabit his temple? This is found in the modern Jewish calendar as well as the Scottish Rite Freemasonry, who, unlike their other brethren, prefer adding 3,760 years to the common date. In order for this superior side of Masonry to arrive at the appropriate number for their finished pyramid and the completed work (the height of the pyramid with its capstone reaching upward of 5,776 inches), they have to add the *future* date, 2016, to the common era, or 3,760+2,016=5,776.

This is important for several reasons, not the least of which is that, if the culmination of the Illuminati enterprise reaches an apex in 2016, it is prophetically related to the infamous year 2012—the rollover of the Mayan and many other ancient pagan calendars that foresaw the conclusion of a dispensation and the beginning of a final Golden Age, which heralds the return of their gods. Disturbingly, some will say the year 2012 could therefore represent in Christian eschatology the beginning of Great Tribulation, with 2016 representing the "midst of the week" when all Hades breaks loose and Apollo (Antichrist) presents himself as God and enters the temple in Jerusalem. Others may see 2016 as the start of this final age.

Recurrence of 2012 and 2016: Did Something Begin in the Year 2012 that will Reach its Apex in 2016?

As the reader will discover, the year-dates 2012 and 2016 appear on more than one occasion in connection to the Masonic prophecy of the coming of Hiram/Osiris/Apollo. We will reveal how these years are encoded on the Great Seal of the United States and several other important Masonic ciphers, including the Lost Symbol, the Capitol Dome in Washington, DC, and the 1st-degree Masonic trestleboard. But first we offer several tidbits related to end-times scenarios that some may find interesting. We mentioned above how the year 2012, being three and one-half years before the Masonic ending date 2016, could thus be viewed as the beginning of the Tribulation period. It is also important to recognize that, based on Daniel chapter 9 and related texts, scholars believe a period of not more than seventy years (a biblical generation) will elapse between the reformation of Israel as a nation and the return of Jesus Christ. When seventy years is added to 1948—the year Israel was formally recognized as an independent nation by the United Nations—it brings us through the year 2018. Does this mean the year 2019—exactly seven years after 2012—would mark the year that Jesus Christ returns with the armies of heaven to establish His rule over earth? Interestingly, some Islamic scholars seem to hold a parallel view. The author of *The Day of Wrath*, Safar Ibn ʿAbd Al-Rahman Al-Hawali, writes at www. IslamicAwakening.com:

> When Daniel specified the period between its distress and relief, between the era of anguish and the era of blessing, he put it as forty-five years! We have already seen that he specified the time of the establishment of the abomination of desolation as the year 1967, which is what in fact occurred. Therefore, the end—or the beginning of the end—will be 1967 + 45 = 2012.

What is the most remarkable connection between these dates is that the Maya themselves recognized a direct link between the number thirteen and the years 1776 and 2012 in cycles and illustrations in a way that academic Richard N. Luxton found to be similar to prophecies of the "Christian Last Judgment." He translated and annotated *The Book of Chumayel: The Counsel Book of the Yucatec Maya 1539–1638*, and noted on katun 13 Ahau:

> The dates that accompany the illustrations approximate real counts. Katun 13 Ahau ended in 1539 and began in the Colonial Count in 1776…. The traditional theme of agreement as the end of the eastern katun cycle in 13 Ahau is

intermingled here with elements of the Christian Last Judgment. Whether this paradigm was also intended for the end of the Long Count in 2012 is open to question.[263]

Religious ceremonies and prophecies accompanied Mayan katuns, and Luxton's connection to the "Christian Last Judgment" and the thirteen katuns (a katun is approximately 19.7 years) between 1776 and 2012 is drawn from the prophecies of the Mayan prophet Chilam Balam. Written down in about the year 1595, the oracular Chilam Balam, or "jaguar" shaman, said the end of this period would witness the judgment of God in the form of social collapse, epidemics, plagues, and famine. The same period would see the coming of two great prophets, one after the other, according to the Mayan prophecy. Is this the False Prophet paving the way for the Antichrist?

It may be no coincidence that the start and ending dates of the final thirteen katuns of the Mesoamerican Mayan Long Count calendar are reflected in the thirteen steps of the pyramid on the United States' Great Seal. That the steps of the pyramid were intended to convey units of time has been an open secret for many years. Though he was not sure what to make of it himself, Paul Foster Case wrote many years ago that:

Since the date, 1776, is placed on the bottom course of the pyramid, and since the number thirteen has been so important in the symbolism of the seal, it is not unreasonable to suppose that the thirteen courses of the pyramid may represent thirteen time periods.[264]

John Kehne made an even more intriguing observation, directly coupling the Great Seal's trestleboard date, 1776, and the Mayan ending date 2012:

This Seal shows a thirteen-step pyramid with 1776 in Roman numerals.… [The year] 1776 was not only the year that the Declaration of Independence was signed, but was also a special year in the Mayan calendar. Just as the last katun in the Great Cycle is "katun 2012," the first katun in the cycle of thirteen was "katun 1776." In fact, the katun ended thirty-three days before the signing. So 1776 is the bottom level of the pyramid, where the date is actually inscribed—the top of the pyramid is therefore 2012.[265]

As we shall show, early Freemasons were aware of the significance of these dates—1776, 2012, and 2016 respectively—and while the thirteen steps of the unfinished pyramid on the Great Seal account for the timeframe 1776–2012 using the slightly less than twenty-year periods (19.7) of the katun, the Gregorian twenty-year cycle produces 1776–2016, both of which fit perfectly within the trestleboard dating on the US Great Seal cipher and the first Masonic tracing board, as we will reveal.

1st-Degree Tracing Board Shows the Way

When research began for this book and I became aware of the nearly five hundred-year-old Mayan prophecies connecting the "colonial count 1776" with the final thirteen katuns of their calendar ending in the year 2012 (and how academia viewed this as a mirror of the countdown to the "Christian Last Judgment"), I wondered if early American scholars—and specifically architects of Freemasonry involved in the design of Washington, DC, the Great Seal of the United States, and other iconic artifacts important to the founding of this country—were aware of this Mesoamerican timeline. It seemed too much of a coincidence that the final thirteen katuns ending in 2012 would match the starting and ending date on the Great Seal by chance. My investigation into the matter resulted in numerous examples of the year 2012 related to America (and other places of the world), which I will summarize in the following chapter. But due to the nature of the present chapter, I will list here two of the findings directly connected with Freemasons and the designers of the capital city in Washington, DC that illustrate their knowledge of the ending date 2012.

The first discovery came as a result of Dr. Robert Lomas of the University of Bradford in the UK openly posting on the school's website an archive on Freemasonry that he had received from the Masons.[266] The reason behind the decision to make this information available is unknown, but thankfully it included the tracing board of the 1st-degree Freemasons. When I discovered this page at the college, I was amazed that the galactic alignment that New Agers claimed to have occurred in 2012 is clearly depicted on the tracing board. Even more surprising, it is connected with the ladder that the enlightened Mason may use to reach the location of the Great Architect of the Universe in 2012—shown to be *the seven-star Pleiades system of Apollo/Osiris!* The tracing board is stunning in its symbolism, depicting nearly everything we have stated thus far concerning the god of Freemasonry, the myths associated with him, and the date on which he is prophesied to return.

When interpreting the symbolism of this tracing board, it is important to remain faithful to the information provided on the University's website, which in turn is consistent with Scottish Rite Freemasonry. Specific language from the site, therefore, has been used in deciphering the tracing board's meaning, including the following:

> The Blazing Star, or glory in the centre, refers us to the Sun, which enlightens the earth, and by its benign influence dispenses its blessings to mankind in general. The Indented or Tessellated Border refers us to the Planets, which, in their various revolutions form a beautiful border or skirtwork round that grand luminary, the Sun....
>
> In all regular, well-formed, constituted Lodges, there is a point within a circle round which the Brethren cannot err. This circle is bounded between North and South by two grand parallel lines.... On the upper part of this circle rests the Volume of the Sacred Law, supporting Jacob's ladder, the top of which reaches to the heavens.
>
> The three great pillars supporting a Freemason's Lodge are emblematic of those Divine attributes, and further represent Solomon King of Israel, Hiram, King of Tyre and Hiram Abiff.... Solomon King of Israel for his wisdom in building, completing, and dedicating the Temple at Jerusalem to God's service; Hiram King of Tyre [Lucifer of

Ezekiel 28:11–19?] for his strength in supporting him with men and materials; and Hiram Abiff [Osiris, according to Freemasonry] for his curious and masterly workmanship in beautifying and adorning the same.

[The] Mason who is possessed of this virtue in its most ample sense may justly be deemed to have attained the summit of his profession; figuratively speaking, an ethereal mansion, veiled from mortal eyes by the starry firmament, emblematically depicted in our Lodges by seven Stars, which have an allusion to as many regularly made Masons; without which number no Lodge is perfect, neither can any candidate be legally initiated into the Order…

The Sun and Moon are messengers of His will.

Using the descriptions of the symbols provided by Masons, the first thing one notes at the bottom of the ladder is the point within the circle: the symbol of Ra, Osiris, and Isis joined in procreation, "bounded between North and South by two grand parallel lines." The blazing star near the center of the board represents the Dog Star Sirius, which is related to Lucifer and the Osiris epic at length, according to Albert Pike in *Morals and Dogma*. He noted that the 1st-degree Masons who would use this tracing board would be ignorant of this connection; they would think the blazing star represents the "sun," as they are instructed to believe according to guidelines on the university website.

But those adepts "initiated into the mysteries" understand it is Sirius—connected to Lucifer, Isis, Osiris, and the all-seeing eye of Osiris—as "his is the All-Seeing Eye in our Lodges," according to Pike.

Concerning this deity, instructions on the University website to the 1st-degree Freemasons go on to explain that the sun and moon at the top of the board are "messengers" of the god. Understanding this, the solstice sun in the upper left corner does in fact tell us something very clearly about "time" and its relationship with the Isis/Osiris symbolism. The sun is depicted sitting in the "dark rift" of the Milky Way, while the moon on the right is joined by the seven stars of the Pleiades. Simply put, this is the arrangement that some claim happened when the Mayan Long Count calendar rolled over and the winter solstice sun aligned with the "dark rift," a place the Maya described as being the "Road to the Underworld." The tracing board thus conveys that at the moment this galactic alignment occurred, the dawn of a new age of Osiris began when the ladder to heaven joined the devout Masons with their Great Architect December 21, 2012.

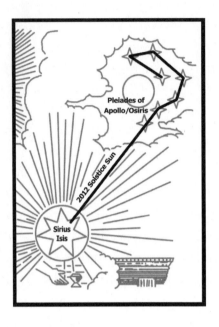

What Brumidi Revealed in the Capitol Dome

Fabulous and irrefutable evidence that early Freemasons and those working with them were aware of the Mesoamerican belief system and the calendar ending date of 2012 is actually incorporated directly into the design of the Capitol Dome in Washington, DC (more on the Dome later), and is vividly illustrated in the commissioned artwork of Constantino Brumidi. Born July 26, 1805, in Rome, Brumidi was an Italian/Greek painter who made his name restoring sixteenth-century Vatican frescos, as well as artwork in several Roman palaces. Following the French occupation of Rome in 1849, Brumidi immigrated to the United States, where he became a citizen and began work for the Jesuits in New York (viewed at that time as the "hidden power and authority" of the Roman Catholic Church). This work included frescos in the Church of St. Ignatius in Baltimore, Maryland; the Church of St. Aloysius in Washington, DC; and St. Stephen's Church in Philadelphia, namely, the Crucifixion, the Martydom of St. Stephen, and the Assumption of Mary.

Abruptly in 1854, the Jesuits financed a trip for Brumidi to Mexico, where he painted a representation of the Holy Trinity in the Mexico City Cathedral. However, while there, he engaged in the curious task of making copious notes of the ancient Aztec Calendar Stone (also known as the "Stone of the Sun"), which rolled over in the year 2012.

Immediately upon his return from Mexico, Brumidi took his collection of notes and drawings to Washington, DC, where he met with Quartermaster General Montgomery C. Meigs, supervisor of construction over the wings and Dome of the United States Capitol. Brumidi was quickly commissioned to be the "government painter," and began adorning the hallways and Rotunda of the Capitol with pagan frescos sacred to Freemasonry, including the *Apotheosis of George Washington* and the famous *Frieze of American History*. Brumidi died in 1880 and three other artists completed the frieze, but not before Brumidi attached to his historic work—sometime between 1878–1880—a scene called *Cortez and Montezuma at Mexican Temple*, featuring the Aztec Calendar Stone and other important symbolism.

The Stone of the Sun depicted in Brumidi's frieze (the circular object behind the figures on the right) is based on the actual twelve-foot tall, four-foot thick, twenty-four-ton, monolithic Aztec Calendar Stone. During the pinnacle of Aztec civilization when the Aztec dominated all other tribes of Mexico, this Stone rested atop the Tenochtitlan Temple in the midst of the most powerful and largest city in Mesoamerica. Today, Mexico City's Cathedral, where Brumidi worked, occupies this site. The Spaniards buried the Stone

Cortez and Montezuma at Mexican Temple, by Brumidi

there, and it remained hidden beneath the Cathedral until it was rediscovered in 1790. Then it was raised and embedded into the wall of the Cathedral, where it remained until 1885. Today, the Stone of the Sun is on display in the National Museum of Anthropology in Mexico City's Chapultepec Park.

The inclusion of this symbolism and its accompanying idols in the US Capitol Dome is important. The sun god Tonatiuh, whose face and protruding tongue are seen at the center of the Sun Stone, is the god of the present (fifth) time, which began in 3114 BC and rolled over in 2012. The Aztec solar calendar is second only in accuracy to the Mayan calendar, which also started over December 21, 2012. Tonatiuh—who delivered important prophecies and demanded human sacrifices (more than twenty thousand victims per year were offered to him, according to Aztec and Spanish records, and in the single year of 1487, Aztec priests sacrificed eighty thousand people to him at the dedication of the reconstructed temple of the sun god)—was also known as the lord of the thirteen days (from 1 Death to 13 Flint), a number sacred to Aztec, Maya, *and Freemasons* for prophetic and mystical reasons.

The Stone of the Sun

Like the Maya, Aztecs believed the first age, or "First Sun," was a time when giants had lived on earth who were destroyed by a great flood or deluge long before the Mayan or Toltec civilizations came along. (The significance of this is detailed in the next chapter.) The final age, or "Fifth Sun," would end in 2012. While the Aztecs assimilated such knowledge from the Maya, they built their culture primarily on Toltec ideas. Their great city of Tenochtitlan, on an island in Lake Texcoco with its causeways, canals, marketplaces, and vast towers and temples rising majestically into the air, was so spectacular that when the conquistador Bernal Díaz del Castillo, who wrote an eyewitness account of the conquest of Mexico by the Spaniards, saw it, he exclaimed:

> When we saw so many cities and villages built in the water and other great towns on dry land we were amazed and said that it was like the enchantments…on account of the great towers and cues and buildings rising from the water, and all built of masonry. And some of our soldiers even asked whether the things that we saw were not a dream…. I do not know how to describe it, seeing things as we did that had never been heard of or seen before, not even dreamed about.[267]

Not only was the Aztec culture so advanced in engineering, astronomy, and mathematics, but the warriors of Montezuma outnumbered the expedition of Cortez by a thousand to one. How then did the Spaniards conquer the Aztecs so easily? Toltec prophecy had told of Quetzalcoatl, who would come from the east as a light-skinned priest to rule their civilization. Nezhaulcoyotl, a great astrologer who supported Montezuma, believed this vision, and when Cortez arrived exactly when the prophecy said the god would return, Montezuma received him as the coming of Quetzalcoatl, and surrendered. This event is symbolized in the *Cortez and Montezuma* frieze by Brumidi.

Another connection between Brumidi's prophetic Stone of the Sun depiction and Freemasonry can be seen in the serpent coiled around the sacred fire, toward which Montezuma's left hand intentionally gestures. The sacred fire was connected to the seven-star Pleiades (Tianquiztli, the "gathering place") by the Aztecs, and represented the final year in a fifty-two-year cycle called "calendar round," which ended when the Pleiades crossed the fifth cardinal point at midnight that year. At this time, the Aztecs would let the fires go out and conduct the "dance of the new fire" to start the cycle again. When the priests lit the new "sacred fire" as well as the hearth fires, it ensured the movement of the sun (the serpent coiled around the sacred fire in Brumidi's painting) along the precession anew. In the year 2012, not only was the Pleiades in this zenith over Mesoamerica, but the alignment came into full conjunction with the sun, as depicted on the Freemason 1st-degree tracing board. This sacred knowledge is why the Pyramid of the Sun at Teotihuacan near Mexico City also corresponds with the Pleiades. Its west side and surrounding streets are aligned directly with the setting point of the Pleiades, a configuration held in high esteem by the Maya as well. They built the Kukulcan pyramid at Chichen Itza so that during the spring and autumn equinox, at the rising and setting of the sun, a slithering, snake-like shadow representing Kukulcan (Quetzalcoatl, the plumed serpent) would cast along the north stairway to the serpent's head at the bottom. Sixty days later, when the sun rises over the Pyramid at midday, it aligns with the Pleiades again.

By portraying the Stone of the Sun that rolled over in 2012, the sacred fire that was extinguished and relit in 2012, and the astrological alignment with the Pleiades in the *Frieze of American History*, Brumidi was telling us quite clearly that the designers of the Capitol were aware of the implications of 2012. This adds clarity to the reasons the designers of the Great Seal of the United States similarly incorporated the Mayan 13 katun system—which started in 1776 and ended in 2012—on the nation's primary cipher.

Yet a deeper and related message is also openly hidden in the Capitol Dome. A third piece of imagery from Brumidi's *Cortez and Montezuma* scene that not only connects Mesoamerican belief to the Freemasons and prophecy, but to the Vatican, can be found in the drum behind the kneeling Aztec. The drum bears the shape of the Maltese cross, a symbol connected in history with the empire of Osiris as starting on the island of Malta. The Maltese cross was adopted by the Knights of Malta (connected with Freemasonry) and the Vatican (where Brumidi first worked and found favor). We believe this is not by chance. Captain Montgomery C. Meigs, the engineer who placed Brumidi over the paintings for the new Dome, wanted artwork reminiscent of that at the Vatican. With Brumidi's ties to the Vatican and the Jesuits, it was a match "made in heaven." By including this well-known Mayan, Illuminati, and Freemasonic symbol, Brumidi cleverly connected the design of the Capitol Dome in Washington, DC with the Vatican, Masonic mysticism, and the year 2012 in more ways than one.

The Dome of America's Temple, the Obelisk, and the Lost Symbol

Undoubtedly the vast majority of people, when looking at Washington, DC and at the Vatican, never comprehend how these cities constitute one of the greatest open conspiracies of all time. There, reproduced in all their glory and right before the world's eyes, is an ancient talismanic diagram based on the history and cult of Isis, Osiris, and Horus, including the magical utilities meant to generate the deity's return.

The primeval concept—especially that of sacred Domes facing Obelisks—was designed in antiquity for the express purpose of regeneration, resurrection, and apotheosis, for deity incarnation from the underworld to earth's surface through union of the respective figures—the Dome (ancient structural representation of the womb of Isis) and the Obelisk (ancient representation of the erect male phallus of Osiris).

This layout, as modeled in antiquity, exists today on the grandest scale at the heart of the capital of the most powerful government on earth—the United States—as well as in the heart of the most politically influential Church on earth—the Vatican. Given this fact and the pattern provided by the apostle Paul and the Apocalypse of John (the book of Revelation) that the end times would culminate in a marriage between political (Antichrist) and religious (False Prophet) authorities at the return of Osiris/Apollo, it behooves open-minded researchers to carefully consider this prophecy in stone, as it defines the spiritual energy that is knowingly or unknowingly being invoked at both locations with potential ramifications for Petrus Romanus, the year 2012, and beyond.

The US capital has been called the "Mirror Vatican" due to the strikingly similar layout and design of its primary buildings and streets. This is no accident. In fact, America's forefathers first named the capital city "Rome." But the parallelism between Washington and the Vatican is most clearly illustrated by the Capitol building and Dome facing the Obelisk known as the Washington Monument, and at St. Peter's Basilica in the Vatican by a similar Dome facing a familiar Obelisk—both of which were, according to their own official records, fashioned after the Roman Pantheon, the circular Domed Rotunda "dedicated to all pagan gods." This layout—a Domed temple facing an Obelisk—is an ancient, alchemical blueprint that holds significant esoteric meaning.

For those who may not know, the US Capitol building in Washington, DC is historically based on a pagan Masonic temple theme, Thomas Jefferson, who shepherded the antichristian "Roman Pantheon" design, wrote to the Capitol's architect, Benjamin LaTrobe, defining it as "the first temple dedicated to…embellishing with Athenian taste the course of a nation looking far beyond the range of Athenian destinies"[268] (the "Athenian" empire was first known as "Osiria," the kingdom of Osiris). In 1833, Massachusetts Representative Rufus Choate agreed, writing, "We have built no national temples but the Capitol."[269] William Henry and Mark Gray in their book, *Freedom's Gate: Lost Symbols in the U.S. Capitol*, add that, "The U.S. Capitol has numerous architectural and other features that unquestionably identify it with ancient temples."[270] After listing various features to make their case that the US Capitol building is a "religious temple"—including housing the image of a deified being, heavenly beings, gods, symbols, inscriptions, sacred geometry, columns, prayers, and orientation to the sun—they conclude:

> The designers of the city of Washington DC oriented it to the Sun—especially the rising Sun on June 21 and December 21 [the same day and month as the end of the Mayan calendar in 2012]. The measurements for this orientation were made from the location of the center of the Dome of the U.S. Capitol, rendering it a "solar temple." Its alignment and encoded numerology point to the Sun as well as the stars. A golden circle on the Rotunda story and a white star

in the Crypt marks this spot.... It is clear that the builders viewed the Capitol as America's sole temple: a solemn...
Solar Temple to be exact.[271]

To understand what these statements may soon mean for the
future of the world, one needs to comprehend how these aparati—
the Dome and the Obelisk facing it—facilitate important archaic
and modern protocols for invigorating *prophetic* supernatural
alchemy. In ancient times, the Obelisk represented the god Osiris'
"missing" male organ, which Isis was not able to find after her hus-
band/brother was slain and chopped into fourteen pieces by his evil
brother Seth (or Set). The story involves a detailed account of the
envious brother and seventy-two conspirators tricking Osiris into
climbing inside a box, which Seth quickly locked and threw into
the Nile. Osiris drowned, and his body floated down the Nile River,
where it snagged on the limbs of a tamarisk tree. In Byblos, Isis
recovered his body from the river bank and took it into her care. In
her absence, Seth stole the body again and chopped it into fourteen
pieces, which he threw into the Nile. Isis searched the river bank
until she recovered every piece, except for the genitals, which had
been swallowed by a fish (Plutarch says a crocodile). Isis recombined
the thirteen pieces of Osiris' corpse and replaced the missing organ
with a magic facsimile (Obelisk), which she used to impregnate herself, thus giving rise to Osiris again in the person of his son, Horus.
This legendary ritual for reincarnating Osiris formed the core of
Egyptian cosmology (as well as the Rosicrucian/Masonic dying-and-
rising myths) and was fantastically venerated on the most imposing
scale throughout all of Egypt by towering Obelisks (representing
the phallus of Osiris) and Domes (representing the pregnant belly
of Isis) including at Karnak where the upright Obelisks were "vital-

ized" or "stimulated" from the energy of the masturbatory Sun god Ra shining down upon them.

There is historical evidence that this elaborate myth and its rituals may have been based originally on real characters and events. Regarding this, it is noteworthy that in 1998, former secretary general of Egypt's Supreme Council of Antiquities, Zahi Hawass, claimed to have found the burial tomb of the god Osiris (Apollo/Nimrod) at the Giza Plateau. As referred to earlier in this work, in the article, "Sandpit of Royalty," from the newspaper *Extra Bladet* (Copenhagen), January 31, 1999, Hawass was quoted saying:

> I have found a shaft, going twenty-nine meters vertically down into the ground, exactly halfway between the Chefren Pyramid and the Sphinx. At the bottom, which was filled with water, we have found a burial chamber with four pillars. In the middle is a large granite sarcophagus, which I expect to be the grave of Osiris, the god.... I have been digging in Egypt's sand for more than thirty years, and up to date this is the most exciting discovery I have made.... We found the shaft in November and began pumping up the water recently. So several years will pass before we have finished investigating the find.[272]

As far as we know, this discovery did not ultimately provide the physical remains of the deified person. But what it did illustrate is that at least some very powerful Egyptologists believe Osiris was a historical figure, and that his body was stored somewhere at or near the Great Pyramid. Manly P. Hall, who knew that the Masonic legend of Hiram Abiff was a thinly veiled prophecy of the resurrection of Osiris, may have understood what Zahi Hawass (not to mention

Roerich, Roosevelt, and Wallace with their sacred Osiris Casket [see previous chapter]) was looking for, and why. Consider that he wrote in *The Secret Teachings of All Ages*: "The Dying God [Osiris] shall rise again! The secret room in the House of the Hidden Places shall be rediscovered. The Pyramid again shall stand as the ideal emblem of...resurrection, and regeneration."[273]

In Egypt, where rituals were performed to actually "raise" the spirit of Osiris into the reigning Pharaoh, political authority in the form of divine kingship or theocratic statesmanship was established (later reflected in the political and religious doctrine of royal and political legitimacy or "the divine right of kings," who supposedly derived their right to rule from the will of God, with the exception in some countries that the king is subject to the Church and the pope). This meant, among other things, the Egyptian Pharaoh enjoyed extraordinary authority as the "son of the sun god" (Ra) and the incarnation of the falcon god Horus during his lifetime. At death, Pharaoh became the Osiris, the divine judge of the netherworld, and on earth, his son and predecessor took his place as the newly anointed manifestation of Horus. Thus each generation of pharaohs provided the gods with a spokesman for the present world and for the afterlife while also offering the nation divinely appointed leadership.

Yet the observant reader may wonder, "Was there something more to the Pharaoh's deification than faith in ritual magic?" The cult center of Amun-Ra at Thebes may hold the answer, as it was the site of the largest religious structure ever built—the temple of Amun-Ra at Karnak—and the location of many extraordinary mysterious rites. The great temple with its one hundred miles of walls and gardens (the primary object of fascination and worship by the nemesis of Moses—the Pharaoh of the Exodus, Ramses II) was the place where each pharaoh reconciled his divinity in the company

of Amun-Ra during the festival of Opet. The festival was held at
the temple of Luxor and included a procession of gods carried on
barges up the Nile River from Karnak to the temple. The royal family accompanied the gods on boats while the Egyptian laity walked
along the shore, calling aloud and making requests of the gods. Once
at Luxor, the Pharaoh and his entourage entered the holy of holies,
where the ceremony to raise the spirit of Osiris into the king was performed and Pharaoh was transmogrified into a living deity. Outside,
large groups of dancers and musicians waited anxiously. When the
king emerged as the "born again" Osiris, the crowd erupted in gaiety.
From that day forward, the Pharaoh was considered to be—just as
the god ciphered in the Great Seal of the United States will be—the
son and spiritual incarnation of the Supreme Deity. The all-seeing
eye of Horus/Apollo/Osiris above the unfinished pyramid on the
Great Seal represents this event.

Modern people, especially in America, may view the symbols
used in this magic—the Dome representing the habitually pregnant belly of Isis, and the Obelisk, representing the erect phallus of
Osiris—as profane or pornographic. But they were in fact ritualized fertility objects, which the ancients believed could produce tangible reactions, properties, or "manifestations" within the material
world. The Obelisk and Dome as imitations of the deities' male and
female reproductive organs could, through government representation, invoke into existence the being or beings symbolized by them.
This is why inside the temple or Dome, temple prostitutes representing the human manifestation of the goddess were also available
for ritual sex as a form of imitative magic. These prostitutes usually
began their services to the goddess as children, and were deflowered
at a very young age by a priest or, as Isis was, by a modeled Obelisk
of Osiris' phallus. Sometimes these prostitutes were chosen, on the

basis of their beauty, as the sexual mates of sacred temple bulls who were considered the incarnation of Osiris. In other places, such as at Mendes, temple prostitutes were offered in coitus to divine goats. Through such imitative sex, the Dome and Obelisk became "energy receivers," capable of assimilating Ra's essence from the rays of the sun, which in turn drew forth the "seed" of the underworld Osiris. The seed of the dead deity would, according to the supernatural-ism, transmit upward from out of the underworld through the base (testes) of the Obelisk and magically emit from the tower's head into the womb (Dome) of Isis where incarnation into the sitting pha-raoh/king/president would occur (during what Freemasons also call *the raising [of Osiris] ceremony*). In this way, Osiris could be habitu-ally "born again" or reincarnated as Horus and constantly direct the spiritual destiny of the nation.

This metaphysical phenomenon, which originated with Nim-rod/Semiramis and was central to numerous other ancient cultures, was especially developed in Egypt, where Nimrod/Semiramis were known as Osiris/Isis (and in Ezekiel chapter 8 the children of Israel set up the Obelisk ["image of jealousy," verse 5] facing the entry of their temple—just as the Dome faces the Obelisk in Washing-ton, DC and in the Vatican City—and were condemned by God for worshipping the Sun [Ra] while weeping for Osiris [Tammuz]). The familiar Masonic figure of the point within a circle is the symbol of this union between Ra, Osiris, and Isis. The "point" represents Osiris' phallus in the center of the circle or womb of Isis, which in turn is enlivened by the sun rays from Ra, just as is represented today at the Vatican, where the Egyptian Obelisk of Osiris sits within a circle, and in Washington, DC, where the Obelisk does similarly, situated so as to be the first thing the sun (Ra) strikes as it rises over the capital city and which, when viewed from overhead, forms the magical point within a circle known as a *circumpunct*. The sorcery is further amplified, according to ancient occultic beliefs, by the presence of the Reflecting Pool in DC, which serves as a mirror to heaven and "transferring point" for those spirits and energies.

And just what is it the spirits see when they look downward on the Reflecting Pool in Washington? They find a city dedicated to and built in honor of the legendary deities Isis and Osiris complete with the thirteen gathered pieces of Osiris (America's original thirteen colonies); the required Obelisk known as the Washington Monument; the Capitol Dome (of Isis) for impregnation and incarnation of deity into each Pharaoh (president); and last but not least, the official government buildings erected to face their respective counterparts and whose cornerstones—including the US. Capitol Dome—were dedicated during astrological alignments related to the zodiacal constellation Virgo (Isis) as required for the magic to occur.

Where the Vitality of Osiris/Apollo (the Beast that Was, and Is Not, and Yet Is) Pulsates in Anticipation of His Final "Raising"

The three-hundred-thirty ton Obelisk in St. Peter's Square in the Vatican City is not just any Obelisk. It was cut from a single block of red granite during the Fifth dynasty of Egypt to stand as Osiris' erect phallus at the Temple of the Sun in ancient Heliopolis (Ἡλιούπολις, meaning city of the sun or principal seat of Atum-Ra sun-worship), the city of "On" in the Bible, dedicated to Ra, Osiris, and Isis. The Obelisk was moved from Heliopolis to the Julian Forum of Alexandria by Emperor Augustus and later from thence (approximately 37 AD) by Caligula to Rome to stand at the spine of the Circus. There, under Nero, its excited presence maintained a counter-vigil over countless brutal Christian executions, including the martyrdom of the apostle Peter (according to some historians). Over fifteen hundred years following that, Pope Sixtus V ordered hundreds of workmen under celebrated engineer-architects Giovanni and Domenico Fontana (who also erected three other ancient obelisks in the old Roman city including one dedicated to Osiris by Rameses III—at the Piazza del Popolo, Piazza di S. Maria Maggiore, and Piazza di S. Giovanni in Laterano) to move the phallic pillar to the center of St. Peter's Square in Rome. This proved a daunting task, which took over four months, nine hundred laborers, one hundred forty horses, and seventy winches. Though worshipped at its present location ever since by countless admirers, the proximity of the Obelisk to the old Basilica was formerly "resented as something of a provocation, almost as a slight to the Christian religion. It had stood there like a false idol, as it were vaingloriously, on what was believed to be the center of the accursed circus where the early Christians and St. Peter had been put to death. Its sides, then as now, were graven with dedications to [the worst of ruthless pagans] Augustus and Tiberius."[274]

The fact that many traditional Catholics as well as Protestants perceived such idols of stone to be not only objects of heathen adoration but the worship of demons (see Acts 7:41–42; Psalms 96:5; and 1 Corinthians 10:20) makes what motivated Pope Sixtus to erect the phallus of Osiris in the heart of St. Peter's Square, located in Vatican City and bordering St. Peter's Basilica, very curious. To ancient Christians, the image of a cross and symbol of Jesus sitting atop (or emitting from) the head of a demonic god's erect manhood would have been at a minimum a very serious blasphemy. Yet Sixtus was not content with simply restoring and using such ancient pagan relics (which were believed in those days to actually house the pagan spirit they represented) but even destroyed Christian artifacts in the process. Michael W. Cole, Associate Professor in the Department of the History of Art at the University of Pennsylvania, and Professor Rebecca E. Zorach, Associate Professor of Art History at the University of Chicago, raise critical questions about this in their scholarly book *The Idol in the Age of Art* when they state:

> Whereas Gregory, to follow the chroniclers, had ritually dismembered the city's *imagines daemonem* [demonic images], Sixtus fixed what was in disrepair, added missing parts, and made the "idols" into prominent urban features. Two of the four obelisks had to be reconstructed from found or excavated pieces... The pope was even content to destroy *Christian* antiquities in the process: as Jennifer Montagu has pointed out, the bronze for the statues of Peter and Paul came from the medieval doors of S. Agnese, from the Scala Santa at the Lateran, and from a ciborium at St. Peter's.
>
> [Sixtus] must have realized that, especially in their work on the two [broken obelisks], they were not merely repairing injured objects, but also restoring a *type*... In his classic book *The Gothic Idol*, Michael Camille showed literally dozens of medieval images in which the freestanding figure atop a column betokened the pagan idol. The sheer quantity of Camille's examples makes it clear that the device, and what it stood for, would have been immediately recognizable to medieval viewers, and there is no reason to assume that, by Sixtus's time, this had ceased to be true.[275]

The important point made by Professors Cole and Zorach is that at the time Sixtus was busy reintroducing to the Roman public square restored images and statues on columns, the belief remained strong that these idols housed their patron deity, and further that, if these were not treated properly and even placed into service during proper constellations related to their myth, it could beckon evil omens. Leonardo da Vinci had even written in his Codex Urbinas how those who would adore and pray to the image were likely to believe the god represented by it was alive in the stone and watching their behavior. There is strong indication that Sixtus believed this too, and that he "worried about the powers that might inhabit his new urban markers."[276] This was clearly evident when the cross was placed on top of the Obelisk in the midst of St. Peter's Square and the pope marked the occasion by conducting the ancient rite of exorcism against the phallic symbol. First scheduled to occur on September 14th to coincide with the liturgical Feast of the Exaltation of the Cross and not coincidently under the zodiacal sign of Virgo (Isis), the event was delayed until later in the month and fell under the sign of Libra, representing a zenith event for the year. On that morning, a pontifical High Mass was held just before the cross was raised from a portable altar to the apex of Baal's Shaft (as such phallic towers were also known). While clergy prayed and a choir sang Psalms, Pope Sixtus stood facing the Obelisk and, extending his hand toward it, announced: "Exorcizote, creatura lapidis, in nomine Dei" ("I exorcize you, creature of stone, in the name of God"). Sixtus then cast sanctified water upon the pillar's middle, then its right side, then left, then above, and finally below to form a cross, followed by, "In nomine Patris, et Filij, et Spiritus sancti. Amen" ("In the Name of the Father and of the Son and of the Holy Ghost. Amen"). He then crossed himself three times and watched as the symbol of Christ was placed atop Osiris' erect phallus.

Washington Dome Facing Obelisk

Vatican Dome Facing Obelisk

Yet if what Sixtus established in the heart of Vatican City gives some readers pause (numerous other signature events by Sixtus aligned the Sistine city with constellations sacred to Osiris and Isis, which we are not taking time to discuss here but that caused Profs. Zorach and Cole to conclude that, in the end, Sixtus wanted to remain *in the good graces of the pagan gods*), in Washington, DC near the west end of the National Mall, the Obelisk built by Freemasons and dedicated to America's first president brings the fullest meaning to the Nephilim-originated and modern porn-industry impression that "size matters." This is no crude declaration, as adepts of ritual sex-magic know, and dates back to ancient women who wanted to give birth to the offspring of the gods and who judged the size of the male generative organ as indicative of the "giant" genetics or divine seed needed for such offspring. While such phallic symbols have been and still are found in cultures around the world, in ancient Egypt, devotion to this type "obscene divinity" began with Amun-Min and reached its crescendo in the Obelisks of Osiris.

Throughout Greece and Rome the god Priapus (son of Aphrodite) was invoked as a symbol of such divine fertility and later became directly linked to the cult of pornography reflected in the more modern sentiments about "size." This is important because, in addition to the Washington Monument being intentionally constructed to be the tallest Obelisk of its kind in the world at 6,666 (some say 6,660) inches high and 666 inches wide along each side at the base, one of the original concepts for the Washington Monument included Apollo (the Greek version of Osiris) triumphantly returning in his heavenly chariot, and another illustrating a tower "like that of Babel" for its head. Any of these designs would have been equally appropriate to the thirty-three-hundred-pound pyramidal capstone it now displays, as all three concepts carried the meaning necessary to accomplish what late researcher David Flynn described as "the same secret knowledge preserved by the mystery schools since the time of the Pelasgians [that] display modern Isis Osiris worship."[277] This is to say, the "seed" discharged from a Tower-of-Babel-shaped head would magically issue forth the same as would proceed from the existing Egyptian capstone—the offspring of Apollo/Osiris/Nimrod.

The greatest minds in Freemasonry, whose beliefs set the tone for the design of the capital city, its Great Seal, its Dome, and its Obelisk, understood and wrote about this intent. Albert Pike described it as Isis and Osiris' "Active and Passive Principles of the Universe…commonly symbolized by the generative parts of man and woman,"[278] and Freemason writer Albert Mackey described not only the Obelisk, but added the importance of the circle around its base, saying, "The Phallus was an imitation of the male generative organ. It was represented…by a column [Obelisk] that was surrounded by a circle at the base."[279]

In Egypt, where the parodies and rituals for raising Osiris to life through these magical constructs was perfected, Pharaoh served as the "fit extension" for the reborn god to take residence in as the "sex act" was ritualized at the temple of Amun-Ra. The all-seeing eye of Horus/Osiris/Apollo above the unfinished pyramid on the Great Seal forecasts the culmination of this event—that is, the actual return of Osiris—for the United States closely following the year 2012, and the Dome and Obelisk stand ready for the metaphysical ritual to be performed in secret by the elite. We use the phrase "performed in secret" because what the vast majority of people throughout America do not know is that the "raising" ceremony is still conducted inside the headquarters of the Scottish Rite Freemasonry in the House of the Temple by the Supreme Council 33rd Degree over Washington, DC for at least two reasons. First, whenever a Mason reaches the Master level, the ritual includes a parody representing the death, burial, and future resurrection of Hiram Abiff (Osiris). The world at large finally caught a glimpse of this custom when Dan Brown, in his book *The Lost Symbol*, opened with a scene depicting the start of the tradition:

> The secret is how to die.
>
> Since the beginning of time, the secret had always been how to die.
>
> The thirty-four-year-old initiate gazed down at the human skull cradled in his palms. The skull was hollow, like a bowl, filled with bloodred wine.
>
> Drink it, he told himself. You have nothing to fear.
>
> As was tradition, he had begun his journey adorned in the ritualistic garb of a medieval heretic being led to the gallows, his loose-fitting shirt gaping open to reveal his pale chest, his left pant leg rolled up to the knee, and his right sleeve rolled up to the elbow. Around his neck hung a heavy rope noose—a "cable-tow" as the brethren called it. Tonight, however, like the brethren bearing witness, he was dressed as a master.
>
> The assembly of brothers encircling him all were adorned in their full regalia of lambskin aprons, sashes, and white gloves. Around their necks hung ceremonial jewels that glistened like ghostly eyes in the muted light. Many of these men held powerful stations in life, and yet the initiate knew their worldly ranks meant nothing within these walls. Here all men were equals, sworn brothers sharing a mystical bond.
>
> As he surveyed the daunting assembly, the initiate wondered who on the outside would ever believe that this collection of men would assemble in one place...much less this place. The room looked like a holy sanctuary from the ancient world.

The truth, however, was stranger still.

I am just blocks away from the White House.

This colossal edifice, located at 1733 Sixteenth Street NW in Washington, D.C., was a replica of a pre-Christian temple—the temple of King Mausolus, the original mausoleum…a place to be taken after death. Outside the main entrance, two seventeen-ton sphinxes guarded the bronze doors. The interior was an ornate labyrinth of ritualistic chambers, halls, sealed vaults, libraries, and even a hallow wall that held the remains of two human bodies. The initiate had been told every room in the building held a secret, and yet he knew no room held deeper secrets than the gigantic chamber in which he was currently kneeling with a skull cradled in his palms.

The Temple Room.[280]

While such drama makes for excellent fiction, *The Lost Symbol* turns out to be at best a love fest and at worst a cover up between Dan Brown and the Freemasons. However, one thing Brown said is true—the Temple Room in the Heredom does hold an important *secret*. We've been there, stood inside and prayed for protection under our breath, because according to our sources (who provided facts that have not been denied when we were interviewed by a US Congressman, US Senator, and even a 33rd-Degree Freemason on his radio show), in addition to when a Mason reaches the Master level, the ancient raising ceremony is conducted following the election of an American president—just as their Egyptian forefathers did at the temple of Amun-Ra in Karnak—in keeping with the tradition of installing within him the representative spirit of Osiris until such time as the god himself shall fulfill the Great Seal prophecy and return in flesh.

In the prologue of 33rd-Degree Freemason Manly P. Hall's book, *The Lost Keys of Freemasonry*, detailed recounting of the underlying and familiar story of Hiram Abiff (Osiris) is told, who sets out to construct the temple of the Great Architect of the Universe, but is killed by three spectres. This story, impersonated every time an initiate reaches the level of Master Mason, is by admission of Freemasons a retelling of the death-epic of the god Osiris. In *Lost Keys*, Hall narrates how the Great Architect gives Hiram (Osiris) the trestleboard for the construction of the great temple, and when he is killed by three ruffians, the Great Architect bathes him in "a glory celestial," as in the glory surrounding the all-seeing eye of Osiris above the pyramid on the Great Seal. The Great Architect follows this by charging those who would finish the building with the task of finding the body of Hiram (Osiris) and raising him from the dead. When *this* has been accomplished, the great work will conclude and the god will inhabit the (third) temple:

Seek ye where the broken twig lies and the dead stick molds away, where the clouds float together and the stones rest by the hillside, for all these mark the grave of Hiram [Osiris] who has carried my Will with him to the tomb. This eternal quest is yours until ye have found your Builder, until the cup giveth up its secret, until the grave giveth up its ghosts. No more shall I speak until ye have found and raised my beloved Son [Osiris], and have listened to the words of my Messenger and with Him as your guide have finished the temple which I shall then inhabit. Amen.[281]

Thus the appearance of the uncapped pyramid of Giza on the Great Seal of the United States echoes the ancient pagan as well as Masonic beliefs concerning the old mysteries and the prophecy of the return of Osiris/Apollo/Nimrod. In *Rosicrucian and Masonic Origins*, Hall, who had said in *The Secret Teachings of All Ages* that the Great Pyramid was "the tomb of Osiris,"[282] explains that Preston, Gould, Mackey, Oliver, Pike, and nearly every other great historian of Freemasonry were aware of this connection between Freemasonry and the ancient mysteries and primitive ceremonials based on Osiris. "These eminent Masonic scholars have all recognized in the legend of Hiram Abiff an adaptation of the Osiris myth; nor do they deny that the major part of the symbolism of the craft is derived from the pagan institutions of antiquity when the gods were venerated in secret places with strange figures and appropriate rituals."[283] In *Morals and Dogma*, Albert Pike even enumerated the esoteric significance of the Osiris epic at length, adding that lower-level Masons (Blue Masonry) are ignorant of its true meaning, which is only known to those who are "initiated into the Mysteries."[284] Pike also spoke of the star Sirius—connected to Isis and at length to Lucifer/Satan—as "still glittering" in the Masonic lodges as "the Blazing Star." Elsewhere in *Morals and Dogma*, Pike reiterated that the "All-Seeing Eye…was the emblem of Osiris"[285] and that the "Sun was termed by the Greeks the Eye of Jupiter, and the Eye of the World; and his is the All-Seeing Eye in our Lodges."[286]

Magic Squares, 666, and Human Sacrifice?

While finding the body of Osiris and resurrecting it—either figuratively or literally—is central to the prophetic beliefs of Freemasonry, until Apollo/Osiris return, formal procedures will continue in secret for installing within America's national leader the divine right of Kingship through the raising of Osiris ceremony. It is very important to note how, when this ritual is carried out in the Temple Room of the Heredom, it unfolds below a vast thirty-six-paneled skylight that forms a stylized Magic 666 Square. Around the four sides of the skylight can be seen the Winged Sun-Disc. This positioning above the altar is in keeping with historical occultism. Egyptian magicians employed the same symbolism above the altar for invoking the sun deity. In the St. Martin's Press book *Practical Egyptian Magic* it is noted: "Emblematic of the element of air, this consists of a circle or solar-type disk enclosed by a pair of wings. In ritual magic it is suspended over the altar in an easterly direction and used when invoking the protection and co-operation of the sylphs."[287] The Renaissance occultist Paracelsus describes these sylphs as invisible beings of the air, entities that the New Testament book of Ephesians (2:2) describes as working beneath "the prince [Lucifer/Satan] of the power of the air, the spirit that now worketh in the children of disobedience." In applied magic, the "magic square of the sun" itself was associated in antiquity with binding or loosing the sun god Apollo/Osiris and was the most famous of all magical utilities because the sum of any row, column, or diagonal is equal to the number 111, while the total of all the numbers in the square from 1 to 36 equals 666. In the magical Hebrew Kabbalah, each planet is associated with a number, intelligence, and spirit. The intelligence of the Sun is Nakiel, which equals 111, while the spirit of the Sun is Sorath and equals 666. It makes sense therefore that Freemasons built the Washington Monument Obelisk to form a magic square at its base and to stand 555 feet above earth, so that when a line is drawn 111 feet directly below it toward the underworld of Osiris, it equals the total of 666 (555+111=666)—the exact values of the binding square of the Sun God Apollo/Osiris installed in the ceiling above where the Osiris raising ceremony is conducted in the House of the Temple.

6	32	3	34	35	1
7	11	27	28	8	30
19	14	16	15	23	24
18	20	22	21	17	13
25	29	10	9	26	12
36	5	33	4	2	31

Magic 666 Square

The 36-Paneled Magic-Square Skylight Above
the Altar in the House of the Temple

Freemason and occultist Aleister Crowley practiced such Kabbalah and likewise connected the number 111 with the number 6, which he described as the greatest number of the Sun or sun god. He employed the magic square in rituals to make contact with a spirit described in *The Book of the Sacred Magic of Abramelin the Mage*, a work from the 1600s or 1700s that involves evocation of demons. In Book Four of the magic text, a set of magical word-square talismans provides for the magician's Holy Guardian Angel who appears and reveals occult secrets for calling forth and gaining control over the twelve underworld authorities including Lucifer, Satan, Leviathan, and Belial. In addition to Crowley, the most influential founding father and Freemason, Benjamin Franklin, not only used such magic squares, but according to his own biography and numerous other authoritative sources even created magic squares and circles for use by himself and his brethren. Yet the gentle appearance and keen astuteness of America's most famous bespeckled Freemason might have hidden an even darker history than the story told by those magic squares, which his strong, deft hands once held. Award-winning filmmaker Christian J. Pinto explains:

One of the most influential founding fathers, and the only one of them to have signed all of the original founding documents (the Declaration of Independence, the Treaty of Paris, and the U.S. Constitution) was Benjamin Franklin. Franklin was…without question, deeply involved in Freemasonry and in other secret societies. He belonged to secret groups in the three countries involved in the War of Independence: America, France, and England. He was master of the Masonic Lodge of Philadelphia; while over in France, he was master of the Nine Sisters Lodge, from which sprang the

French Revolution. In England, he joined a rakish political group founded by Sir Francis Dashwood (member of Parliament, advisor to King George III) called the "Monks of Medmenham Abbey," otherwise known as the "Hellfire Club." This eighteenth-century group is described as follows:

> The Hellfire Club was an exclusive, English club that met sporadically during the mid-eighteenth century. Its purpose, at best, was to mock traditional religion and conduct orgies. At worst, it involved the indulgence of satanic rites and sacrifices. The club to which Franklin belonged was established by Francis Dashwood, a member of Parliament and friend of Franklin. The club, which consisted of "The Superior Order" of twelve members, allegedly took part in basic forms of satanic worship. In addition to taking part in the occult, orgies and parties with prostitutes were also said to be the norm.

Pinto continues this connection between Benjamin Franklin and dark occultism:

On February 11, 1998, the Sunday Times reported that ten bodies were dug up from beneath Benjamin Franklin's home at 36 Craven Street in London. The bodies were of four adults and six children. They were discovered during a costly renovation of Franklin's former home. The Times reported: "Initial estimates are that the bones are about two hundred years old and were buried at the time Franklin was living in the house, which was his home from 1757 to

1762 and from 1764 to 1775. Most of the bones show signs of having been dissected, sawn or cut. One skull has been drilled with several holes."

The original Times article reported that the bones were "deeply buried, probably to hide them because grave robbing was illegal." They said, "There could be more buried, and there probably are." But the story doesn't end there. Later reports from the Benjamin Franklin House reveal that not only were human remains found, but animal remains were discovered as well. This is where things get very interesting. From the published photographs, some of the bones appear to be blackened or charred, as if by fire… It is well documented that Satanists perform ritual killings of both humans and animals alike.[288]

While many students of history are aware of the magic 666 square and its use by occultists down through time to control the spirit of Apollo/Osiris, what some will not know is how this magical binding and loosing of supernatural entities also extends to the testes of Washington's 6,666 inch-high phallic Obelisk, dedicated by Freemasons seventy-two years following 1776 (note the magic number 72), where a Bible (that Dan Brown identified as the "Lost Symbol" in his latest book) is encased within the cornerstone of its 666-inch-square base. One wonders what type of Bible this is. If a Masonic version, it is covered with occult symbols of the Brotherhood and Rosicrucianism and the purpose for having it so encased might be to energize the Mason's interpretation of Scripture in bringing forth the seed of Osiris/Apollo from the testes/cornerstone. If it is a non-Masonic Bible, the purpose may be to "bind" its influence inside the 666 square and thus allow the seed of Osiris/Apollo to prevail. The dedication of the cornerstone during the astrological alignment with Virgo/Isis as the sun was passing over Sirius indicates a high degree of magic was indeed intended by those in charge.

The First American Osiris

Through Masonic alchemistry, presidential *apotheosis*—that is, the leader of the United States (America's Pharaoh) being transformed into a god within the Capitol Dome/womb of Isis in sight of the Obelisk of Osiris (the Washington Monument to those whom Masons call "profane," the uninitiated)—actually began with America's first and most revered president, Master Freemason George Washington. In fact, Masons in attendance at Washington's funeral in 1799 cast sprigs of acacia "to symbolize both Osiris' resurrection and Washington's imminent resurrection in the realm where Osiris presides."[289] According to this Masonic enchantment, Osiris (Horus) was rising within a new president in DC as Washington took his role as Osiris of the underworld. This is further simulated and symbolized by the three-story design of the Capitol building. Freemasons point out how the Great Pyramid of Giza was made up of three main chambers to facilitate Pharaoh's transference to Osiris, just as the temple of Solomon was a three-sectioned tabernacle made up of the ground floor, middle chamber, and Holy of Holies. The US Capitol building was thus designed with three stories—Washington's Tomb, the Crypt, and the Rotunda—capped by a Dome. Each floor has significant esoteric meaning regarding apotheosis, and the tomb of Washington is empty. The official narrative is that a legal issue kept the government from placing Washington's body there. However, just as the tomb of Jesus Christ was emptied before His ascension, Washington is not in his tomb because he has travelled to the home of Osiris, as depicted high overhead in the womb/Dome of Isis.

When visitors to Washington, DC tour the Capitol, one of the unquestionable highlights is to visit the womb of Isis—the Capitol Dome—where, when peering upward from inside Isis' continuously pregnant belly, tourists can see hidden in plain sight Brumidi's 4,664-square-foot fresco, *The Apotheosis of George Washington*. The word "apotheosis" means to "deify" or to "become a god," and explains part of the reason US presidents, military commanders, and members of Congress lay in state in the Capitol Dome. The womb of Isis is where they go at death to magically reach apotheosis and transform into gods.

Those who believe the United States was founded on Christianity and visit the Capitol for the first time will be surprised by the stark contrast to historic Christian artwork of the ascension of Jesus Christ compared to the "heaven" George Washington rises into from within the energized Capitol Dome/womb of Isis. It is not occupied by angels, but with devils and pagan deities important to Masonic belief. These include Hermes, Neptune, Venus (Isis), Ceres, Minerva, and Vulcan (Satan), of course, the son of Jupiter and Juno to which human sacrifices are made and about whom Manly Hall said brings "the seething energies of Lucifer" into the Mason's hands.[290]

For high-degree Masons and other illuminatus, the symbolism of Washington surrounded by pagan entities and transformed into a heathen god is entirely appropriate. Deeply rooted in the mysteries of ancient societies and at the core of Rosicrucianism and those rituals of the Brotherhood that founded the United States is the idea that chosen humans are selected by these supernatural forces and their earthly kingdoms are formed and guided by these gods. As a Deist, George Washington believed that by following the enlightened path guided by principles of Freemasonry, he would achieve apotheosis and become deified. Affirming this widespread belief among America's founding fathers are numerous works of art throughout

Washington, DC. On an 1865 card titled "Washington and Lincoln Apotheosis," Abraham Lincoln is depicted transcending death to meet Washington among the gods. What god did Lincoln become? Humanist and American poet Walt Whitman eulogized him as the "American Osiris." Horatio Greenough's 1840, government-commissioned statue of George Washington shows the first president enthroned as the god Jupiter/Zeus. On one side of Washington/Zeus is his son Hercules clutching two serpents, and on the other side is his son Apollo. Greenough admitted this vision was based on presenting Washington as a deified figure, the father of Apollo similar to what the Hebrew God is to Jesus. Another representation of Washington as Jupiter/Zeus is a painting by Rembrandt Peale that hangs in the Old Senate Chamber. Peale painted it in a "poetic frenzy" in a stone oval window atop a stone sill engraved "PATRIAE PATER" ("Father of His Country"). The window is decorated with a garland of oak leaves, which was sacred to Jupiter, and is surmounted by the "Phydian head of Jupiter" (Peale's description) on the keystone. The symbol of Jupitor/Zeus, the father of Apollo above Washington's head, reflects the same conviction scripted on America's Great Seal—that the divine being watching over Washington and the founding of the country was Jupiter/Zeus (Lucifer in the Bible), whose son is coming again to rule the *novus ordo seclorum*. Even the name "Capitol Hill" for Government Center in Washington originated with this concept. Thomas Jefferson selected it to reflect Capitoline Hill from ancient Rome, where Jupiter (Jove) was the king of the gods. In more recent times, the Congressional Prayer Room was set up next to the Rotunda, where representatives and senators can go to meditate. The centerpiece in this room is a large, stained-glass window with George Washington between the two sides of the Great Seal of the United States. What is striking about this feature is that the order of the seal is inverted against protocol, with the reverse side of the seal, which should be at the bottom, above Washington's head, and the front of the seal, which should be at the top, under his feet. In this position, Washington is seen on his knees praying beneath the uncapped pyramid and the all-seeing eye of Horus/Osiris/Apollo. I leave the reader to interpret what this clearly is meant to signify.

Beside those pagan gods which accompany Washington inside the Capitol Dome, the scene is rich with symbols analogous with ancient and modern magic, including the powerful trident—considered of the utmost importance for sorcery and indispensable to the efficacy of infernal rites—and the caduceus, tied to Apollo and Freemasonic Gnosticism in which Jesus was a myth based on Apollo's son, Asclepius, the god of medicine and healing whose snake-entwined staff remains a symbol of medicine today. Occult numerology associated with the legend of Isis and Osiris is also encoded throughout the painting, such as the thirteen maidens, the six scenes of pagan gods around the perimeter forming a hexagram, and the entire scene bounded by the powerful Pythagorian/Freemasonic "binding" utility—seventy-two five-pointed stars within circles.

Much has been written by historians within and without Masonry as to the relevance of the number seventy-two (72) and the alchemy related to it. In the Kabbalah, Freemasonry, and Jewish apocalyptic writings, the number equals the total of wings Enoch received when transformed into Metatron (3 Enoch 9:2). This plays an important role for the Brotherhood, as Metatron or "the angel in the whirlwind" was enabled as the guiding spirit over America during George W. Bush's administration for the purpose of directing the *future* and *fate* of the United States (as also prayed by Congressman Major R. Owens of New York before the House of Representatives on Wednesday, February 28, 2001).

The Apotheosis of George Washington Above 72 Pentagrams

But in the context of the Capitol Dome and the seventy-two stars that circle Washington's apotheosis in the womb of Isis, the significance of this symbolism is far more important. In sacred literature, including the Bible, stars are symbolic of angels, and within Masonic Gnosticism, seventy-two is the number of fallen angels or "kosmokrators" (reflected in the seventy-two conspirators that controlled Osiris' life in Egyptian myth) that currently administer the affairs of earth. Experts in the study of the Divine Council believe that, beginning at the Tower of Babel, the world and its inhabitants were disinherited by the sovereign God of Israel and placed under the authority of seventy-two angels (the earliest records had the number of angels at seventy, but this was later changed to seventy-two) which became corrupt and disloyal to God in their administration of those nations (Psalm 82). These beings quickly became worshipped on earth as gods following Babel, led by Nimrod/Gilgamesh/Osiris/Apollo. Consistent with this tradition, the designers of the Capitol Dome, the Great Seal of the United States, and the Obelisk Washington Monument circled the *Apotheosis of Washington* with seventy-two pentagram stars, dedicated the Obelisk seventy-two years after the signing of the Declaration of Independence, and placed seventy-two stones on the Great Seal's uncapped pyramid, above which the eye of Horus/Osiris/Apollo stares. These three sets of seventy-two (72), combined with the imagery and occult numerology of the Osiris/Obelisk, the Isis/Dome, and the oracular Great Seal, are richly symbolic of the influence of Satan and his angels over the world (see Luke 4:5–6, 2 Corinthians 4:4, and Ephesians 6:12) with a prophecy toward Satan's final earthly empire—the coming *novus ordo seclorum*, or new golden pagan age.

In order for the "inevitable" worship of Osiris to be "reestablished" on earth, the seventy-two demons that govern the nations must be controlled, thus they are set in magical constraints on the Great Seal, the Washington Obelisk, and the pentagram circles around the *Apotheosis of Washington* to bind and force the desired effect.

In *The Secret Destiny of America*, Hall noted as well that the seventy-two stones of the pyramid on the Great Seal correspond to the seventy-two arrangements of the Tetragrammaton, or the four-lettered name of God in Hebrew. "These four letters can be combined in seventy-two combinations, resulting in what is called the Shemhamforesh, which represents, in turn, the laws, powers, and energies of Nature."[291] The idea that the mystical name of God could be invoked to bind or loose those supernatural agents (powers and energies of nature, as Hall called them) is meaningful creed within many occult tenets, including Kabbalah and Freemasonry. This is why the seventy-two stars are pentagram-shaped around the deified Freemason, George Washington. Medieval books of magic, or grimoires such as the Key of Solomon and the Lesser Key of Solomon not only identify the star systems Orion (Osiris) and Pleiades (Apollo) as the "home" of these powers, but applies great importance to the pentagram shape of the stars for binding and loosing their influence. Adept Rosicrucians and Freemasons have long used these magical texts—the Key of Solomon and the Lesser Key of Solomon—to do just that. Peter Goodgame makes an important observation about this in "The Giza Discovery":

> One of the co-founders of the occult society known as the Golden Dawn[292] was a Rosicrucian Freemason named S. L. MacGregor Mathers, who was the first to print and publish the Key of Solomon (in 1889) making it readily available to the public. Mathers describes it as a primary occult text: "The fountainhead and storehouse of Qabalistic Magic, and

the origin of much of the Ceremonial Magic of mediaeval times, the 'Key' has been ever valued by occult writers as a work of the highest authority." Of the 519 esoteric titles included in the catalogue of the Golden Dawn library, the Key was listed as number one. As far as contents are concerned, the Key included instructions on how to prepare for the summoning of spirits including…demons.… One of the most well-known members of the Golden Dawn was the magician [and 33rd-degree freemason] Aleister Crowley. In 1904 Crowley published the first part of the five-part Lesser Key of Solomon known as the Ars Goetia,[293] which is Latin for "art of sorcery." The Goetia is a grimoire for summoning seventy-two different demons that were allegedly summoned, restrained, and put to work by King Solomon [according to Masonic mysticism] during the construction of the Temple of YHWH.[294]

Unlike other grimoires including the sixteenth-century *Pseudomonarchia Daemonum* and the seventeenth-century *Lemegeton*, the Key of Solomon does not contain the "Diabolical Signature" of the devil or demons, which the Ars Goetia describes as numbering seventy-two and who were, according to legend, constrained to assist King Solomon after he bound them in a bronze vessel sealed by magic symbols. Such books routinely contain invocations and curses for summoning, binding, and loosing these demons in order to force them to do the conjurers will. Even members of the Church of Satan sign letters using the Shemhamforash, from the Hebrew name of God or Tetragrammaton, producing a blasphemous reinterpretation of the seventy-two entities. And then there is Michelangelo, who painted what we have called the "Sign of the Sixth Knuckle" inside the Sistine Chapel (mentioned elsewhere in this book) that tied the prophecy on the Great Seal of the United States from the Cumaean Sibyl to the return of the Nephilim Apollo. But incredibly, Michelangelo also produced the Shemhamforash on the Vatican's famous ceiling, as his fresco has "an architectural design of 24 columns. On each of these columns are two cherubs, which are mirror imaged on the adjoining column totaling 48 cherubs figures. Then on the 12 triangular spandrels flanking the ceiling borders are an additional 24 nude figures (two bronze nude figures per triangular spandrel) also mirror imaging each other. This totals to 72 cherub figures or the 72 angels of God or names of God [or conversely, the 72 angels that fell and are now the demons or kosmokrators over the nations of the earth]."[295] Once one understands the importance that these mystical keys hold in Kabbalah, Rosicrucianism, Freemasonic mysticism, and other mystery traditions, there can be (and is) but one reasonable interpretation for the connection in the Vatican and the seventy-two pentagrams at the base of the Apotheosis of Washington. These are there to bind and control the demons over the nations to honor the dedication made by early American Freemasons and certain Roman devotees for a New Atlantis and New World Order under the coming antichrist deity Osiris/Apollo.

From Seventy-Two Demons to Feathered Serpents: What You Do—and Do Not—Learn in School about American History

In public school, children are taught how a world map was created in 1507 by German cartographer Martin Waldseemüller. On this map, the lands of the Western Hemisphere are first called "America," named so after an Italian explorer and navigator named Amerigo Vespucci. According to the official account, the United States of

America received the latter part of its name when Waldseemüller used the feminized Latin version of *Amerigo* to call this land *America*.

Or, at least that's what we are told.

What kiddies in public education are not taught, however (and which mainstream academia has yet been willing to accept), is a rival explanation for the origin of "America" related to Mesoamerican serpent-worship, biblical giants, Freemasonry, and even the year 2012.

The story begins long before the Spaniards arrived on this continent and was chronicled in the hieroglyphic characters (and repeated in oral history) of the sacred, indigenous Maya narrative called the Popol Vuh. Sometime between 1701 and 1703, a Dominican priest named Father Francisco Ximénez transcribed and translated the Mayan work into Spanish. Later his text was taken from Guatemala to Europe by Abbott Brasseur de Bourbough where it was translated into French. Today the Popol Vuh rests in Chicago's Newberry Library, but what makes the script interesting is its creation narrative, history, and cosmology, especially as it relates to the worship of the great "feathered serpent" creator deity known as *Q'uq'umatz*; a god considered by scholars to be roughly equivalent to the Aztec god *Quetzalcoatl* and the Yucatec Mayan *Kukulkan*. According to Freemasons like Manly P. Hall, no other ancient work sets forth so completely the initiatory rituals of the great school of philosophic mystery, which was so central to America's Baconian dream of the New Atlantis, than the Popol Vuh. What's more, Hall says, it is in this region where we find the true origin of America's name and destiny.

In *The Secret Teachings of All Ages*, Hall writes:

This volume [Popol Vuh] alone is sufficient to establish incontestably the philosophical excellence of the red race.

"The Red 'Children of the Sun,'" writes James Morgan Pryse, "do not worship the One God. For them that One God is absolutely impersonal, and all the Forces emanated from that One God are personal. This is the exact reverse of the popular western conception of a personal God and impersonal working forces in nature. Decide for yourself which of these beliefs is the more philosophical [Hall says sarcastically]. These Children of the Sun adore the Plumèd Serpent, who is the messenger of the Sun. *He was the God Quetzalcoatl in Mexico, Gucumatz in Quiché; and in Peru he was called Amaru. From the latter name comes our word America. Amaruca is, literally translated, 'Land of the Plumèd Serpent.'* The priests of this [flying dragon], from their chief centre in the Cordilleras, once ruled both Americas. All the Red men who have remained true to the ancient religion are still under their sway. One of their strong centres was in Guatemala, and of their Order was the author of the book called Popol Vuh. In the Quiché tongue Gucumatz is the exact equivalent of Quetzalcoatl in the Nahuatl language; quetzal, the bird of Paradise; coatl, serpent—'the Serpent veiled in plumes of the paradise-bird!'"

The Popol Vuh was discovered by Father Ximinez in the seventeenth century. It was translated into French by Brasseur de Bourbourg and published in 1861. The only complete English translation is that by Kenneth Sylvan Guthrie, which ran through the early files of The Word magazine and which is used as the basis of this article. A portion of the Popol Vuh was translated into English, with *extremely valuable commentaries*, by James Morgan Pryse, but unfortunately his translation was never completed. The second book of the Popol Vuh is largely devoted to the initiatory rituals of the Quiché nation. *These ceremonials are of first importance to students of Masonic symbolism and mystical philosophy, since they establish beyond doubt the existence of ancient and divinely instituted Mystery schools on the American Continent.* (emphasis added)[296]

Thus from Hall we learn that Freemasons like him believe "ancient and divinely instituted" mystery religion important to students of Masonry came to Amaruca/America—*the Land of the Plumèd Serpent*—from knowledge that the Red Man received from the dragon himself. What Hall conceals is that when he refers to those "extremely valuable commentaries" made by James Pryes, he is referencing an article from Helena Blavatsky's *Lucifer* magazine, which was published by the Theosophical Society and that illuminated the inner doctrine of Rosicrucianism, Freemasonry, and all the secret orders— that Lucifer is the "angel of light" who, in the form of a serpent, bids mankind to partake of the "Tree of Knowledge of Good and Evil" so that their eyes would be open and they could become as gods. Even to this day, in the secret societies, Lucifer is considered this benevolent serpent-god who has nothing more than the best intentions for man, while Jehovah is an evil entity who tries to keep mankind in the dark and punishes him if he seeks the truest wisdom. Since these ancient serpent legends include the Mesoamerican feathered serpent gods and can be looked upon as a historical testament of that Angel thrown down by God, "then perhaps The Land of the Plumèd Serpent may also be known as *the Land of Lucifer,*" concludes Ken Hudnall in *The Occult Connection II: The Hidden Race.*[297]

This raises serious questions about what type of "divinely instituted" wisdom Hall had in mind for Amaruca/America, as part of the legitimate concern revolving around this disclosure stems from the fact that the Inca, Aztec, and Maya were either unquestionably gifted mathematicians and astronomers, or they really did receive advanced knowledge from *someone or something*. They measured the length of the solar year far more accurately than did the Europeans in their Gregorian calendar, and precisely oriented their sacred buildings and cities with stars and star clusters, particularly Pleiades and the Orion Nebula associated throughout the ancient Middle East with Osiris/Apollo/Nimrod. The pre-Columbian book, *Codex Dresdensis* (a.k.a. the *Dresden Codex*) by the Yucatecan Maya is famous for its first-known related illustrations of advanced calculations and astronomical phenomena. But how were the pre-telescopic Mesoamericans uniquely aware of such important knowledge? They themselves—like other archaic cultures did—credited ancient "gods" with bringing the heavenly information to Earth.

In 2008, fellow researcher David Flynn may have uncovered important information related to this legend, the size and scope of which simply surpass comprehension. It involves mammoth traces of intelligence carved in stone and covering hundreds of square miles: possibly the strongest evidence ever detected of prehistoric engineering by those who were known and feared throughout the ancient world as gods—the giant offspring of the Watchers.

In the same way modern archeologists only recently found the ruins of hidden Mayan temples in the Guatemalan jungle by using satellites, Flynn employed above-Earth orbiting satellites to image a vast network of patterns that surround Lake Titicaca in Bolivia, South America, which extend for more than one hundred miles south into the Bolivian desert. The patterns display geometric repetition and intelligent designs, including interlocking rectangular cells and mounds, perfectly straight lines, and repeated sharp-angle turns that do not occur naturally. These cover every topographical feature of the high plateau surrounding the lake, over flood plains, hills, cliffs, and mountains. The full report of this remarkable research plus numerous satellite images is available at RaidersNewsUpdate. com/giants.

Twelve miles south of Lake Titicaca, located within the center of the array of geoglyphs, lies the megalithic ruins of Tiahuanaco. Known as the "American Stonehenge" or the "Baalbek of the New World," its architecture exhibits technological skill that exceeds modern feats of building. At Tiahuanaco, immense stone works were joined with modular fittings and complex breach-locking levels that have never been seen in any other ancient culture. According to engineers, one of the largest single stones ever to be moved and put into a building anywhere on earth (about four hundred tons) was transported to Tiahuanaco from a quarry over two hundred miles away. This feat is even more incomprehensible when one realizes the route of transport was through a mountain range up to fifteen thousand feet.

Conventional historians try to assign the age of the structures at Tiahuanaco to around 600 BC, postulating that a pre-Inca civilization, without benefit of the wheel, modern tools, or even a written language constructed these architectural marvels. But historian Arthur Posnansky studied the area for more than fifty years and observed that sediment had been deposited over the site to the depth of six feet. Within this overburden, produced by a massive flood of water sometime around the Pleistocene age (thirteen thousand years ago), fossilized human skulls were unearthed together with seashells and remnants of tropical plants. The skulls have nearly three times the cranial capacity of modern man and are displayed in the La Paz museum in Bolivia.

In addition, when the first Spanish chroniclers arrived with the conquistador Pizaro, the Inca explained that Tiahuanaco had been constructed by a race of giants called "Huaris" before *Chamak-pacha*, the "period of darkness," and was already in ruins before their civilization began. They said these giants had been created by Viracocha ("Kukulkan" to the Maya and "Quetzalcoatl" to the Aztecs), *the god who came from the heavens* (a.k.a. the Watchers).

> He (Viracocha) created animals and a race of giants. These beings enraged the Lord, and he turned them into stone. Then he flooded the earth till all was under water, and all life extinguished. This flood was called uñu pachacuti, by the Inca which means "water that overturns the land." They say that it rained sixty days and nights, that it drowned all created things, and that there alone remained some vestiges of those who were turned into stones. Viracocha rose from the bosom of Lake Titicaca, and presided over the erection of those wondrous cities whose ruins still dot its islands and western shores, and whose history is totally lost in the night of time.[298]

Near Lake Titicaca in the Hayu Marca Mountain region of Southern Peru at fourteen thousand feet exists a huge, mysterious, door-like structure carved into a solid rock face in an area long revered by Peruvian Indians as the "City of the Gods." Shamans still come to perform rituals at this site, which they call *Puerta de Hayu Marca* or the Gate of the Gods. It measures exactly twenty-three feet in height and width, with a recess in the center slightly smaller than six-feet high. Native Indians say the site is "a gateway to the lands of the Gods" through which, in their ancient past, great heroes arrived and then departed with a "key" that could open the mysterious doorway. Another legend tells of the first Incan priest—the Amaru Meru (note again the

Amaru-ca/America connection)—who used a golden disk to open the portal, which turned the solid rock into a stargate. According to local legend, this priest was the first of other "kings" who came to Earth from heavenly locations specifically associated with the Pleiades (Apollo) and Orion (Osiris). This disc-key section of the Gate of the Gods may be depicted by a small, circular depression on the right side of the recess of *Puerta de Hayu Marca*, which in turn could be related to another "portal" not far away—the Gate of the Sun at Tiahuanaco, identified by some historians and archaeologists as the gate of the god Viracocha who created the race of giants.

Mythology involving such giants, followed by world deluge, is universally recorded in the legends of the Inca, Maya, Olmec, and Aztec cultures of Mexico. These stories are consistent with Sumerian and Hebrew accounts of the Great Flood and of the subsequent destruction of giant Nephilim whose history of human sacrifices parallel Mayan rituals (victims of Maya had their arms and legs held down while a priest cut their chests open and ripped out their hearts). The Greeks likewise recorded how prehistoric giants were responsible for the creation of megalithic structures discovered around the world, and Islamic folklore ascribes this prehistoric "building" activity to a race of super beings called "jinn" (genies):

> The Jinn were before Adam: They built huge cities whose ruins still stand in forgotten places.[299]
>
> In Egypt, the Edfu temple texts, believed to predate the Egyptians themselves, explain something of additional significance, reminiscent of Nephilim activity before and after the Flood:
>
> The most ancient of earth's temples and monuments were built to bring about the resurrection of the destroyed world of the gods.[300]

Within the Inca religious paradigm, the oldest record of the Andean region available, the Tiahuanaco geoglyphs are therefore viewed as the vestiges of a lost civilization that knew its destiny…to be destroyed by world cataclysm. In this regard, the geoglyphs serve not only as a memorial of an ancient existence, but also as a warning for future humanity and the return of a destructive epoch, or as David Flynn concluded:

> The geoglyphs seem to be physical evidence that supports the Middle and South American myths of world deluge and giants. Their discovery in modern times fits Inca and Mayan prophecies of an "awakening" to knowledge of the ancient past, of the "builder gods" and of their return. It is perhaps testament to the accuracy of these prophecies that the date, December 21, 2012, is known so widely in modern times… the end of the Mayan calendar.[301]

CHAPTER 20:12

FINAL PART OF THE LAST MYSTERY

2012–2016, 2019, and the End?

When in the course of history the threat of extinction confronts mankind, it is necessary for the people of the United States to declare their interdependence with the people of all nations and to embrace those principles and build those institutions which will enable mankind to survive and civilization to flourish. Two centuries ago our forefathers brought forth a new nation; now we must join with others to bring forth a New World Order. —World Affairs Council of Philadelphia, "A Declaration of Interdependence"

A couple of points need clarification at the beginning of this final chapter having to do with 1) date-setting; and 2) extra-biblical sources for interpreting end-times prophecy. Setting dates in particular for eschatological affairs (such as the beginning of sorrows, the return of Christ, or the battle of Armageddon) have been illustrated historically to be unwise, discrediting those who make such predictions concerning the exact timing of future events. In general, Christians should simply always be ready for the end of the age and the coming of Christ, because, "Ye know not what hour your Lord doth come" (Matthew 24:42). Jesus further told His followers that the exact date of His arrival would be known by "no man, no, not the angels of heaven, but my Father only" (Matthew 24:36). While the particular moment of His appearance thus remains a mystery, elsewhere Jesus explained that the "signs of the times" can be discerned (Matthew 16:3), and when His closest disciples asked Him frankly, "What shall be the sign of thy coming, and of the end of the world?" He provided a long list of specific indicators that would herald His arrival. He then added that, "When ye shall see these things, know that it is near, even at the doors. Verily I say unto you, This generation shall not pass, till all these things be fulfilled" (Matthew 24:3, 33–34). Therefore, while most Christians agree they cannot know the exact "hour" of Christ's coming or the end of the age, they can know the "season."

Another issue when interpreting end-time "signs" comes from the use of non-canonical sources. This is obviously problematic when it includes occult sources such as the writings of famous seers like Edgar Cayce or Jeane Dixon. However, aside from such spirit mediums, it is helpful to recall other bona fide revelations that arrived from sources that today would not set well in our denominational boxes. For instance, Nebuchadnezzar's dream from Daniel 2. God chose to reveal a prophecy spanning from 605 BC through the second coming of Christ to an arrogant narcissistic pagan king and then required his holy servant, Daniel, to interpret the dream for him. Similarly, God used Balaam, a darkened wizard who now lives in prophetic infamy (2 Peter 2:15; Jude 11; Revelation 2:14) to prophesy, "I shall see him, but not now: I shall behold him, but not nigh: there shall come a Star out of Jacob, and a Sceptre shall rise out of Israel, and shall smite the corners of Moab, and destroy all the children of Sheth" (Numbers 24:17), a text which scholars today believe spoke unmistakably of the coming of the Messiah.

This Pethorian prediction was well over one thousand years before the birth of Christ and from a hostile source, yet it is probably what led the Magi to Bethlehem. The nameless author of the allegedly lost *La profezia* used Balaam as an example as well, remarking that the gift of prophecy "is essentially a free supernatural gift, in which God certifies the truth of His faith by communicating to different souls, sometimes even infidels like Balaam, in whom altered states have occurred inspiring them spontaneously to speak marvelously of the most sublime mystery of God."[302] Of course we are instructed in the New Testament not to despise prophesying (1 Thessalonians 5:20) as it is a part of the Church Age.

Having stated the above, not everybody accepts the wisdom of discussing ancient extra-biblical texts or dates such as the years 2012 and 2016 in particular, most publicly identified with the end of the Mayan Calendar Long Count and Precession Cycle. Yet we do so precisely because this book and others we have written intend to unveil not just what Bible scholars believe about the end times, but what occultists are convinced of and are dedicated to fulfilling. Knowledge is power, we believe, and prayer is most effective when the target is understood. Our enemy is definitely scheming over particular dates, and from Scripture we learn that demons know something about times and dispensations and plot within them, something they most assuredly want Christians to remain ignorant of. For instance, recall when Jesus went into the valley of the Gadarenes and two exceedingly fierce men possessed with devils came out of the tombs crying, "What have we to do with thee, Jesus, thou Son of God? art thou come hither to torment us *before the time?*" (Matthew 8:28–29; emphasis added). The Greek word for "time" in this verse is *kairos*, and means a fixed and definite period of days, a decisive epoch waited for. Somehow the evil spirits knew the dispensation of their judgment had not yet arrived, and knowing they perceive such things, it is not hard to imagine extra-biblical prophecies by those such as the Maya or the Cumaean Sibyl having been infused with occult energy providing supernatural perception and *deception*. This was illustrated again in the story of Jannes and Jambres (2 Timothy 3:8), who withstood Moses in the Old Testament, and the Pythian priestess in the New Testament (Acts 16:16–17), who somehow knew that God had sent Paul. This fact—that demons can prophesy, know something of times and seasons, and want true Christians to remain ignorant of their schemes related to those specific periods—is especially important at this juncture because while the first part of the "final mystery of the Great Seal" involves *who* is prophesied to rule the *novus order seclorum*, the second, more disturbing, aspect of the US national cipher has to do with *when* this deity—and its Nephilim army—are predicted to arrive.

From Christians to New Agers, skeptics to historians, the world was enthralled until recently with the meaning of the year 2012. In general, the excitement (or dread, as the case may be) surrounded a variety of predictions made by ancient and modern sources concerning a portentous moment in time. Mankind was on course toward unprecedented global upheaval, according to these experts, when the Earth, and all life upon it, will undergo apocalyptica marked by the end of the "thirteenth baktun" of the Mesoamerican Mayan Long Count. The exact end date of this calendar was December 21, 2012, when during the winter solstice at 11:11 GMT (Greenwich Mean Time), the sun supposedly aligned with the galactic center of the Milky Way galaxy, an event that occurs only every thirteen thousand years. The precession of the equinoxes concluded a twenty-six-thousand-year cycle, bringing the astrological Age of Pisces to an end and introducing the beginning of Aquarius, when the next cycle began and the sun arose out of the mouth of the Ouroboros (great serpent of the Milky Way). This was the sun rising in Sagittarius, the centaur with a bow—the symbol for Nimrod coming out from the mouth of Leviathan and the sun "god" rising again—Nimrod/Osiris/Apollo. The Mayans predicted this conjunction, interpreting it as a harbinger of the end of the world as we know it and the beginning of a new era. While the Maya were not alone among ancient cultures in this regard—for instance, the Hindu Kali Yuga calendar started approximately during the Mayan Fifth Great Cycle and also predicted global Earth changes following the year 2012—it is the Maya who were mostly credited with fixing the importance of this date. Researchers say cataclysmic events associated with this final dispensation have already started, including geologic upheaval, drought, famine, mass extinction, and the arrival of solar maximum following the year 2012. Like the Aztec and Inca, the Maya believed Earth seasons and celestial cycles were affected by otherworldly and prophetic significance. Mayan priests interpreted such activity and coupled it with the mathematics of their calendars, making predictions based on the terrestrial and celestial cycles.

Early on, the only known Mayan inscription that elaborated on the specific significance behind the end of the thirteenth baktun—December 21, 2012—was discovered on Monument 6 at Tortuguero, in Tabasco, Mexico. Though defaced from area construction and previous looting of the archaeological location, scholars were able to partially translate the monument, finding that it referred to the year 2012 and a return of the spirit of Bolon Yokte K'u, the underworld lord who represents the solar system and the nine support gods orbiting the Sun.

The inscription: Tzuhtz-(a)j-oom u(y)-uxlajuun pik (ta) Chan Ajaw ux(-te') Uniiw. Uht-oom ? Y-em(al)?? Bolon Yookte' K'uh ta ?

The interpretation: "The Thirteenth 'Bak'tun" will be finished (on) Four Ajaw, the Third of Uniiw (K'ank'in). ? will occur. (It will be) the descent (??) of the Nine Support? God(s) to the ?."

While New Agers admitted the end of the Mayan calendar thus heralded the return of the spirit of Bolon Yokte K'u to Earth beginning in 2012 (the date the Toltec prophesied the return of the spirit Quetzalcoatl), a few rightly claimed this advent and the roll-over of the Mayan calendar and Jaguar prophecies accompanying it did not forecast the end of the world but rather a new dispensation or Golden Age of ascended consciousness.

And the Maya were not the only ancient society to foresee the beginning of a new epoch starting in 2012.

For instance, the "Cherokee Rattlesnake Prophecies," also known as the "Chickamaugan Prophecy" or the "Cherokee Star Constellation Prophecies," are part of a series of apocalyptic prophecies made by members of the Cherokee tribe during 1811–1812. The prophecies are very similar to Mesoamerican belief, and are viewed by scholars as likely referring to the return of Quetzalcoatl in 2012–2016. Like the Maya, the Cherokee calendar ended mysteriously in the year 2012 when astronomical phenomena related to Jupiter, Venus, Orion, and Pleiades caused the "powers" of the star systems to "awaken."

A portion of the "Rattlesnake Prophecy" reads:

At this time [the end of 2012] of the fingers striking Jupiter that Orion Star System will awaken. And the Pleiades and Orion will war once again as in old. Jupiter and Venus will awaken to its destiny of Time/Untime of cycles. Orion will war with Pleiades, Jupiter will war with Venus....

[Following] the year...2012 an alignment will take

place both on the Cherokee calendar and in the heavens of the Rattlesnake Constellation.… It is the time of the double headed serpent stick. It is the time of the red of Orion and Jupiter against the white blue of Pleiades and Venus… the Cherokee Rattlesnake Constellation will take on a different configuration. The snake itself will remain, however; upon the Rattlesnake shall be added upon its head feathers, its eyes will open and glow, wings spring forth as a winged rattlesnake. It shall have hands and arms and in its hands shall be a bowl. The bowl will hold blood. Upon its tail of seven rattles shall be the glowing and movement of Pleiades.

The Rattlesnake shall become a feathered rattlesnake or feathered serpent of Time/Untime [Quetzalcoatl?].

And upon the Rattlesnake is also the Milky Way. A crossing of the Milky Way shall be seen at these times.

And the Cherokee calendar shall end in the year 2012… [heralding] the coming of the Pale One once again.[303]

2012 and Prophecy from the *Zohar* on Messiah's Return

Widely considered the most important work of Jewish Kabbalah, the *Zohar* is a collection of books written in medieval Aramaic over seven hundred years ago containing mystical commentary on the Pentateuch (five books of Moses, the Torah). In addition to interpreting Scripture, the Vaera section (volume 3, section 34) includes, "The signs heralding Mashiach," or, "The coming of the Messiah." The fascinating date for "his" appearance is set in the *Zohar* during 2012–2013. Given the rejection of Jesus by orthodox Jews as Messiah, this seven-hundred-year-old prediction indicates the Antichrist "arrived" circa 2012–2013.

The Eight-Hundred-Year-Old Prophecy of
Rabbi Judah Ben Samuel

Will the years immediately following 2016 be prophetically important for Israel and the world? Earlier we noted when seventy years (a
biblical generation) is added to 1948—the year Israel was formally
recognized as an independent nation by the United Nations—it
brings us through the year 2018. Does this mean the year 2019—
exactly seven years after 2012—would mark the year that Jesus Christ
returns with the armies of heaven to establish His rule over Earth?
According to an eight-hundred-year-old prophecy, it certainly could.
Before he died of cancer, J. R. Church analyzed the ancient predictions of Rabbi Judah Ben Samuel and noted:

> Ludwig Schneider, writing for *Israel Today* (March 2008)
> said, "Some 800 years ago in Germany, Rabbi Judah Ben
> Samuel was a top Talmudic scholar with an inclination for
> the mystical. Before he died in the year 1217, he prophesied
> that the Ottoman Turks would conquer Jerusalem and rule
> the Holy City for 'eight Jubilee Years.'" A biblical Jubilee
> year consists of 50 years. Fifty multiplied by eight equals 400
> years.
>
> Afterwards, according to Ben Samuel, the Ottomans
> would be driven out of Jerusalem, which would remain a
> no-man's land for one Jubilee year. In the tenth Jubilee year
> [2017]...the Messianic end times would begin....
>
> Looking back at Ben Samuel's prediction, we should
> note that the Ottoman Empire did conquer Jerusalem in
> 1517, exactly 300 years after the rabbi's death, and was
> defeated 400 years later in 1917.

In *Israel Today*, Ludwig Schneider continues, "This came to pass 300 years after Ben Samuel's death. He could not have based this prophecy on events that could be foreseen, but only on the results of his study of the Bible.

"According to Leviticus 25, the nation is reunited with its land in the year of Jubilee. Therefore, the Jubilee year plays an important role in Israel's history. In this case, the Jubilee began with the defeat and conquest of the Mamelukes in Jerusalem by the Ottoman Kingdom in 1517. The Turks reigned over Jerusalem until the British General Edmund Allenby defeated them exactly eight Jubilees later in 1917.

"Ben Samuel's prophecy was fulfilled precisely because 1517 to 1917 is exactly 400 years. Afterward, Jerusalem was a no-man's land for 50 years during the time of the British Mandate (1917–1967) and the time of Jordanian rule (1947–1967), another Jubilee year. During the Six Day War in 1967, Israel captured Jerusalem from Jordan and the city returned to the Jewish people after nearly two millennia of exile. After that, the countdown for the Messianic age began."

Schneider assumes that since Rabbi Judah Ben Samuel's prediction appears to be fulfilled to date, then 2017 should launch the beginning of the Messianic era.[304]

2012 and Matthew 24

Is it possible that Jesus marked the year 2012 as the start of the final age? When His disciples asked, "Tell us, when shall these things be? And what shall be the sign of thy coming, and of the end of the world [*aion*]?" (Matthew 24:3), Jesus answered, "As the Days of Noe

[Noah] were, so shall also the coming of the Son of man be" (Matthew 24:37).

The word *aion* in this text is not the general word for "time" (*chronos*) in Greek. *Aion* is the word the Greeks used to designate an actual cycle of the Milky Way alignments or the span of an age. Before he passed away, David Flynn said of this: "The answer Jesus provided His apostles for 'when' the end of the *aion* would occur was specific. The astronomical signs in the heavens would be just as those during the days of Noah when Leviathan encircled the horizon in the dawn of the Summer solstice. There could have been no more accurate comparison made between our present time than the age of Noah.... The present aion is coming to a close. Like the *sunteleia* before, there will be great upheaval and change."[305]

Protestant Reformers and the Years 2012–2016

Among the turn-of-the-century protestant reformers, there were an astonishing number of theologians that believed the False Prophet and Antichrist would take the stage between the years 2012 and 2016! The famous preacher Jonathan Edwards was convinced of this possibility and held a postmillennial view based on the twelve hundred and sixty days the woman is in the wilderness in Revelation 12:6. He interpreted those days as the years that the true Church was to be oppressed by the papists. Clarence Goen writes of this, "Edwards considered that the most likely time for the...reign of Antichrist was 1260 years after AD 756 (the acceding of temporal power to the Pope),"[306] which would place the apex of Antichrist's power squarely in 2016 (and it seems judicious to observe that 2016 falls in range of 3.5 years from June, 2012). When we were doing research for the book, *Petrus Romanus: The Final Pope Is Here*, we learned of this belief by Edwards and sought to verify it by examining a collection of his personal voluminous writings. We found confirmation within a series of his sermons, preached at Northampton, Massachusetts in 1739, on how history and prophecy coincide:

> I am far from pretending to determine the time when the reign of Antichrist began, which is a point that has been so much controverted among divines and expositors. It is certain that the twelve hundred and sixty days, or years, which are so often in Scripture mentioned as the time of the continuance of Antichrist's reign, did not commence before the year of Christ four hundred and seventy-nine; because if they did, they would have ended, and Antichrist would have fallen before now. The rise of Antichrist was gradual. The Christian church corrupted itself in many things presently after Constantine's time; growing more and more superstitious in its worship and by degrees bringing in many ceremonies into the worship of God, till at length they brought in the worship of saints, and set up images in their churches. The clergy in general, and especially the bishop of Rome, assumed more and more authority to himself. In the primitive times, he was only a minister of a congregation; then a standing moderator of a presbytery; then a diocesan bishop; then a metropolitan, which is equivalent to an archbishop; then a patriarch. Afterwards he claimed the power of universal bishop over the whole Christian church; wherein he was opposed for a while, but afterwards was confirmed in it by the civil power of the emperor in the year six hundred and six. After that he claimed the power of a temporal prince, and so was wont to carry two swords, to signify that both the temporal and

spiritual sword was his. He claimed more and more authority, till at length, as Christ's vice-regent on earth, he claimed
the very same power that Christ would have done, if he was
present on earth reigning on his throne; or the same power
that belongs to God, and was used to be called *God on earth*;
to be submitted to by all the princes of Christendom.[307]

We also found this letter by Edwards which addresses the 1260
days specifically:

To the Rev. Mr. M'Culloch.
Northampton, Oct. 7, 1748.
Rev. and Dear Sir,
[edited out first section]
    With respect to your very ingenious conjectures, con-
cerning the period of *forty-two months*, or *one thousand two
hundred and sixty days*, of the outer court and holy city's being
trodden under-foot of the Gentiles; you know, Sir, that that
forty-two months, or one thousand two hundred and sixty
days, spoken of Rev. xi. 2. has been universally understood,
as being the very same period with the 1260 days of the
witnesses prophesying in sackcloth, spoken of in the next
verse; and the one thousand two hundred and sixty days of
the woman's being led in the wilderness, chap. xii. 6. and
the time, times, and half a time, of her being nourished in
the wilderness from the face of the serpent, ver. 14. and the
forty-two months of the continuance of the beast, chap. xiii.
5. But it does not appear to me probable that these forty-two
months of the continuance of the beast, means the sum of
the diverse periods in which the *plat of ground*, whereon the
ancient literal Jerusalem stood, was under the dominion of

the Romans, Saracens, Persians, and Turks; but the space of time during which the reign of antichrist or the popish hierarchy continues; and as to the particular time of the downfall of antichrist, you see my reasons in the forementioned pamphlet, why I think it certain that it will not be known till it be accomplished: I cannot but think that the Scripture is plain in that matter, and that it does, in effect, require us to rest satisfied in ignorance till *the time of the end* comes.

However, I should be very foolish, if I were dogmatical in my thoughts concerning the interpretation of the prophecies: especially in opposition to those who have had so much more opportunity to be well acquainted with things of this nature. But since you have insisted on my thoughts, I conclude you will not be displeased that I have mentioned them, though not altogether agreeable to yours. I am nevertheless greatly obliged to you for your condescension in communicating your thoughts to me. If we do not exactly agree in our thoughts about these things, yet in our prayers for the accomplishment of these glorious events in God's time, and for God's gracious presence with us, and his assistance in endeavours to promote his kingdom and interests, in the meantime, we may be entirely agreed and united. That we may be so, is the earnest desire of, dear Sir,

Your Affectionate Brother and Servant,

In Our Common Lord,

Jonathan Edwards[308]

As Cris Putnam endeavored to demonstrate in our book *Petrus Romanus*, the pope's rise to temporal power began when Pope Stephen began courting Pepin around 751 and then became a reality in 756 with the expulsion of the Lombards. Putnam quickly broke out his calculator and saw that 756 placed the target sometime in 2016 which can also be thought of as in the range of three and a half years from 2012. Around that same time during our investigation, a friend named Trey Clark emailed after doing some digging of his own and made us aware of a sermon collection from the 1800s, titled, "Lectures on the Revelation," by the Reverend William J. Reid, pastor of First United Presbyterian Church in Pittsburgh, Pennsylvania, which were given over a period of time ending in March of 1876. Like Jonathan Edwards had over a hundred years earlier, Reid deduced the False Prophet and Antichrist would arrive sometime around 2012–2016. Soon we uncovered numerous other ancient examples in which the years 2012 and 2016 specifically were foreseen as when the False Prophet and the Antichrist would appear, followed by the destruction of Rome. These included:

- *The Theological Dictionary of Princeton University* (1830)
- *Critical Commentary and Paraphrase on the Old and New Testament* by Lowth and Lowman (1822)
- *The American Biblical Repository* (1840)
- *Notes on the Revelation of St. John* by Lowman (1773)
- *The Christian Spectator,* "The Monthly" (1885)
- *Abridgement of Ecclesiastical History* (1776)
- *The Works of the Rev. P. Doddridge, DD* (1804)
- *The International Sunday School Lessons Pub* (1878)
- *Character and Prospects on the Church of Rome in Two Discourses by the Rev. William Mackray* (1829)
- *The Panoplist and Missionary Magazine* (1809)
- *Lectures on Romanism* by Joseph F. Berg (1840)
- *The Congregational Magazine for the Year* (1834)
- *The Presbyterian Magazine* (1858)

Blood Moons and the Years 2012–2016

Many assume when God created the Sun and the Moon that He did so for light, heat, gravity, and other natural mechanisms. While those facts seem obvious, when looking at Genesis 1:14, we learn of four other purposes behind why the lights in the heavens were created and placed where they are. The Bible says these are for "signs," "seasons," "days," and "years." The Hebrew word for signs in this context is *owth*, a word meaning a "miraculous sign," "omen," or "warning." It signifies, among other things, that God created the heavenly bodies to communicate important matters at particular times to His covenant people.

The next reason God created the sun and the moon is for "seasons." Again, in our Western mindset, we figure God is talking about winter, spring, summer, and fall. This is the farthest from the truth. In Hebrew, the word here is *mow'ed* and is accurately translated as "an appointed time" or "divine appointment" especially related to "sacred seasons" or Feast days. This same Hebrew word is translated into English in Leviticus 23 as "feast" where it talks about the Feasts of the Lord. At first, these two words—appointments and feasts— seem about as far apart as you can get. This is why one needs to keep the Hebrew language in perspective so as not to miss the deeper conveyances of this text. The word *mow'ed* implies that God has a day timer or calendar on which He keeps predetermined "appointments" with human history and that are connected with His Feasts or Holy Days. For example, in the Book of Revelation it says that the Messiah was slain "from the foundations of the world." This means God the Father knew the year, the month, the day, and the exact time His Son would die and how this event would be played out in fulfillment of the Levitical feasts of Israel.

Finally, God declares that the sun and the moon were created to determine "days and years." Obviously, this has nothing to do with our modern calendar, which was created by a pagan Roman ruler and is based on the sun. The Muslim calendar is based on the moon. But the biblical calendar—the one that God uses according to Genesis—is based on the sun *and* the moon. So when the Scripture refers to "days and years" in Genesis 1:14, it is pointing to biblical days and years or "holy days" as well as Shemittah years and Jubilee years (every seventh year the land in Israel was to rest. This is why the Jewish people went into captivity because they did not observe the seventh year. Every fiftieth year was to be a year of Jubilee when captives were set free and received their land back).

With this in mind, a whole new discovery is made concerning how God created the sun and the moon and the stars as harbingers or "signal-senders" of His appointed times. This is confirmed throughout the Bible in places like the books of Joel, Isaiah, Revelation, as well as Jesus, Himself, in the Gospels confirming there would be signs in the sun and the moon and the stars that would herald the last days.

While solar and lunar eclipses are common occurrences and for the most part have no great prophetic significance, when they fall on the biblical Feast days, we should pay close attention. In Revelation 6:12, the Bible declares that the sun will become black as sackcloth of hair, and the moon as red as blood. Most scholars believe this important end-times sign is speaking of solar and lunar eclipses. The significance of a total solar eclipse or total lunar eclipse, if it happened on one of God's Feast days would be a powerful message. Knowing this, be advised there are four total blood moons coming, back to back, right in a row, all falling on Feast days. Equally incredible is how within the very same timeframe, two solar eclipses are scheduled to arrive. Read that again and let the significance of these comments sink in. Prophetically speaking, we are talking about the equivalent of six grand-slam homeruns in a row—a mathematical improbability that stands out against the randomness of natural cycles and strongly suggests a miraculous sign or "omen" of intelligent design is coming. Of significance to this book is how these "grand slams" are set to unfold between the years 2012–2016, specifically 2014 and 2015.

When examining NASA's website, we find these specific types or strings of total eclipses are called a "tetrad" and are very rare. According to their own calculations, a similar string of four total lunar eclipses did not happen at all in the 1800s, 1700s, or even the 1600s. Amazingly, in the 1500s it happened around seven times but not once did all four eclipses fall on the Jewish Feast days. When *was* the last time four blood moons not only occurred back to back but fell on the Feasts? The shocking dates were 1967 and 1968 when Israel recaptured Jerusalem! What about the time before that? Right on the heels of Israel becoming a nation in May of 1948. The following two years in 1949 and 1950 again saw four blood moons on Passover and the Feast of Tabernacles and then again on Passover and the Feast of Tabernacles! In other words, not only were there four blood moons in a row, but all four of them fell on the Feast days and were accompanied by historically prophetic implications of divine proportions.

What does all this have to do with the future and the timespan 2012–2016? From the Books of Revelation and Joel (2:31), we understand that the sun shall be turned into darkness, and the moon into blood, before the great and the terrible *day* of the Lord. In Exodus (chapter 12), God told Moses that Passover (roughly March-April in the Gregorian calendar) would be the point at which the religious year would begin. It just so happens that after the two blood moons on Passover and Tabernacles in 2014, this Jewish New Year in 2015 will be met with a total solar eclipse. Two weeks later on Passover we have the next total lunar eclipse. Then on the Feast of Trumpets, also known as Rosh HaShana, there is a partial solar eclipse followed two weeks later by the next total lunar eclipse on the Feast of Tabernacles. There will not be another such tetrad of four blood moons landing on biblical holidays this century. Keep your eyes on global events as these blood moons mark God's prophetic calendar. Of course, only time will tell, but these suggested apocalyptic scenarios may soon begin falling like dominoes across the world scene in anticipation of the second coming of Jesus Christ.

Deeper Secrets: The Watchers and 33, 2012, 2016

In May of 2005, I commissioned David Flynn to write another study for my daily news service (www.RaidersNewsUpdate.com) based on mutual research we were investigating at that time. The article, "An Occult Translation of the Roswell Event: Countdown to 2012," was truly unprecedented and later formed the basis of Flynn's presentation at the 2005 Ancient of Days Conference in Roswell, New Mexico. The feature article has since been quoted hundreds of times by media and republished in magazines and print publications around the world, yet what the extraordinary findings actually foretell remains hidden to most of the world.

Like Dr. I. D. E. Thomas, Dr. Jacques F. Vallée, Chuck Missler, and others, Flynn became fascinated with the mysterious connection between Watchers, so-called "aliens," the coming of Antichrist, the Mayan date 2012, and the hidden occult aspiration of Freemasons and other Illuminatus related to these subjects.

Starting out, Flynn cited how in 1928, the occult visionary, Manly P. Hall, wrote:

> European mysticism was not dead at the time the United States of America was founded. The hand of the mysteries controlled in the establishment of the new government for the signature of the mysteries may still be seen on the Great Seal of the United States of America. Careful analysis of the seal discloses a mass of occult and Masonic symbols, chief among them, the so-called American eagle.... The American eagle upon the Great Seal is but a conventionalized phoenix.[309]

"Phoenix," the last word of Hall's statement of the founding of America, was key to the "secret destiny" of civilization, for as occultists understand, the word "phoenix" is derivative of "Phoenicians" and refers to the ancient people who inhabited the very land recorded in the book of Enoch as the entry point for Watcher influence from Mt. Hermon in Phoenicia. Intriguingly, the consonants in Hebrew that make up the word "Hermon" are *ch-r-m* or the noun *cherem*, meaning "devoted to destruction." And as Elizabeth van Buren acknowledged in *The Secret of the Illuminati*, the great significance of this Phoenician Watcher location could be understood through the occult value of the numbers three and thirty-three when combined with the most important science of Freemasonry, navigation, and sacred location.[310]

The compass and square, the most visible emblems of Masonry, are the symbols of this navigation and mapmaking process. The number three is essential because without the geometry of the three-sided triangle, establishing location and distance on a map ("triangulation") is impossible. Navigation not only predicts the destination of a traveler on the Earth but also the time the traveler will arrive. As the navigator can use increments of Earth's latitude and longitude to determine location in space and time, these increments can be measured in the Earth itself according to mystics to reveal the appointed time of humanity's destiny. This is one of the main reasons the number thirty-three and the compass and square are such important symbols of the illumined elite.

With this in mind, Flynn made the unprecedented disclosure that 33.33 degrees of the great circle of the Earth represents 2,012 nautical miles, the identical number at the end of the Mayan calendar. Flynn further revealed that Mount Hermon in Phoenicia, the first location of the descent of the Watchers, lies precisely at 33.33 degrees north, 33.33 degrees east, 2,012 miles from the equator, and 2,012 miles from the prime meridian, a location of Mt. Hermon in longitude based on the Paris 0 meridian 2.20 degrees east of Greenwich.

To be even more accurate, the number of nautical miles in 33.33 degrees of the Earth is 2,012 ".9." This actually corresponds more precisely with the ending year date of the Mayan calendar—December 21, 2012.

Did the chosen location of the first connection of Watchers on Mt. Hermon at 33.33 degrees north and 33.33 east set in time the commencement of a luciferian plan for a final New World Order beginning in 2012? In light of the ancient history of Mt. Hermon and the Mayan buildings and cities having been intentionally aligned with the Pleiades and Orion Nebula, the return to Earth of the god these terrestrial and celestial locations are historically connected with—Apollo/Osiris/Nimrod—literally seems to have been set in stone. The highest sacred number (thirty-three) of the occultists who encoded the return of Apollo on the Great Seal of the United States also: 1) equals the exact location where the Watchers first descended to Earth and; 2) triangulates the mile measurement 2012—the end date of the Mayan countdown to the return of their bloodthirsty god.

A related matter that is equally disturbing and perhaps validates the concerns of Dr. Thomas, Vallée, Flynn, and others whose research produced repetitive connections between Watchers and so-called "probing aliens," is the most celebrated ufological location on Earth—the impact site near Roswell, New Mexico, which sits incredibly at 33 degrees north latitude, at a distance 2,012 miles from the equator! Furthermore, when the latitude of the Roswell impact site, 33 degrees north, is multiplied by the universal mathematical constant pi (3.1415926572...), the result is 104 degrees, the longitude of the impact site!

Scientists at the Search for Extraterrestrial Intelligence (SETI) know that a radio message from intelligent extraterrestrial life would use such redundant universal mathematical constants, which are not dependent on calibration systems, but on ratios. Any signal coming from space that has these numbers would stand out against the randomness in the background of space noise and would define itself as intelligent and deliberate. This is the case with the location of the Roswell incident, as the odds against a crash location occurring "by chance" precisely at the whereabouts that are the product of pi x 33 are astronomical...on the order of millions to one. The location appears to have been chosen to show deliberate and intelligent coordinates related to the occult values thirty-three (= the Masonic prophecy) and 2012 (= the year the god returned) in precise parallel to the fixed location where Watchers first descended.

It might seem beyond mere chance therefore that the United States recovered the debris and "alien" bodies of the Roswell crash on the Fourth of July, 1947. America was founded on the same date in 1776 (also the year the Order of the Illuminati was established), chosen by the elite behind the formation of America for a special reason, which we discussed earlier, related to 33.33 as the ultimate number of earthly luciferian government. Is it therefore coincidence that important ancient structures were built around the world on or near the Earth's thirty-third parallel—including Great Pyramids, Megiddo, Tyre (where Ezekiel compared the ancient king to Lucifer), the Temple of Marduk, Babylon, Baalbeck, and dozens more? Reason may be shed in the book of Revelation concerning why this number in particular seems to be so important to occultists, ancient pagans, and the messengers of Mt. Hermon and Roswell:

> And there appeared another wonder in heaven; and behold a great red dragon.... And his tail drew the third part [33.33 percent] of the [angels] of heaven, and did cast them to the earth. (Revelation 12:3–4)

Of course, the correlation between the Masonic number thirty-three and the year 2012, plus the matching of these numbers to the exact coordinates of the arrival of Watchers on Mt. Hermon and the date that the Maya predicted the return of the gods in spirit or form, could be nothing more than a coincidence. An amazing and mathematically incomprehensible coincidence…and yet the rabbit hole goes deeper…

Petrus Romanus and the Final Conclave

While a magnificent amount of material has been published in recent years involving the Mayan date 2012, until this book, the world at large was unaware of the connection between this year and the Great Seal regarding the arrival of Apollo/Osiris/Nimrod and the start of a final World Order.

This includes the prophecies of the Cumaean Sibyl—whose predictions concerning the return of Apollo is encoded on the Masonically designed Great Seal of the United States—who was (and is) so highly regarded as a true prophetess among the occult hierarchy as well as holding occasions of sacred esteem in the Vatican's holy places, including the Sistine Chapel. It therefore bears repeating here the concerns of several church fathers concerning end-times great deception, and what they said about Masonic involvement in the religious institution ultimately paving the way for the coming of the False Prophet and Antichrist.

To start with, among scholars of the implications of the years 2012–2016, more than a few have pointed to the contemporaneous prophecy of St. Malachy regarding "the last pope." The prophecy, taken from St. Malachy's "Prophecy of the Popes," is among a list of verses predicting each of the Roman Catholic popes from Pope Celestine II to the final pope, "Peter the Roman," whose reign would end in the destruction of Rome. First made public in 1595, the prophecies were attributed to St. Malachy by a Benedictine historian named Arnold de Wyon, who recorded them in his book, *Lignum Vitæ*. Tradition holds that Malachy had been called to Rome by Pope Innocent II, and while he was there, he experienced the vision of the future popes, including the last one, which he wrote down in a series of cryptic phrases. According to the prophecy, the current pope (Francis) is the final pontiff, *Petrus Romanus*.

> In persecutione extrema S. R. E. sedebit Petrus Romanus, qui pascet oues in multis tribulationibus: quibus transactis ciuitas septicollis diruetur, et Iudex tremendus iudicabit populum. Finis.

> In extreme persecution, the seat of the Holy Roman Church will be occupied by Peter the Roman, who will feed the sheep through many tribulations; when they are over, the city of seven hills will be destroyed, and the terrible or fearsome Judge will judge his people. The End.

As stated in our bestselling book, *Petrus Romanus: The Final Pope Is Here* (Defender Publishing, 2012) we held the title Petrus Romanus (Peter the Roman) from Malachy's prophecy as symbolic of the pontificate and meaning that the final pope (Francis) will reaffirm the authority of the Roman pontiff over the Church and will emphasize the supremacy of the Roman Catholic Faith over all other religions around the world. As the first Jesuit elected to the papacy, Francis is not only uniquely qualified, but under oath to accomplish this very thing.

The idea by some Catholics that this final pope from St. Malachy's list heralds the beginning of "great apostasy" followed by "great tribulation" sets the stage for the imminent unfolding of apocalyptic events, something many non-Catholics would agree with. This could give rise to the False Prophet, who, according to the book of Revelation, leads the world's *religious* communities into embracing a *political* leader known as the Antichrist. This marriage of Church and secular government would give unprecedented global influence to the Man of Sin during the period known as the Great Tribulation.

In recent history, several Catholic priests—some deceased now—have been surprisingly outspoken on what they have seen as the inevitable danger of the False Prophet rising from within the ranks of Catholicism as a result of secret satanic "Illuminati-Masonic" influences. These priests—as we have done in this book—used the term "Illuminati" not strictly as a reference to the Bavarian movement founded May 1, 1776 by Jesuit-taught Adam Weishaupt, but as indicative of a modern multinational power elite, the occult hierarchy operating behind current supranatural and global political machinations. According to Catholic priests such as Father John F. O'Connor, Father Alfred Kunz, Father Malachi Martin, and others, among this secret society are sinister false Catholic infiltrators who understand that, as the Roman Catholic Church represents one-sixth of the world's population and over half of all professing Christians, it is indispensable for controlling future global elements in matters of church and state.

In a two-hour presentation (available on DVD and at You-Tube[311]), Father O'Connor gave a homily titled, "The Reign of the Antichrist," in which he described how changes within society and in the institution were already at work before his death to provide for the coming of Antichrist. In this sermon and elsewhere, O'Connor outlined the catalyst for this scheme unfolding as a result of "Masonic Conspirators" within the organization whose plan, called "Alta Vendetta," would essentially take control of the papacy and help the

False Prophet deceive the world's faithful (including Catholics) into worshipping Antichrist.

O'Connor was not alone as whistleblower to the vast Masonic conspiracy within the Vatican's ranks covertly working toward an anti-Christian New World Order. Retired professor of the Pontifical Biblical Institute, eminent Catholic theologian, and former Jesuit priest, Malachi Martin, was a close personal friend of Pope Paul VI and worked within the Holy See doing research on the Dead Sea Scrolls, publishing articles in journals on Semitic paleography, and teaching Aramaic, Hebrew, and Sacred Scripture. In 1965, Paul VI granted Martin a dispensation from his Jesuit and priestly duties, and Martin moved to New York, where he dedicated himself to writing about—and sometimes speaking out on—a variety of issues stemming from the Second Vatican Council, to detailed insider accounts of papal history, Catholic dogma, and geopolitics. As a member of the Vatican Advisory Council and personal secretary to renowned Jesuit Cardinal Augustin Bea, Martin had privileged information pertaining to secretive Church and world issues, including the Third Secret of Fátima, which many believe has never been released and that Martin hinted spelled-out parts of a plan to formerly install the dreaded False Prophet during a "Final Conclave." In light of Pope Benedict's resignation and the election of the first Jesuit to the pontificate, Martin's book, *Windswept House*—in which he depicted how a pope would be secretly forced from office (Benedict?) and replaced by a Jesuit-backed leader who would help them establish a New World Order (Francis?)—comes vividly into view. Martin's claim that this Illuminati-empowered group had infiltrated the highest levels of Vatican administration and were working to bring about this New World Order may also have led to involvement by operatives of the same group concerning his untimely, some say "suspicious" death in 1999.

This raises questions as well about John Paul I, who was elected pope in 1978 but who died only thirty-three days later (33: an occult Masonic marker). Shortly after becoming pope, John Paul I learned of cardinals, bishops, and high-ranking prelates that were Freemasons. He may have been murdered to keep him from exposing these men's plans and/or to deter an investigation he had launched into the Vatican bank connected with Roberto Calvi, a Grand Orient Freemason and the Chairman of the Ambrosiano Bank, which the Vatican Bank was primary shareholder of. When in 1978 it was discovered that monies had been illegally laundered for the Mafia through that bank, Calvi fled Italy and, three days later, the Bank's shares crashed. One day after that, Calvi's secretary conveniently committed suicide, and on June 18, Calvi himself was found hanging beneath the Blackfriar Bridge (connected to Freemasons) in London with a Masonic Cabletow around his neck and chunks of masonry (left as a symbol?) in his pockets. John Daniel says of this in *Scarlet and the Beast*: "At Masonic ritual murders, Masonic symbols are left at the scene for several reasons: (1) to show Masons that this was a Masonic murder; (2) to warn Masons to follow the Masonic code, or suffer like fate; and (3) to prove to Masonic paymasters that the 'hit' was accomplished."[312]

But was John Paul I, like Calvi may have been (and like Malachi Martin infers in *Windswept House*), murdered by a Masonic "Superforce" too large and too powerful for him to contain; one that Martin would later claim was behind the scenes, secretly working to use the Vatican to bring about a global Antichrist system? "Suddenly it became unarguable that now… the Roman Catholic organization carried a permanent presence of clerics who worshipped Satan and liked it," wrote Martin. "The facts that brought the Pope to a new level of suffering were mainly two: The systematic organizational links—the network, in other words that had been established between certain clerical homosexual groups and Satanist covens. And the inordinate power and influence of that network."[313]

Ten years before something "pulled his feet" out from under Martin while he was preparing for an exorcism (which caused him to fall, bringing about his death later; at the time he was working on what he promised would be his most explosive book yet under the telling title: *Primacy: How the Institutional Roman Catholic Church became a Creature of The New World Order*), he had become increasingly outspoken about pedophilic Satanism at the heart of the Vatican throughout the College of Cardinals and all the way down to local parishes, which he said were in league with a secret Masonic *diabolicus* that began following the "enthronement of the fallen Archangel Lucifer" in the Roman Catholic Citadel on June 29, 1963. This horrid *rituale*, as Martin had called it, had two primary objectives: 1) to enthrone Lucifer as the Prince over Rome; and 2) *to assure the sorcerous inception and embodiment in flesh of that immaterial spirit that would fill Petrus Romanus.*

In his book, *The Keys of This Blood: The Struggle of World Dominion*, Martin had written:

> Most frighteningly for John Paul, he had come up against the irremovable presence of a malign strength in his own Vatican and in certain bishops' chanceries. It was what knowledgeable Churchmen called the "superforce." Rumors, always difficult to verify, tied its installation to the beginning of Pope Paul VI's reign in 1963. Indeed Paul had alluded somberly to "the smoke of Satan which has entered the Sanctuary"…an oblique reference to an enthronement ceremony by Satanists in the Vatican.[314]

Martin concealed even greater detail of this luciferic "enthronement ceremony by Satanists in the Vatican" in his book, *Windswept House.*

The Enthronement of the Fallen Archangel Lucifer was effected within the Roman Catholic Citadel on June 29, 1963; a fitting date for the historic promise about to be fulfilled. As the principal agents of this Ceremonial well knew, Satanist tradition had long predicted that the Time of the Prince would be ushered in at the moment when a Pope would take the name of the Apostle Paul [Pope Paul VI]. That requirement—the signal that the Availing Time had begun—had been accomplished just eight days before with the election of the latest Peter-in-the-Line.[315]

The specific date given by Martin—June 29, 1963—and the combination of the specific names Peter (whom the pope is successor of in Catholicism) and Paul, is important. June 29 is the Feast or Solemnity of both apostles, Peter and Paul. This is a liturgical feast in honor of the martyrdom of both saints and a holy day of obligation in the universal Church in which the faithful are "obliged" to participate in mass. Among other things, this means that on this specific date, a perfectly timed sacrilegious parody of the Catholic mass was completed during the Enthronement of the Fallen Archangel Lucifer (which occultists know would hold high satanic energy) as well as simultaneously an offense made against the martyrdom of Peter and Paul during the Church's Feast in their names.

Martin stated publicly on more than one occasion that this enthronement of Lucifer in Rome was based on fact, and that to facilitate the black magic, a parallel ceremony was conducted simultaneously in the United States in Charleston, South Carolina. The reason this location was selected has remained obscure to many, but given what Malachi said about the Masonic connection, it makes sense that South Carolina was chosen: It is the site of the first

Supreme Council of the Scottish Rite Freemasonry in the United States, called "the Mother Lodge of the World," where in 1859, champion of luciferian dogma for the Masonic-Illuminatus, Albert Pike became Grand Commander of the Supreme Council, where he served the Order of the Quest until his death in Washington, DC on April 2, 1892. Pike was known as a Satanist in his adopted state of Arkansas and loved to sit naked in the woods astride a phallic throne while participating for days in drunkenness and debauchery. Today, his body is proudly entombed at the House of the Temple, headquarters of the Southern Jurisdiction of the Scottish Rite Free-masonry in Washington, DC.

According to the logic of former Sirhan Sirhan attorney, Day Williams, this makes Charleston, at the thirty-third parallel, even more perfect for the sacrifice and parallel ceremony described by Martin because, "If a life is taken close to the…33rd Parallel, this fits with the Masons' demonic mythology in which they demonstrate their worldly power by spilling human blood at a predetermined locale."[316] Martin added additional reasons for the South Carolina location:

> Such unobtrusive elements as the Pentagram and the black candles and the appropriate draperies could be part of the Ceremonial in Rome. But other Ruberics—the Bowl of Bones and the Ritual Din, for example, the sacrificial ani-mals and the victim—would be too much. There would have to be a Parallel Enthronement. A Concelebration could be accomplished with the same effect by the Brethren in an Authorized Targeting Chapel. Provided all the participants in both locations "targeted" every element of the Event on the Roman Chapel, then the Event in its fullness would be

accomplished specifically in the target area. It would all be a matter of unanimity of hearts, identity of intention and perfect synchronization of words and actions between the Targeting Chapel and the Target Chapel. The living wills and the thinking minds of the Participants concentrated on the specific Aim of the Prince would transcend all distance.[317] Martin's chilling description in *Windswept House* of the methodical profanation of everything virtuous and innocent during the "Parallel Enthronement" between the Targeting Chapel and the Target Chapel included indescribably foul Invocations, sadistic animal sacrifices, and repeated violations of a young "Ritual Victim" on an altar. For the uninitiated, the very idea this happened strains credulity. Yet when John F. McManus (for *The New American*, June 9, 1997) asked Father Martin if the Black Mass in South Carolina had actually occurred, it led to an enlightening Q and A:

McManus: Your book begins with a vivid description of a sacrilegious "Black Mass" held in 1963 in Charleston, South Carolina. Did this really happen?

Martin: Yes it did. And the participation by telephone of some high officials of the church in the Vatican is also a fact. The young female who was forced to be a part of this satanic ritual is very much alive and, happily, has been able to marry and lead a normal life. She supplied details about the event....

McManus: In addition...you depict numerous other cardinals and bishops in a very bad light. Are these characterizations based on fact?

Martin: Yes, among the cardinals and the hierarchy there are satanists, homosexuals, anti-papists, and cooperators in the drive for world rule.[318]

Even more explosive, near the end of *Windswept House* there is an often overlooked section providing explicit details of the enthronement ceremony and its true purpose to create a satanic pope. Martin provides details of the "Roman Phalanx," another name for the Vatican satanic cult, as well as describing their ultimate goal:

As a body, they had sworn "the Sacred Oath of Commitment" administered by the Delegate. Then each man had approached the Altar to give "Evidence" of his personal dedication. With blood drawn by the prick of a golden pin, each had pressed his fingerprint beside his name on the Bill of Authorization. Henceforth, the life and work of every member of the Phalanx in the Roman Citadel was to be focused on the transformation of the papacy itself. No longer was the Petrine Office to be an instrument of the "Nameless Weakling" [Jesus]. It was to be fashioned into a willing instrument of the Prince, and a living model for "the New Age of Man."[319]

Thus, it appears frighteningly evident that, like in the movie *Rosemary's Baby* and in the visions and fears of so many Catholic seers, a ceremony for invoking the incarnation of Satan's seed—or installing it ritualistically inside a chosen priest—was indeed performed, and a blood oath of dedication enacted for its goals by highly placed Satanists inside the Roman Catholic Citadel did take place a little less than fifty years ago.

Whether Martin was killed and his death covered up for revealing this satanic scheme to use the Catholic Church as a launching pad for a luciferic *novus ordo seclorum* may never be known. One year before he died, however, Martin's very good friend, Father Alfred Kunz, was brutally murdered at his St. Michael Catholic Church in Dane, Wisconsin. Kunz had been investigating the same Satanism among priests that Martin had warned about, and had told Martin in the weeks before his murder that he feared for his life.

When Kunz was found dead with his throat slit, Martin claimed in various media that he had "inside information" and that the Vatican "luciferians" had murdered him because he was getting ready to blow the lid off their conspiracy. The satanic animal sacrifice described by Martin in *Windswept House* as part of the "enthronement of the Fallen Archangel Lucifer in the Vatican" seems eerily comparable to what was indeed discovered in Dane County during the first hours of the murder investigation, including a calf which had been found sacrificed on a farm near St. Michael's Church exactly twenty-four hours before Kunz was last seen alive. According to police reports, the calf's throat was slit, as was the throat of Father Kunz, and its genitals cut off. There are details we will not discuss in this book due to their horrific nature, but deep within occultism there are reasons for removing the genitals of a sacrifice having to do with blasphemy of the Old Testament description of animals being accounted unworthy as offerings to the Lord if their testicles are bruised, crushed, torn, or cut (Leviticus 22:24). According to survivors of ritual satanic abuse (including Egyptian-Masonic Satanism), human sacrificial victims are sometimes laid on a table and their genitals likewise removed in order to make them "unworthy" or unfit for salvation (though versions of such abuse in South Africa are called "muti" murders, and some people pay large sums of money for genitalia from these human sacrifices in the belief it will bring them fertility, health, and good fortune). Then there is the ancient occult idea that decapitated persons cannot partake in the resurrection, thus dark rituals can include mutilation of the head, throat, and genitals where damnation of the victim is meant as a magical curse. In the case of the Dane County murder, was a black ritual performed between the hours of 10 p.m. on March 2, and 4 a.m. on March 3, 1998, to "target" Father Kunz and to "mark" him unfit for redemption?

During our investigative research for the book *Petrus Romanus*, we made formal requests of the Dane County Sheriff's Office for pertinent case files (DCSO Case # 98011295) pertaining to the ongoing investigation of the Father Kunz homicide. After first being told the files we requested would be given us, on December 15, 2011 we received a letter from the office of Lieutenant Mark Twombly signed by Sheriff Mahoney that the District Attorney would need to approve the release of the files (in other words it would take a court order) and therefore the request had been denied. Since this is an active, ongoing case, the sensitive records are not to be made public at this time and this is understandable. In filing a second request for less delicate documents, we were able to obtain a packet of files, but none of these provided solid clues to the larger question of conspiracy related to the murder of Father Kunz—specifically, was evidence discovered at the crime scene that his murder was somehow connected to his conservative position on Vatican II and, more importantly, that he had information on certain pedophile priests and Satanists (that had earned him fierce enemies within the Church) reaching all the way to the Catholic hierarchy in Rome involved in ceremonies or behavior related to the enthronement of Lucifer and a ritual conducted for the purpose of transmigrating a particular spirit into Petrus Romanus?

"In the absence of an arrest, the Kunz case has developed into a sinister religious Rorschach for many—certainly among those close to the case who consider themselves traditionalists within the troubled Roman Catholic Church,"[320] wrote Chuck Nowlen in the 2001 cover story for *Las Vegas Weekly*, "The Devil and Father Kunz." At that time, Nowlen had interviewed Peter Kelly, a Monroe, Wisconsin attorney and master's divinity student who had produced Kunz's weekly radio show. Given that Kelly was a good friend of Kunz and had spent substantial time with him in private conversations, his response to Nowlen's questions reveal a lot about what Kelly personally believed lay at the root of the murder: "This is a time of major crisis within the church, and the breakdown tends to be along traditional and conservative versus liberal lines. I think it's getting almost to the point of complete collapse. And, yeah, I know: Some people delve into a so-called satanic influence in the church, and everybody sort of rolls their eyes and laughs. But, I tell you, the nexus is really there."[321]

Still, Nowlen wondered, could someone within the Church really have killed Kunz—or ordered him killed?

"Absolutely," the lawyer confirmed, "as unbelievable as that might sound to some people."[322]

Finally, from the Q and A with McManus, Martin revealed the end-game behind those who may have murdered Father Kunz and infiltrated the Catholic Church:

McManus: Your book claims that subversive influences in the highest clerical positions of the Church are working to bring it into the New World Order. What do you mean by "New World Order?"

Martin: In its completely planned form…the governments of the world will be directed by those who have climbed their way into the capstone.

McManus: What do you mean by the "capstone"?

Martin: The underlying force I have written about in *Windswept House* is structured very much like a pyramid. It is wide at the bottom where many individuals work for its goals and hope to be elevated to a higher place. There are fewer and fewer inhabitants in each of the ascending steps in the structure. Only a very few form its ultimate directorate, the capstone of the pyramid.[323]

Long before popular author Dan Brown (*The Da Vinci Code, Angels and Demons, The Lost Symbol*) characterized an Illuminati scheme to destroy the Vatican, Malachi Martin had pointed to the familiar pyramid symbolism from the Great Seal of the United States associated with the New World Order and had accurately directed investigators toward the conspirators, as well as to the prophetic references of the *novus ordo seclorum* as arriving when the capstone would be figuratively filled and fitted atop the unfinished pyramid. Whether Martin perceived the year that the conspirator's plan would reach its zenith is uncertain, but the occult elite have always had their date, which, as the reader has discovered, is cleverly encoded alongside the other details of the complete cipher in the Great Seal of the United States. It indicates that something began in 2012 and will reach its zenith in 2016. Is it thus coincidental that the Vice President of the United States just called for the creation of "the New World Order"?[324]

The "Fourth Turning" and 2012–2016

I learned recently that our good friend Sue Bradley, an investigative journalist and blogger, had gone home to be with Jesus early in the morning on April 26, 2013. In 2008, and again in 2012, with input from Steve Quayle and me, Sue had started work on what would be one of her last articles. It was titled "The Fourth Turning: The Protocols and The Gray Champion." A couple months before she departed this life, she had emailed me from her hospital room and said she was about to expand her Fourth Turning work based on some *Zenith 2016* material I had just shared with her. Unfortunately, like with the passing of David Flynn, the world will probably never know what Sue was about to reveal. What we do understand is that her research would be partially based on a book published in 1997, *The Fourth Turning*, which describes itself as "a book that turns history into prophecy." It explains cycles of life and generational archetypes through the examination of Western historical paradigms over the past five centuries. By surveying the past and identifying contemporary markers, William Strauss and Neil Howe, the authors of the study, determined an astoundingly prescient forecast in which they saw a cascade of incidents that would ultimately lead to chaos and the "Fourth Turning." Keep in mind they made these predictions over sixteen years ago, long before the September 11, 2001 attacks on America or the financial issues of today. Among the scenarios they foresaw were:

The first could be economic distress with a government beset by fiscal crisis, the state laying claim to federal tax monies, federal marshals enforcing orders, tax rebellions, special forces, and an ensuing constitutional crisis;

The second is a terrorist attack, involving an airliner, a military response, authorization for house-to-house searches, and false flag accusations against the administration;

The third scenario is an economic disaster involving Wall Street and a federal budget impasse which results in a stalemate;

The fourth consideration is eco-environmental malaise with the Centers for Disease Control announcing the spread of a new communicable virus with quarantines and relocations;

The fifth projection is geopolitical in nature with growing anarchy throughout the former Soviet republics prompting Russia to conduct training exercises around its borders, a Russian alliance with Iran, soaring gold and silver prices and global military responses.

In describing these insightful scenarios, Strauss and Howe felt a catalyst would unfold as a result of a specific dynamic and, "An initial spark will trigger a chain reaction of unyielding responses and further emergencies"[325] (the war on terror?).

According to Strauss and Howe in 1997, this chain reaction was already prepped to unfold as the result of natural cycles or "Turnings" in which generations are doomed to forget—and thus to repeat—the mistakes of the past. The authors describe a Turning as "an era with a characteristic social mood, a new twist on how people feel about themselves and their nation. It results from the aging of the generation [before it]."[326] A society enters a Turning once every twenty years or so, when all living generations begin to enter their next phases of life. The living generations, or *saeculae*, comprise four cyclical "Turnings," characterized as:

The First Turning (THE HIGH): an era of enthusiastic collective strengthening and civic development, having burned the brush and swept the ashes of preceding structure.

The Second Turning (THE AWAKENING): built on the energies and accomplishments of the High but finds increasing yearning for introspection with a high tolerance for spiritual expression outside the parameters of predetermined standards.

The Third Turning (THE UNRAVELING): begins as the "society-wide embrace of the liberating cultural forces" loosed by the Awakening shows signs of civic disorder and decay, a heightened sense of self-reliance and an increasing withdrawal of public trust. This builds to a near crisis of downcast pessimism and a palpable pall that can only be remedied by yielding to the next.

The Fourth Turning (THE CRISES and the era we have now entered): by far, the most perilous as societies pass through the greatest and most dangerous gates of history. As desperate solutions are sought for "sudden threats" on multiple cultural fronts, confrontation is passionate and decisions are often reactive, aggressive. "Government governs, community obstacles are removed, and laws and customs that resisted change for decades are swiftly shunted aside. A grim preoccupation with civic peril causes spiritual curiosity to decline... Public order tightens, private risk-taking abates, and...child-rearing reaches a smothering degree of protection and structure. The young focus their energy on worldly achievements, leaving values in the hands of the old. Wars are fought with fury and for maximum result."[327]

Through the examination of an enormous amount of political and cultural history, Strauss and Howe processed over five hundred years of Anglo-American cultural nuance into remarkable, well-organized, and predictable cycles and it is from this reservoir they finally stake an uncanny claim:

> Just after the millennium, America will enter a new era that will culminate with a crisis comparable to the American Revolution, the Civil War, the Great Depression, and World War II. The very survival of the nation will almost certainly be at stake.[328]

Strauss and Howe saw the United States of that time (1997) in the Third Turning, "midway through an Unraveling," roughly a decade away from the next Crisis or Fourth Turning:

> America feels like it's unraveling. Although we live in an era of relative peace and comfort, we have settled into a mood of pessimism about the long-term future, fearful that our superpower nation is somehow rotting from within.
>
> The next Fourth Turning is due to begin shortly after the new millennium… Real hardship will beset the land, with severe distress that could involve questions of class, race, nation, and empire…
>
> The very survival of the nation will feel at stake.
>
> Sometime before the year 2025, America will pass through a great gate in history, commensurate with the American Revolution, Civil War, and twin emergencies of the Great Depression and World War II.
>
> The risk of catastrophe will be very high. The nation could erupt into insurrection or civil violence, crack up geo-

graphically, or succumb to authoritarian rule. If there is a war, it is likely to be one of maximum risk and efforts—in other words, a TOTAL WAR.[329]

The striking details contained within *The Fourth Turning* illustrate the precision that was distilled with a close examination of historical patterns and contemporary application.

Although the authors note that the events described are not absolute, they also insist that the cycles, these Turnings, cannot be interrupted. As summer follows spring, an Unraveling precedes a Crisis of Faustian proportions:

> It will require us to lend a new seasonal interpretation to our revered American Dream. And it will require us to admit that our faith in linear progress has often amounted to a Faustian bargain with our children.
>
> Faust always ups the ante, and every bet is double-or-nothing. Through much of the Third Turning, we have managed to postpone the reckoning. But history warns that we can't defer it beyond the next bend in time.[330]

While a "Faustian bargain" sounds ominous, there is little evidence that the Anglo-American "Dream" has undergone the introspection and discipline necessary to buffer the arrogant recklessness of this generation and its administration.

NBC's Chuck Todd noted, on the evening of November 4, 2008, that Barack Obama was a changing of the guard in the United States from the Baby Boomer presidencies of William Clinton and George W. Bush. The *Toronto Globe and Mail* referred to President-elect Obama as being a member of Generation X, being born in 1961. And Strauss and Howe assigned Generation X—

the Thirteenth Generation—to those who have now brought us to chaos and the start of the Fourth Turning.

When the Constitution Hangs by a Thread, Will Romney Ride in on a White Horse?

Mirroring the premise of the Fourth Turning is a controversial Mormon prophecy ascribed to Joseph Smith. The 1843 divination is called the "White Horse Prophecy" and is named after the White Horse of the book of Revelation. It predicts a time when the US Constitution will be in crisis only to be saved by a member of the LDS (Latter Day Saints, more commonly called "Mormons"). If Mitt Romney runs again for president in 2016 (barring any end-run around the Twenty-Second Amendment to the United States Constitution by Obama), the controversial prediction allegedly made by Mormonism's founder could have a disturbing way of coming to pass.

According to history, after their expulsion from Missouri in 1838, the Mormon prophet Joseph Smith traveled to Washington, DC where he made an appeal to the national government for redress of wrongs suffered in that state. Judge Elias Higbee traveled with him and they were met by leading statesmen of the United States including "Henry Clay, John C. Calhoun, President Martin Van Buren, different members of the Cabinet, Senators, and Representatives."[331] After hearing their grievances, Van Buren admitted their cause was just, but said that he could do nothing about it lest he lose the vote in Missouri. Smith found this outrageous, and uttered divine judgments against the United States Government. Mormon historian, Marvin S. Hill, wrote of this: "To secure legal sanction for his call to arms, Smith petitioned Congress to form Nauvoo [a small city established by early Mormons in Hancock County, Illinois, along a great bend in the Mississippi River] into a federal district and grant him authority to command federal troops in defense of the city. He warned his closest friends [in the Nauvoo City Council] that 'if Congress will not hear our petition and grant us protection, they will be broken up as a government, and God shall damn them, and there shall be nothing left of them—not even a grease spot.'"[332] Approximately four years later, Smith prophesied again, this time speaking of a day when the US Constitution would "hang by a thread" and would barely be "preserved and saved" by a rider of a White Horse or representative of the Mormon Church. The "White Horse Prophecy," as it has come to be known, bares a dubious distinction because it was not given in public but rests mostly on the testimonies of two other Mormons—Edwin Rushton and Theodore Turley—who wrote it down as Smith delivered the prophecy at his home in May, 1843. The following year, Smith would run as an independent candidate against James Polk and Whig Henry Clay for the presidency of the United States. At that time he was advocating the overthrow of the US government and its replacement by a Mormon-led theocracy with himself as leader of "the army of God," but his hopes were cut short when he and his brother Hyrum were attacked and killed by a mob. While the White Horse prophecy he gave (which, also of contemporary interest, states that "the two Popes, Greek and Catholic, will come together and be united"[333]) is not considered undisputable by all Mormons, it has, at least in part, been repeatedly affirmed as genuine in general conference messages, including in October 1918, when the sixth LDS president, Joseph F. Smith, said, "Joseph Smith, the prophet…predicted that the time would come, when the Constitution of our country would hang as it were by a thread, and that the Latter-day Saints above all other people in the world would come to the rescue of that great and glorious palladium of our liberty."[334]

Other famous Mormons that have spoken in favor of the White Horse Prophecy include:

- In 1855, Brigham Young declared at the Tabernacle in Salt Lake: "When the Constitution of the United States hangs, as it were, upon a single thread, they will have to call for the Mormon Elders to save it from utter destruction; and they will step forth and do it."[335]
- Again in 1868, Young stated: "How long will it be before the words of the prophet Joseph will be fulfilled? He said if the Constitution of the United States were saved at all it must be done by this people. It will not be many years before these words come to pass."[336]
- The Mormon Apostle, J. Reuben Clark, repeated this belief again in a 1942 conference message, saying, "You and I have heard all our lives that the time may come when the Constitution may hang by a thread. I do not know whether it is a thread, or a small rope by which it now hangs, but I do know that whether it shall live or die is now in the balance."[337]
- In 1961, Mormon Apostle Ezra Taft Benson, who would later become the thirteenth president of the LDS, agreed, saying, "The Lord told the Prophet Joseph Smith there would be an attempt to overthrow the country by destroying the Constitution. Joseph Smith predicted that the time would come when the Constitution would hang, as it were, by a thread, and at that time 'this people will step forth and save it from the threatened destruction.'"[338]
- Two years later, Benson mentioned the prophecy again as he addressed the conference: "The Prophet Joseph Smith said the time would come when the Constitution would hang as

it were by a thread. Modern-day prophets for the last thirty years have been warning us that we have been rapidly moving in that direction. Fortunately, the Prophet Joseph Smith saw the part the elders of Israel [Mormons] would play in this crisis. Will there be some of us who won't care about saving the Constitution, others who will be blinded by the craftiness of men, and some who will knowingly be working to destroy it? He that has ears to hear and eyes to see can discern by the Spirit and through the words of God's mouthpiece that our liberties are being taken."[339]

The list above goes on and on among various Mormons throughout history that have held the prophecy of a constitutional crisis and its salvation via a Mormon to be true. In more recent years, Utah Senator Orrin Hatch made an oblique reference to the prophecy during his year 2000 bid for the US presidency, saying, "I've never seen it worse than this, where the Constitution literally is hanging by a thread,"[340] and talk-show host, Glenn Beck, mentioned the "hang by a thread" portion of the White Horse Prophecy when he was on the Bill O'Reilly show on November 14, 2008.[341]

This brings us to the present hour. The clock is ticking down toward the year 2016 when some expect a constitutional crisis to unfold right in time for a Mormon savior to appear on his white horse.[342] Romney has already made his 2016 presidential ambitions public,[343] and he isn't just any Mormon. He is the miracle baby of a woman who was told by her doctor she could never bear a fourth child. Born anyway in 1947, he became the star-child of George W. Romney, the most prominent Mormon in American politics (as governor of Michigan) and a seventh-generation direct descendant of Parley Parker Pratt, Sr., one of Mormonism's founding twelve apostles. Named after the close family friend John Willard Marriott (one of the richest Mormons in history), Romney received his patriarchal blessing at nineteen years of age and was told by the Church that the Lord expected great things from him. Shortly thereafter, while helping his mother (Lenore Romney) in the 1970 campaign against Democrat Phillip A. Hart in the Michigan general election, "Mitt" Romney—as he was then being called and whose name can be made to equal 666—began hearing prophetic insinuations about his future role as a national leader. This included whispers among Mormons about the White Horse Prophecy, as author Sally Denton noted for Salon Magaine:

> That same year [1970], the Cougar Club—the all male, all white social club at Brigham Young University in Salt Lake City (blacks were excluded from full membership in the Mormon church until 1978)—was humming with talk that its president, Mitt Romney, would become the first Mormon president of the United States. "If not Mitt, then who?" was the ubiquitous slogan within the elite organization. The pious world of BYU was expected to spawn the man who would lead the Mormons into the White House and fulfill the prophecies of the church's founder, Joseph Smith Jr., *which Romney has avidly sought to realize.* (emphasis added)[344]

Though Romney has publically sought to downplay the White Horse Prophecy whenever raised in media,[345] he is aware that fellow students at BYU not only idolized him as the "alpha male" of their fraternity but commonly referred to him as "the One Mighty and Strong"—a direct line from the prophecy by Joseph Smith, Jr., the founder of the Latter Day Saints. This grandiose and prophetic title is taken from Isaiah 28:2, "The Lord hath a mighty and strong one, which as a tempest of hail and a destroying storm, as a flood of mighty waters overflowing, shall cast down to the earth with the hand." Smith predicted this Mighty and Strong One would not only save the US Constitution but use his political office to bring about the "inheritances of the [Latter Day] Saints." What that implies could be of significance for the future of the United States according to former candidate for Nevada governor and television newsman, Mike Moody.

As a young man, Moody was a personal friend of Romney and a member of the prestigious Cougar Club at Brigham Young University that held "Mitt" in such prophetic esteem. In his memoir, *Mitt—Set Our People Free*, he describes how the White Horse Prophecy motivated him personally "to seek a career in government and politics" because he believed that he and other Mormons were being divinely directed to expand the Mormon "kingdom" by helping Romney—whom he says is under a sacred blood-oath to the Mormon Church to actually *replace* the US Constitution—to advance the goal of a one-world government under Mormon paternalistic priesthoods and the "political Kingdom of God and Joseph Smith's version of the Millennial Kingdom on Earth."[346]

"We were taught that America is the Promised Land," Moody told me on the phone, adding that, "the Mormons believe they are the Chosen People and that the time has come for a Mormon leader to usher in the second coming of Christ and a political Kingdom of God in Washington, DC."[347]

After our discussion, Moody mailed me a copy of his book, *Mitt—Set Our People Free*, and I found it to be an intriguing and rare insight into Mormon theology and philosophy. I was already familiar with the LDS belief involving pre-mortal existence where they, as "spirit children," existed in heaven and were sent by God to Earth to go through trials in bodies of flesh in order to be perfected like the Father. That is to say, following their time on this planet, worthy Mormons may also become gods and rule over their own worlds where they—just like the God of the Bible—can be served and worshipped throughout eternity by lesser humans (you and me) who fail to attain such divinity. What I had not realized, however, was the extent to which some Mormons—including those devoted to Mitt Romney—saw their place in the deity-building scheme unfolding within American politics. Early in his work, Moody reflects this creed when republishing personal correspondence between himself and the 2016 presidential hopeful. In his open letter to Romney, the former Mormon says:

At eighteen, my Patriarchal Blessing rattled through my brain like a coronation and a call to arms. Patriarch J. Harold Brinley laid his hands on my head in 1963 and told me I was a valiant, true son in the preexistence with important earthly responsibilities. He said when I raised my voice in defense of the truth [Mormonism] the Lord would magnify and enhance me in the eyes of my fellow men. The instructions in my blessing, which I believed came directly from Jesus, motivated me to seek a career in government and politics… My foreordained destiny had called me, and the words of my blessing swelled in my chest. I did my duty to the Mormon Gods and ran for Governor to expand our kingdom and help you [Romney] lead the world into the Millennium.[348]

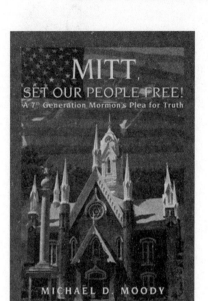

Front Cover of Michael Moody's Book

Whether it be Mitt Romney or another LDS member, the chances of a Mormon American president in 2016 is stronger than many think, as this religion—once widely held as a cult—is among the fastest growing in the world. What makes this prophetically interesting in light of the larger scope of this book and the occultist dream of a deified man in the role of a national leader (the second coming of Apollo), is how perfectly fitting Mormon theology balances with scriptural revelations concerning the arrival of the Antichrist. As with Joseph Smith's prophecy, the Man of Sin will ride in on a white horse (Revelation 6:2), having preexisted before coming (again) in a body of flesh (Revelation 17:8). He will be a god-man, as Mormonism aspires to, and the embodiment of Jesus' bad-boy "brother," the Devil. Yes—despite the flack presidential candidate Mike Huckabee took in 2007[349] for asking the question—members of the LDS do

believe Jesus and Satan are brothers and you can read this for yourself
on the LDS website in chapter three of their "Gospel Principles."[350]
Mike Moody adds, "Mormons were taught as children that Lucifer is our big brother—the second born after Jesus—who presented
God the Father with an earthly plan to force humanity into righ-
teousness and mandatory salvation.[351] In response, Jesus countered
with his plan of 'free agency,' which our Heavenly Father accepted for
his spirit children over [the other son] Lucifer's plan."[352] Mormonism
even provides for the posthuman technology known as "transhumanism" that some believe is necessary to incarnate the Lord's "brother"
as the end-times Man of Sin, and a Mormon Transhumanist Association[353] exists to syncretize LDS religion with these goals.

End-Times Cult or Just Another Christian Denomination?

This is where I may lose some readers, but I must be straight forward
on this issue. Mormonism is not just another Christian denomination. It is a cult and one of the earliest American forms of transhumanism. This is readily demonstrated in their doctrines concerning
Jesus where His deity is minimized as not so unlike other glorified
men. He is eternal, but the spirits of all men are eternal in the same
way. Mormon theology teaches that the gods produced spirit children from eternity, but that they had to wait for men on Earth to
provide bodies for their incarnation via human procreation. Jesus
Christ was merely one of these spirit children along with His brother,
Lucifer, who received a body and became a god. The only difference
between Christ and other men is one of progression over time rather
than ontology. A partial transcript from a documentary by Jeremiah
Films on the Belief of Mormonism explains:

Mormons believe that Elohim is their heavenly father and that he lives with his many goddess wives on a planet near a mysterious star called Kolob.

Here, the god of Mormonism and his wives, through endless celestial sex, produced billions of spirit children. To decide their destiny, the head of the Mormon gods called a great heavenly council meeting. Both of Elohim's eldest sons were there, Lucifer, and his brother, Jesus.

A plan was presented to build planet earth, where the spirit children would be sent to take on mortal bodies and learn good from evil.

Lucifer stood and made his bid for becoming savior of this new world. Wanting the glory for himself, he planned to force everyone to become gods. Opposing the idea, the Mormon Jesus suggested giving man his freedom of choice as on other planets. The vote that followed approved the proposal of the Mormon Jesus, who would become savior of the planet earth.

Enraged, Lucifer cunningly convinced one third of the spirits destined for earth to fight with him in revolt.

Thus Lucifer became the Devil and his followers the Demons. Sent to this world, they would forever be denied bodies of flesh and bone.

Those who remained neutral in the battle were cursed to be born with black skin. This is the Mormon explanation for [persons of black ancestry or appearance].

The spirits that fought most valiantly against Lucifer would be born into Mormon families on planet earth. These would be the lighter skinned people, or white and delightsome, as the Book of Mormon describes them.

Early Mormon prophets taught that Elohim and one of his goddess wives came to earth as Adam and Eve to start the human race. Thousands of years later, Elohim, in human form once again, journeyed to earth from the star base Kolob, this time to have sex with the Virgin Mary in order to provide Jesus with a physical body.[354]

Facsimile No. 2 from the Book of Abraham, which
Joseph Smith Said Discusses the Planet Kolob

Building on the necessity of divinity via endless sex and conception, Mormon doctrine teaches that "Jesus" was also a polygamist and married the two Marys and Martha of the New Testament, producing children with them. This was necessary for him to do, they say, in order to become a divine being because the LDS doctrine of exaltation requires procreation in order to attain godhood. This is readily seen in the writing of Mormon apostle, Bruce R. McConkie, where he says:

Of those who enter the Lord's order of matrimony and who keep their covenants…the Lord says: "They shall pass by the angels, and the gods…to their exaltation and glory in all things…which glory shall be a fulness and a continuation of the seeds forever and ever." That is to say, eternal life consists of two things: (1) the continuation of the family unit in eternity, which means a continuation of the seeds or the everlasting begetting of children; and (2) the receipt of the fulness of the glory of the Father, which is all power in heaven and on earth.[355]

In his journal, dated July 22, 1883, LDS apostle, Wilford Woodruff, reaffirmed this commonly held belief by LDS leaders that Jesus was married[356] and Mormon Apostle Orson Hyde went even further, actually quoting the famous Bible story of the marriage at Cana in Galilee (John 2:1–11) to suggest that it was Jesus who was joined in matrimony that day. Hyde writes:

Now there was actually a marriage; and if Jesus was not the bridegroom on that occasion, please tell who was. If any man can show this, and prove that it was not the Savior of the world, then I will acknowledge I am in error. We say it was Jesus Christ who was married, to be brought into the relation whereby he could see his seed, before he was crucified.[357]

Mormon Apostle Orson Pratt continues this profane belief, writing:

One thing is certain, that there were several holy women that greatly loved Jesus—such as Mary, and Martha her sister, and Mary Magdalene; and Jesus greatly loved them, and associated with them much; and when He arose from the dead, instead of showing Himself to His chosen witnesses, the Apostles, He appeared first to these women, or at least to one of them—namely, Mary Magdalene. Now it would be natural for a husband in the resurrection to appear first to his own dear wives, and afterwards show himself to his other friends. If all the acts of Jesus were written, we no doubt should learn that these beloved women were His wives.[358]

These Da Vinci Code-like doctrines are just the tip of the sacrilegious iceberg and even include the story of Italian fascist dictator Benito Mussolini, a genocidal confederate of Hitler, who was given the Mormon "baptism for the dead" and made a Saint in the LDS Church. Why? Because he shared the Mormon belief that Jesus Christ was married and procreated a line of descendants inclusive of himself and, of course, according to LDS sources, Joseph Smith.

Mormonism, Freemasonry, and Transhumanism

Joseph Smith, the founder of LDS, was a known occult practitioner in his home town, and his involvement in Freemasonry (as discussed earlier in connection with the spirit of occultism) has been thoroughly documented. When former Wheaton College president, Dr. Jonathan Blanchard, wrote his treatise exposing Scottish Rite Masonry concerning the thirteenth degree, he included:

The power of this degree, long as it has befooled its thousands, is the power of Mormonism, of Alchemy, of Astrology, of Spiritism, Mesmerism and whatever holds the mind steady for Satan to demoralize it. It is the power of that spirit whose coming is with lying wonders. The wonders may be real, but they land men in the lie, that they may be saved without Christ.[359]

References to Mormonism are ubiquitous throughout this scholarly work regarding the degrees of Scottish Rite. In the second volume, Blanchard concludes, "The two institutions are morally and legally the same."[360] While this may be news to some, it shouldn't be too surprising. It is a matter of record that Smith became a Mason in 1842 along with at least twelve hundred other Mormons.[361] They appropriated the Masonic rituals and rebranded them as Mormon temple rites. Indeed, there is ample scholarly consensus that the Mormon temple formalities were plagiarized directly from Freemasonry, including the LDS endowment ceremonies.

For example, consider the Masonic "five points of fellowship" which is virtually identical in Mormonism:

FOR MASONS: He (the candidate) is raised on what is called the five points of fellowship.... This is done by putting the inside of your right foot to the inside of the right foot of the person to whom you are going to give the word, the inside of your knee to his, laying your right breast against his, your left hands on the back of each other, and your mouths to each other's right ear (in which position alone you are permitted to give the word), and whisper the word Mahhah-bone.... He is also told that Mahhah-bone signifies marrow in the bone.

FOR MORMONS: The five points of fellowship are given by putting the inside of the right foot to the inside of the Lord's, the inside of your knee to his, laying your breast close to his, your left hands on each other's backs, and each

one putting his mouth to the other's ear, in which position
the Lord whispers: "Lord—'This is the sign of the token:
Health to the navel, marrow in the bones.'"[362]

While the "borrowing" example listed above is self-evident, it is
important to note that in the Mormon version of the secret ritual,
the LDS member plays the role of God. What mysteries might these
deified plagiaristic cult members whisper in each other's ears? Mormon founder Joseph Smith said, "God Himself was once as we are
now, and is an exalted man, and sits enthroned in yonder heavens!
That is the great secret. If the veil were rent today, and the great God
who holds this world in its orbit, and who upholds all worlds and all
things by His power, was to make Himself visible,—I say, if you were
to see Him today, you would see Him like a man in form—like your-
selves in all the person, image, and very form as a man."[363] In other
words, God was not always God, but developed into an exalted state.
Accordingly, God began with and still has a human body of flesh
and blood just like everyone else. This, too, is a system of belief taken
directly from Freemasonic occultism. As one of the order's most celebrated mystics, 33rd degree Mason, Manly P. Hall, wrote: "Man is a
god in the making, and as in the mystic myths of Egypt, on the pot-
ter's wheel he is being molded. When his light shines out to lift and
preserve all things, he receives the triple crown of godhood, and joins
that throng of Master Masons…"[364] Even more descriptive, English
author and Freemason Walter Leslie Wilmshurst described this process in his 1922 book, *The Meaning of Masonry*:

From grade to grade the candidate is being led from an old
to an entirely new quality of life. He begins his Masonic
career as the natural man; he ends it by becoming through

its discipline, a regenerated perfected man. To attain this transmutation, this metamorphosis of himself, he is taught first to purify and subdue his sensual nature; then to purify and develop his mental nature; and finally, by utter surrender of his old life and losing his soul to save it, he rises from the dead a Master, a just man made perfect...

This—the evolution of man into superman—was always the purpose of the ancient Mysteries, and the real purpose of modern Masonry is, not the social and charitable purpose to which so much attention is paid, but the expediting of the spiritual evolution of those who aspire to perfect their own nature and transform it into a more god-like quality. And this is a definite science, a royal art...[365]

Mormonism—thus an alternative form of Masonic occultism and transhumanism—teaches that men can evolve into gods through self-determination and personal will. "Therefore," writes Carl Teichrib, editor and CEO of the highly recommended *Forcing Change Magazine*, "becoming a God is not only possible, but the implied goal of the LDS believer."[366] Furthermore, if faithful churchmen work hard to become such co-creators with the Father, they are promised the opportunity of reigning over alien worlds. In his *Doctrines of Salvation*, Joseph Smith adds:

The Father has promised us that through our faithfulness we shall be blessed with the fulness of his kingdom. In other words we will have the privilege of becoming like him. To become like him we must have all the powers of godhood; thus a man and his wife when glorified will have spirit children who eventually will go on an earth like this one we are on and pass through the same kind of experiences, being subject to mortal conditions, and if faithful, then they also will receive the fulness of exaltation and partake of the same blessings. There is no end to this development; it will go on forever. *We will become gods and have jurisdiction over worlds, and these worlds will be peopled by our own offspring. We will have an endless eternity for this.* (emphasis added)[367]

Mormon theologians, thinking like philosophical materialists, thereby distort biblical passages to support an apostate view of countless alien worlds ruled by extraterrestrial gods (for more on this particular point, read the best-selling book *Exo-Vaticana* from Defender Publishing, 2013). Of course, Mormons run into difficulty with passages like, "God is not a man, that he should lie; neither the son of man, that he should repent" (Numbers 23:19a), and similar passages including 1 Samuel 15:29 and Hosea 11:9. Mormons typically respond that the passage in Numbers is simply contrasting the exalted posthuman state against the less evolved human condition. But Jesus taught that God is Spirit (John 4:24), and that Spirit is not made of flesh and bone (Luke 24:39). Modern LDS members have no coherent answers for these clear contradictions with the Bible but are quietly laying the philosophical groundwork to merge the two systems—theological and biotechnological (and astrobiological)—with modern fatalistic arguments in favor of employing emerging fields of technology (including genetics) to fashion a new form of man—a transhuman deity and ultimately a posthuman god. As the president of the Mormon Transhumanist Association has written:

Most Mormon Transhumanists consider our religion to be remarkably compatible with transhumanism. We consider

Mormonism to be a religious transhumanism. Eternal progression is a central doctrine of Mormonism. Basically, the idea is that we have all existed in some form or another into the indefinite past; that we have been and are progressing toward becoming like God in a creative and benevolent capacity, and that we should each help others do the same into the indefinite future. Mormon scripture asserts the work of God to be that of bringing about immortality and eternal life, and invites us all to participate in that work.[368]

Given Mormonism's embrace of the biotechnological posthuman paradigm as the most powerful modem of radically producing supermen, could a man like Romney, with the necessary hubris and financial resources, be uniquely qualified to realize the outrageous goal of incarnation into flesh of that diabolical "brother of Jesus" and end-times leader of the New World Order, the Devil? Time will tell, and whether a Mormon will ride in on his white horse in 2016 to save the US Constitution will also soon be known. Likewise, it won't be long before we see whether turn-of-the-century protestant reformers like the great Jonathan Edwards, medieval Catholic mystics including Saint Malachy, and Jewish sages who wrote the Zohar seven-hundred years ago saw correctly in their visions of the arrival of the False Prophet and Antichrist in the years 2012–2016.

Whatever happens, this writer firmly believes events unfolding around the globe do indeed suggest a near future in which a man of superior intelligence, wit, charm, and diplomacy could emerge on the world scene as a savior. He will seemingly possess transcendent wisdom that enables him to solve problems and offer solutions for many of today's most perplexing issues. His popularity will be widespread and his fans will include young and old, religious and non-religious, male and female. Talk show hosts will interview his colleagues, news anchors will cover his movements, scholars will applaud his uncanny ability at resolving what has escaped the rest of us, and the poor will bow down at his table. He will, in all human respects, appeal to the best idea of society. But his profound comprehension and irresistible presence will be the result of an invisible network of thousands of years of collective knowledge. He will, quite literally, represent the embodiment of a very old, super-intelligent spirit. As Jesus Christ was the "seed of the woman" (Genesis 3:15), he will be the "seed of the serpent." Moreover, though his arrival in the form of a man was foretold by numerous Scriptures, the broad masses will not immediately recognize him for what he actually is—paganism's ultimate incarnation; the "beast" of Revelation 13:1.

I must ask, therefore: Are you prepared spiritually, mentally, and physically for what may be just ahead? Ancient and modern occultists obviously have plans for the near future, including strategies to install the dreaded Man of Sin who will, for a short period of time, conquer and then betray the human race. Thankfully it is the Father of heaven and His Son, Jesus Christ, which will have the final word and ultimately determine the fate of mankind. Therefore, knowing Jesus as Savior is the first and most important "emergency planning step" you can take for your future security and survival. With Christ as your Lord, you will be able to "enter thou into thy chambers, and shut thy doors about thee: hide thyself as it were for a little moment, until the indignation be overpast" (Isaiah 26:20).

To learn more, please visit:

www.RaidersNewsUpdate.com
www.Zenith2016.com

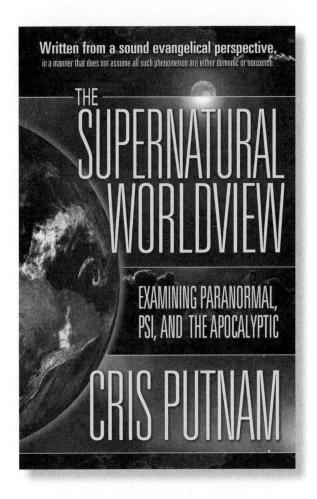

COMING IN 2013
THE SUPERNATURAL WORLDVIEW

Far from the reach of conventional science, when mind overtakes matter and the paranormal becomes normal, then the numinous will manifest. From the internationally renowned author of *Petrus Romanus* and *Exo-Vaticana* comes *The Supernatural Worldview*, apocalyptic apologetics for the impending paradigm shift.

Also NEW From Tom Horn!

Following the release of their 2012 best-seller *Petrus Romanus: The Final Pope Is Here*, Tom Horn and Cris Putnam were inundated with invitations from around the world to be interviewed on radio, television, and in print media. These included segments in The History Channel's "Countdown to Apocalypse," a special feature on Canada's largest Christian channel VisionTV titled "I Prophesy: The Apocalypse Series," invitations to Rome to discuss with Italian media their findings on René Thibaut (a Belgian Jesuit whose meticulous analysis of the Prophecy of the Popes predicted the arrival of Petrus Romanus in this era), and dozens more. But that was just the first part of the story. In *Exo-Vaticana*, the investigation goes into high gear with findings far more disturbing than the authors expected to discover.

Available at www.SurvivorMall.com

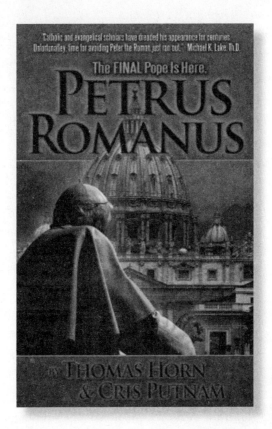

In *Petrus Romanus: The Final Pope Is Here*, internationally acclaimed author Thomas Horn and respected theologian and apologist Cris Putnam predicted the resignation of Pope Benedict XVI and tell readers what to expect to unfold in the coming days, and, more importantly, what they can do to be prepared for the arrival of Petrus Romanus and the kingdom of Antichrist.

Available at www.SurvivorMall.com

Pandemonium's Engine is the vehicle through which Tom Horn, Cris Putnam, and an elite team of commentators inform a still-sleeping public about radical changes coming to our culture… very soon. In particular, the technological advances in genetics, robotics, artificial intelligence, nanotechnology, and synthetics biology (G.R.I.N.S.) that will bring us all to the doorstep of life-altering realities almost too incredible to believe.

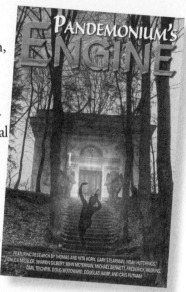

One myth from the history of every great civilization spoke of beings descending from heaven and using human and animal DNA to create giant offspring. Rabbinical authorities, Septuagint translators, and early church fathers understood this as a factual record of history. The phenomenon began with the "Watchers" who spawned "Nephilim" resulting in judgment from God. *Nephilim Stargates and the Return of the Watchers* is a glimpse into this past, present, and future phenomena, with an eye on what sages and scientists believe and what futurists and prophets may fear.

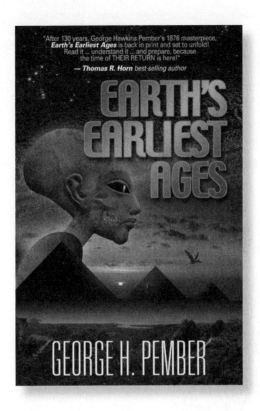

When English theologian George Hawkins Pember, in his 1876 masterpiece, *Earth's Earliest Ages*, analyzed the prophecy of Jesus Christ in Matthew 24 that says the end times would be a repeat of "the days of Noah," he concluded the final and most fearful sign heralding the Lord's Second Coming would be the return of the "Nephilim, the appearance upon earth of beings from the Principality of the Air, and their unlawful intercourse with the human race." It is time for a new generation to discover his warning, as it now appears set to unfold.

Available at www.SurvivorMall.com

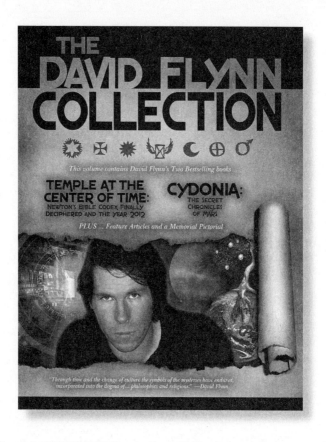

This book is HUGE! With a 8.5" x 11" binding, it's as big as a phone book, containing two complete books, major articles, and a memorial pictorial of the man who, for nearly two decades, was the author of *Temple at the Center of Time, Cydonia: The Secret Chronicles of Mars*, and numerous other works, publishing original and groundbreaking research on his renowned Watchers Website. Best-selling authors and syndicated media often cited his findings.

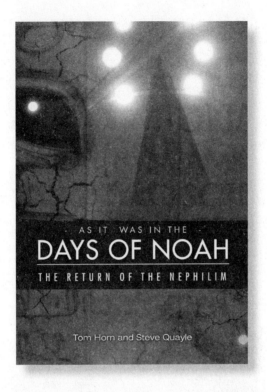

As it Was in the Days of Noah: The Return of the Nephilim has been called "the best ever series" by popular radio personalities Tom Horn and Steve Quayle. This is a fascinating and sometimes frightening exposé on little-known passages from the Bible and apocryphal texts, which speak of an alien agenda, great deception giving rise to the Antichrist, and in the last two parts of this series, the most incredible information ever revealed over the airwaves about the return of the giants in the last days. Tom's newest revelation from the Book of Enoch left Steve Quayle speechless for several seconds and led to newshounds seeking additional information and a feature editorial at WorldNetDaily, the world's #1 online news site.

Available at www.SurvivorMall.com

Mega stores like Barnes & Noble now prominently feature books by prophecy writer Tom Horn.

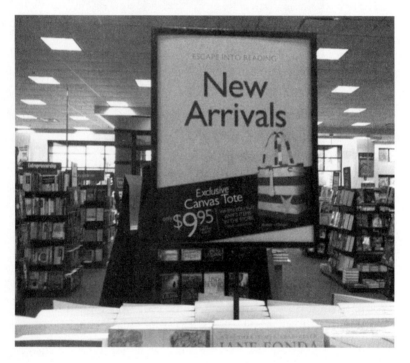

Image of the bookstore's big enriched test ad bet with Tom

NOTES

Preface

1. Elbert Hubbard, "A Little Journey to the Home of Thomas Paine," *Life and Writings of Thomas Paine*, Daniel Edwin Wheeler (Vincent Parke, 1908), 332–333.
2. From the Bauman Rare Books website (http://www.baumanrarebooks.com), on which a copy of Paine's *Common Sense* is offered for $52,000.
3. Thomas Paine, *The Age of Reason*, Part 1, Section 5 (http://www.ushistory.org).
4. Ibid., Part 2, Section 20.
5. Ibid.
6. Andrew A. Lipscomb and Albert Ellery Bergh, eds., *The Writings of Thomas Jefferson*, Vol. XVI (Washington, DC: Thomas Jefferson Memorial Association, 1903), 100-101.
7. Gerard W. Gawalt, ed., *Thomas Jefferson and William Short Correspondence* (Library of Congress Manuscript Division).
8. Lipscomb and Bergh, Vol. XIV, 71–72.
9. Ibid.
10. Samuel E. Forman, *The Life and Writings of Thomas Jefferson* (Bowen-Merrill, 1900), 365.
11. Walter Isaacson, ed., *Benjamin Franklin Reader* (New York: Simon and Schuster, 2003), 492.
12. "Ben Franklin and His Membership in the Hellfire Club: Founding Father or Satanic Killer?" Associated Content News, June 27, 2007 (http://www.associatedcontent.com).
13. "Benjamin Franklin, the Occult, and the Elite," *The Sunday Times*, February 11, 1998 (http://www.infowars.com, January 11, 2005).
14. "Benjamin Franklin," *The Encyclopedia Americana*, Vol. XII (Encyclopedia Americana, 1919), 11.
15. Richard Dawkins, *The God Delusion* (New York: Houghton Mifflin Harcourt, 2006), 43.
16. John E. Remsburg, *Six Historic Americans* (New York: Truth Seeker, 1906), 193 (http://www.infidels.org).
17. Ibid.

18. "A Sly Old Fox: George Washington and Religion," from A Talk for Teachers' Institute at Mt. Vernon (July 21, 1999), citing *The Writings of Thomas Jefferson*, Vol. 1, p. 284.
19. Remsburg.
20. Ibid.
21. Ibid.
22. Peter A. Lillback with Jerry Newcombe, *George Washington's Sacred Fire* (Providence Forum, 2006), 453.
23. David Barton, *The Question of Freemasonry and the Founding Fathers*, 1st ed. (Wallbuilders, 2005), 21.
24. House Resolution 33, as submitted by Congressman and 33rd-Degree Mason Paul Gillmor.
25. *The Secret Mysteries of America's Beginnings* series is available at the Adullam Films website (http://www.adullamfilms.org), or by calling 888-780-5049.
26. W. E. Vine, *Vine's Expository Dictionary of Old and New Testament Words* (1997), 283.
27. Manly P. Hall's obituary, *Scottish Rite Journal* (November 1990), 22, as cited by *Academic Dictionaries and Encyclopedias* (http://www.dic.academic.ru).
28. Manly P. Hall, *The Secret Destiny of America* (Los Angeles: Philosophical Research Society, 1944, 1972), 77.
29. Barton, 82.
30. Johan Huizinga, *Erasmus and the Age of Reformation* (New York: Harper Torchbooks/The Cloister Library, 1957), 171.
31. Barton, 20. Emphasis in original.
32. Jared Sparks, *The Writings of George Washington*, Vol. XII (American Stationers Co., John B. Russell, 1837), 201.
33. James H. Billington, *Fire in the Minds of Men: Origins of the Revolutionary Faith* (Transaction, 1999), 99.
34. Ibid., 100.
35. Ibid.
36. *Riddles in Stone: The Secret Architecture of Washington, D.C.* is the second part of the *Secret Mysteries* series, and is available at http://www.adullamfilms.org.
37. Manly P. Hall, *The Secret Teachings of All Ages*, Diamond Jubilee Edition (Los Angeles: Philosophical Research Society, 2000), CIV.
38. Johanne Wolfgang von Goethe, *Faust*, translated by George Madison Priest, *The Alchemy Website* (http://www.levity.com).
39. *Freemasonry Today*, Issue 16 (Spring 2001), Grand Lodge Publications (http://www.freemasonrytoday.com).

Chapter 1

40. Congressman Major R. Owens (http://www.house.gov/owens/rap010228. htm).

41. *The Possessed* (http://etext.library.adelaide.edu.au/d/Dostoyevsky/d72p/).

42. Bruce Lincoln, *Holy Terrors* (Chicago: University of Chicago Press, 2003), 30-32.

43. Bruce Lincoln, "The Rhetoric of Bush and Bin Laden," excerpt from *Holy Terrors,* posted online at University of Chicago Library Digital Collections (http://fathom.lib.uchicago.edu/1/7777777190152/).

44. Kevin Phillips, *American Dynasty: Aristocracy, Fortune, and the Politics of Deceit in the House of Bush* (New York: Penguin, 2004), 225.

45. Lincoln, "The Rhetoric of Bush and Bin Laden."

46. Christopher Findlay, "Millenarianism in U.S. Domestic Politics," *ISN Security Watch* (April 22, 2005).

47. "Bush: 'God Told Me to Invade Iraq'," *The Independent* (October 7, 2005).

48. Clive Hamilton, "Bush's Shocking Biblical Prophecy Emerges: God Wants to 'Erase' Mid-East Enemies 'Before a New Age Begins'," *CounterPunch* (May 25, 2009).

49. Ezekiel 32:27, The Message.

50. Office of the Press Secretary, *President's Remarks at National Day of Prayer and Remembrance* (September 14, 2001) (http://www.whitehouse.gov/news/releases/2001/09/20010914-2.html).

51. Bob Woodward, *Bush at War* (New York: Simon and Schuster, 2002), 67.

52. Phillips, 239.

53. Ibid.

54. Debora Caldwell, "George W. Bush, Presidential Preacher," *Beliefnet* (February 17, 2003), 1.

Chapter 2

55. John Coleman, *Committee of 300* (America West Publishers, 1993), 159–160.

56. Gershom G. Scholem, *Major Trends in Jewish Mysticism* (1941/1961), 67.

57. "Metatron," *Encyclopedia Mythica* (created December 29, 1999, last modified November 27, 2003, Revision 2) (http://www.pantheon.org/articles/m/Metatron.html).

58. Mark Stavish, *Freemasonry: Rituals, Symbols and History of the Secret Society,* illus. ed., Lon Milo DuQuette, contributor (Llewellyn Worldwide, 2007), 177.

59. *Spiritual Warfare: The Invisible Invasion,* 103.

60. Christopher Knight and Robert Lomas, *The Second Messiah: Templars,*

The Turin Shroud, and the Great Secret of Freemasonry (Fair Winds, 2001), 204–205.

61. Albert G. Mackey and William R. Singleton, *History of Freemasonry Part 1:V* (Kessinger, 2003), 49.

62. Albert Pike, *Morals and Dogma* (Charleston: Supreme Council of the 33rd Degree for the Southern Jurisdiction of the United States, 1871), 210.

63. Jason Keyser, "Jerusalem's Old City at Risk in Earthquake," Associated Press (January 19, 2004) (http://www.msnbc.msn.com/id/3980139/).

64. Ohr Margalit, "A New Vision for God's Holy Mountain" (http://newsweek. washingtonpost.com/onfaith/guestvoices/2009/06/a_new_vision_for_gods_ holy_mountain.html).

Chapter 3

65. H. Freedman and Maurice Simon, trans., *Midrash Rabbah: Genesis*, Vols. 1–2 (London: Soncino Press, 1939).

66. David Bay, "Masonic Symbols of Power in their Seat of Power—Washington, D.C.," (http://www.cuttingedge.org/news/n1040.html).

67. David Stevenson, *The Origins of Freemasonry: Scotland's Century, 1590–1710,* illust. ed.,(London: Cambridge University, 1990), 148.

68. Adel Awadalla, *The Prophecy and the Warnings Shine through the Mystifying Codes of the Holy Quran: The Prophecy of World War III* (Bloomington, IN: Trafford Publishing, 2004), 90).

69. Apollodorus, *The Twelve Labors of Hercules, Labor 11—Apples of Hesperides*, trans. Sir James G. Frazer (1921).

70. Pike, 592.

71. Manly P. Hall, *The Lost Keys of Freemasonry* (Richmond, VA: Macoy and Masonic Supply), 48.

72. J. C. Cirlot, *Dictionary of Symbols* (New York: Routledge, 1990), 362.

Chapter 4

73. President George H. W. Bush, Address before Joint Session of Congress on the State of the Union (January 29, 1991).

74. (http://www.realclearpolitics.com/articles/2009/01/the_chance_for_a_new_ world_ord.html).

75. Transcribed from a tape recording made by one of the Swiss delegates.

76. President George W. Bush, Second Inaugural Address (January 20, 2005).

77. Pat Robertson, *The New World Order* (Dallas: Word, 1991), 5.

78. Barry M. Goldwater, *With No Apologies: The Personal and Political Memoirs of United States Senator Barry M. Goldwater*, 1st ed. (New York: Morrow, 1979), 284.

79. "The Global Ruling Class," *The Economist* (April 24, 2008) (http://www.economist.com/books/displaystory.cfm?story_id=11081878).

80. Stanley Monteith, "The Occult Hierarchy: Part 1" *Radio Liberty* (May 2005) (http://www.radioliberty.com/nlmay05.html).

81. Samuel P. Huntington, *Who Are We? The Challenges to America's National Identity*, illus. ed. (New York: Simon and Schuster, 2004), 268.

82. "Famous exorcist: 'The devil loves to take over those who hold political office' *Catholic News Agency* (June 6, 2008) (http://www.catholicnewsagency.com/new.php?n=12861).

83. Mark Morford, "Is Obama an Enlightened Being?" *San Francisco Gate* (June 6, 2008) (http://www.sfgate.com/cgi-bin/article.cgi?f=/g/a/2008/06/06/notes060608.DTL).

84. Dahleen Glanton, "Some See God's Will in Obama Win," *Chicago Tribune* (November 29, 2008) (http://www.chicagotribune.com/news/nationworld/chi-obama-godsend_glantonnov29,0,7660180.story).

85. Dinesh Sharma, "Obama's Satyagraha: Or, Did Obama Swallow the Mahatma?" *OpEdNews* (June 27, 2008) (http://www.opednews.com/articles/Obama-s-Satyagraha—Or—Di-by-Dinesh-Sharma-080626-187.html).

86. Steve Davis, "Barack's Appeal Is Actually Messianic," *Journal Gazette* (March 31, 2008) (http://www.jg-tc.com/articles/2008/03/31/opinion/letters/doc47f0586a2fflb441328510.txt).

87. Chris Matthews, *MSNBC* (February 12, 2008) (http://newsbusters.org/stories/Matthews-obama-speech-caused-thrill-going-my-leg.html?q=blogs/brad-wilmouth/2008/02/13/Matthews-obama-speech-caused-thrill-going-my-leg).

88. *Daily Kos* (April 26, 2008) (http://www.dailykos.com/storyonly/2008/4/26/83118/7371/654/503796).

89. Lynn Sweet, *Chicago Sun Times* (March 21, 2008) (http://blogs.suntimes.com/sweet/2008/03/sweet_richardson_in_endorsing.html#comments).

90. Gary Hart, *Huffington Post* (February 13, 2008) (http://www.huffingtonpost.com/gary-hart/politics-as-transcendence_b_86490.html).

91. Ezra Klein, "Obama's Gift," (January 3, 2008) (http://www.prospect.org/csnc/blogs/ezraklein_archive?month=01&year=2008&base_name=obamas_gift).

92. Gerald Campbell, "Obama: On Toughness and Success in Politics," *First Things First* (December 22, 2007) (http://geraldcampbell.typepad.com/impact/2007/12/recently-on-npr.html).

93. Janny Scott, "In 2000, a Streetwise Veteran Schooled a Bold Young Obama," *New York Times* (September 9, 2007) (http://www.nytimes.com/2007/09/09/us/politics/09obama.html?pagewanted=print).

94. Micah Tillman, "Plato, Obama, and Peters on the Question of Mighty

Pens," *The Free Liberal* (July 10, 2008) (http://www.freeliberal.com/archives/003418.html).

95. Representative Jesse Jackson, Jr., "On Obama's Winning the Democratic Presidential Nomination," *Politico* (June 5, 2008) (http://dyn.politico.com/printstory.cfm?uuid=55D13D94-3048-5C12-00E851454E822F1E).

96. J. R. Church, *Guardians of the Grail* (Oklahoma City, OK: Prophecy Publications, 1989), 307.

97. Michelle Boorstein and Jacqueline Salmon, "A Rush of Spiritual Outreach, Spirited Partying," *Washington Post* (January 11, 2009), C04.

98. Bob Unruh, "CNN Likens Inauguration to 'Hajj,'" *WorldNetDaily* (January 24, 2009).

99. Drew Zahn, "Obama Triumphal Entry: Gentle, Riding on a Donkey," *WorldNetDaily* (January 24, 2009).

100. "Doorway Anointed with Oil for Obama," *EURweb* (January 12, 2009) (http://www.eurweb.com/story/eur50011.cfm).

101. Jim L. Cunningham, "Ceremony Purges White House of Evil Spirits," *DC Progressive Examiner* (January 21, 2009).

102. See (http://uk.youtube.com/watch?v=LXcvbnzNIjg&feature=related).

103. Terry Neal, "A New Faith Needed to Unify Humankind as We March Into Future" *Hamilton Spectator* (February 14, 2009) (http://www.thespec.com/Opinions/article/513536).

104. http://www.amazon.com/The-Gospel-According-Apostle-Barack/dp/1468587021

105. We might even have one of our most noteworthy leaders be asked to give the prayer at a Presidential Inauguration.

106. Hitler spoke of bringing about the New Order as did Franklin D. Roosevelt.

107. Item #24 of the German Worker's Party "Program" circa 1920s.

108. Adolf Hitler, in his speech to the Reichstag on 23 March 1933.

109. http://www.christianpost.com/news/john-brennan-chooses-not-to-use-bible-for-swearing-in-as-cia-director-91633/

110. "Many Have Asked: Is Obama the Anti-Christ? Famed Novelist Michael O'Brien Answers," *LifeSiteNews.com* (November 3, 2008) (http://www.lifesitenews.com/ldn/2008/nov/08110307.html).

111. Michael D. O'Brien, "Globalization and the New World Order," *Mother of All Peoples* (March 21, 2009) (http://www.motherofallpeoples.com/articles/our-lady-and-christian-culture/globalization-and-the-new-world-order.html).

112. "Is Obama Speech Site Contaminated by Nazi Past?" *Spiegel Online* (July 20, 2008) (http://www.spiegel.de/international/germany/0,1518,566920,00.html).

113. Ibid.
114. As quoted by J. R. Church, *Prophecy in the News* (December 2008), 36.
115. Ibid.
116. Ibid.
117. See (http://www.youtube.com/watch?v=Zr4VZ8xCzOg&eurl=http%
3A%2F%2Fwww%2Eraidersnewsupdate%2Ecom%2F&feature=pla
yer_embedded).

Chapter 5
118. Gary Lachman, *Politics and the Occult: The Left, the Right, and the Radically Unseen* (Wheaton, IL: Theosophical Publishing House, 2008), 39.
119. Manly P. Hall, *Secret Teachings of All Ages: An Encyclopedic Outline of Masonic, Hermetic, Qabbalistic and Rosicrucian Symbolical Philosophy* (Lulu. com, 2005), 589.
120. "The Most Approved Plan: The Competition for the Capitol's Design" (http://www.loc.gov/exhibits/us.capitol/s2.html).
121. Lachman, 97–98.
122. David Ovason, *The Secret Architecture of Our Nation's Capital: The Masons and the Building of Washington, D.C.* (New York: HarperCollins, 2000), 71.
123. Ibid., 361.
124. Ibid., 373.
125. Julie Duin, "Ergo, We're Virgo" (October 16, 2000) (http://findarticles. com/p/articles/mi_m1571/is_38_16/ai_66241134).
126. Ovason, 71.
127. Foster Bailey, *The Spirit of Freemasonry* (New York: Lucis Press, 1957).
128. Pike, 89–90.

Chapter 6
129. Hall, *Secret Destiny*, chapter 18.
130. Ibid.
131. Mitch Horowitz, *Occult America* (New York, NY: Bantam Books, 2010), 172.
132. John C. Culver and John Hyde, *American Dreamer: The Life and Times of Henry A. Wallace* (W. W. Norton & Company, 2001), 135.
133. Helena Petrovna Blavatsky, *The Secret Doctrine: The Synthesis of Science, Religion, and Philosophy, Volume 1* (New York: NY, Newman, Cowell & Gripper, Ltd., 1893), 332.
134. John C. Culver and John Hyde, American Dreamer, 136.
135. "How the Great Seal Got on the One Dollar Bill," *GreatSeal.com*, last accessed January 23, 2012, http://www.greatseal.com/dollar/hawfdr.html.
136. Mitch Horowitz, *Occult America*, 173.

137. Frederick S. Voss, *The Smithsonian Treasury: Presidents* (Random House Value Publishing, 1991), 72.

138. Henry A. Wallace, *Statesmanship and Religion* (New York, NY: Round Table, 1934), 78–79.

139. John C. Culver and John Hyde, *American Dreamer*, 134.

140. William Henry, *Cloak of the Illuminati: Secrets, Transformations, Crossing the Stargate* (Kempton, IL: Adventures Unlimited, 2003), 13.

141. John Dryden, trans., as published by Georgetown University Online; also appears in: Thomas Horn, *Apollyon Rising 2012*.

142. Peter Goodgame, *The Giza Discovery, Part Nine: The Mighty One*, last accessed January 23, 2012, http://www.redmoonrising.com/Giza/Asshur9.htm.

143. Thomas and Nita Horn, *Forbidden Gates: How Genetics, Robotics, Artificial Intelligence, Synthetic Biology, Nanotechnology, and Human Enhancement Herald the Dawn of TechoDimensional Spiritual Warfare* (Crane, MO: Defender Publishing, 2011), 55.

144. Benedict XVI, *Light of the World: The Pope, the Church, and the Signs of the Times* (San Francisco: Ignatius Press, 2010), 19.

145. Rachel Donadio and Nicholas Kulish, "A Statement Rocks Rome, Then Sends Shockwaves Around the World," *New York Times*, February 11, 2013, last accessed February 13, 2013, http://www.usatoday.com/story/weather/2013/02/12/lightning-bolt-strikes-vatican-pope-benedict-resignation/1913095/.

146. "Lightning Strikes St. Peters Basilica," YouTube video, 0:10, posted by congaspot, last updated February 12, 2013, last accessed March 25, 2013, http://youtu.be/Q6olT4ozDyk.

147. Nicole Winfield, "Pope's Retirement Plan Revealed," *Reuters*, last accessed March 25, 2013, http://www.3news.co.nz/Popes-retirement-plan-revealed/tabid/417/articleID/286573/Default.aspx.

148. "Holy Smoke! Is This Final Pope before Jesus?" *World Net Daily*, last accessed March 25, 2013, http://www.wnd.com/2013/03/holy-smoke-is-this-final-pope-before-jesus/#oImqawiZUvBPwORI.99.

149. René Thibaut, *La Mystérieuse Prophétie des Papes* (Paris: J. Vrin, 1951), 25.

150. http://www.catholicculture.org/news/headlines/index.cfm?storyid=17490

151. Shlomo Cesana, "Vatican, Israel Reach Historic Deal on Last Supper Site," *Israel Hayom*, January 30, 2013, last accessed March 25, 2013, http://www.israelhayom.com/site/newsletter_article.php?id=7230.

152. Hal Lindsey, "News from Hal Lindsey Ministries," email dated March 22, 2013 to author Cris Putnam.

153. Ethelbert W. Bullinger, *Number in Scripture* (Pleasant Places Press, 2004), 208.

154. Ethelbert W. Bullinger, *Number in Scripture*, 225 (bolding added).

155. This authoritatively explains why all popes are false prophets. See: John MacArthur, "The Pope and the Papacy," http://www.gty.org/resources/sermons/90-291/the-pope-and-the-papacy.

156. "Why the pope chose the name Francis," YouTube video, 3:12, posted by CatholicNewsService, last updated March 16, 2013, last accessed March 26, 2013, https://www.youtube.com/watch?feature=player_embedded&v=t2XiT76tgCo.

157. *Works of the Seraphic Father St. Francis of Assisi* (1182–1226), Washbourne, 1882 AD, 248 (also as quoted on page 389 of this book). Also see http://www.realclearreligion.com/index_files/ac206ecae86856da08a615cb61987e74-643.php.

158. W. C. Brownlee, *Secret Instructions of the Jesuits* (1857) 7. See: http://archive.org/stream/instructiosecret00browrich#page/7/.

159. "Papal Address to Members of Jesuit General Congregation," *Zenit*, March 4, 2008, http://www.zenit.org/en/articles/papal-address-to-members-of-jesuit-general-congregation.

160. W. C. Brownlee, *Secret Instructions of the Jesuits*, 6. See: http://archive.org/stream/instructiosecret00browrich#page/6/.

161. Journals of the 62nd Congress, 3rd Session, of the United States Congressional Record (House Calendar No. 397, Report No. 1523, 15 February, 1913, pp. 3215–3216). Text available here: http://www.redicecreations.com/specialreports/2006/04apr/jesuitbloodoath.html.

162. "Ian Paisley Teaches on the Jesuits," YouTube video, 52:01, posted by tlthe5th, last updated November 28, 2007, last accessed March 25, 2013, http://youtu.be/4wfQbVaRv18 (time of quoted material, 42:50–7).

163. Malachi Martin, *The Jesuits* (New York, NY: Simon & Schuster, 1988), 13.

164. Francis X, Rocca "Cardinal Jorge Bergoglio: A Profile," *Catholic Herald*, March 13, 2013, last accessed March 23, 2013, http://www.catholicherald.co.uk/news/2013/03/13/cardinal-bergoglio-profile/.

165. José Gabriel Funes, "The Extraterrestrial Is My Brother," *L'Osservatore Romano*, May 14, 2008 (English translation of article viewable here: http://padrefunes.blogspot.com/).

166. Patricia Zapor, "Jesuits Surprised that First of Their Brethren Is Elected Pope," *Catholic News Service*, last accessed March 23, 2013, http://www.catholicnews.com/data/stories/cns/1301160.htm.

167. "Pontifical Academy Studies Possibility of Extraterrestrial Life," *Catholic World News*, November 11, 2009, http://www.catholicculture.org/news/headlines/index.cfm?storyid=4568.

Chapter 7

168. Dr. James Kennedy, *The Real Meaning of the Zodiac* (Fort Lauderdale, FL: TCRM, 1993), 6–8.
169. Thomas R. Horn, *Spiritual Warfare: The Invisible Invasion* (Lafayette, LA: Huntington House, 1998), 21–22.
170. Ibid., 23–24.
171. Richard Cavendish, *Man, Myth, & Magic*, s.v. "Apollo."
172. Euripides, *The Bacchantes*, Dramatis Personare (Messenger to Pentheus concerning the Bacchantes), 410 BC.
173. Walter F. Otto, *Dionysus Myth and Cult* (Indianapolis, IN: Indiana University, 1965), 114.
174. Philip J. King, Michael David Coogan, J. Cheryl Exum, Lawrence E. Stager, *Scripture and Other Artifacts: Essays on the Bible and Archaeology in Honor of Philip J. King* (Westminster John Knox, 1994), 121.
175. See (http://www.redmoonrising.com/Giza/DomDec6.htm).

Chapter 8

176. Stephen Quayle, *Genesis 6 Giants*, (End Time Thunder, 2002), 60.
177. Jacques Vallée, *The Invisible College: What a Group of Scientists Has Discovered About UFO Influences on the Human Race* (New York: Dutton, 1975), 233.
178. Ibid., 143–144.
179. Annette Yoshiko Reed, *Fallen Angels and the History of Judaism and Christianity: The Reception of Enochic Literature* (Cambridge, 2005), 214.

Chapter 9

180. Hugo de Garis, *The Artilect War: Cosmists vs. Terrans: A Bitter Controversy Concerning Whether Humanity Should Build Godlike Massively Intelligent Machines* E(Palm Springs, CA: ETC, 2005) 11–12, 15, 84.
181. Theodore Kaczynski, "Industrial Society and Its Future," Wikisource, http://en.wikisource.org/wiki/Industrial_Society_and_Its_Future.
182. Joe Garreau, *Radical Evolution: The Promise and Peril of Enhancing Our Minds, Our Bodies—and What It Means to Be Human* (New York: Broadway, 2005) 71–72)
183. Ray Kurzweil, *The Singularity is Near* (New York: Penguin, 2006) 7–8.
184. Abou Farman, "The Intelligent Universe," *Maison Neuve* (8/2/10) http://maisonneuve.org/pressroom/article/2010/aug/2/intelligent-universe/.
185. Kurzweil, 9.
186. "The Coming Technological Singularity," presented at the VISION-21 Symposium sponsored by NASA Lewis Research Center and the Ohio Aerospace Institute (3/30–31/93).

187. Jerome C. Glenn, "The State of the Future" (7/14/10) www.kurzweilai.net/the-state-of-the-future, emphasis added.

188. Ibid, emphasis added.

189. Case Western Reserve University, "Case Law School Receives $773,000 NIH Grant to Develop Guidelines for Genetic Enhancement Research: Professor Max Mehlman to Lead Team of Law Professors, Physicians, and Bioethicists in Two-Year Project (April 28, 2006).

190. Jane Picken, "Medical Marvels," *The Evening Chronicle* (April 13, 2007).

191. Joseph Infranco, "President Barack Obama Warped and Twisted Science with Embryonic Stem Cell Order," *LifeNews* (4/13/09) http://www.lifenews.com/bio2823.html.

192. Nick Bostrom, "Transhumanist Values," www.nickbostrom.com.

193. "Facing the Challenges of Transhumanism: Religion, Science, Technology," *Arizona State University*, http://transhumanism.asu.edu/.

194. http://lach.web.arizona.edu/Sophia/.

195. Leon R. Kass, *Life, Liberty, and the Defense of Dignity: The Challenge for Bioethics* (New York: Encounter, 10/25/02).

196. Rick Weiss, "Of Mice, Men, and In-Between," *MSNBC* (11/20/04) http://www.msnbc.msn.com/id/6534243/.

197. http://news.yahoo.com/s/cq/20090315/pl_cq_politics/politics3075228.

198. *American Journal of Law and Medicine*, vol. 28, nos. 2 and 3 (2002), 162.

199. As quoted by Margaret McLean, PHD., "Redesigning Humans: The Final Frontier," http://www.elca.org/What-We-Believe/Social-Issues/Journal-of-Lutheran-Ethics/Book-Reviews/Redesigning-Humans-by-Gregory-Stock/Redesigning-Humans-The-Final-Frontier.aspx.

200. "The Coming Technological Singularity," presented at the VISION-21 Symposium sponsored by NASA Lewis Research Center and the Ohio Aerospace Institute (3/30–31/93).

201. Noah Shachtman, "Top Pentagon Scientists Fear Brain-Modified Foes," *Wired* (6/9/08) http://www.wired.com/dangerroom/2008/06/jason-warns-of/.

202. Nigel M. de S. Cameron, *Human Dignity in the Biotech Century* (Downers Grove, IL: InterVarsity, 2004) 75.

203. Ibid., 87, emphasis added.

204. Mihail Roco, *Converging Technologies for Improving Human Performance* (U.S. National Science Foundation and Department of Commerce, 2002) 6.

205. http://www.newamerica.net/events/2010/warring_futures_a_future_tense_event.

206. Chris Floyd, "Monsters, Inc.: The Pentagon Plan to Create Mutant 'Super-Soldiers,'" *CounterPunch* (1/13/03).

207. Garreau, *Radical Evolution:* 269–270.
208. Katie Drummond, "Holy Acronym, Darpa! 'Batman & Robin' to Master Biology, Outdo Evolution," *Wired* (7/6/10) http://www.wired.com/dangerroom/2010/07/holy-acronym-darpa-batman-robin-to-master-biology-outdo-evolution/.
209. Katie Drummond, "Darpa's News Plans: Crowdsource Intel, Edit DNA," *Wired* (2/2/10) http://www.wired.com/dangerroom/2010/02/darpas-new-plans-crowdsource-intel-immunize-nets-edit-dna/.
210. Katie Drummond, "Pentagon Looks to Breed Immortal 'Synthetic Organisms,' Molecular Kill-Switch Included," *Wired* (2/5/10) http://www.wired.com/dangerroom/2010/02/pentagon-looks-to-breed-immortal-synthetic-organisms-molecular-kill-switch-included/.
211. Chuck Missler, "An Alternative View: The Return of Nimrod?" *Koinonia House* (http://www.khouse.org/articles/2002/433/).
212. "Sandpit of Royalty," *Extra Bladet* (Copenhagen, January 31, 1999).
213. Hall, Secret Teachings, 104.
214. Alexander Hislop, *The Two Babylons*, 20.
215. Chuck Missler and Mark Eastman, *Alien Encounters* (Coeur d'Alene, ID: Koinonia House, 1997), 275.
216. Louis Pauwells and Jacques Bergier, *The Dawn of Magic* (first published as "Le Matin des Magiciens") (Paris: Editions Gallmiard, 1960), 68.
217. Augustine, *City of God*, 23:15.
218. Fr. Ludovicus Maria Sinistrari de Ameno, *De Daemonialitate, et Incubis, et Succubi* (1622–1701), English translation of this portion provided by Jacques Vallee in Passport to Magonia (Contemporary Books, 1993), 127–129.

Chapter 10
219. *Institute for Responsible Technology,* http://www.responsibletechnology.org/GMFree/Home/index.cfm.
220. Waclaw Szybalski, *In Vivo and in Vitro Initiation of Transcription*, 405. In A. Kohn and A. Shatkay (eds.), *Control of Gene Expression,* 23–24, and Discussion 404–405 (Szybalski's concept of Synthetic Biology), 411–412, 415–417 (New York: Plenum, 1974).
221. "First Self-Replicating Synthetic Bacterial Cell," *J. Craig Venter Institute,* http://www.jcvi.org/cms/research/projects/first-self-replicating-synthetic-bacterial-cell.
222. Peter E. Nielsen, "Triple Helix: Designing a New Molecule of Life," *Scientific American* (12/08) http://www.scientificamerican.com/article.cfm?id=triple-helix-designing-a-new-molecule&ec=su_triplehelix.

223. Charles W. Colson, *Human Dignity in the Biotech Century* (Downers Grove, IL: InterVarsity, 2004) 8.

224. C. Christopher Hook, *Human Dignity in the Biotech Century* (Downers Grove, IL: InterVarsity, 2004) 80–81.

225. Garreau, Radical Evolution, 116.

226. Francis Fukuyama, *Our Posthuman Future: Consequences of the Biotechnology Revolution* (New York: Picador, 2002) 6.

227. Garreau, 106.

228. Garreau, Radical Evolution, 113–114.

229. "Carried Away with Convergence," New Atlantis (Summer 2003) 102–105, http://www.thenewatlantis.com/publications/carried-away-with-convergence.

230. (Summer 2003 issue of The New Atlantis, http://www.thenewatlantis.com/publications/carried-away-with-convergence)

231. Bill Joy, "Why the Future Doesn't Need Us," Wired (April 2000) http://www.wired.com/wired/archive/8.04/joy.html), emphasis added.

232. Mark Walker, "Ship of Fools: Why Transhumanism is the Best Bet to Prevent the Extinction of Civilization," Metanexus Institute (2/5/09) http://www.metanexus.net/magazine/tabid/68/id/10682/Default.aspx.

233. Tom Mangold and Jeff Goldberg, *Plague Wars: The Terrifying Reality of Biological Warfare*, xi, 225.

234. Jim Wilson, "When UFOs Arrive," *Popular Mechanics* (February 2004).

235. *Millennium*, Episode #203, "Sense and Antisense," Fox Entertainment (October 3, 1997).

Chapter 11:11

236. Hall, *Lost Keys,*19.

237. Pike, 819.

238. Bailey, 20.

239. Manly P. Hall, *Lectures on Ancient Philosophy: An Introduction to Practical Ideals* (Philosophical Research Society, 1984), 433.

240. Hall, *Secret Destiny*, 26.

241. Hall, *Secret Teachings,* 91.

242. Hall, *Secret Destiny*, Chapter 18

243. Ovason, 236.

244. Ibid., 139.

245. Ibid., 49.

246. See (http://en.wikipedia.org/wiki/Statue_of_Liberty).

247. Pike, 335.

248. Ibid., 16.

249. Ibid., 472.

250. Ovason, 237.

251. Ibid.

252. Hall, *Lost Keys*, Prologue.

253. See (http://www.redmoonrising.com/Giza/DomDec6.htm).

254. http://en.wikipedia.org/wiki/Nimrod.

255. Daniel Beresniak, *Symbols of Freemasonry* (New York: Assouline, 2000), 60.

256. Hall, *Secret Teachings*, 116–120.

257. Manly P. Hall, "Rosicrucianism and Masonic Origins," from *Lectures on Ancient Philosophy—An Introduction to the Study and Application of Rational Procedure* (Los Angeles: Hall, 1929), 397–417.

258. Mircea Eliade and Willard R. Trask, *Yoga: Immortality and Freedom* (Princeton, NJ: Princeton University, 1970), 221–222.

259. N. W. Hutchings, *Prophecy in Stone* (Fort Worth, TX: Harvest, 1974), Introduction.

260. J. L. Lightfoot, *The Sibylline Oracles* (London: Oxford University, 2008), 423.

261. Ibid., 325–330.

262. See (http://www.masonicdictionary.com/doubleeagle.html).

263. *The Book of Chumayel: The Counsel Book of the Yucatec Maya 1539–1638*, Richard N. Luxton, trans., Series: "Mayan Studies 7" (Laguna Hills, CA: Aegean Park, 1995), 307.

264. Paul Foster Case, *The Great Seal of the United States*, 10th ed. (Los Angeles: Builders of Adytum, 1976), 29.

265. See (http://www.december212012.com/join_the%20believers_list.htm).

266. See (http://www.brad.ac.uk/webofhiram/?section=lectures_craft&page=1Lec.html).

267. See (http://en.wikipedia.org/wiki/Tenochtitlan).

268. "Growth of a Young Nation," *U.S. House of Representatives: Office of the Clerk*, last accessed January 30, 2012, http://artandhistory.house.gov/art_artifacts/virtual_tours/splendid_hall/young_nation.aspx.

269. "1964–Present: September 11, 2001, The Capitol Building as a Target," *United States Senate*, last accessed January 30, 2012, http://www.senate.gov/artandhistory/history/minute/Attack.htm.

270. William Henry and Mark Gray, *Freedom's Gate: Lost Symbols in the U.S.* (Hendersonville, TN: Scala Dei, 2009), 3.

271. Ibid., 4.

272. "Sandpit of Royalty," *Extra Bladet* (Copenhagen, January 31, 1999).

273. Manly P Hall, *Secret Teachings*, 104.

274. James Lees-Milne, *Saint Peter's: The Story of Saint Peter's Basilica in Rome* (Little, Brown, 1967), 221.

275. Rebecca Zorach and Michael W. Cole, *The Idol in the Age of Art* (Ashgate, 2009), 61.

276. Rebecca Zorach and Michael W. Cole, *The Idol in the Age of Art*, 63.

277. David Flynn, *Cydonia: The Secret Chronicles of Mars* (Bozwman, MT: End Time Thunder, 2002),156.

278. Albert Pike, *Morals and Dogma: Of the Ancient and Accepted Scottish Rite of Freemasonry*, (Forgotten Books), 401.

279. Albert Mackey, *A Manual of the Lodge* (1870), 56.

280. Dan Brown, *The Lost Symbol* (Anchor; Reprint edition, 2010), 3–4.

281. Manly P. Hall, *Lost Keys*, Prologue.

282. Manly P. Hall, *Secret Teachings*, 116–120.

283. Manly P. Hall, "Rosicrucianism and Masonic Origins," from *Lectures on Ancient Philosophy—An Introduction to the Study and Application of Rational Procedure* (Los Angeles: Hall, 1929), 397–417.

284. Albert Pike, *Morals and Dogma*, 335.

285. Ibid., 16.

286. Ibid., 472.

287. Hope, Murry, Practical Egyptian Magic (New York: St. Martin's Press), 1984 p. 107. Quoted by Fritz Springmeier, The Watchtower & the Masons, 1990, 1992 pp. 113, 114.

288. Thomas Horn, *Apollyon Rising 2012*,, 7-10.

289. Martin Short, *Inside the Brotherhood: Explosive Secrets of the Freemasons* (UK: HarperCollins, 1995), 122.

290. Manly P. Hall, *The Lost Keys of Freemasonry*, 48.

291. Manly P. Hall, *Secret Destiny of America* (Penguin Group, 2008), chapter 18.

292. See: http://en.wikipedia.org/wiki/Hermetic_Order_of_the_Golden_Dawn.

293. See: http://en.wikipedia.org/wiki/Ars_Goetia#Ars_Goetia.

294. *See: http://www.redmoonrising.com/Giza/DomDec6.htm.*

295. "Shemhamphorasch," *Wikipedia*, last modified December 6, 2011, http://en.wikipedia.org/wiki/Shemhamphorasch.

296. Manly P Hall, *The Secret Teachings of All Ages*, 623–633.

297. Ken Hudnall, *The Occult Connection II: The Hidden Race* (Omega Press, 2004), 207.

298. Pedro Sarmiento De Gamboa, *Acosta, Hint of the New World*, Clements Markham, trans. (Cambridge: The Hakluyt Society, 1907), 28–58.

299. Koran, Surah 89: 9–15, 27.

300. Thomas Horn, *Apollyon Rising 2012*.

301. "Discovery of Vast, Prehistoric Works Built by Giants?: The Geoglyphs of Teohuanaco," *Raiders News Network*, February 24, 2008, http://www.raidersnewsupdate.com/giants.htm.

Chapter 20:12

302. *La profezia dei sommi pontefici* (1794), 15. Translation Cris Putnam.

303. See: http://findarticles.com/p/articles/mi_hb3459/is_199306/ai_n8235230/.

304. J. R. Church, "The 800-Year-Old Prophecy of Rabbi Judah Ben Samuel," (*Prophecy in the News Magazine*, February 2010), 14.

305. In a personal email between David Flynn and Thomas Horn.

306. Clarence Goen, "Jonathan Edwards: A New Departure in Eschatology" (*Church History 28*, 1 Mr 1959), 29. 25–40.

307. Jonathan Edwards, *The Works of Jonathan Edwards, Volume 1* (Utgivare; Logos Bible Software), 594.

308. Jonathan Edwards, *The Works of Jonathan Edwards, Volume 1*, PUBLIC DOMAIN, (Utgivare; Logos Bible Software), chapter XV, page c.

309. Thomas Horn, "Read it Before it's Banned by the US Government," *News With Views*, November 9, 2009, http://www.newswithviews.com/Horn/thomas129.htm.

310. Elizabeth Van Buren, *Secret of the Illumanati* (London: Spearman, 1983), 161–162.

311. "Father John O'Connor: The Reign of the Antichrist," YouTube video, 13:52, posted by enoch7000, last updated August 16, 2010, last accessed May 25, 2013, http://www.youtube.com/watch?v=cIGWOgIHs9U.

312. John Daniel, *Scarlet and the Beast*, Vol 1, 3rd edition (Longview, TX: Day Publishing, 2007), 938.

313. Malachi Martin, *Windswept House: A Vatican Novel* (Doubleday, 1996), 492–493.

314. Malachi Martin, *The Keys of This Blood: The Struggle for World Dominion* (New York, NY: Simon and Schuster, 1991), 632.

315. Malachi Martin, *Windswept House*, 7.

316. Day Williams, "Masons and Mystery at the 33rd Parallel" *Hidden Mysteries E-Magazine*, last accessed January 19, 2012, http://www.hiddenmysteries.org/themagazine/vol14/articles/masonic-33rd.shtml.

317. Malachi Martin, *Windswept House*, 8.

318. "The Catholic Church in Crisis," The New American, *June 9, 1997*, 6–8.

319. Malachi Martin, *Windswept House*, 600.

320. Chuck Nowlen, "The Devil and Father Kunz: An Easter Tale about Murder, the Catholic Church and the Strange Paths of Good and Evil," *Las Vegas Weekly*, April 12, 2001 (Radiant City Publications). Viewable here: http://www.chucknowlen.com/kunz.htm.

321. Ibid.

322. Ibid.

323. Ibid.

324. Lionel, "Lionel: Joe Biden and New World Order" (article with embedded video), *KPLR News*, April 9, 2013, 2:59, posted by Lionel, http://kplr11.com/2013/04/09/lionel-joe-biden-and-new-world-order/.

325. Sue Bradley, "The Fourth Turning: The Protocols and The Gray Champion," *The Sue Bradley Archives*, last accessed May 25, 2013, http://suebradleyarchives.com/have-we-entered-the-fourth-turning/.

326. Ibid.

327. Ibid.

328. Ibid.

329. Ibid.

330. Ibid.

331. See: http://www.boap.org/LDS/History/History_of_the_Church/Vol_IV.

332. Marvin S. Hill, *Quest for Refuge*, viewable here: "Chapter 7, Appeal to a Higher Power,'" *The Signature Books Library*, last accessed May 8, 2013, http://signaturebookslibrary.org/?p=5348.

333. Bill McKeever, "When the Constitution 'Hangs by a Thread—The White Horse Prophecy in Modern Mormonism," *Mormonism Research Ministry*, last accessed Mary 8, 2013, http://www.mrm.org/white-horse-prophecy.

334. Ibid.

335. Ibid.

336. Ibid.

337. Ibid.

338. Ibid.

339. Ibid.

340. "Did Hatch Allude to LDS Prophecy?" (*Salt Lake Tribune*, Nov. 11, 1999).

341. Dana Milbank, "Mormon Prophecy Behind Glenn Beck's Message," *Huffington Post*, October 5, 2010, http://www.huffingtonpost.com/dana-milbank/post_996_b_749750.html.

342. "O'Reilly: 'There Will be a Constitutional Crisis in America,'" video posted by *Real Clear Politics*, January 11, 2013, 3:38, last accessed May 5, 2013, http://www.realclearpolitics.com/video/2013/01/11/oreilly_there_will_be_a_constitutional_crisis_in_america-comments.html.

343. "In Concession Speech Surprise, Romney Kicks Off 2016 Campaign," *The Global Edition*, November 6, 2012, http://www.theglobaledition.com/in-concession-speech-surprise-romney-kicks-off-2016-campaign/.

344. Sally Denton, "Romney and the White Horse Prophecy," *Salon*, January 29, 2012, http://www.salon.com/2012/01/29/mitt_and_the_white_horse_prophecy/.

345. Thomas Burr, "Romney Candidacy has Resurrected Last Days Prophecy of Mormon Saving the Constitution," *The Salt Lake Tribune*, June 4, 2007, http://www.sltrib.com/lds/ci_6055090.

346. Michael D. Moody, *Mitt—Set Our People Free* (New York, NY: iUniverse, 2008); quote viewable here: http://mittsetourpeoplefree.com/book.htm.

347. Michael Moody, in a personal phone conversation between he and Tom Horn, 2013.

348. Michael D. Moody, *Mitt—Set Our People Free*, 2–3.

349. Zev Chafets, "The Huckabee Factor," *The New York Times*, December 12, 2007, http://www.nytimes.com/2007/12/12/magazine/16huckabee.html?_r=2&hp=&pagewanted=print&oref=slogin&.

350. "Gospel Principles: Chapter Three: Jesus Christ, Our Chosen Leader and Savior," *The Church of Jesus Christ of Latter-Day Saints*, last accessed May 8, 2013, http://www.lds.org/manual/gospel-principles/chapter-3-jesus-christ-our-chosen-leader-and-savior

351. Michael D. Moody, *Mitt—Set Our People Free*, quote viewable here: http://www.mittsetourpeoplefree.com/book.htm.

352. Ibid.

353. Mormon Transhumanist Association, last accessed May 8, 2013, http://transfigurism.org/.

354. JTinDC, "Cartoon Explains Mormon Theology," *Daily KOS*, last accessed May 25, 2013, http://www.dailykos.com/story/2012/07/19/1111607/-Cartoon-Explains-Mormon-Theology#.

355. Bruce R. McConkie, *The Millennial Messiah*, p. 708, accessed May 8, 2013 http://www.utlm.org/onlineresources/mormonshopetobecomegods.htm.

356. Wilford Woodruff's Journal 8:187, July 22, 1883.

357. Orson Hyde, *Journal of Discourses*, 2:82.

358. Orson Pratt, *The Seer*, p. 159, accessed May 8, 2013, http://www.archive.org/details/OrsonPratt.

359. Jonathan Blanchard, *Scotch Rite Masonry Illustrated: The Complete Ritual of the Ancient and Accepted Scottish Rite*, profusely illustrated, vol I, 290, accessed May 8, 2013 http://archive.org/stream/scotchritemasonr01blan#page/290/mode/2up.

360. Ibid., 373 http://archive.org/stream/scotchritemasonr02blan#page/372/mode/2up.

361. Larry A. Nichols, George A. Mather, and Alvin J. Schmidt, *Encyclopedic Dictionary of Cults, Sects, and World Religions* (Grand Rapids, MI: Zondervan, 2006), 199.

362. Jerald and Sandra Tanner, *Mormonism—Shadow or Reality?*, Fifth Edition (1987); Reformatted (2008) ed. (Utah Lighthouse Ministry, 1987), 486. See: http://books.google.com/books?ei=6XqKUfzGHYiG9QTa2IHQCw&id=a5vtAAAAMAAJ&dq=Jerald+and+Sandra+Tanner%2C+Mormonism+-+Shadow+or+Reality%3F&q=The+five+points+of+fellowship+#search_anchor.

363. Joseph Smith, *Teachings of Presidents of the Church: Joseph Smith*, accessed May 8, 2013 http://www.lds.org/ldsorg/v/index.jsp?locale=0&sourceId=dc48b00367c45110VgnVCM100000176f620a____&vgnextoid=da135f74db46c010VgnVCM1000004d82620aRCRD.

364. Manly P. Hall, *The Lost Key of Freemasonry* (Richmond, VA: Macoy Publishing and Masonic Supply Company, 1951), 92.

365. W. L. Wilmshurst, *The Meaning of Masonry* (West Yorkshire, England: Gramercy Books, 1922), 47.

366. Carl Teichrib, *Forcing Change*, Volume 7, Issue 4, April 2013, pg. 8

367. Joseph Fielding Smith Jr., *Doctrines of Salvation*, Vol. 2, p. 48: accessed May 8, 2013 http://www.utlm.org/onlineresources/mormonshopetobecomegods.htm.

368. Lincoln Cannon, as quoted in *Mormon Transhumanism: "Eternal Progression towards Becoming Like God"*, by: Hank Hyena, accessed May 8, 2013 http://hplusmagazine.com/2010/08/22/mormon-transhumanism-eternal-progression-towards-becoming-god/.